The Turkish Turn in Contemporary German Literature

Studies in European Culture and History

edited by

Eric D. Weitz and Jack Zipes
University of Minnesota

Since the fall of the Berlin Wall and the collapse of communism, the very meaning of Europe has been opened up and is in the process of being redefined. European states and societies are wrestling with the expansion of NATO and the European Union and with new streams of immigration, while a renewed and reinvigorated cultural interaction has emerged between East and West. But the fast-paced transformations of the last fifteen years also have deeper historical roots. The reconfiguring of contemporary Europe is entwined with the cataclysmic events of the twentieth century, two world wars and the Holocaust, and with the processes of modernity that, since the eighteenth century, have shaped Europe and its engagement with the rest of the world.

Studies in European Culture and History is dedicated to publishing books that explore major issues in Europe's past and present from a wide variety of disciplinary perspectives. The works in the series are interdisciplinary; they focus on culture and society and deal with significant developments in Western and Eastern Europe from the eighteenth century to the present within a social historical context. With its broad span of topics, geography, and chronology, the series aims to publish the most interesting and innovative work on modern Europe.

Series titles

Fascism and Neofascism: Critical Writings on the Radical Right in Europe
Edited by Angelica Fenner and Eric D. Weitz

Fictive Theories: Toward a Deconstructive and Utopian Political Imagination
Susan McManus

German-Jewish Literature in the Wake of the Holocaust: Grete Weil, Ruth Klüger, and the Politics of Address
Pascale Bos

Exile, Science, and Bildung: The Contested Legacies of German Intellectual Figures
Edited by David Kettler and Gerhard Lauer

Transformations of the New Germany
Edited by Ruth Starkman

The Turkish Turn in Contemporary German Literature: Toward a New Critical Grammar of Migration
Leslie A. Adelson

Terror and the Sublime in Art and Critical Theory: From Auschwitz to Hiroshima to September 11
Gene Ray

The Turkish Turn in Contemporary German Literature

Toward a New Critical Grammar of Migration

Leslie A. Adelson

*for Pat,
whose support has been deeply appreciated since the day it all began in 1977!
In admiration and friendship,
Leslie
October 2005*

THE TURKISH TURN IN CONTEMPORARY GERMAN LITERATURE
© Leslie A. Adelson, 2005.

All rights reserved. No part of this book may be used or reproduced in any manner whatsoever without written permission except in the case of brief quotations embodied in critical articles or reviews.

First published in 2005 by
PALGRAVE MACMILLAN™
175 Fifth Avenue, New York, N.Y. 10010 and
Houndmills, Basingstoke, Hampshire, England RG21 6XS
Companies and representatives throughout the world.

PALGRAVE MACMILLAN is the global academic imprint of the Palgrave Macmillan division of St. Martin's Press, LLC and of Palgrave Macmillan Ltd. Macmillan® is a registered trademark in the United States, United Kingdom and other countries. Palgrave is a registered trademark in the European Union and other countries.

ISBN 1–4039–6913–2

Library of Congress Cataloging-in-Publication Data

Adelson, Leslie A.
    The Turkish turn in contemporary German literature : toward a new critical grammar of migration / Leslie A. Adelson.
      p. cm. — (Studies in European culture and history)
    Includes bibliographical references and index.
    ISBN 1–4039–6913–2 (alk. paper)
      1. German literature—20th century—History and criticism.
2. Turks—Germany—Social conditions. 3. Turks in literature.
4. Emigration and immigration in literature. 5. Intercultural communication in literature. I. Title. II. Series.

PT405.A18 2005
830.9′35299435—dc22   2004060156

A catalogue record for this book is available from the British Library.

Design by Newgen Imaging Systems (P) Ltd., Chennai, India.

First edition: August 2005

10 9 8 7 6 5 4 3 2 1

Printed in the United States of America.

for Larry
for Etti, Yos, and Phyl
and
for the birds

Contents

Acknowledgments — ix

Introduction	Toward a New Critical Grammar of Migration	1
Chapter One	Dialogue and Storytelling	31
Chapter Two	Genocide and Taboo	79
Chapter Three	Capital and Labor	123
Postscript		171

Notes — 173
Works Cited — 213
Index — 249

Acknowledgments

This book and its author have benefited from the extraordinary kindness of so many colleagues, students, assistants, strangers, and friends that true acknowledgment can at best take the form of emulation. I hope these generous souls will forgive me for not being able to list their names here and know that their spirited help is no less deeply appreciated. Completion of this study would not have been possible without the gracious support of Cornell University's College of Arts and Sciences and the National Endowment for the Humanities, which provided the author with a Fellowship for University Teachers in the final stage of the project. This award would have been unthinkable without the unflagging encouragement of Patricia Herminghouse, Andreas Huyssen, Dominick LaCapra, and Eric Rentschler, in whose debt I shall long remain. Any views, findings, conclusions, or recommendations expressed in this book do not necessarily reflect those of the National Endowment for the Humanities, Cornell University, or anyone who urged me to write it. I am particularly grateful to Dilip Gaonkar and Benjamin Lee for the invigorating opportunity to participate in a keen interdisciplinary discussion group on "new imaginaries," convened by the Center for Transcultural Studies in Montreal in August 2000. A preliminary version of chapter two was first published in *New German Critique* 80 (2000): 93–124 as "Touching Tales of Turks, Germans, and Jews: Cultural Alterity, Historical Narrative, and Literary Riddles for the 1990s." Revised and expanded arguments based on that article appear here with the cordial permission of *New German Critique*. Elements from an article that appeared in *The Germanic Review* 77.4 (2002): 326–338 as "The Turkish Turn in Contemporary German Literature and Memory Work" have been significantly expanded and figure in chapter three with the kind permission of both *The Germanic Review* and Heldref Publications, 1319 18th Street, N.W., Washington, D.C. 20036–1802. Many thanks are due to Tom Cheesman of the University of Wales (Swansea) for undertaking the English translation of Zafer Şenocak's novel, *Gefährliche Verwandtschaft*, and making *Perilous Kinship* electronically available for both general access and my citations. Whenever possible

I have cited published English translations of source texts in all other instances. Unless otherwise indicated, translations provided are mine.

Indebted to many exceptional individuals at Cornell University, from whom I still have so much to learn, I feel not only grateful but lucky on a daily basis. Among those who have expressed special interest in this book project, I am uniquely beholden to David Bathrick, Dominic Boyer, Susan Buck-Morss, Iftikhar Dadi, Salah Hassan, Peter Hohendahl, Gail Holst-Warhaft, Isabel Hull, Dominick LaCapra, Natalie Melas, and Anette Schwarz. For encouragement sustaining over many years and miles, no words can adequately thank Christine Rinderknecht, Alan Beyerchen, and the late J. J. Reneaux. My deepest gratitude goes to Larry E. Bieri, beloved partner in short- and long-distance mysteries.

Introduction
Toward a New Critical Grammar of Migration

1

"Come on!" a professor once badgered. "If it looks like a duck, walks like a duck, and talks like a duck, don't you damn well think it had better be a duck?" "No!" rallied the student, who happened to be an experienced birdwatcher. "If it looks like a duck, walks like a duck, and talks like a duck, it could be a grebe."[1] Discussion of German literature born of Turkish migration in the latter half of the twentieth century invariably prompts audiences to ask experts to do two impossible things, both predicated on the tacit assumption that the shoe—even a shoe with wings—must be made to fit. The first is to draw a comprehensive picture—on the basis of literary readings—about the social life of those Turks who comprise the largest national and ethnic minority in the Federal Republic of Germany today. The second is to explain these Turks by evacuating the Turkish and German referents altogether, by likening them to more familiar objects on the global stage, usually some constellation of ethnic minorities, powerful nation-states, and transnational economies.[2] This book argues that prevailing analytical paradigms are inadequate to grasp the social dimensions that do inhere in the literature of migration. Because relevant frames of reference for interpreting this literature are often not what they appear, alternative modes of contextualization will be explored. Such exploration is especially important as the interlocking contours of nation, transnation, and postnation shape-change at increasingly accelerated rates. Last but not least, this discussion of the Turkish turn in German culture entails historical claims about the medium of literature and the labor of migration in the 1990s, a dizzying decade of structural transformations affecting Germany, Europe, and what many might call the world at large.

Arjun Appadurai's widely cited study of modernity at large posits "a new role for the imagination in social life" at the crossroads of late-twentieth-century developments in electronic mediation and mass migration (1996: 31).[3] The newness of the global historical moment that the anthropologist has in mind is attributed to an unprecedented constellation of media technologies and mass migration, whereby "electronic mediation transforms preexisting worlds of communication and conduct" (3). This seminal study aims to rethink both modernization theory and area studies beyond a "national-cultural map of the world" and toward "a postnational imaginary" (16, 21). I shall revisit Appadurai's important work, which pays only passing attention to literary texts and less to their medial qualities, in chapter one's discussion of a literary text that maps an especially innovative moment on the arc of the 1990s for German literature written under the sign of Turkish migration. But let us linger a bit—or dabble, as ducks do—in the world of theory.[4]

There are many ways of conjuring a world, and doing so seems indispensable to a wide range of critical and descriptive projects. The trope may suggest an expansive gesture, as when Benedict Anderson imagines the type of serial identification that "has its origins in the print market, especially in newspapers," as "*unbound*," "exemplified by such open-to-the-world plurals as nationalists, anarchists, bureaucrats, and workers" (1998: 29). On the other hand, the world seems a very small place when Anderson lambastes "*bound*" modes of serial identification (e.g., census categories), which "have displaced the cosmos to make way for the world." A restricted sense of worldliness may apply to literary genres or social phenomena, sometimes in relation to each other, as when Michiko Kakutani describes Louise Erdrich's oeuvre "somewhere between the brightly colored world of fable and the grittier world of 20th-century life." One circumscribed world may meet another in an expansive way, as in the Salman Rushdie affair (1989–1998), where "the transnational worlds of liberal aesthetics and radical Islam met head-on" (Appadurai 9). Then there are the First, Second, and Third Worlds of Cold War vintage, which together comprised, for some, the world entire. Guillermo Gómez-Peña defines "millennial topography as the coexistence of five worlds," none of which exists wholly inside or outside the others (Foster 46).[5] There is even a genre of meetings that has been characterized as a world. In a collection of essays on puns Jonathan Culler alerts us to "juxtology"—"a world of yoking" (1988: 6).

One need only allude to the many analyses produced and inspired by scholars such as Benedict Anderson and Homi K. Bhabha to recall that much has been said in the last two decades about national formations and processes of imagination, structures of narration, and patterns of migration in the multiple worlds of modernity. Much work published since the mid-1990s points to the need for qualitatively new modes of imagining and conceptualizing social life in relation to transnational and postnational formations in the age of globalization and amidst ongoing debates about the fate of the nation-state and stateless nationalisms.[6] In Appadurai's narrative of globalization on the bumpy road toward a postnational imaginary, electronic technologies and mass migration together yield "new resources and new disciplines for the construction of imagined selves and imagined worlds" (3). This vast body of scholarship is hardly cast in a humorous vein—because the stakes are so high in world politics—but the "world of yoking" may be closer than we think.

According to Jeanette Winterson's *night screen*, a literary text that has more to do with electronic mediation than mass migration, "a story is a tightrope between two worlds" (141). Popular and scholarly accounts of cultures of migration are often mediated by stories recounted about human beings who move, willingly or under duress, from one place associated with home to another linked to diaspora, and these movements are increasingly multidirectional. With many changes afoot one conceptual paradigm exerts the enormous gravitational pull of a black hole in spite of its historical obsolescence. No rhetorical conceit holds more sway over discussions of migrants and the cultures they produce than that which situates migrants "between two worlds."[7] This is paradigmatic in the sense that the phrase connotes "static logical relations among the elements" in what could become a story (Rimmon-Kenan 10).[8] The locative conceit prompts us to imagine any number of stories involving migrants and any number of dual worlds, but it cannot tell a story alone. The spatial configuration most frequently invoked to situate migrant cultures at the turn to the twenty-first century— an age of accelerated movement and transformation—is one in which nothing happens. This oddity warrants critical attention.

Many fictional and historical subjects navigate complex relations to the worlds of their lives, and we would be hard pressed to find any text or person in the worlds of modernity for which some type of "betweenness" is not constitutive.[9] In postcolonial and post-Holocaust reminiscences of Algeria, for example, Hélène Cixous recalls the name of her aunt's tobacco shop in Oran in the following way: "*Aux Deux Mondes*, The Two Worlds. So the boutique was dedicated, and me with it, to a universe with two worlds. But I never knew in a clear, explicit or decisive way which the two were. The world was two. All the worlds were two and there were always two to begin with. There were so many two-worlds" (271). Cixous's haunting lyrical essay has the high-wire tension of a tightrope straining with the balancing attempts of a historical subject in motion. The problem with situating cultures of migration always and forever "between two worlds" therefore does not reside in the betweenness or worldliness of the conceit. Even its twoness can be opened to a complex multiplicity, as Cixous's phenomenology of historical awareness in Algeria makes abundantly clear. "Between two worlds" becomes conceptually problematic when the conceit is made to function as an analytical paradigm that is effectively incapable of accounting for cultures of migration *as historical formations*. Additional problems arise when whatever worlds are meant are presumed to be originary, mutually exclusive, and intact, the boundaries between them clear and absolute.[10] Envisioning migrant cultures "between two worlds" as a delimited space where two otherwise mutually exclusive worlds intersect is not especially helpful either, since the presumption of originary, essentially intact worlds still applies.[11] It does so to the detriment of our analytical enterprise as so many worlds on the world stage turn to the future, partly because it suggests, contrary to all apparent evidence, that worlds remain stable while unstable migrants are uncertainly suspended between them.

Why does an analytical paradigm so ill-suited to our historical moment have such enduring rhetorical appeal?[12] Could it be underwritten in some far-flung way by residual anxieties or fantasies of first contact? Gayatri Chakravorty Spivak may be suggesting as much when she posits in her critique of postcolonial reason "that an unquestioning privileging of the migrant . . . may also turn out to be a figure of the effacement of the native informant" (1999: 18). Be that as it may, the genre of "the cultural fable," which Laura Brown introduces in her incisive study of literature and history in the English eighteenth century (2001b), helps us understand the attraction of "between two worlds" today. The new world fables studied by Brown collectively comprise what she designates an "imaginative encounter" with the material history of modernity (2001a). These are "stories without a text, imaginative events without an author" about themes such as sanitation, shipping, and finance, just to name a few of those addressed by Brown. She coins the critical term "to yoke the material and historical with the aesthetic" (2001b: 1). The discursive genre of the cultural fable is:

> a formal construct in the sense that it is characterized by a set of related figures that have a distinctive structure or are in a dynamic relationship. These recurrent figures adhere to their own specific texts and develop from their own rhetorical traditions. But beyond that local function, and taken together, they intersect with and elaborate one another so as to project a set of meanings, affects, or even ironies that constitute a common imaginative project. (1)

If "between two worlds" is a paradigmatic conceit in which no narrative can unfold, as I contend, then it becomes a cultural fable only when some succession of events is imagined in reference to it. This is what happens when we hear the phrase and immediately call to mind, without having to recount them, any number of stories involving migrants whose movements are relative to the worlds of their lives. As what I consider a core cultural fable for our increasingly transnational times, "between two worlds"—now in its syntagmatic dimensions—marks an imagined encounter with the material history of modern migrations. To it accrues the beyond-local function elaborated by Brown.[13] To do justice to Brown's terminology in the contemporary setting, one would have to analyze the cultural fable of migrants "between two worlds" in its local function as well, that is to say, in a wide range of specific literary texts. This could be done because the fable in question shadows much of the literature born of migration and not merely discussions of it. Much of the scholarship on this literature already makes the cumulative point without knowing it or having access to Brown's terminology. Instead I argue that a single-minded emphasis on this cultural fable renders scholarship blind to some striking innovations signaled by a complex body of German-language writing that has emerged, especially in the 1990s, in the wake of Turkish migration.

If structural transformations in the German situation are instructive in other contexts as well (a genuine question that only scholars in other fields will be able to answer), the cultural fable we like to tell about migrants "between two worlds" differs with increasing frequency from stories that literary texts born of migration actually set into motion at the turn to the twenty-first century. This is in any case true of the literature of Turkish migration in Germany. Because the gap between these two modes of narration has widened considerably since 1989, I seek a new critical grammar for understanding the configuration of cultural contact and Turkish presence in contemporary German literature. This nontechnical appeal to grammar reflects the need for more critical imagination brought to bear on component elements, textual structures, and cultural relations that figure in the literature of migration in the volatile decade of the 1990s. Such critical reorientation is necessary because "between two worlds" as an explanatory model does more to assuage anxieties about worlds, nations, and cultures in flux than it does to grasp the cultural innovations that migration engenders. If the literature of migration is no longer situated in any predictable sense "between two worlds," then where might it be located, and what is it doing there?

2

In countless debates about the mass migration to Germany that predated 1990, and in much of the international scholarship on "migrants' literature" or "intercultural literature in Germany" (Chiellino 2000), Turks occupy a central representative position, not on a vibrating tightrope, but on an inflexible bridge "between two worlds." One of these worlds is customarily presumed to be European and the other not, while the space between is cast as a site of discriminatory exclusions or the home of happy hybridity.[14] With over two million Turks residing in Germany today, where nearly 9 percent of the population holds non-German citizenship, Turks represent the largest minority in Germany and a growing Muslim population in a country that imagines itself in many ways through the lens of its Christian heritage.[15] Statistically and symbolically, Turks have shouldered the greatest burden of the imagined bridge for migrants in Germany, as they trigger fears of a "clash of civilizations" (Huntington) or spark hopes for a "dialogue of cultures."[16] This is a familiar rhetoric of opposing worlds understood as originary and mutually exclusive. The space "between" is often reserved for migrants inexorably suspended on a bridge leading nowhere. In the broader field of international relations, on the other hand, dialogue is construed as itself a bridge, allowing ostensibly discrete cultures, religions, and civilizations to identify values and interests held in common. When the United Nations declared 2001 the year of "dialogue among civilizations," it attributed such common ground to the universality of human rights. Stressing the importance of dialogue as a powerful means of conflict resolution even (and especially) after the consequential attacks on the United States in September 2001, Secretary-General Kofi Annan listed migration as one key factor contributing to the heightened pace at which "different races, cultures, and ethnicities" encounter each other in today's world writ large (Picco et al. 2001b: 11; see also Tibi 2001: 192, 228).[17] Turkish migrants in Germany occupy a precarious position in this rhetoric of dialogue and conflict. They have long been encoded as inarticulate foreigners in the public imaginary, while dialogue is nonetheless expected of them, albeit as representatives of an alien national culture they are mistakenly held to represent. The dual trajectory of this rhetoric of dialogue between discrete worlds thus tends to yield either a bridge leading nowhere or—with greater frequency in the era of globalization—a bridge leading to a shared future predicated on cultural difference and universal rights. While perennial debates in Germany about Turkey's suitability for full admission to the European Union occasionally reflect the latter sense of a bridge (e.g., Seufert; Şen 2002; Thumann), they often reflect the ongoing intractability of a bridge leading nowhere in many sectors of the public sphere (e.g., Wehler; Schmidt 1989, 2002b).[18] In this more familiar vein "European" is deemed democratic, civilized, and Christian, while "Turkish" is taken to connote the opposite.[19] Although the institutional infrastructure of German society has indeed become increasingly Europeanized since the early 1990s (Katzenstein 1–48; see also Lankowski; Balibar; Berezin and Schain), the rhetorical conceit situating Turkish migrants on a bridge "between two worlds" signals both a German world embedded in a European world and a Turkish world with its proper place outside Europe.

The history of international labor markets that resulted in over two million Turks establishing permanent residence in Germany belies the assumption that any of these worlds have national contours alone. From 1955 to 1973,

German government and industry systematically recruited temporary labor forces from Italy, Greece, Spain, Morocco, Portugal, Tunisia, and Yugoslavia.[20] The relevant agreement signed by the Federal Republic of Germany and the Republic of Turkey in October 1961 followed shortly after the Berlin Wall seriously aggravated the existing labor shortage in the west. If we were to speculate as to why the rhetorical conceit situating Turkish migrants "between two worlds" has so much purchase in Germany, we might note that this historical incarnation of the cultural fable coincided with West Germany's ongoing attempts—in the aftermath of the Third Reich, the Holocaust, and a war of the worlds—to situate itself in relation to the First and Second Worlds of the Cold War and to the so-called Third World in the age of postcolonialism. This speculation is potentially more productive than the common lament that Germans are simply parochial by disposition. There was nonetheless much occasion to hear this lament in the 1990s, when racist and xenophobic violence surged in the wake of unification and when debates raged over German citizenship law, predicated on the legal principle of *ius sanguinis*, a law of blood lineage or familial descent. Part of this law was changed effective January 1, 2000, such that children born on German soil to a non-German parent who has resided legally in the country for eight years are now entitled to German citizenship. Effective January 1, 2005, a significant innovation in laws regulating labor migration and permanent residency paves the way toward recognizing the Federal Republic as a land of immigration (*Einwanderungsland*), even though the law itself speaks only of *Zuwanderung*, migration "to" rather than "into" Germany. The long-range consequences of these legal changes remain to be seen. The cultural effects of Turkish migration have in any case been far more difficult to assess than debates about governmentally sanctioned integration and self-imposed ghettoization imply.

An analytical optic that emphasizes nation-based structures of inclusion and exclusion in German society tends to obscure other structures and processes that shape Turkish life in Germany.[21] Literary texts written under the sign of migration are given short shrift if they are read only in terms of inclusion *versus* exclusion (say, regarding admission to the German canon), especially when these patterns are deemed to mirror approaches to the question of citizenship. A schematic emphasis on inclusion *versus* exclusion also reinforces Germany as a national referent with familiar contours, since citizenship debates in the Federal Republic have been largely framed as a matter of national law.[22] Yet social scientists and political theorists such as Yasemin Soysal (1994, 1998, 2002), Seyla Benhabib (2002a, 2002b), and Joyce Mushaben (2003, 2005) make it clear that absolute precepts of inclusion and exclusion no longer capture the highly diversified structures of political membership affecting migrants in Europe or Germany over the last decade. Stressing the need for a "disaggregated" approach to changing social practices of citizenship in European countries and the European Union, Benhabib targets for critique "the fiction of a 'closed society' " that underwrites many state-centered accounts of citizenship in misleading ways (2002b: 168–169).[23] In *The Limits of Citizenship* Soysal notes the "symbolic intensity" that the "citizen/noncitizen dichotomy" retains in the presence of its institutional erosion but urges scholars "to recognize that national citizenship is no longer an adequate concept upon which to base a perceptive narrative of membership in the postwar era" (166–167).[24] Not all structures of exclusion become inoperative or irrelevant, as the "exclusionary incorporation" experienced by many Black German citizens reveals (Partridge; see also Campt; El-Tayeb; and Grosse). But rightly or wrongly, discussion of migrants often revolves around an axis of inclusion and exclusion precisely because so many migrants in Germany (and especially Turks) have lacked German citizenship. This overdetermined focus in literary studies gives rise to worrisome blind spots that the present study seeks to worry in turn.

Yasemin Soysal directs her wrath toward the category of diaspora in particular, which she finds utterly ineffective in "explaining the contemporary immigration experience" despite its popular and scholarly appeal (2002: 138). In her view, theories of diaspora are inherently ahistorical when they conceptualize diaspora as "the extension of the place left behind" and stress "the presumed rootlessness of immigrant populations in the here and now of the diaspora, and their perpetual longing for then and there" (138–139).[25] In wording that resonates with my arguments about the suspension bridge on which Turks in Germany are allegedly located, Soysal demands that the concept of diaspora be jettisoned because "it suspends immigrant experience between home and host countries, native and foreign lands, homebound desires and losses—thereby obscuring the new topography and practices of citizenship, which are multiconnected, multireferential, and postnational" (149). Soysal and Benhabib stress complex approaches to the local, national, transnational, and postnational contours of the contemporary immigration experience in Europe, and their work highlights two things important for arguments here. The development of postnational structures in the age of globalization does not displace national frames of reference in any simple way, and those national frameworks that endure are historical formations, themselves subject to defamiliarizing change at the turn to the twenty-first century. That is to say, in concert with Saskia Sassen and others who address the shifting structural contours of our times, Soysal and Benhabib regard tensions between the national and the postnational as constitutive of the global order at the end of the twentieth century.[26]

Reflecting on Soysal's emphasis on interlocking systems of political "incorporation" or membership for migrants and nation-states in contemporary

Europe (1994), Benhabib suggests that institutional structures, policies, and economics alone cannot explain why foreigners in a given state enjoy certain rights but not others, or why migrants from non-European countries are regarded differentially within Europe. Her two contrasting examples of political incorporation in the Netherlands and Germany before 1990 underscore the need to account for cultural influences on policy. But the cultural factors she stresses are not those commonly associated with ethnic identities of migrants.

> The incorporation policy of the former Federal Republic of Germany was to integrate guestworkers into the juridical system, not by virtue of their membership in a particular ethnic group, but rather, in the first place, by their status as individual persons and, in the second place, qua workers and employees. (2002b: 77)

By contrast, Turks and other groups in the Netherlands were officially designated as minorities in 1982, which entitled members of these groups to social support and organizational activities relevant to their collective identities (77). As the political theorist elaborates, these differential rights cannot be explained by traditions imported from the migrants' countries of origin. Drawing our attention to the "interaction between the home and the host cultures and traditions," she speaks more pointedly of the differential "historical culture" that pertains in the Netherlands as opposed to the Federal Republic (77–78). If a historical division of Protestantism and Catholicism leads the Dutch to conceive of "cultural groups as confessional unities," Benhabib contends, the catastrophe wrought by the Third Reich left a different imprint on West German policy, which resists "the reintroduction of strong concepts of cultural group identities into public policy and debate" (78). Incorporation cannot be grasped in terms of rights, privileges, and benefits alone. Whereas normative and philosophical questions about "equality and diversity in the global era" remain paramount for Benhabib, the present study has a more modest agenda and perhaps a more elusive object of analysis. If the still emergent literature of Turkish migration functions as a technology of localization in Germany today, what could it mean, beyond simplistic appeals for inclusion, to say that this literature incorporates itself into the historical culture of Germany, a country undergoing rapid change?[27] This is one of the key questions that the book at hand engages.

What are the relevant frameworks in which the literature of migration resonates most deeply? Does articulating one crucial frame of reference obviate the need to consider others that vie more subtly for critical attention? At first blush the interpretive contexts most readily at hand are conventionally national (referring to the Federal Republic in its postwar contours or the Turkish Republic as a Kemalist enterprise) or loosely transnational (in keeping with cosmopolitan claims of hybridity or political claims of globalization). What analytic could yield a more keenly differentiated picture of the interactive cultural contexts in which this literature emerges and intervenes? Benhabib's dual-track defense of a deliberative polity that is at once democratic and multicultural rests on her firm rejection of "strong contextualism" in political theory and "mosaic multiculturalism" in political practice (7–8, 39). Her arguments also rest on a methodological appeal to complex social " 'webs of interlocution' " involving narrative and dialogue.[28] Literary narrative is not Benhabib's concern, however, so her compelling dismissal of strong contextualism in political theory is a good reminder of mistakes to avoid rather than a guide for analyses to pursue in the realm of literature.

Texts to be discussed conjoin historical and literary narrative in particular ways without laying claim to particularist ethnic identities or political rights attaching to them. This sets them apart from debates about evolving norms and infrastructures regarding migration and membership in Europe that Benhabib and Soysal illuminate.[29] On the other hand, this distinction accords with Soysal's impassioned rejection of diaspora as an outdated analytic category on the grounds that "diaspora is a way of theorizing formations that are ethnocultural" (2002: 138). Soysal's critique of this concept is tied to her displeasure with ethnic categories of membership. As she elaborates, "the category of diaspora is an extension of the nation-state model, in that it assumes a congruence between . . . territory, culture, and identity" (138). Two possible criticisms of Soysal's position, one explicit and one merely relevant, raise additional questions about the proper contexts in which German-language stories of Turkish migration are meaningful. The merely relevant criticism is suggested by Brian Axel's anthropological work on violence and transformations in the Sikh diaspora in the age of electronic communication (2001, 2002). Like Soysal, Axel faults diaspora studies for conceptualizing "the homeland as a place of origin and site of departure that constitutes a certain people as a diaspora" (2002: 425–426). Unlike Soysal, who wants to banish the concept of diaspora, Axel proposes to refine it. "In my analysis of the Sikh diaspora," he argues, "the homeland, as a utopian destination for Khalistani activism, is only one element of the diasporic imaginary—and, as such, must be understood as an affective and temporal process rather than a place." This conceptual distinction is important for diaspora studies at large, for "the image of the homeland is only one among several very important aspects of the diasporic imaginary." While shifting the conceptual ground from place to affect may also bear fruit for cultural studies of Turkish migration, Axel's account of diaspora and homeland for Sikhs underscores "the fragile—yet enduring—ground of the nation form" (426).

By this Axel means the real and imagined homeland left behind. If his model applied to the Turkish case in Germany, the affective orientation stressed would be to Turkey. This might apply in some cases, as Azade Seyhan's discussion of Emine Sevgi Özdamar's "tongue stories" demonstrates (2001: 113–124). But it does not necessarily apply, and even when it does, it need not do so exclusively. The question of context is a minefield. Stepping too decisively in one direction might leave us unable to advance methodologically apace with epochal change.

At the crossroads of German Studies and transnational memory studies Andreas Huyssen argues that the "world of the national" endures, even as the parameters of the national change (2003a: 151), but the national world he has in mind in this instance is more or less anchored in Germany. In an essay on Zafer Şenocak's novel of genocidal legacies concerning Germans, Jews, Turks, and Armenians Huyssen contends, "Soysal goes overboard when she dismisses diaspora as a critical category" (150).

> For just as a reified notion of diaspora may block out the real present, exclusive focus on issues of citizenship and everyday life in the present may prematurely block out issues of memory, history, and, yes, nostalgia which should be seen both in its affirmative delusional and its critical dimension rather than simply being dismissed. . . . It is particularly the relationship between diasporic memory and the memory formations of the national culture within which a given diaspora may be embedded that remains seriously understudied. And here the notion of diaspora itself may assume new meanings in line with the changes of nationhood that Soysal and others have so cogently analyzed. (150–151)

My juxtaposition of Axel, Huyssen, and Soysal has three main implications for a discussion of interpretive contexts. First and foremost, some proclamations of the postnational are simply premature. Second, a scalar understanding of interactive contexts—as opposed to a dichotomous model of discrete worlds—is likely to yield more precise accounts of the interventions signaled by German literature of Turkish migration at the turn to the twenty-first century, especially if we recall that the relevant interactive contexts are not congruent with national formations as we have known them.[30] Third, Soysal might be throwing the baby out with the bathwater when she jettisons ethnocultural categories along with the concept of diaspora. Cultural concepts of *ethnos* are themselves undergoing a historic transformation. Ethnicity can hardly be analytically passé with so many conflicts crystallizing around ethnic signifiers, but it behooves us to consider that familiar concepts of ethnic cohesion may have lost whatever explanatory power they once held.[31] Figural functions of ethnicity will therefore be prodded and probed in the chapters to follow.

The proper placement of migrant cultures on a scale of categorical distinctions recalls the sorites paradox of vagueness, whereby a series of transitions eventually makes one item look categorically distinct from another without the precise point of transformation being clearly ascertainable. At what point does the literature of migration acquire contours more German than Turkish in structure, more transnational than national, more postnational than anything else? These terms are scalar rather than absolute, historically variable rather than ontological. One of several philosophers to have wrestled with the paradox of vagueness, Diana Raffman makes a persuasive case for contextualization as a possible solution to the philosophical dilemma. In the primary fields of analysis that concern me—literary and historical—contextualization is what Dominick LaCapra calls a necessary but insufficient condition of analysis (2003; 2004a: 72; see also 2004b). The present study argues that no cultural frames of reference are pre-given in any authoritative sense for the literature of Turkish migration, and that each text must be interpreted for relevant frames of reference or contexts to be rendered meaningful. Stemming from the 1990s, most of the literary narratives addressed in this book involve a *preponderance* of interventions into and beyond national archives of twentieth-century German culture. (To date most of the authors responsible for these interventions, which take their cue from the phenomenon of Turkish migration, have been predominantly though not exclusively Turkish-born. While this situation is likely to change, the relative attention paid to minority and majority writers in the present study reflects an imbalance characteristic of the 1990s.) Because these interventions are easily overlooked if one focuses on the Turkish national archive, transnational literatures with an "accent" (Modarressi), or even postcolonial difference, the analyses here focus precisely on reconfigurations of the German national archive, though others will occasionally be discussed too.[32] The appeal for a new critical grammar of migration is not intended to displace all previous studies, but to expand and sharpen the critical repertoire brought to bear on literatures of migration, especially in the interdisciplinary field of German Studies.

Why should the question of proper context interest a broader audience as well? Some speculations come to mind. A wan but forceful specter of twentieth-century Germany enlivens many theoretical claims about modernity, globalization, and immigration without being in any way quickened with German context. This can be traced in analytical enterprises as disparate as Homi K. Bhabha's seminal account of the modern national narrative (1990a), Steven G. Kellman's assessment of "the translingual imagination" (2000), and Emily Apter's invocation of "the global onslaught of English as a universal language ... *über alles*" (2001b: 7). This ghostly German presence often wears a Turkish mask. This is especially the case for Bhabha, for whom the verbally challenged Turkish guest worker in Germany signals "the radical incommensurability of translation" in the modern national narrative *tout court* (317), while Kellman loosely conjures Turkish guest worker literature in Germany as emblematic of the "translingual writing" that characterizes "the literature of immigration" generally at the millennium (17).[33] But what does it mean to invoke Turks in Germany as a cipher for global change if the landscape of meaning in which Turkish figures intervene is sketched in only the faintest of lines? If this German landscape is one of the "'process' geographies" (Appadurai 2000: 7) perplexing area studies and migration studies today, scholars who build theoretical claims in reference to this landscape would be well advised to consider what processes of transformation are underway there.

Let me pause to recapitulate what seems counterintuitive in this book's approach to contemporary German literature written in the transitional decade of the 1990s but born of the Turkish migration that began on a large-scale basis in the 1960s. While individual texts may allude to greater and lesser degrees to the Republic of Turkey, the national culture of Turkey is not a necessary or primary frame of reference for the literature in question.[34] The commonplace that authors of Turkish birth or descent represent a miniature or otherwise discrete Turkish world in Germany is not supported by the literature of migration, and it would be overstated to speak of these texts generally or necessarily as a diasporic phenomenon.[35] Neither does this literature in its recent configuration signal Turkish identity politics in a German or European metropole.[36] This would have to be distinguished from other spheres of public life, where one could make a stronger, though possibly still problematic case for the centrality of identity politics, for example, in soccer clubs, street gangs, and some religious organizations.[37] As Georg Stoll observes, references to Islam are few and far between in this literature, so my discussion of the latter can hardly account for all the important aspects of Turkish cultural production in the new Germany.[38] Partly for this reason, my larger argument goes to the need for medium-specific and context-specific vocabularies that allow us to grasp the varied cultural effects of Turkish migration in increasingly refined ways. Finally, as the essays and images in *Unpacking Europe* highlight (Hassan and Dadi), the center of Europe is no longer Eurocentric. If German worlds figure pivotally in the literature of Turkish migration, they too are configured in newly imagined ways.

3

If literature of migration does not revolve around contested rights and identities, why bother with it at all? One central premise here is that these literary narratives provoke us to ponder the historical intelligibility of our time, to become more historically literate by reading against the grain of existing categories, concepts, and statistics of migration in order to ask what worlds we inhabit as the millennium turns. (Readers should note the scalar emphasis.) This is not to suggest that this literature illuminates historical developments in expository, informative fashion or that its substance could be recounted *as* historical narrative subject to factual verification.[39] On the contrary, the labor of imagination that I ascribe to this literature is enabled by decidedly literary strategies of transformation.[40] Collectively these stylistic turns signal the emergence of something new in German literary history. This goes well beyond the introduction of transnational migration as a new theme reflecting a demographically altered landscape. In this restricted sense the texts in question participate in the broader phenomenon of "emergent literatures" associated with minority populations in liberal nation-states. More than this, however, much of the literature of migration takes up historical phantasms that circulate mischievously today. This taking up does not necessarily serve the recuperation of past losses, but rather the reworking of cultural matter from which historical narrative is fashioned and forged.[41] This labor often renders palpable those residual affects of historical experience that vex relations between Germans and the Turks among them today. But this imaginative labor has been increasingly oriented toward a shared future history as well. As Yasemin Soysal observes, Turkish membership in the German polity is now "grounded in a shared public social space" rather than blood lineage or even constitutional patriotism, to use a phrase made famous by Jürgen Habermas (Soysal 1994: 166). Remarking on "emerging forms of Turkish identification *with* the host country," Mushaben similarly alerts us to over forty years of lived history that is now shared (2003). German literature of Turkish migration marks and advances a shared imaginative project as well. The labor entailed in this literary project and the imaginative work of community formation that Appadurai adduces as evidence for "a new role for the imagination in social life" are different. The anthropologist means largely that newly proliferating electronic media give rise to new ways of imagining lived social practice for real migrants with simultaneous ties to multiple communities in different places. In this respect Appadurai probes newly diasporic forms of long-distance affiliation. The labor of imagination enabled by the literature of Turkish migration more frequently probes short-distance modes of cultural affiliation in Germany.[42] The material effects of this labor are far more elusive than the political effects of postnational diasporas discussed by Appadurai. There are no sustained sociological studies of this literature's reception in Germany or elsewhere, so it is difficult to say exactly who reads this literature, let alone predict what the social consequences of such reading might be.[43]

The literature of Turkish migration functions as a kind of cultural archive, where changing perceptions and phantasms of sociality are both tracked and imagined. By means of this archive, questions about the historic contours of our time may be variously entertained, depending on which methods one brings to the task if one considers the material at all.[44]

Common wisdom has long held that the literature of migration, especially the "guest worker literature" that peaked modestly in the 1980s, reflects the social disorientation of hapless foreign laborers in Germany.[45] I submit instead that the literature of Turkish migration archives "an epochal sense of disorientation" (Adelson 1997a: 123). Shared by Germans, Turks, and many others too, the epoch is characterized by categorical disorientation and historic reorientation. Teetering between the postwar contours of the Federal Republic during the Cold War and the era of globalization, the Berlin Republic is one site among many where transnational labor patterns of the 1950s and 1960s contributed to a heightened sense of reorientation in the 1990s.[46] In Germany the decade marked, first and foremost, the multifaceted and rocky transition from national division to unification, a development to which people still refer colloquially as *die Wende*, the turn. German literature that reflects on this structural transformation and its cultural consequences is commonly called *Wende-Literatur* (see Brockmann; Boa and Wharton; Fischer and Roberts; Fröhling, Meinel, and Riha). Although texts by Turkish-born authors are generally excluded from this category without commentary (with the notable exception of Yeşilada 2000), there is a *Wende-Literatur* inflected by Turkish migration (Adelson 2002). Beyond this, a broader Turkish turn in German literature has been underway since roughly the 1970s. The literature of Turkish migration indexing national unification (in the narrow sense of a thematic turn) participates in but does not inaugurate the more wide-ranging Turkish turn that informs this book. (See, e.g., Kara.) This broader Turkish turn began to acquire critical mass in German-language fiction in the 1990s as well, when ethnic signifiers, memory cultures, and tectonic shifts in transnational conflicts loomed disorientingly large, not only in Germany but on a global stage in dramatic transition.[47] This book thus focuses jointly on this broader turn toward new modes of orientation in German literature and on work published in the final decade of the twentieth century.[48]

4

Well known for its portrayal of a topsy-turvy world in the mid-nineteenth century, Lewis Carroll's *Alice in Wonderland* figures importantly in a short story discussed at length in chapter one. One passage from the sequel to this curious tale of wonderment seems uncannily apt to a discussion of the literature of migration since the Berlin Wall was toppled in 1989. "Humpty Dumpty was sitting with his legs crossed, like a Turk, on the top of a high wall—such a narrow one that Alice quite wondered how he could keep his balance—and, as his eyes were steadily fixed in the opposite direction, and he didn't take the least notice of her, she thought he must be a stuffed figure" (154).[49] Humpty Dumpty fell no less famously than the wall dividing German states, Cold War Europe, and much of the rest of the world. In many popular and scholarly tales of transnational migration to Germany in the late twentieth century, however, the figure of "a Turk" appears unshakably intact, intractably referential. Even Alice recognizes that an anthropomorphic egg sitting "like a Turk" must be a figure of sorts rather than a social actor or historical agent. Readers concerned with literatures of migration have something to learn from this. Assessing the confluence of literary and historical narrative in the German fiction of Turkish migration requires keener attention than has been paid to the use of figural language that palpitates these literary texts. Such assessments require more differentiated accounts of the various ways in which these largely fictional tales advance the manifold story of migration, often in reference to Turkish figures that are not, strictly speaking, socially referential.[50] In this sense it is important to distinguish between a "Turkish figure" as a character in a fictional text and a rhetorical figure that becomes coded in a given text as some type of Turkish cipher that propels the narrative.

To what exactly do we refer when we speak of a Turkish presence in German culture? Commentators in wide-ranging venues commonly assume that the literature of migration depicts Turks literally and represents them politically (thus conflating the German sense of *darstellen* and *vertreten*).[51] This referential presumption dovetails easily with the perception that public figures of Turks represent self-evident categories of cultural difference, social unassimilability, or incommensurable strangeness.[52] The country's leading weekly news magazine once captured this tendency by characterizing German Turks as "icons of the foreign" (*Spiegel* 17). While the visual repertoire of Turkish images in the German public sphere has grown more diverse over time—including a once prominent Green parliamentarian who considers himself an Anatolian from Swabia (Özdemir 1997)—the presumption of self-evident codes of representation is still widespread across the political spectrum. For this reason, Turks are often perceived both *as* and *on* what I call *the face of things*. (This helps explain why intercultural dialogue is so often stressed in Germany and so rarely achieved. It may also explain why counting Turks is such a favored analytic pastime.) The allegedly self-evident thingliness ascribed to Turkish figures—rather than the substantive ascription of cultural difference—is what I wish to indict here, though the two often appear joined at the hip. A counterexample clarifies the point.

A Guatemalan journalist in the 1980s described the problem he posed to many Germans simply by having "undecipherable hair" (Godoy); they could not tell by looking at him how to categorize the difference he represented. For many Turks in Germany, the opposite applies. "What you see is what you get" seems to rule the day when it comes to Turkish figures in social spaces, as if appearances alone could provide definitive answers to questions about social cohesion or compatability.[53] Since no group has a monopoly on the propensity to take systems of representation at face value or base beliefs about strangers on stereotypes, I am less interested in making any claims about German attitudes toward Turks than I am in criticizing the presumption that Turks figure a cultural difference and a social reality that are a priori known and knowable only in predetermined ways. This presumption easily spills over into discussions of literature of migration, especially when this literature is taken to represent Turkish migrants "between two worlds."

This clarification is necessary to explain what I mean by the riddle of referentiality. My exploration of the Turkish turn is motivated by curiosity about specific ways in which Turkish figures of rhetorical coin allow contact narratives in the literature of migration to unfold. What are the figures in reference to which literary tales of migration are told? By what means are these figures constituted? What cultural labor do they facilitate in a literary framework? If I do not entertain these questions as open-ended, I run too great a risk of reinscribing an anachronistic social referent "between two worlds" into the literary analysis. My operative definition of referentiality is thus the conjoined effect of literary figuration and narrative development. This definition has a thematic component in that it is anchored in literary texts that take up the subject of Turkish migration to Germany in some fashion. But this thematic component can be understood only in conjunction with structural components of figuration and narrative on which the definition also rests. This linkage of thematic and structural elements distinguishes the operative approach to referentiality here from a strict narratological differentiation among textual features that refer to real as opposed to fictional worlds.[54] My emphasis on the narrative nexus of literary structures and historical phantasms also leads me to acknowledge only in passing the influential work of Paul de Man, who has written so famously on the chasm between figural language and referential meaning in literary texts (1979).[55] The present study shares some basic premises with Hayden White's seminal defense of literary and historical discourses as constitutively linked. For example, the putative thingliness of Turkish figures mentioned above is related to the somewhat different "quality of 'thinginess' " that White identifies in poetic and historical discourses. "Like poetic discourse," White contends, "historical discourse is intensional, that is, is systematically intra- as well as extrareferential. This intensionality endows the historical discourse with a quality of 'thinginess' similar to that of the poetic utterance" (1999: 7).[56] But White's account of "figural realism" and "emplotment" in historical narrative is ultimately too schematic to yield insights into structures of figuration and reference at work in the German literature of Turkish migration.[57] Like Katrin Sieg's analysis of "ethnic drag" as "a symbolic contact zone between German bodies and other cultures" in performance, including one dramatic work of Turkish migration, the present study challenges models of reading persons or texts that "mistake appearances for essence" (2–3). Because Sieg's concept of referentiality in theater differs in key respects from my use of the term regarding fictional narrative, it remains to clarify where the differences lie and why they are significant.

In *Ethnic Drag* Sieg astutely analyzes a play featuring stock figures from children's literature, opera, and theater that interact while impersonating Turkish migrants, a range of vegetables, and a bottle of salad dressing (Özdamar 1991, 2000a). The analysis is embedded in an extended treatise on medium-specific structures of "ethnic drag" subtending high and low performance cultures, especially German theatrical scenarios since 1945. Combining feminist theories of gender and masquerade, queer theories of sexuality and transvestitism, critical theories of race and minstrelsy, postcolonial theories of ambivalence and mimicry, and dramatic theories of mimesis and impersonation, Sieg coins her central term to address deep structures of theater and history at play when members of one ethnic group perform emphatically in the guise of another. She wields it deftly to refine our understanding of how collective anxieties and representational paradigms collaborate—sometimes oppositionally, sometimes affirmatively—to mediate responses to historical legacies and historic change. For example, chapters on the evolution of "Indian" impersonation in annual festivals and among German hobbyists identify a triangulated structure of performative surrogation whereby the Nazi past is simultaneously remembered and forgotten.[58]

The concept of ethnic drag refers to a theatrical "technique of estrangement" that defies facile claims of social reference. On this Sieg and I agree, and she accurately cites my distinction between *proximate historical narratives* and *historical narrative by proxy* in reference to the fiction of Turkish migration in order to elaborate her argument (14, 11–12).[59] I have learned much from this scholar's insights into mimesis, masquerade, and surrogation in German theater, and I am clearly interested in the phantasmatic residue of historical experience reforged by literature of migration. These intersections notwithstanding, Sieg's understanding of referentiality in ethnic drag departs from my understanding of referentiality in the literature of migration. Her operative concept has two primary trajectories. First and foremost, *Ethnic Drag* challenges presumptions of any "direct relationship between symbolic practices and social effects" (10). This is one reason why a Brechtian theory of estrangement figures so pivotally in Sieg's study. At the same time and second, Sieg does not want to cede "an ontological ground from which oppressive systems can be denounced, alternative knowledges accumulated, truth claims made, and the social order reimagined" (17). Brecht's dramatic theory is also important for these emphases, as is Amy Robinson's theory of spectatorship and race. Sieg musters both to criticize what she considers Judith Butler's "recipe for purchasing subversion at the cost of a subject position" (17). By this account, Brecht insists "on a referent that anchors performance" (16). At one point Sieg seems to define referentiality as "the representation of clearly recognizable social and ethnic milieux" (10). This definition may be intended to explain only how presumptions of referentiality functioned in a conflict over casting discussed in Sieg's introduction, for the parenthetical definition otherwise contradicts a stated emphasis on estrangement unsettling any supposition that social referents can be rendered directly recognizable in performance. Sieg concludes with phrasing that only appears to echo my understanding of proximate historical narratives: "Some masquerades translate high cultural icons into local forms of engagement and activism. Others evoke the shared memories of displacement and ostracization, as well as proximate histories of pride and resilience, for a politics of dialogue, trialogue, and coalition" (260).

Sieg's invocation of a "trialogue" harkens back to a passage from Şenocak's novel *Gefährliche Verwandtschaft* [in Tom Cheesman's translation, *Perilous Kinship*], which I cited in an earlier version of what appears as chapter two here (Adelson 2000).[60] Sieg references the novel and my discussion of it immediately after introducing my distinction between proximate historical narratives and historical narrative by proxy (14–15), but this is where trouble ensues. Although I had described Şenocak's rhetorical figure of a trialogue involving Turks, Germans, and Jews as one readers are encouraged to regard as "highly suspect" (2000: 124), I apparently did not make it clear enough that the combined effect of figuration and narrative in the novel precludes social reference indexing political claims tied to ethnic identities or antiracist coalitions.[61] Chapter two clarifies what I understand to be the riddle of referentiality in Şenocak's novel. For the moment it suffices to note that the confluence of literary structures and historical experience in the German fiction of Turkish migration has in the first instance an archival effect, as discussed above. Historical experience circulates in these texts figuratively and phantasmatically, but not in a way that could underwrite political projects with normative claims on behalf of particularist social groups. This may lessen the interest that some readers bring to the literature of migration, while it may spark greater curiosity about the cultural effects of Turkish migration in others. The distinction between Sieg's understanding of referentiality and my own allows me to underscore two arguments advanced here: (1) the literature of Turkish migration is not anchored in a politics of identity and (2) the cultural effects of Turkish migration to Germany manifest themselves variously in medium-specific ways.

5

Because this study argues for the historical obsolescence of the cultural fable suspending migrants "between two worlds," it introduces the concept of *touching tales* as an alternative organizing principle for considering *"Turkish" lines of thought*. These lines of thought have been quietly shifting the ground on which German-language literature of the 1990s responds to historic changes at the millennial turn. Deriving from a comparison of work by Şenocak and Zaimoğlu in particular, both terms inform my critical project more broadly and warrant explication at the outset. The concept of touching tales informs the analyses presented here in several ways. First, it suggests that Germans and Turks in Germany share more culture (as an ongoing imaginative project) than is often presumed when one speaks of two discrete worlds encountering each other across a civilizational divide. Touching tales thus takes conceptual leave from a model of incommensurable differences to stress a broad range of common ground, which can be thicker or thinner at some junctures.[62] Second, it acknowledges affective dimensions that shadow the literature of Turkish migration, which in varying configurations reflects German guilt, shame, or resentment about the Nazi past, German fears of migration, Turkish fears of victimization, national taboos in both countries, and Turkish perceptions of German fantasies. As chapter one demonstrates, other affects point to something approximating postnational intimacy. Most important, touching tales denotes literary narratives that commingle cultural developments and historical references generally not thought to belong together in any proper sense. Prime examples of this involve Turkish migration and the Holocaust, the Cold War, European modernity, or the Armenian genocide. The proposed interpretations of such touching tales move beyond political, social, or historical analogy to address aesthetic innovations that reframe German and transnational pasts, presents, and futures from the vantage of the 1990s. How are we to read the literature of migration if familiar points of reference (such as Turks, the Holocaust, or the Cold War) are unsettled by the disorienting web of cultural narratives in which they serve *as* points of reference for interpretive and historical orientation alike? Finally, drawing attention to touching tales in the literature of migration allows us to trace the intersection of metanarratives about twentieth-century German history and literary history on the cusp of a new marking of time.

Nonetheless, touching tales should not be confused with basic features of either literary narrative or historical scholarship. Many literary texts have plots with multiple and related story lines. "A story-line is structured like the complete story, but unlike the latter it is restricted to one set of individuals," Rimmon-Kenan explains (16). The German literature of Turkish migration involves many intersecting story lines in this sense, but the concept of touching tales targets structures of figural reference and narrative progression that impinge on each other as enumerated above. Even the material that historians weave into a story, Jürgen Kocka tells us, entails entangled plots in some measure, to the extent that historians rely on "narrative forms of presentation" (41). His summary of recent disciplinary trends highlights a growing interest in transnational phenomena as opposed to those centered in easily circumscribed contexts. According to Kocka, historians the world over are called upon more than ever to consider new methodological approaches to account systematically for " 'entangled histories' " (42). The touching tales discussed here bespeak historical and cultural entanglements to which the transnational labor migration of the 1950s and 1960s has given rise in Germany. But the historical *Gestalt* of these literary tales cannot be captured by systematic accounts of historical causation or even sequence. The combined effects of figural reference and narrative structures in the literature of migration have more to do with cultural matters of orientation that are no less significant for being intangible or irregular. The sustained combination of story lines about Turkish migration and twentieth-century German history is still a relative novum in German literature.[63] While some scholars speak of intercultural "intersections" (Durzak 1993; Petersen 1995; Özoğuz 2001) or even "new narrative alliances" (Gerstenberger 236) in this regard, the concept and phenomena of touching tales are elucidated here in an effort to refine the critical vocabulary available to studies of literature and migration.

"Turkish" lines of thought is an abstraction rather than a thing, a critical conceit made to function like a tool, and nothing more. If some confuse the concept with beliefs held by a minority population in Germany (or a majority population in Turkey), it may not even be a very good tool. The phrase "lines of thought" is also a common figure of speech. The potential for misleading appropriations of the combined term makes me introduce it with some trepidation. As an abstraction, however, the concept helps clarify the claim that German literature of Turkish migration probes the historical intelligibility of our time. The term is deployed to consider transfigurative dimensions of contemporary literature at a pivotal moment in German as well as transnational cultures and histories. "Turkish" lines of thought in this sense are cast, not in terms of identity politics, ethnic difference, or national mentalities, but as figurative story lines reshaping key points of

reference and orientation in German and transnational cultures through the looking glass of Turkish migration. The 1990s saw the German nations of Cold War vintage unexpectedly unified and the contours of unified Germany teased by rapid Europeanization, globalization, and ongoing migration effects. Construed as an agonal clash of ethnic or national differences, the notion of contact inhering in the two-worlds approach is ill equipped to capture the cultural complexity of this moment. This is one reason why the concept of touching tales seems a necessary intervention. These tales touch by figural and narrative means, but they also mediate abstract lines of thought pointing readers toward newly imagined (and newly imaginable) cultural effects of Turkish migration.

For theoretical reflections on the philosophical and epistemological significance of "drawing a line" as a historically significant act, I am indebted to Claudia Brodsky Lacour's inspired study of Descartes.[64] Although Brodsky Lacour devotes her attention to ways in which the Cartesian method inaugurates modern European philosophy, her distinction between figural representation and lines drawn in thought is salutary in a radically different context. The modern line of Descartes's discursive architectonics is "without plastic reality." That is to say, "[i]t reiterates nothing and represents no preexisting process, but commits an unprecedented form to being." This is, as Brodsky Lacour puts it, "discourse with no worldly analogue" (1996: 7). The notion that German literature of Turkish migration could articulate something not yet otherwise known, or even something with as yet "no worldly analogue," has not been broadly considered in German Studies or migration studies to date. One might surmise that this habit of thought implicitly relegates Turks in Germany to a place imagined to be outside Germany and outside modernity. The present study asks whether the figure of "things Turkish" is a thing in reference to which only a predictable story can be told or an abstraction—a narrative effect—by means of which something unprecedented begins to emerge. Such a narrative effect would also have to be acknowledged as a thing, but only in the sense in which Brodsky Lacour speaks of a line of thought as "an iconoclastic line." As she elaborates, "The discursive beginning of modern philosophy, the founding of the subject of thinking, occurs not as a linguistic picture or image but as line, an iconoclastic line, a 'line of thought.' Dependent for its own manifestation on the discursive means with which it is never identical, the thinking of thought as line—medium and manifestation of science as well as art—dispels every regressive and recurrent myth of cognition as the effect of resemblance, whether the coin of imitation be categorized as copy, type, or archetype, just as it demonstrates the impurity of nonimitative, 'pure' thought" (8). For Descartes, Brodsky Lacour continues, the discourse of European modernity is "writing which conceals its own status as line in its intelligibility as representation." This is writing characterized by the figurative and the iconoclastic as interdependent formations. By introducing the concept of "Turkish" lines of thought, I propose to understand the literature of migration as writing that the figurative and iconoclastic cohabit as well, albeit to varying degrees of cohabitation depending on the texts considered. I emphasize abstract dimensions as a counterpoint to the supposed "thingliness" of Turkish figures in the civic sphere. But to highlight abstract features of the literature is not to say that referentiality (as the conjoined effect of figuration and narration) is relegated to a social vacuum. The interactive contexts in which these literary texts intervene can be mediated only by interpretation. These iconoclastic lines of thought and mediation are by no means linear.[65]

6

Throughout this introduction "literature of migration" appears in reference to what many since the 1980s have called "guest worker literature," "foreigners' literature," or "migrants' literature" instead. The progressive displacement of one term by another has signaled shifting themes, emphases, and norms in literature, media, and scholarship. As I understand it, the literature of Turkish migration does not necessarily revolve around the guest worker phenomenon, though guest workers sometimes figure in this literature and long-range effects of labor migration are entertained whether individual authors were once guest workers or not. Because this study focuses on cultural effects of Turkish migration, to which heightened symbolic status accrues in Germany, and because major Turkish writers are now German citizens, the category of "foreigners' literature" would be similarly misplaced. The literature of migration is not necessarily written by migrants alone. Beyond this, I emphasize a "literature of migration" in contradistinction to what many have taken to calling "intercultural" literature (e.g., Chiellino 2000; Blioumi; Howard; Shafi).[66] Why does this distinction matter? First, conceptualizing the field as a literature of migration allows us to keep transnational migration and its long-range cultural effects keenly in sight as historical formations, without limiting these effects to the initial influx of guest workers. The second reason explains why the rubric of "intercultural literature" allows for such historical perspectives far less reliably, for "intercultural" is often wielded to stress an encounter between communitarian traditions taken to replicate what Benhabib decries as the figure of "seamless wholes" (2002b: 25), even if scholars allow for the heterogeneity of a given tradition considered in isolation. Because intercultural rubrics do not necessarily preclude historical concerns or analytical complexity, however, additional explanation is required.[67] The argument now turns to related critiques of the hermeneutic enterprise levied by literary scholars working in disparate venues. This resurrects the problematic rhetoric of dialogic communication discussed above.

The hermeneutic circle of understanding variously articulates and negotiates structural, philosophical, and historical relationships between parts and wholes. This often entails a kind of dialogic encounter between an object of analysis and its interpreter, one that seeks to bridge a gap inherent in the initial relationship. In the late twentieth century Hans-Georg Gadamer's influential philosophy of hermeneutics emphasized historical understanding as a "fusion of horizons" (*Horizontverschmelzung*) in this sense. At the intersection of literary studies and ethnic studies, Doris Sommer has articulated the most sustained and impassioned critique of hermeneutic models of understanding from the vantage of minority writing and bilingual literary games in the Americas (1999, 2003, 2004). Charging Gadamer with treating rhetoric as "always a bridge" to understanding through dialogue and fusion (1999: 25), Sommer proposes a negative hermeneutic focusing on impediments to understanding that must be acknowledged and respected before any genuinely cross-cultural dialogue can occur. The "rhetoric of particularism" so forcefully advanced by Sommer is intended as a corrective to the "rhetoric of universalism" undergirding literary and philosophical analysis alike. "To understand is to establish identity; and this requires conceptualization that generalizes away otherness," Sommer contends (27).[68] By this account, dialogue and fusion in the hermeneutic model become euphemisms for the erasure of difference (24). By contrast, the Latin Americanist submits, minority writing engages readers with particularist difference, insistently refusing the preemptive embrace of understanding. Sommer's operative term, it should be noted, is not "intercultural." She also identifies her particularist rhetoric as fitting into "a broadly hermeneutical project" of interpretation and acknowledges that even Gadamer's concept of historical fusion entails "an engagement with difference rather than its elimination" (25). Sommer's textual analyses also link particularist rhetoric and historical questions. Her discussion of Toni Morrison, for example, would be nonsensical if one were to strip the analysis of its references to African American history.

With regard to minority concerns in Germany, the country's first public intellectual of note to have been born in Turkey also calls for "something like a negative hermeneutic" to heal "the wounds of communication" (Şenocak 2000: 42, 68).[69] With this Şenocak indicts only a particular kind of understanding rather than a philosophy of hermeneutics.[70] He lambastes "the sort of hermeneutic approach to the Turkish minority that thwarts rather than fosters more profound understanding of the current situation" to the extent that it is "obsessed with 'intercultural' exchange or dialogue" (Adelson 2000a: xxix–xxx). His essays on Turkish and German entanglements challenge a schematic rhetoric of self and other predicated on incommensurable partners in dialogue. Two scholars of German literature have launched independent critiques of hermeneutic philosophy that share Şenocak and Sommer's displeasure with feigned dialogue.[71] Ülker Gökberk also takes aim at the philosophical tradition of hermeneutics where minority writing is concerned. Instead of rejecting the hermeneutic enterprise altogether or insisting on a negative hermeneutic, Gökberk advocates an emphatically "intercultural" variant (1991, 1997a, 1997b). Unlike Sommer but with Tzvetan Todorov and Yüksel Pazarkaya (in Chiellino 1988: 100–110), Gökberk stresses "the possibility of genuine intercultural communication" (1997b: 42) as an ideal to which speakers and readers should aspire.[72] Dialogic approximations—rather than impediments or exchange—are key to this model of understanding, which underscores universality and diversity as compatible principles (Gökberk 1991: 166; Mecklenburg 1999: 131–134). Arguing that difference is hence not an insurmountable impediment to genuinely "*dialogic* communication" (Gökberk 1991: 163), Gökberk nonetheless finds Gadamer's concept of "fusion" in understanding woefully inadequate to account for really existing cultural difference. If an interpreter from Gadamer's perspective must bridge the gap between present and past (without necessarily acknowledging cultural differences as such), an intercultural hermeneutic appeals to Gökberk because it recognizes the gap to be bridged as an "experience of foreignness" beyond a temporal divide (1997b: 22). Methodologically this entails shifting from historical questions to spatial configurations, and to my mind, this is where problems arise. "The intercultural method is primarily concerned with the transfer of literature from one cultural space into another," Gökberk notes (22).[73] Her remarks on "the writing of immigrants in Germany" are consequently figured in spatial terms. "The language is often fused with images, idioms, and proverbs that are obviously transmitted from another language realm and cultural space. The majority of these works are set in Germany itself; the homeland sphere (*Heimat*) is generally present in memory only. Nevertheless, the German reader's own cultural realm is now viewed from without, from another cultural space" (27).[74] As my discussion of relevant frameworks indicates, the cultural space in question is not always accurately captured by references to the national culture of Turkey.

Unlike Gökberk, Azade Seyhan does not especially advocate an intercultural approach to transnational literature in her multifaceted account of "writing outside the nation" (2001). But like Sommer and Gökberk, she faults Gadamer's philosophy of hermeneutics for positing historical understanding as "the fusion of familiarity and foreignness," whereby "this fusion comes very close to consuming the foreign" (6). Seyhan too appeals to dialogue without fusion as a corrective to this impasse.[75] This is how she describes transnational narratives authored under conditions of bi- and multilingualism by Turkish, Syrian, and Czech writers in Germany or Chinese American, Cuban American, and Chicana writers in the United States. "Born of crisis and change, suffering alternately from amnesia and too much remembering, and precariously positioned at the interstices of different spaces, histories, and languages, they seek . . . to enter novel forms of inter/transcultural dialogue" (4). Taking recourse to a heuristic distinction between native and foreign, Seyhan foregrounds dialogue that is somehow still anchored in different national cultures. "The ontological ground of understanding in language, the fusion of horizons in interpretation," she argues, "cannot explain other, vastly different cultures that do not share our histories" (6). The "irreducible untranslatability" (148) of Seyhan's literary examples appears as a cultural chasm between national archives, a requisite object of study that brooks no "fusion" of understanding. This configuration of cultural specificity illuminates some features of newly transnational literatures, but it cannot illuminate the significance of some crucial features found in the literature of Turkish migration. Touching tales at the center of this study are a case in point, for structural and affective dimensions in much of this literature highlight histories and cultures shared in some fashion.

By and large, an intercultural approach to literature of migration stresses dialogic communication as a process in which readers and characters engage as representatives of discrete worlds. This approach is ill equipped to account for the relevant contexts and historical impetus of a genuine novum, the German literature of Turkish migration that emerged in the 1990s. My critical project has a hermeneutic streak of its own, inasmuch as I understand the literature of Turkish migration as a historical phenomenon, and inasmuch as I propose to interpret literary structures partly in terms of their transfigurative historic significance. This includes the transfiguration of ethnic signifiers. But no circle of understanding will be closed here. The "Turkish" lines of thought brought into focus are iconoclasts, not to be confused with lines of communication between social agents in civic spheres of contestation. Many different functions accrue to the literature of migration. This book addresses some that merit attention and analysis.

7

"Touching tales" and " 'Turkish' lines of thought" are heuristic tools for conceptualizing some of the more innovative effects of a growing Turkish presence in German literature and culture. There are assuredly other lines of reorientation to be studied in the manifold cultural effects of Turkish migration in the 1990s and beyond, and my hope is that this book will encourage others to undertake medium-specific analyses of them. Most of the literary analyses here focus on narrative phenomena that emerged in the transitional decade with which the twentieth century ended and a new telling of time began to take shape in diverse and sometimes divergent ways. Nodal points of cultural contact at which touching tales converge and interpretive dilemmas arise are key to the chapters that follow. *Dialogue and storytelling, genocide and taboo*, and *capital and labor* represent major pivot points in the history of migration where interpretive dilemmas regarding the figure of cultural contact become especially acute. Beyond the "dialogue of cultures" and migrants suspended "between two worlds," *chapter one* examines functions of *dialogue and storytelling* in prose works that have made literary history by different means. Published in 1990, Sten Nadolny's *Selim oder Die Gabe der Rede* [Selim or the Gift of Speech] is the first novel by a mainstream German author in which Turkish migration figures as more than a blip on the narrative screen. New meaning accrues to national frames of reference in *Selim* when the story of Turkish migration and the legacy of the Nazi past converge around a West German speech problem, one still beholden to the postwar era even as the novel rewrites the story of that epoch. Originally written in 1999, "Der Hof im Spiegel" [The Courtyard in the Mirror] is the title story in a collection published in 2001 by the first Turkish-born author to have won the Ingeborg Bachmann Prize, a decade earlier, for literature written in German. Here Özdamar reconfigures imaginative vectors of reference, inference, and affiliation in an ethnoscape transformed by migration. Focalized through the eyes and ears of a Turkish migrant observing her neighbors in Düsseldorf, this courtyard tale breaks new ground by prompting readers to imagine something approximating postnational intimacy in the here and now of reading.

A prominent political scientist asks, in reference to German Turks and the Nazi Holocaust, "how immigrants deal with their host country's 'burden of the past' " (Leggewie 2002, 2005: 94–97). Huyssen poses the question more broadly when he suggests that trans- or postnational categories of diaspora and memory cannot fully account for changing relationships between diasporic communities and national traditions as new cultures of memory are formed. Not coincidentally, both scholars are prompted to entertain questions about migration and memory by Şenocak, whose political essays and literary prose have garnered him far greater recognition and acclaim outside Germany (especially in the United States, France, Great Britain, and Turkey) than in the Federal Republic. As early as January 1990, together with Bülent Tulay, this versatile writer asked, "Doesn't immigrating to Germany also mean immigrating to, entering into, the arena of Germany's recent past?" (2000: 6).[76] Unlike Huyssen, Leggewie overlooks literature as one of the myriad means by which Turks in Germany enter the thicket of German culture, including its thorny historical legacy.[77] By contrast, *chapter two* examines the nexus of *genocide and taboo* as configured in Şenocak's first novel (1998). While this fictional biography conjoins twentieth-century German and Turkish histories, including the genocide of Jews and Armenians in the first half of the century, the texture of Şenocak's prose is maddeningly difficult to grasp. Is it laughably thin or impossibly dense? Why does the order of things seem to disappear behind the *trompe l'oeil* of referential extensions in this novel? The first German narrative of Turkish migration to figure the Armenian genocide, still a largely taboo and in any event highly controversial subject in Turkey (Taner Akçam 2001, 2002), *Perilous Kinship* also tells an entangled tale of German taboos. Addressing figures of history that haunt dramatic work by Peter Weiss in the 1960s and inventive prose by Feridun Zaimoğlu in the 1990s, chapter two probes the riddle of referentiality at the core of Şenocak's novel and the transnational—but still predominantly German—context in which it boldly intervenes. If Holocaust memory has "migrated" into national contexts at considerable remove from where the genocidal practices of the Nazis were conceived and implemented (Huyssen 2003b: 14–16), this chapter probes the cultural effects of Turkish migration to the democratic successor state to Nazi Germany.

Because gender difference and criminal behavior have been discursive and ideological staples in many accounts of Turkish migration as it bears on human rights, German modernity, and European integration, the final chapter examines the surprising configuration of ethnic "personhood" in stylistically diverse works by Aras Ören, Özdamar, and Şenocak. These texts—a novella, a short story, and two essays—stage pivotal encounters between Turkish migration and capitalist reconstruction in postwar Germany, a Cold War divide, and national unification under the triumphal sign of capital. Because agonal forces of *capital and labor* are often thought to determine the story of Turkish migration and the trajectory of German history since 1945, however, *chapter three* considers ethnicity and gender, not as self-evident signposts of embodied identities and cultural experience, but as a strategic nexus of historical narration at a moment of historic transformation. What imaginative labors accrue to anthropomorphic figures of ethnicity and gender in the recent literature of migration? What forms of cultural capital can they be said to underwrite? Hinging at first glance on the would-be personhood of a hapless laborer, Ören's *Bitte nix Polizei* (1981, or *Please, No Police* in the English translation of 1992) alerts us to an early attempt by a Turkish author living in Germany to rework the imaginative terms of labor and capital binding Germans and the Turks among them together. Best known for his poetic "Berlin Trilogy" of the 1970s, Ören is often invoked for his skilled depiction of the lived aporias of Turkish migrants trapped between two worlds. An analysis of touching tales of transgression in his work demonstrates how much more lived—but hardly embodied—history is at stake in his prototypical configuration of epochal disorientation. While later publications by many of the authors discussed reforge the legacy of the Cold War on the anvil of Turkish migration (e.g., Zaimoğlu 2002 or Özdamar 2003), chapter three revisits the "tongue stories" with which Özdamar made her literary debüt in 1990 and then turns to two essays from 1991 and 1995 in which Şenocak weaves migration into the fabric of German memory with the minutiae of his writing craft, sometimes with no Turkish figure in sight. A gendered division of labor that one might associate with Şenocak and Özdamar—one body of writing predominantly western, masculinist, and reflective, the other seemingly eastern, feminist, and naïve—upon examination defies any mirror logic at all. The nexus of capital and labor with which large-scale Turkish migration to Germany began in the 1960s yields to a disaggregated cultural economy of losses and gains. This is a landscape where historical remainders never add up to seamless wholes and where the meaning of ethnoscape no longer relies on ethnicity as strong multiculturalism defines it. As world upon world turns, this too is part of the ongoing labor of imagination, which is not confined to diasporic public spheres alone.

Reading the literature of Turkish migration beyond a conceptual lens that situates migrants "between two worlds" and national cultures, we see that the future of Germany lies ahead no less than its past and that the *Gestalt* of both is one in which the literature of migration is deeply invested. The process of determining whether the cultural vectors of imaginative reorientation in any given case are predominantly national, transnational, postnational, or something else altogether is an uncertain interpretive enterprise, but this is no reason not to undertake it. Iconoclastic lines of thought direct us to where we had not thought to go, but curiosity has its rewards. How does a world in flux ascribe meaning to its experiences, values, fears, and goals? More than any other country in the world at large, Germany in all its postwar variants has been profoundly shaped by historical and demographic divides associated with the Holocaust and the Cold War. If cultural effects of Turkish migration are a by-product of transnational or global economies, they are hardly a by-product of these factors alone. Beyond all the historic caesuras evoked by 1945 and 1989, what labor does German culture perform in the new Europe? How are the analytic contours of this question shaped by the imaginative lens of Turkish migration? This book turns a curious eye to literary means of orientation in order to pursue these and other questions elaborated in the introduction.

Thanks in no small measure to Appadurai's seminal study of modernity at large, mass migration and electronic mediation often serve the critical imagination as twinned ciphers of innovation. The Turkish turn in contemporary

German literature suggests that electronic media have no monopoly on the culture of transformation. The editors of *Reading Matters* remind us of this in another context (Tabbi and Wutz). Literature today is assuredly "one of many information processing technologies vying for position in the field of available representation" (15). The imaginative labor of cultural reorientation in the 1990s and beyond takes place in myriad ways and in many venues. Reading the literature of migration as a historical formation in the diversified medial economy of our time has much to teach us about some unanticipated aspects and effects of this labor. Recalling for my own readers the avian figure with which this introduction began, I turn again to *Reading Matters*, which opens with a description of Anselm Kiefer's sculpture *Das Buch*, a book with huge and ponderously leaden wings. The copy of *Alice in Wonderland* that readers encounter in Özdamar's tale of a courtyard in Düsseldorf at one crucial point falls from the sky, an apparent victim of gravity, only to take flight in a turn of phrase that reorients readerly imagination. If it looks like a duck, walks like a duck, and talks like a duck, let us now imagine, perhaps it is a story of an altogether different feather, one whose patterns of flight and landing we have only begun to fathom.

Chapter One
Dialogue and Storytelling

1

The story of Selim and Alexander begins in the Bavarian village of Rosenheim with minimalist dialogue. When a train reserved for migrant laborers from Turkey stops briefly in January 1965, a young German soldier defies the stationmaster's admonitions not to board the northbound train. Concerned only with returning to base on time, Alexander initially ignores the welcoming gestures made by one of the five Turkish men sharing a compartment for six. The absentminded interloper finally responds to a tap on his shoulder and the German word for "please" by occupying the sixth seat and greeting his traveling companions as custom warrants. They all reply in kind, but then silence sets in. Quickly burying himself in his newspaper, the awkward newcomer spends the remainder of the journey exchanging stolen glances with the Turks around him, especially Selim, the most attentive observer in the compartment. When another traveler intones the laborers' destination as a question, to ask whether Alexander is also headed for Kiel, the uncomprehending soldier merely shrugs his shoulders, says nothing, and wonders to himself what the presumably foreign utterance could mean. Eventually the industrial recruits resume their Turkish conversation, and Alexander reads on. The two protagonists of Sten Nadolny's *Selim oder Die Gabe der Rede* [Selim or The Gift of Speech], a novel that made literary history in 1990, do not cross paths again until 1967, when circuitous routes and diverse experiences in postwar Germany lead them to the same bar in West Berlin. The deep friendship that ensues spans two continents and three decades in which Alexander experiences Selim as "the genius of storytelling" and "a story" that Alexander wants to tell (318, 47). The novel is in turn narrated by a writer reflecting on the pitfalls of rhetoric, narration, and epistemological hubris. In the novel within the novel the unwitting Alexander is characterized by his narrating self as the complete tourist in Turkey: "money, diarrhea, a bad mood and not a clue" (447). Obsessed throughout his life with rhetoric and oratory, Alexander functions in neither narrative frame as a master storyteller or even a good conversationalist. Recounting their first verbal exchange over two years after the fact, Selim laughingly notes that the train conversation had consisted of "hello," "good bye," and Alexander reading the newspaper in between (225). Dialogue and storytelling are clearly centrifugal motifs in *Selim*. This is the third of several novels by a mainstream German author whose bestseller about an Arctic explorer has been translated into over a dozen languages (1997a; Günther 36). How can we best evaluate the dialogic and storytelling functions of *Selim*, by all accounts the first German literary work to address the phenomenon of Turkish migration in sustained fictional narrative?[1]

Scholars agree that *Selim* marks a sea change in German literary production since 1945 (Durzak 1993; Günther 1993; Adelson 1994; Von Dirke 1994; Kuruyazıcı 1995; Bosse 1996; Adelson 1997c; Gökberk 1997a; Mecklenburg 1999: 135; Hoffmann 2001; Mani 2001). Offering "the panorama of a quarter century of German history,"[2] the novel breaks with a longstanding tendency by majority writers in the Federal Republic simply to overlook Turkish migration as a phenomenon warranting literary reflection. Anke Bosse suggests that German public consciousness of Turks over the last several decades has been inversely proportional to the increased visibility of Turks in German social life. While prolific writers and long-term residents such as Aras Ören and Güney Dal have authored many Turkish-language novels weaving narrative strands about Turkish migration into complex tapestries of German history and European fiction, their work is often relegated to the sociological category of "guest worker literature" by critics in Germany, despite its availability in excellent translations.[3] On those occasions when Turkish migrants do appear in mainstream German literature of the last forty years, they tend to serve as background ciphers of incoherence or symbolic victims of discrimination (Teraoka 1987; Durzak 1980, 1993).[4] If one considers Turkish themes in recent novels by well established Jewish writers such as Katja Behrens and Maxim Biller, a longstanding oversight seems far less entrenched around 2000 than it did a decade earlier. With a major publisher announcing Thorsten Becker's new novel as a "greatly conceived guest worker epic" (Becker 2003), and with Dal's imminent publication of an " 'old-fashioned Gastarbeiter novel' " (Clarke 12), the sea change begun with *Selim* may soon give rise to more frequent waves.[5] Yet Nadolny's novel occupies a lonely position on the German literary landscape at the end of the postwar era. Even in the wake of public outrage over murderous xenophobia in the early 1990s, one famous writer remarks, "in our works one seldom encounters the people for whose civil rights we have committed ourselves" (Schneider 1995: 487).[6] What role then accrues to an indispensable Turk and genial *raconteur* in Nadolny's panoramic sweep of postwar German history?

Although scholars agree that the story of Selim and Alexander signaled something new in contemporary literature, analytical assessments of the innovation vary. Critical differences indicate two common points of departure. One approach situates the metacritical narrative, multiperspectival focalization, and Alexander's growing humility in the broader context of Nadolny's aesthetic oeuvre (Günther 1993; Wittstock 1994; Bohnenkamp 1996; Bunzel 1996a; Überhoff 2002). From this vantage *Selim* is a good example of Nadolny's overall preference for stories bespeaking "victory in failure" (Bunzel 1996a: 167). This focus is sometimes tied to Nadolny's categorization as a postmodernist writer (Wittstock 272–275), but it is rarely linked to intercultural themes. Instead "the stranger's gaze" is deemed characteristic for all of Nadolny's protagonists (Günther 40), and the motif of storytelling in *Selim* is understood in terms of Nadolny's overall attempts to revive epic narration in the 1980s (Überhoff 2002: 5–6; Günther 37).[7] Nadolny subsequently published a novel about Hermes (1997b), which prompted one scholar to liken the impertinent messenger of the gods to Selim, "a peppy teller of tales" (Überhoff 8).

In contrast to analyses stressing narrative experimentation with virtually no attention to cultural difference in *Selim*, other scholars offer pointedly intercultural interpretations by focusing on the Turkish identity of the friend whom Alexander seeks to know and the ostensibly Turkish story that the German wants to tell. This approach is usually underwritten by the notion that two distinct worlds encounter each other in the friendship between the two men. Nilüfer Kuruyazıcı's account of the novel's reception in Germany and Turkey characterizes the protagonists as "representatives of two worlds," who enable readers from "both cultures" to read the novel in culturally specific ways (23).[8] An emphasis on dialogic communication is often key to interpretations that see two distinct worlds meeting in the story of Selim and Alexander. First to note the novel's innovative status in German literary history at the "intersections of intercultural experience," Manfred Durzak considers *Selim* a utopian novel in which "different cultural–historical paradigms enter into a dialogue, in which both sides learn and benefit" (1993: 303–304). Sabine von Dirke asks, "Does the novel develop a dialogical structure that allows the foreigner's voice to articulate itself?" (62). She then contends that the novel only feigns dialogue, because the Turkish Selim at best represents the German Alexander's "idealized projection of the Oriental storyteller" (62). Bosse, Gökberk, and Mani all take issue with von Dirke's reproach of Orientalism for reasons that revolve around the role of dialogue in intercultural understanding. For Mani, Selim is the subaltern who "speaks" when his German interlocutor presents their joint "narraphasia" (2001: 32, 39).[9] The most sustained intercultural reading of *Selim* comes from Gökberk, who bemoans the lack of a genuinely "dialogic model" in minority studies as they intersect with German cultural studies (1997a: 101).[10] In her view Nadolny offers an alternative model of understanding, whereby Alexander and Selim relate to one another as "complementary, brotherly possibilities" transcending any putatively absolute divide between Orient and Occident while respecting differences that matter (103). Citing Wierlacher on intercultural hermeneutics, Gökberk speaks of a " 'process of approximation' " with considerable utopian potential (see also Blioumi 33). By this account cultural differences between Selim and Alexander are partial rather than absolute, though significant enough for understanding to be always partial too. Alexander's "failed encounter with Turkish culture" fuels the narrator's self-critical reflections on the necessarily "fragmentary nature of understanding," especially where "the gap" between Turkish and German mentalities is concerned (113–114). Alexander sheds the Eurocentric stereotypes with which he began, Gökberk argues, and the frame novel reflects on this process. According to this mode of analysis, talking and narrating alike function in the novel in complementary ways to advance the approximation that intercultural attempts at understanding at best entail. Hoffmann similarly characterizes Nadolny's narrative as a bridge advancing the "dialogue between cultures" (132).

For Durzak, the novel's "intercultural contribution to knowledge" is cemented when Alexander travels to Turkey, where he learns how to understand strange behaviors in Germany on the basis of living situations in Turkey (298). Gökberk likewise identifies the chapter "In Turkey" as the hinge on which the novel turns (1997a: 110), for there Alexander confronts and abandons his prejudices. Much justifies this recourse to Turkey as a decisive point of reference for understanding the story of Selim and Alexander as an encounter between two national cultures. When the narrator characterizes Selim, months before the military coup that rocked Turkey in 1980, as both "a story" Alexander wants to tell and someone to whom he is "duty-bound," for example, a lone sentence fragment refers to "anarchy and terror, many dead" in Turkey (47). This seems to suggest that the story the German narrator feels duty-bound to tell is indeed a Turkish story, more specifically, a Turkish story emanating from the Republic of Turkey. Yet the competing claim that Nadolny's novel "renders postwar German history intelligible in previously uncharted ways" (Adelson 1997c: 280) rests on a different fulcrum: the dialogic scenario with which the story of Selim and Alexander begins.[11] Revisiting the train scene demonstrates how the story of Selim that Alexander wants to tell is in some pivotal respects a fundamentally German story, albeit one enabled by Turkish migration. In telling this "Selim" story, Alexander writes his postwar self into the German national narrative by way of the Turkish figure around which the novel revolves. This is not another example of a Eurocentric Self projecting its fantasies onto an Orientalized Other (Von Dirke, Akbulut). If the novel acknowledges social transformations sparked by postwar labor migration—"The wide world came to us, and with it we continued the journey" (42)—Alexander's reflections on Selim's gift of speech situate the figure of the Turkish migrant at the core of a decidedly German cultural dilemma. How does this work?[12]

As Selim observes, the initial dialogue with Alexander consists of "hello," "good bye," and something not especially communicative in between. Burying himself in his newspaper, Alexander scans several articles, among which only one longer item captures his attention.[13] The piece that he tears out and tucks into his pocket is "about the Auschwitz trial" (48). This unelaborated reference indexes what most German readers would recognize as a major turning point in West Germany's attempts to come to critical terms with the Nazi past. After the Nuremberg trials of 1946 and the Eichmann trial of 1961, the "Auschwitz trial" in Frankfurt on the Main preoccupied the German public from December 1963 to August 1965 (Pendas 2000). Resulting from inquiries launched by the Central Office for Investigation of National Socialist Crimes (founded in 1958), these legal proceedings against former members of the SS were the first highly publicized trials undertaken by the West German state on its own behalf. By the time Alexander busies himself with newspaper coverage of the trial, the German media had devoted extensive attention to the proceedings for over a year. In October 1965, a controversial play based on trial transcripts and other documentation would grip the German public when it premiered on fifteen different stages in West and East simultaneously (Weiss 1965a, 1966). The unarticulated significance of the reading material that competes with migrant laborers for Alexander's attention in the train scene looms large, even if Alexander never comments on this significance as character or narrator in any time frame.[14] Many elements underscore the haunting presence of a difficult German legacy in the encounter between Alexander and Selim, including the town where the military recruit boards the "special train" reserved for Turkish laborers. The Nuremberg trials are explicitly indexed when the narrator conjures an image of Göring, the "much touted 'great son' " of Rosenheim, as the Nazi *Reichsmarschall* faced his victorious accusers "with headphones before the court" (18). As the narrator subsequently reveals in the frame novel, one of the burning questions for Alexander in the 1960s is "the question of [his] intellectual relationship with those who had worked for Hitler" (263).[15] Scholars for whom Selim and Alexander represent a generic contrast between the storytelling gifts of premodern cultures and the storytelling failures of the industrialized west (Durzak 1993: 302) overlook something important about the function of dialogue in the novel, even as they stress its dialogic contributions to intercultural understanding. For the inaugural dialogue between Selim and Alexander is emblematic in historically particular ways. This particularity—encapsulated in the news "about the Auschwitz trial"—transforms the rhetorical figure of Selim into a German story that Alexander struggles to tell by weaving himself and the Turkish migrant into the fabric of the national narrative simultaneously.[16]

There are two primary means by which historical particularity accrues to dialogic scenarios in the novel. One involves dialogic exchange in which the spoken or unspoken topic of conversation is the problematic legacy of the Nazi past, which is cast as a speech problem for Alexander and his generational cohort, born around 1945 and raised in the West German state founded in 1949. The other involves extended narrative descriptions of physical gestures, facial expressions, and behavioral affects that underwrite conversations in which Alexander is emotionally invested. The minimalist dialogic structure of the early train scene ("hello," "good-bye," and a lot of something else in between) includes both, which makes it a seminal if implicit point of reference for many dialogues and stories that follow. Alexander's reluctance to converse with his Turkish traveling companions in 1965 stems only in part from arrogance, ignorance, and prejudice. Speech is a life-long obsession for him; it stymies him at every turn.[17] Two examples of dialogic exchange in which the fascist legacy emerges as a topic and a problem for Alexander help clarify the nature of his dilemma. Encountering the former Nazi who had taught him Greek and rhetoric in high school, Alexander virtually cringes at having to exchange any words with him: "He didn't want to speak with that one" (16). The polite words that the two men exchange in actual conversation bespeak harmless pleasantries, leaving the former student, who experiences everything about his teacher "as a type of camouflage" (17), to fume inside, as internal focalization reveals. Imagining the older man committing suicide, a young girl begging for her life in the Warsaw Ghetto, and Göring brought to justice in Nuremberg, Alexander experiences this conversation as a personal "defeat" (18). He knows "why he wanted to be able to speak: he wanted to intimidate, wound, send all these well-meaning toads into flight, . . . to strike jovial blabbermouths dumb" (18). The discrepancy between the semantic register of "toads" and "blabbermouths" and the affective range of shame and rage is a symptom of Alexander's decidedly historical speech problem in the Third Reich's democratic successor state, where atonement had been institutionalized and institutions normalized. One of these institutions provides the setting for a bedtime conversation in which the topic of Hitler's renowned powers of speech exposes an attitudinal rift in the antifascist military of the 1960s. As one critical bunkmate groans, " 'To still want to be a public speaker after Hitler, I can't imagine that.' " The rejoinder comes quickly from another bed: " 'That's exactly my opinion,' " the final speaker echoes and turns out the light: " 'he'll always be the greatest in that' " (93). No voice comments on this ironic twist, but readers later learn that the young Alexander aspires to become the officer "responsible for conversation" (101), for he dreams of arming himself with effective speech against the Nazi past.[18]

This eludes him, as the second type of dialogic scenario makes clear. While the Turkish men in the train compartment talk animatedly among themselves, Alexander signals nonverbal interest in their conversation, however faintly. "The German read but looked as though he were listening, even smiled a little when everyone laughed" (46). His reading is therefore wedded to interest and inefficacy in conversation. During a later argument about antifascist resistance with the same soldier who admires Hitler's rhetorical powers, Alexander feels again defeated in conversation and thinks back to the Turks on the train.

> How nice it would be, he thought, for a limited time not to understand any language, not even one's own. He thought of the Turkish conversations on the train.
>   He thought he could again remember the time when he was still too little to understand language. But he had enjoyed listening: one word fit into another, the pauses into movements, and it kept going on. Sometimes one person spoke, then another, everything hung together, and everyone took joy in it. The voices climbed high up, deep down, figures emerged from sounds and interesting noises. To this they moved hands and heads, adjusted their chairs, kept showing new, odd folds around their eyes and mouth. The best was when everyone laughed about a word and showed their teeth, then a light came into their faces. (84)

Alexander's underlying fascination with conversation is not about ideological content or communicative substance at all. It stems instead from formative childhood scenes in which he had first admired his biological brother, "a born speaker" (84), and then tragically lost him. The quotation above is immediately followed by this brotherly story, which ends in 1949 when the German boy with the gift of speech finds live German munitions and an untimely death in a creek near his home. When the narrator finishes this story, we are privy to Alexander "freezing" and resuming his reading on resistance (85). A young soldier in the German *Wehrmacht* in 1944, another story line has it, Alexander's father was sent to "certain death" at the front for having criticized Hitler "too loudly" (206). Alexander's speech problem is a tangled web of personal and institutionalized trauma, grief, shame, and accountability. The inaugural dialogue with migrant laborers is to be located within this web, and Alexander's affective investment in "the Turkish conversations on the train" is central to the story that *Selim* has to tell.

When Bunzel refers to Selim as Alexander's "surrogate brother" (1996a: 162) and Gökberk characterizes the friends as "brotherly possibilities" (1997a: 103), they come close to capturing an important aspect of Alexander's narrative relationship to Selim. Reflecting on this relationship after learning belatedly of Selim's death, however, Alexander uses the phrase "almost a brother to me" (474). Attending to modes of indirection in the novel allows us to understand dialogic and storytelling functions obscured in a rhetoric of complementarity. If Alexander experiences Selim "almost" like a brother, then he also experiences Turks in dialogue *almost* like a conversation in which he could do more than stumble and freeze. Turkish characters eventually learn to speak flawless German, but it is "the Turkish conversations" that Alexander cannot understand which speak most importantly to him. A subsequent description of Turks talking animatedly among themselves echoes the attention to affect that characterizes the time when Alexander was "still too little to understand language." This is the bar dialogue that Alexander observes when Selim reenters his life in Berlin:

> The lecture [by Mesut] seemed to have no effect on Selim, for suddenly he burst out laughing and went up to the bar without explaining himself in order to change a ten-spot. Mesut sat there stunned and waited for the other man to listen again. When the wrestler came back, he gave himself over to a song of complaint, but probably meant it in scorn. Then he sat down and spoke a single sentence, laconic and hard. Mesut now seemed to want to defend himself, poked back in scorn, got excited. Two other southern-looking men had stopped near the table and listened. Mesut raised his voice and delivered a chain of apodictic sentences. In the meantime the wrestler took off his right shoe and inspected it like a shoemaker, straightened his sock and mumbled an excuse. But then he immediately took over, spoke quickly and very distinctly, became louder, yelled downright, and stood up. As in the opening of a feud, he threw his shoe onto the floor in front of Mesut, then picked it up again and couldn't hold back his laughter. The other Turks laughed too. Then the wrestler became serious again and, while he slowly sat down again, began to tell a longer story in a musical rhythm. Mesut kept shaking his head scornfully and asking questions, to which the wrestler apparently responded not at all or only later. He concluded his speech with a word that took effect and he paused so that Mesut could answer. Mesut didn't. He was impressed, or else nothing else occurred to him. Selim grabbed Mesut's forearm and shook it, said something cheering and added a joke that everyone laughed at. Even Mesut managed a sour smile.
> "Excuse me," the new guy said to Alexander. "We were chatting a bit." (219)

Two things are striking about this dialogic scenario as compared with the one on the train and the idyllic childhood scenario in which joy prevails. For one, Alexander does not bury himself in text but follows a conversation he does not understand with keen and sustained interest. For another, the conversational affects described incorporate elements of conflict. When "the new guy" then explains to Alexander what has just transpired— " 'We were chatting a bit' "—he indeed functions as a kind of speech teacher for the German protagonist. But this role ultimately accrues to Selim as a rhetorical figure in the novel's narrative economy, not as a character.[19]

The Turkish "genius of storytelling"—as a narrative figure rather than a character's identity—allows Alexander to revisit the stunted dialogic scenes of his past and his nation's past. This does not mean that Turkish laborers arriving in the 1960s brought exculpatory salvation to the German youth whose affect and intellect erupted into social movements associated with 1968.[20] Nadolny rather refashions the national narrative of postwar vintage as the shared story of Selim and Alexander. The recognition that the character Selim shares unequally in this story (Gökberk 1997a: 102) is not incompatible with the realization that Nadolny makes Turkish migration indispensable to the complex German story Alexander is drawn to tell. The German national context remains the primary frame of reference here in ways that will have less clear purchase in the decade following *Selim*'s publication and national unification.[21] Authors such as Şenocak and Özdamar, who began to make their literary mark in Germany only in this decade of rapid transformation, write Turkish subjects of German culture and remembrance into being in ways that Nadolny did not yet envision for Selim. After all, this character is deported to Turkey as early as 1982, while Turkish characters, immigrants, and authors in the 1990s are less easily displaced from a rapidly changing German landscape in an era when cultural questions are no longer overdetermined by postwar discourse. In the 1960s, Nadolny's narrator observes, "One still lived in two different parts of the earth, Europe and Asia. One wanted to hold on to that. It had a somehow calming effect" (117). While this observation belies the cultural innovation that *Selim*'s deployment of dialogue and storytelling signifies, the novel overall teeters precariously between two competing paradigms. This is why intercultural analyses by scholars such as Durzak, Gökberk, and Kuruyazıcı yield insights into certain aspects of the story of Selim and Alexander, but it is also why an intercultural paradigm presupposing dialogue between "two worlds" cannot account for other affective and stylistic dimensions of the novel. There are other dialogues and stories in *Selim* that scholars have discussed at length elsewhere. The analysis here illuminates instead those dialogic and storytelling functions that signal a watershed event in West German literature around 1990.

2

What does it mean to speak of a Turkish presence in German literature on the cusp of the twenty-first century? Roughly ten years after Nadolny made literary history with *Selim*, a seemingly minor piece of literary prose by Emine Sevgi Özdamar challenges us to pose this question anew.[22] Arguably the most widely read author of German-language literature to have been born in Turkey, Özdamar represents a formidable literary talent on the contemporary landscape generally.[23] While she entered the annals of German literary history in 1991 when she became the first Turkish-born author to win the coveted Bachmann Prize—for an excerpt from her novel about coming of age in modern Turkey (2000b)—this writer made her prose debut in 1990 with a collection called *Mother Tongue*, the two lead stories of which unfold on the seam of divided Germany.[24] A German citizen since 1996 (Özdamar 2001: 121), Özdamar first came to Germany as an industrial laborer in 1965 for a two-year stint in West Berlin, followed by three years of theatrical training in Istanbul. In the crushing wake of the military coup of 1971 political reasons compelled her to leave Turkey for Europe again, but it was not until 1976 that Özdamar began working extensively in German theaters—first in the East German theaters of Berlin and later in the West German city of Bochum—as an actor, dramaturge, and playwright.[25] Two major novels have appeared in the interim. *Die Brücke vom Goldenen Horn* [The Bridge of the Golden Horn] revolves around 1968 from Turkish, German, and French perspectives, while *Seltsame Sterne starren zur Erde* [Strange Stars Stare Toward Earth] revisits the two Berlins of the 1970s with a German–Jewish bohemian artist from another era as the author's muse.[26] For her first decade of creative work in German Özdamar received the Adelbert von Chamisso Prize in 1999.[27] Written in the same year for a literary competition but published only in 2001 as the title story in a collection of short prose, "The Courtyard in the Mirror" (*Der Hof im Spiegel*) will receive sustained attention here.[28] Unlike Nadolny's extended novelistic and largely masculinist reflections on a Turkish guest worker in the decades just prior to unification, Özdamar's "Courtyard" is deceptively short, an intricately crafted tale of a Turkish woman living in Germany in the 1990s.[29] The lines of the story chart a "personal city map" (17) in a West German city clearly identifiable, without being named, as Düsseldorf. If new meaning accrues to national frames of reference in Nadolny's *Selim*, the rest of this chapter demonstrates how something approximating postnational intimacy manifests itself in Özdamar's "Courtyard in the Mirror." It does so by virtue of narrative and dialogic functions having little to do with the communicative exchange and entrenched binarisms associated with sociopolitical calls for a "dialogue of cultures" between Germans and Turks (or between the civilizational paradigms that these groups are often taken to signify when they encounter each other). Neither do these functions have much in common with the willed refusal to be understood that Sommer associates with the negative hermeneutics of "bilingual games" in multicultural contexts of the western hemisphere, largely because the politics of identity developed in those contexts does not underwrite Özdamar's prose.[30] When Şenocak called for "something like a negative hermeneutic" in an essay on Salman Rushdie (2000: 42), the Turkish-born writer had what he later called the "wounds of communication" (68) in mind. Although Şenocak and Sommer use a similar terminology to reject related modes of presumptive cross-cultural understanding, Şenocak's literary projects of the 1990s can no more be grasped in terms of ethnic identity politics than Özdamar's. Chapter two is devoted to an analysis of the differently transnational strategies that Şenocak develops in *Perilous Kinship*. For the present we turn to Özdamar's "Courtyard in the Mirror," a short text that labors to lengthen the ties that bind.

3

The transition from the friendly gift of gab in *Selim* to neighborly figures of reference in "The Courtyard" necessitates a brief return to Appadurai. In *Modernity at Large*, this critical anthropologist posits, "an unprecedented constellation" of electronic techonologies and mass migration at the end of the twentieth century has given rise to "a new role for the imagination in social life" (3–4). Appadurai is necessary for my discussion of "The Courtyard," but not because *Modernity at Large* has anything to say about the medium of literature. Like many social scientists, Appadurai offers expository readings of literary excerpts to illustrate points that could be made without any discussion of literature at all. He is conjured here for important conceptual work entailed in his discussion of "ethnoscapes" and "the production of locality." In spite of his frequent rhetorical invocation of various worlds, "world" is not a central term in his analysis of the new role accruing to imagination in social life today. Rejecting the national–cultural frames of reference that animated area studies prior to globalization, he stresses disjunctive features in global cultural flows. By this account, "the work of the imagination" (9 and passim) in social life proceeds by breaks and ruptures, not in terms of communal continuity or contiguity. "[T]he break caused by the joint force of electronic mediation and mass migration is explicitly transnational—even postnational," Appadurai claims. This distinguishes his theory of "the global modern" from classical theories of modernization, which privilege the nation-state as a frame of reference (9–11; see also Beck). Appadurai's main concern is newly diasporic modes of social interaction in a postnational world. Diaspora is less relevant to the literature of Turkish migration in Germany than it may be to other arenas of Turkish social life in Europe. But I am interested in the terminology Appadurai develops to capture proliferating interactive contexts in and through which new roles accrue to the social labor of imagination.[31]

Modernity at Large calls for more rigorous approaches to "*intercontextual* relations" in the discipline of anthropology (187). Toward this goal Appadurai contributes five key terms to designate interactive dimensions of a "global cultural economy" understood "as a complex, overlapping, disjunctive order" superseding models predicated on center and periphery (32). These five "building blocks" of social imagination are designated as ethnoscapes, mediascapes, technoscapes, financescapes, and ideoscapes (33). Only the first is of primary concern here.[32] Appadurai defines *ethnoscape* as "the landscape of persons who constitute the shifting world in which we live" (33). Applying this definition to the Turkish situation in Germany should not be taken to mean that the social landscape of a multicultural Germany is simply characterized by ethnic diversity, with each ethnoscape representing a distinct ethnic identity. It would mean instead that—in some instances— Turks and Germans (and others, too) occupy the same ethnoscape.[33] Özdamar's stories warrant critical readings through this lens.

Appadurai's final chapter highlights "the production of locality," which some critics have confused with "the local" as a counterpoint to "the transnational" (e.g., Ong 4).[34] Appadurai's discussion of the production of locality is an extended reflection on the crisis of anthropology in "a dramatically delocalized world" (178). Bypassing his disciplinary concerns, I focus on the definition of locality as "a complex phenomenological quality, constituted by a series of links between the sense of social immediacy, the technologies of interactivity, and the relativity of contexts" (178). Appadurai reserves "neighborhood" for "actually existing social forms" in which locality is produced in variable ways (178–179). Özdamar's tale of Düsseldorf, which features a Turkish woman negotiating complex yet indistinct relations with neighbors in her building and the one across the courtyard, almost demands to be read with an eye to the production of locality as defined in *Modernity at Large*. Yet I do not propose to read this literary gem as an exposition of Appadurai's thesis. The medial economy of the text beckons.

At first glance the courtyard vectors of sociality seem to mimic the "long-distance" affinities that Benedict Anderson associates with imagining the nation and those that Appadurai associates with the postnation of diasporic public spheres.[35] The Turkish woman who narrates the story from the vantage point of her apartment in Düsseldorf evidences the closest emotional ties to her interlocutors in Turkey, and the ethnoscape of her German environment is peopled with Moroccan, South African, and Yugoslavian figures in addition to German figures—who predominate—and a Black African family whose national origin is not specified. These transnational ciphers also seem situated in an instantiation of the local, given that most of these figures reside in the narrator's immediate neighborhood. But spatial vectors of imagined affinities are not what they seem. If Turkey is a national frame of reference in "The Courtyard," it is mediated through the figures of the narrator's parents, both of whom die, and a close friend who is a poet identified in the text proper only as Can.[36] The narrator had grown to love these figures while living in Turkey under circumstances characterized by "short-distance" rather than "long-distance" identification. From her distanced location in Düsseldorf, she speaks frequently by telephone with her mother and later her friend. These are people whom she knows intimately but cannot see, though she can hear them by telephone. This is in contrast to figures in her immediate environment, whom she sees and hears but does not know intimately. The narrator is the only Turkish figure in Düsseldorf to which we are privy in "The Courtyard." For these reasons, the story warrants reading against the grain of "long-distance" identifications in the age of mass migration and globalization. Rather than celebrating the local as a counterpoint to nation, transnation, or postnation, "The Courtyard" articulates an opportunity to reflect on "the production of locality"—the production of the "here and now" (Appadurai 1–23). This transpires through the medium of a literary text written under the sign of Turkish migration nearly forty years after its onset.

Given the frequency with which mass migration is coupled in the critical imagination with electronic mediation "at the close of the mechanical age" (Tabbi and Wutz 2), the nearly complete absence of references to electronic media in Özdamar's "Courtyard" is striking. A lone reference to computerized photography pales amidst the many medial leitmotifs in reference to which the narrator's tale unfolds. These include mirrors, windows, doors, telephones, televisions, and books. Even allusions to television redirect attention to literary or social mediation rather than invoking the electronic reproduction of images. The occupants of the apartment directly below the narrator repair televisions for the neighborhood, which makes them privy to all kinds of information about what is happening to whom. In punning fashion that proves pivotally characteristic for this piece, Özdamar designates these repairmen as a *Fernsehnachrichtendienst*, a "long-distance-viewing news service" (22). Textual elaboration clarifies that no televised images are at stake and the news provided concerns people living close by. "They knew everything about the people who lived on the street, because many people brought them their television sets to be fixed, bought a new television set from them, or the two of them made house calls to the people's apartments. When I wanted to know something, I went to them" (22). This news service also has blind spots. When the narrator wants to find a former neighbor who has disappeared, the "long-distance-viewing news service" falters. " 'He was a very interesting man,' " the repairmen tell her, " 'but he did not have a television set, so we don't know anything about him' " (40).

The repairmen, who had previously been pilots in South Africa, also indict any long-distance imaging capabilities associated with documentary television. " 'What goes on there, no television can report' " (21).[37]

"The Courtyard" alludes to only a single specific television image, and this is introduced through an extended simile when the narrator describes a sad German cashier whose shoulders she offers to massage. "Her eyes looked like the eyes of a chicken that I had seen on television" (34). This was a very unhappy chicken indeed, one among many being led to slaughter after a living death in cramped industrial cages. The image seems just as forlorn as the poor chicken, for the simile quickly yields to another comparison, one that makes the television image recede into the distant background. "[This chicken] had such tired eyes, as tired as those of a wise grandmother who wants to prevent a war but whose words no longer had any value. That is how the cashier's eyes looked in the little supermarket now" (34). Such referential overlay is intensified when comparative references are invoked but unmoored from any particular antecedent. For example, when the narrator travels to Istanbul after learning of her mother's death, she searches everywhere for women who resemble her mother. She finds one at a small train station. "Sitting on the ground there were Kurdish women and children who had been brought there as seasonal laborers. But it had rained a great deal, and the cotton that they were supposed to pick had become wet. One of the Kurdish women was crying loudly. Her crying was similar to the crying of my mother, but the train pulled out, and I still heard her crying voice" (13). Does the voice heard at the end of this passage belong to the seasonal laborer or the narrator's deceased mother?

The referent cannot be syntactically resolved, a detail that reverberates with other ways in which Özdamar mediates the vibrant production of the here and now in text. A telephone conversation between the narrator in Düsseldorf and her grieving father in Istanbul echoes both referential indeterminacy and the deictic production of locality.

—Father, what are you doing?
—I am sitting here in the dark.
—So am I, father. (16)

Readers might justifiably understand that the daughter is sitting in the dark in Düsseldorf while her father sits in the dark in Istanbul. But the linked "here" of the father's utterance and the "too" of the daughter's in the German original (*Ich auch, Vater*) cannot be resolved geographically on the text's narrative terms as such. Production of a here and now is both substance and medium of this story. What are the figures of mediation and structures of narration that lend this tale such referential vibrancy of deictic detail?[38]

The three mirrors in the narrator's apartment and the telephone near the mirror in her kitchen are central to the first-person perspective of narration and reciprocally referential. "I always stood in front of the mirror whenever I used the telephone" (25). Whenever this "I" talks with her mother by telephone in front of the mirror, she hears background noises from the city streets of Istanbul while she describes to her mother what her neighbors are doing in Düsseldorf.[39] She has access to this information because she observes her neighbors across the courtyard, as she regularly does, not through the window but by means of the mirrors in her apartment.[40] We rarely see her looking out the window or directly into the courtyard at all. The neighbors across the way of greatest interest to the narrative are nuns in the main building and tenants to whom they rent the basement apartment.

> The three mirrors gathered all the windows and floors and the garden of the nuns' house together from three different perspectives. When I stood with my back to the courtyard, I saw all the nuns' windows and their garden in the three mirrors. We all lived in three mirrors nose-to-nose together. When I woke up, I did not look into the courtyard from the balcony, but looked in the mirror instead. (26)

This Turkish "I" even hears her own voice only when looking in the mirror (27). This seems odd, since she never looks for her own face in the mirror and only sometimes happens to catch a glimpse of it while looking at or for someone else. This disqualifies Özdamar's deployment of the mirror from inclusion in Jenijoy LaBelle's feminist account of the modern literary tradition of women looking at themselves in reflective surfaces. According to LaBelle, "What women want is not the world's mirror, but a mirror of their own" (185). This is no more applicable to the courtyard narrator than LaBelle's emphasis on relations mediating "interiority and exteriority" in the semiotics of the literary self (9, 12).[41] Is the narrating persona of the courtyard story a medium of some sort rather than an implied self? As a textual function, the narrating "I" presents information to readers about the configuration of the textual world, and the human being to whom readers imagine the "I" refers tries to make sense of this information. What else is there to say about this referential indeterminacy, which characterizes many first-person narratives?[42]

Despite the affect of mourning infusing this story, in which eventually all the dead take up residence with the living in the mirror over the kitchen table, it would be difficult to say whether the narrating persona of "The Courtyard" has an inner life in any self-constituting sense.[43] Such a life seems closest when the "I" mourns her Turkish mother in Düsseldorf. But most of the narrative is devoted to recounting habitual behaviors of

German neighbors who live above, across, and otherwise near the narrator, whose own observational habits connote an emotive investment in social relations with her neighbors, especially the Germans among them, without denoting any relational substance. This suggests that the narrator—in both the abstract and the characterological functions attached to the "I"— reproduces and produces complex structures of social affinity without filling them with content otherwise associated with ethnic identities or national archives. This emphasis on behavioral patterns allows the narrator to notice ruptures in her neighbors' quotidian habits. She invariably reacts to these breaks as significant phenomena, but what they signify is often left as a question mark in the minds of readers.[44]

Even when the text provides ostensible answers regarding the significance of rupture events, many questions remain as to what they mean to the narrator. For example, Mr. Volker lives directly above her. She monitors his movements by the sound of footsteps and patterns of light in the stairwell, which filter through the milk-glass door to her apartment. She infers his presence on the stairs from the regularity of his habits. But then an observation signals something amiss. "His steps used to be much louder than they are now" (11). Even when we learn that his lover has left him and his Turkish neighbor acts in a manner signaling compassion, the emotional content of this interaction is not substantiated. The narrating "I" also observes a change of pattern in the butcher shop nearby, which was run by an elderly woman together with her son and daughter-in-law. We read of the elderly butcher, "Normally the butcher shop was always full of customers, but on this evening she was standing there alone" (19). The narrator had not intended to buy anything but enters the butcher shop when the butcher catches her eye.

> Kling, kling. The door opened and shut. In the glass refrigerator I saw nothing but a few frozen chickens.
> "Don't you have any fresh chickens today?"
> "No."
> The old woman looked into my eyes for a long time. After an hour I went back and bought a frozen chicken. (19)

Much remains unsaid in this dialogue and the framing narrative. This electrically charged exchange is apparently pregnant with meaning, as is the surrounding narrative, but meaning is withheld.[45] Even when we learn that the young butchers have been killed in a traffic accident and that the Turkish "I" cries about this with her mother on the telephone, the emotional content of these affective affinities is left to our imagination. The same could be said of the Turkish woman's considerable investment in Hartmut, a down-and-out aristocrat whose disappearance from the basement apartment across the courtyard prompts her to search the city frantically for him. A bus driver offers one explanation for her agitated disorientation when he asks, " 'Girl, are you in love?' " (39). But the emotional content of this unconventional relationship is never disclosed.

The most important rupture event in the neighborhood's daily routine concerns the old nun across the way, whose hand the narrator regularly sees dispensing crumbs to birds in the garden. References to this nun structure the progression of the narrative, yet the nun is introduced as a referential enigma, with which the story begins.

> I thought she had died. I was standing in the kitchen with my back against the radiator, waiting for the sad light in her room, in the house across the way, where she lived, to go on in the large mirror that was attached to the wall over my kitchen table. For years her light from the house on the other side of the courtyard had been my setting sun. (11)

The emotional content of any possible relationship between the Turkish woman and the old nun is left to readerly speculation, while the "she" of the inaugural speculation acquires referential substance only in the middle of the story with emphasis on the nowness of the speculation. "And now, now I think, the old nun in the courtyard has also died" (24). The ending of the story is signaled structurally by substantive confirmation of the nun's death. Referentiality immediately takes flight again when the narrator dreams of the nun's death as a kind of transubstantiation in which the old nun joins the narrator's deceased mother, father, and grandmother as they fly off into the sky.

The German word *Himmel* does double duty here signifying both *heaven* and *sky*. This homonymous pun is underscored at the story's end when the narrator describes the garden birds, now searching for crumbs in vain, flying off into the sky. A poem about a *Himmel* that is thoroughly soaked getting caught in fishing nets and turning all anglers sky blue has the last word.[46] Whether this is a sky soaked with rain or a heaven soaked with tears is unresolved by either the poem or the story. Acts of crying pepper the latter, as do tagged and untagged puns.[47] *Blau* refers to the color blue, but in common parlance the word also connotes the disoriented state of drunkenness.[48] The combined *Himmelblau* of the poem entails a relational inversion. What was up is down, what was down is up, and the worlds of affect and meaning are topsy-turvy.

Punning figures in another key aspect of the nun's unsubstantiated relationship to the narrator. The old nun was reading *Alice in Wonderland* when she died, her Turkish neighbor acquires this book (a favorite of her own) upon the nun's death, and the narrator dreams that the old nun flies up into the heavens while reading *Alice in Wonderland*. Here the book's trajectory and that of the nun separate. "The book fell out of her hands and flew into the sky. I screamed: 'Alice, Alice, Alice . . .'" (45). To recall the discussion of rhetorical conceits of contact in the introduction, we are in the "world of yoking" now. In analytical terms this is a world where absolute difference has no place. As Jonathan Culler observes in "The Call of the Phoneme," puns "use related forms to connect disparate meanings," and "the surprising coupling" that results often yields "new configurations of meaning" (2–3). *Alice in Wonderland* is famously full of puns, and the title *Alice im Wunderland* can be read as a double pun. *Wunderland* in Özdamar's German original conjures associations with Germany as the land of the *Wirtschaftswunder*, the "economic miracle" that paved the way for large-scale migration involving a Turkish labor force. For decades *Ali* has been the stereotyping moniker in Germany for Turks and other migrants.[49] If one lends the name *Alice* a Turkish pronunciation, we have *Ali-ce*, which means in Turkish "in the manner of Ali" or "in the language of Ali." One could cite many other examples to demonstrate that referential perturbations can be found throughout "The Courtyard in the Mirror."

Özdamar's literary mediation of suspended referentiality differs from any generic suspension of referential substance that one might ascribe to language from a structuralist or poststructuralist perspective. It also differs decisively from the conceptual suspension of migrants on a rhetorical bridge between two mutually exclusive worlds. Özdamar grounds referential suspension in a historical moment in which readers are called upon to situate themselves. On the one hand, this moment is easily identified in calendrical terms as the 1990s. Temporal contours of the courtyard present are established largely by allusion to the general collapse of communism. The narrator situates her father's grief over his wife's death in the historical past, a term that Agnes Heller reserves for structures of social life no longer current. "At that time many Bulgarian Turks were fleeing into Turkey, especially from Bulgaria" (14). Such large-scale flight of Bulgaria's Turkish minority was possible only after 1989. The reference to an earthquake in Turkey cannot refer to the disastrous earthquake of August 17, 1999, because one of the historical personages alive at the time of narration (Can Yücel) died nearly a week before this seismic event occurred. The time of narration can therefore be identified as the 1990s prior to August 1999. On the other hand, the 1990s mark a historical moment widely characterized by epistemological anxiety about the social worlds in which we live and analytical uncertainty about the interlocking contexts in which analysis remains meaningful. Özdamar's particular mode of literary figuration and narrational reference begins to chart the structural contours of a "here and now," a historical context in which the very meaning of referential context has taken flight.

With a nod to Appadurai I submit that literary qualities allow this text to function—in this historical moment—in terms of a technology of localization (1996: 180).[50] This entails no celebration of the local as a facile counterpoint to the national, transnational, or postnational. In a nuanced critique of Anderson's influential work on the novel in relation to long-distance processes by which nations could be imagined, Culler rightly cautions us not to confuse a textual form as "a structural condition of possibility" with historically instantiated perspectives on particular nations that might or might not be mediated through that form ("Anderson" 37). This caution also applies to "The Courtyard," even though I have no name for the textual form by means of which Özdamar prompts us to imagine something approximating a postnational world. Formally this text works the boundary between the world of the text and the world of its contexts with considerable ardor. Additionally, what appears as a migrant subject in this text is both a thematic figure and an abstract function palpitating this boundary and being palpitated by it in turn. What this means requires elaboration. We begin by noting that this thematically infused boundary work cannot be grasped by models of "border culture" that rely on traditional concepts of ethnic identity, national culture, or even "colonial difference" (Mignolo 2000a).[51]

4

David Herman introduces "contextual anchoring" to address a matter of reference to which narratologists have paid insufficient attention, the "boundary work" whereby stories "rely on and challenge the border between text and context" (332, 338). "Contextual anchoring" is Herman's term for "the process whereby a narrative, in a more or less explicit and reflexive way, asks its interpreters to search for analogies" between the textual world of the story and the lived worlds of the interpreters (331). Herman speaks of textual and lived worlds, but we must not confuse these constellations with the two worlds between which migrants are so often presumed to be suspended. Herman's emphasis on "deictic reference" (332)— the storied production of the here-and-now—as one major medium of contextual anchoring in literary narrative is just as important to my reading of "The Courtyard" as Appadurai's anthropological emphasis on "the production of locality." German literature written under the sign of Turkish migration does not simply stand in for twentieth-century contexts of mass migration, national unification, and postnational globalization. But neither can these texts and contexts be read in isolation. They are mutually constitutive. The ways in which this meeting ground is constituted can be articulated only through the boundary work of reading historically in the diversified medial economy of our time.

To say that "The Courtyard" works the boundary between its textual and contextual worlds with considerable ardor is to say two things about the cultural labor signaled by this text. First, the text performs an act of labor by highlighting and teasing this boundary explicitly and implicitly. Second, because of this feature the text prompts readers to reflect critically on the contextual here and now in which text and readers meeting at the millennial turn may be localized. Such historical reflections require the labor of reading quizzically. The ensuing discussion of "The Courtyard" draws attention to key strategies with which the text foregrounds the boundary work associated with contextual anchoring. How the labor of reading the boundary between text and context yields interpretive possibilities that could be characterized as both historical and quizzical will then be elaborated. Doing so allows us to articulate what it means to understand this text as prompting readers to imagine something approximating a postnational world.

According to Herman, "interpreters rely on story logic to make moment-by-moment decisions concerning what constitutes text and what constitutes context" (336). This differs from the interactivity that Marie-Laure Ryan discusses in reference to narrative modes influenced by digital media, given that the boundary work foregrounded by Herman—and Özdamar—does not involve readerly decisions affecting the plot or outcome of the story (2001: 352). Yet the boundary work described by Herman actively engages readers in the "transgression of boundaries assumed to separate the actual and the virtual, the fictional and the real" (338). If Dorrit Cohn insists on an absolute distinction between referentiality and non-referentiality as an indispensable criterion for establishing the fictionality of a given text, Ryan stresses a "continuum" of referential and fictional modes rather than mutually exclusive categories or practices (2002: 357–358). Courtyard referential strategies—and the narrative they enable—play this continuum in such a way that a note struck in one register reverberates in the other. A certifiable reference to the extratextual world resonates with referential parameters of the textual world—as when the really existing *Alice in Wonderland* becomes a virtual figure of reference in Özdamar's tale—but virtual references to the textual world also resonate outward into the contextual world. The deictic features of this text are to be found along this vibrant continuum.

Özdamar's narrator bears no name that would unequivocally distinguish her from or identify her with the author.[52] While the city in which the courtyard is located never is named, an explicit reference to "Germany" identifies the country in which the city may be found (15). The urban environment is also readily identifiable as Düsseldorf (where the author long maintained a residence) by dint of so many verifiable references to historical persons and actual sites that readers seem forcefully directed to situate themselves in the real world (as opposed to a strictly fictional one) and the specific locale to which the narrative refers. References to a busy train station could evoke any large German city, but references to the house where Heinrich Heine was born, the city where Joseph Beuys used to live, and a particular movie theater collectively ground the courtyard narrative in the real city of Düsseldorf. The text does not shy away from mentioning other real cities by name (e.g., Berlin, Istanbul, Munich, Paris, Vienna), and it likewise makes explicit reference to historical persons such as Kurt Weill, Fredric Chopin, Charles Baudelaire, Joseph Conrad, Greta Garbo, and the Marx Brothers in addition to Heine and Beuys. The Turkish poet with whom the "I" is befriended and whose telephone conversations help sustain her after her mother's death is assigned only a first name (Can) in the text, yet the inclusion of some of his poems in the narrative—together with the book's partial dedication to Can Yücel and a bibliographical reference to Yücel's work at the end of the book—render this figure identifiable as Can Yücel.[53] The " 'German song' " that the narrator sings to her mother in one telephone call is similarly identifiable as Bertolt Brecht's "Sailors' Song" (30; Brecht 1990: 76–78), and several poems by Heine and Baudelaire are explicitly tagged as such.[54] Why is the city of Düsseldorf rendered identifiable but nameless? Why does this matter?

The double deixis of the phrase "in this city here" (17, 21) helps us begin to answer these questions. When the text refers explicitly to the house and implicitly to the city where Heine was born, Düsseldorf is referenced as an urban environment that exists verifiably in the extratextual world. When readerly attention is drawn to "this city here," that attention is contextually anchored in Herman's sense. The text goes to some lengths to identify the city to which "this city here" refers as a real one (Düsseldorf), but readers cannot resolve the deictic reference absolutely, since it points to a city in the textual world.[55] The emphatic combination of *this* and *here* encourages readers to seek analogies between what they are made to see in the story world and what they know can be seen in the world outside the text. The entire text probes what it means to live in the here and now, not in a presentist sense (as all the dead living in the kitchen mirror attest) but in terms of a technology of localization. This is a fundamentally relational enterprise.

References to the old nun underwrite many features of "The Courtyard," even the basic structure of the narrative. They do so in such a way that readers are guided to imagine themselves in the positions from which the focalizing "I" narrates the relational quality of the courtyard. The text's inaugural speculation about a possible death is immediately followed by a passage belaboring "here" in decidedly relational terms.

> I was standing in the kitchen with my back against the radiator, waiting for the sad light in her room, in the house across the way, where she lived, to go on in the large mirror that was attached to the wall over my kitchen table. For years her light from the house on the other side of the courtyard had been my setting sun. (11)

The directional signals demand such concentration that readers must imagine each relational turn as the narrative proceeds. The paragraph continues:

> Whenever I saw her lighted window in the kitchen mirror, only then did I turn on the light in the apartment. Now I was standing in the dark and had a biscuit in my hand, but didn't eat, was afraid that I would make too much noise. If she had died . . . (11)

This line of narrative is abandoned until the middle of the story when we read, "And now, now I think, the old nun in the courtyard has also died" (24). The narrator's speculation continues several sentences later: "I waited a while longer in the dark, my back up against the radiator, but the light of the old nun didn't go on again in the kitchen mirror" (25). If the old nun acquires referential substance (as the female who is dying) only in this section, the vantage point of narrative focalization is also recalled here in perspectival detail. As readers we too stand here "in the dark" with our backs up against the radiator. Are we standing in the world of text or context? Just as the deictic reference to "here in the dark" could not be geographically resolved in the narrator's conversation with her father, the here that readers are positioned to share with the "I" of narration is a textual function. It signals the boundary work of contextual anchoring.

Additional boundary work is implied when the narrator claims that the "light from the house on the other side of the courtyard"—which we later learn comes from the old nun's room—has long been her own "setting sun" (11). Nothing indicates that "the house on the other side of the courtyard" is physically situated to the west of the narrator's apartment, and yet the metaphorical invocation of a "setting sun" points to a conventional cipher of physical orientation in the extratextual world. At the same time the possessive pronoun that precedes "setting sun" to yield "my setting sun" stresses relational rather than geographical aspects that might attach to this figure of speech. In contrast to all the German neighbors and establishments referenced by name (e.g., *Herr Volker, Herr Kürten, Hartmut, Renate, Metzgerei Carl*) the six nuns and the priest across the way are not tagged in a way that would identify them as German, unless one takes this to be the default designation in Düsseldorf. More significantly, the female object of reference in this opening passage is literally rendered western when the narrator refers to her as her own "setting sun." Given the many puns that enliven Özdamar's text, this rhetoric of orientation and occidentation evokes the discourse of Orientalism with a double twist. Here a woman from Turkey, a land otherwise associated with "the Orient," directs her gaze to the west. And yet this is hardly cast as defiance, anger, or even critique.[56] For the Turkish woman also orients herself affectionately toward the Christian nun who feeds crumbs to the birds in the garden, reads *Alice in Wonderland*, and is dying. Given the punning on *Himmel* that proves so pivotal in this text, one might even wonder whether the narrator's habitual orientation toward the nun is meant to be depicted as *anhimmelnd* (subserviently adoring). Such a reading would overlook key affective dimensions of the narrative yet to be discussed. The rhetorical figure of "my setting sun" does conjure broadly influential debates about the Orient and the Occident. The author's tongue-in-cheek deployment of this figure of reference represents another instance of boundary work that keeps readers oscillating between the rhetorical world of the text and the contextual worlds of their lives.

This implicit boundary work must be distinguished from the explicitly deictic strategies discussed earlier, but it also contributes to contextual anchoring. Other implied instances of boundary work demand to be read with a grain of salt, such that a text infused with the affect of mourning also tickles our funny bone.[57] A prime example of this concerns a parrot shop, which the narrator designates as the first item she would draw on her personal map of the city. " 'Excuse me, how many languages does your parrot speak?' The saleswoman said, 'We speak German' " (17). Here the sales clerk uses the first-person plural to circumscribe a community of speech from which the Turk who has just asked a question in fluent German is ostensibly excluded. This conjures any number of situations and paradigms in which incoherence is ascribed to Turkish migrants and intelligibility claimed for native Germans (Teraoka 1987, 1989, 1996b).[58] Özdamar spoofs this context when she has the narrator refer to the parrot "that had spoken such unintelligible German to me" (24). Yet this is no mere witty indictment of discriminatory stereotypes, for we also learn that the dead parrot takes up residence with everyone else in the kitchen mirror.[59]

The same cannot be said of a drunk connoting a contextual world of hostility toward Turks in Germany. Seeking clues as to the whereabouts of an evicted neighbor, the narrator approaches a woman sitting at a bar and poses a question.

"Where is the owner of the bar?" She looked at me and screamed:
"Whaaattt!" I ran outside immediately, my heart between my hands, and outside in the night I swore to myself that, from now on, I would never speak with another German again. (41)

This German voices only a howl of indignation in response to an articulate Turk. This reaction distresses the would-be interlocutor greatly, which in turn marks one of the few instances in which readers are privy to a distinctly emotional response ascribed to the narrator. Only after risking contact with ten more Germans—on Can's insistently calming advice—and encountering none who hurt her does this Turkish "I" abandon her vow never to speak with another German again. If both the parrot and the drunk invoke a xenophobic context in Germany, why does the former take up residence in the kitchen mirror but not the latter? And again, why should such details matter?

One apparent explanation is that the drunk is very much alive without being part of the courtyard. The parrot must have died, readers infer, because this bird lives "in this mirror" along with "all the dead" (24), in addition to the living whose daily habits the narrator observes in the mirror. Greater interpretive and affective significance accrues to the parrot because this figure connotes the cultural fable of "the nonhuman being" that Laura Brown analyzes as inextricably linked to the modern "encounter with cultural difference" (2001b: 245).[60] The courtyard narrative turns on key references to birds more generally. The boundary work signaled by the parrot pales in comparison to that tethering text and context through references to birds of a more quotidian feather. These include the garden beneficiaries of the nun's crumbs and others to which the argument soon turns. Relational effects and affects mediated through these avian figures carry far more textual weight than the discriminatory slights that the Turkish narrator experiences in the German bar or the parrot shop, which may explain why the parrot is listed among the dead rather than the living who reside in the kitchen mirror and why the indignant woman in the bar has no place in the mirror at all.

5

What structures of affinity are at stake in the courtyard? Why does the life of emotions have so little heft in this text overall despite frequent allusions to tears, laughter, and loss? These questions appear misguided if one focuses on literal references to love, as several examples attest. The first mention of the word "love" (*Liebe*) coincides with the first reference to birds (*Vögel*). Entering her German apartment for the first time after her mother's funeral in Turkey, the narrator spies the telephone through which she and her mother had spoken on so many occasions, and only then does the daughter begin to cry. This brief reference to crying is immediately followed by the narrator's recollection of the restless use of the telephone she had observed in her grieving father. This prompts her to reflect: "For years I . . . had always spoken with my parents or friends by telephone. As if the birds that alight on the telegraph poles could pick up the love of these human beings and bring them to me in their mouths and with their feet" (15).[61] One of the nuns has skin "like unloved leather" (33), while the sight of the youngest nun drinking a glass of red wine and the sound of her laughing move the narrator to remark: "I was always happy whenever she laughed, and then I always wanted to go out and give my love to other people" (34).

Two Yücel poems from which Özdamar includes isolated sections in German translation reference "love" as a noun or a verb. One follows on the heels of the conversation in which the narrator reports to Can that she found no one who treated her badly the day after her distressing encounter with the drunk. Can responds with a poem, which readers may identify without much difficulty as the last verse of Yücel's "Public Enemy Number One/Bir Numaralı Halk Düşmanı" (Fergar 48–53). Having confessed his transgressions to a judge, a laborer concludes his reflections:

> I've neither robbed nor murdered
> No, I've done something much worse
> You know what, Your Honor?
> I simply loved human beings. (42)[62]

In a doubly rare moment when the Turkish woman looks directly into the courtyard and becomes the object of a neighborly gaze, the old nun who sees her struggles to find facial muscles that would allow her "to express her joy." The narrator continues: "Then she drew my attention to the birds, which were picking at their bread crumbs down on the ground, as if I were her child, and she showed me how nicely the birds ate together. We both watched until the birds flew away" (29).

Some readers may conclude that "The Courtyard" cultivates a welcome or unwelcome sentimentality in the persona of the Turkish narrator. After all, this figure invests great interest in her German neighbors in particular, especially the impoverished aristocrat and the old nun.[63] Can once asks his Turkish friend in Germany to give him " 'a German word' " (42). Her reply is an incantation of yearning as she parses the German compound for longing (*Sehnsucht*), then segues into a portentous anecdote about her grandmother. " 'You know, Can, my grandmother had told me in Istanbul, don't look into the mirror at night, otherwise you'll travel to a strange land. . . . Now I live only in the mirror. I'm talking to you in the mirror' " (42). Emotional ties to one's homeland and the loneliness of exile similarly appear to shadow excerpts from poems by Heinrich Heine shortly after the nun acts as if the Turkish neighbor were her child (29). A cited verse from Heine's "Abroad" (*In der Fremde*) speaks of a "tender word" on the wind as an indeterminate something "drives you for fair, now here, now there" (Draper 362; Heine II 71). The next verse, which Özdamar does not cite but many readers of the German text will know, speaks of "love you left behind" (Draper 362; Heine II 71). A verse taken from Heine's "The Homecoming" (*Die Heimkehr*) gives us a lonely wanderer along the shore, where many a "sweet" if watery word is heard (Draper 173; Heine I.1 488). One might imagine that the "I" of narration is a lonely and grieving Turkish woman who longs for other Turks close to her heart and yearns wistfully for German neighbors who would love her as she is inclined to love them, in spite of the few unfriendly ones she encounters.

This is decidedly not the reading I wish to advance. Some readers might welcome the reassurance that they remain lovable in the eyes of a minority not infrequently targeted for aggression in Germany. Proponents of identity politics might argue that the Turkish narrator cultivates false objects of affection by extending love to Germans rather than stressing bonds of fellowship with other migrants in her neighborhood and likely coalition partners in a politics of enfranchisement. Some readers might be offended by the seeming—and seemingly exaggerated—emotionality of the female narrator, who shares many tears with another Turkish woman on the telephone. For all its wit and wonder, does "The Courtyard" merely recycle tired stereotypes of women and "Orientals" as highly emotional beings, the repositories and agents of love in the cold world of western rationality? Although the author of one cultural history of German tears indicts what she calls a "taboo against tears" in German society (Berkenbusch 15), the emotive vectors of Özdamar's narrative cannot be located along a stereotypical divide between Turkish warmth and German coldness. German characters cry and suffer in this text and Turkish characters do many other things far more frequently than they cry. And yet, the narrator is quite unrealistically the only Turkish figure in the text to reside in the German city. She lavishes far more attention on the comings and goings of her German neighbors than those of the Moroccan cobbler or the South African television repairmen. Some form of social intimacy is activated by the figural references, narrative structures, and boundary work of this text, but what kind of "short-distance" intimacy might this be?

The operative word here is form, which must be distinguished from any emotional content otherwise associated with love. Love too is an abstraction, the realization of which takes literally countless forms. This might entail the socialist embrace of humankind (associated with poetry by Yücel), the problematic bonds of nation (or "fatherland," as implied by allusions to Heine), or the experiential kinship of family (represented by Turkish and German figures alike).[64] Thematic references to "love" signify no emotional content as such. They mark a moment of abstraction where a sociality of affirmation is intended but not substantiated. As discussed, the narrative stresses behavioral patterns in the neighborhood and significant departures from them in such a way that the Turkish narrator's relationships with her German neighbors are never accounted for in substantive terms. Rupture events are structurally indexed as significant, while the nature of their significance is at its root broadly open to interpretation. Social significance is marked textually by a series of implied questions.

This emphasis on patterns of behavior and forms of interaction is underscored by the theme of mediation joined to technology. This is partly why affect attaches to things in key passages. The distraught Mr. Volker lies down on his apartment floor next to the telephone, "so that the telephone will take pity on him" (16), but the lover who has deserted him does not call. His Turkish neighbor, who had gone upstairs because Mr. Volker had been banging on the floor and crying, returns to her own apartment to place a call. " 'Mr. Volker, your telephone is taking a little pity on you after all' " (17). The kitchen mirror, we read, indicates how the narrating "I" feels about the people with whom she speaks by telephone while standing in front of the mirror.

> The mirror showed me whether I loved the person I happened to be talking to or not. When I didn't love someone, I began to see the dust on the kitchen shelves or on the picture frames in the mirror, or I saw that a picture was hanging crooked on the wall. I'll have to straighten it later. (25)

The narrator's examples tell us only what behaviors indicate that she does not love her partner in conversation. What forms of interaction signal love? The syntactical logic of the passage leads readers to expect an affirmative counterpart, an explicit account of behaviors that indicate to the narrator that she loves the person with whom she is speaking by telephone. No such account is provided. The mental reminder to straighten a crooked picture is immediately followed instead by a reference to the mirror that culminates in an image of active extension across a shared space. "In the mirror I saw myself again, heard my voice, saw the kitchen, and the kitchen extended itself (*verlängerte sich*) to the nuns' house in the courtyard" (25). The notion of spatial extension stands in where an index of love should be. By means of the kitchen mirror figures of spatial extension connote social extensions as well, a tentative lengthening or stretching of the ties that bind.[65]

This mode of extension—at once architectural and social—is explicitly associated with "the residential aesthetic of the Orient" (25).

> The people there extended their houses into alleys. In this way a window suddenly found itself in front of the neighbors' window. The houses got all mixed up together, and so something resembling labyrinths came into being. The neighbors woke up nose to nose. (25)

Whether architectural historians would ultimately assign such group housing to "the Orient" as distinct from "the Occident" is far less clear than the fact that the courtyard narrative links this "residential aesthetic" to an ostensibly Oriental mode of connectivity.[66] Because the narrator is coded as "Oriental" by virtue of her Turkish history and the vantage point from which she speaks of the old nun as her "setting sun," the act of extending oneself spatially is rendered not only as a social gesture in the text's economy, but also as a gesture actively imported by the Turkish "I" into her neighborhood in Düsseldorf. She too, we read, "had extended this apartment with three mirrors to the house in the courtyard" (25–26). When we read further that the narrator and everyone in the nuns' house live in three mirrors "nose to nose together" (26), the German courtyard reverberates with a form of intimacy rhetorically coded in Özdamar's diction as Turkish and "Oriental." This is the narrative elaboration of how the telephone in the mirror signals love. But why does the courtyard narrative go to such lengths to stress forms of intimacy and structures of affinity rather than interpersonal relations with emotional content? Why does the migrant persona direct so many gestures of intimacy toward her German neighbors and the old nun in particular? Thematic references to love are insufficient to answer these questions. For that we turn again to the medial features of the courtyard narrative.

Its many puns and extensive boundary work rely structurally on a linked sense of common ground and partial difference. Puns would be neither amusing nor illuminating if absolute difference applied. The same might be said of the boundary work that Herman characterizes as "a playing with . . . boundaries assumed to separate the actual and the virtual, the fictional and the real" (338). Different readers will understand the textual punning and engage in contextual anchoring to different degrees and with different frames of reference in mind. Micro-textual provocations to seek referential and affective similarity where difference might otherwise prevail recall LaCapra's critique of absolute notions of incommensurability "between culture-specific groups" (1998: 193). "Any complex, diversified (perhaps even any conceivable) political entity would manifest a dynamic combination of the incommensurable and the shared that would vary over time," he suggests instead (194).[67] Because the lengthening of the ties that bind is textually coded as a Turkish or "Oriental" impulse in "The Courtyard," and because the Turkish "I" devotes so much attention to her German neighbors, readers might hastily assume that familiar national or cultural frames of reference hold firm. The "labyrinths" (25) that result from "the residential aesthetic of the Orient" and the migrant's application of it to the German courtyard connote multiple challenges to orientation instead. We would be hard pressed to say that the courtyard ethnoscape represents "culture-specific groups" at all. If familiar German and Turkish frames of reference shadow the narrative in minor ways, this is because the tale of the courtyard marks a historic moment between national and postnational worlds. This is neither a moment of suspension between national cultures nor a way station on any teleological route. If the nineteenth-century novel has been widely discussed in connection with the "construction of a national intimacy" (Sommer 1991: ix), "The Courtyard in the Mirror" probes the parameters of what might become a postnational world of affinity.[68] This is a tentative enterprise at best. Not to be confused with cosmopolitan solidarity or diasporic community, the imaginative extensions prompted by the courtyard narrative entail the production of locality across short rather than long distances in space, in constellations where the grounds for shared feeling are neither pre-given nor self-evident. The Turkish "I" only begins to map the relational contours of the world she inhabits "in this city here." Readers are implicitly but repeatedly called upon to trace these structures with her without knowing where this boundary work will lead. The substantive bonds of social intimacy that might yield genuinely new communities are thus a historic project to which readers are subtly summoned.

6

In her study of the "phenomenology of reading" in the digital age, Marie-Laure Ryan recalls the media studies of Marshall McLuhan, whose characterization of immersion and interactivity "as polar opposites" she upends (2001: 2, 347). She argues that "medium-aware immersion" is not altogether incompatible with the interactivity associated with electronic media (351–352). Although Ryan characterizes interactivity as a " 'windowed' structure" (352), the text in which Özdamar's narrator establishes multiple windows on her courtyard world does not yield to Ryan's terminology. This is partly because readers of the courtyard narrative do not affect the plot (as they do with interactive texts, as Ryan defines them) and partly because the fluid sense of "wholeness" associated with immersion is counter-indicated by extensive boundary work. Ryan's revisitation of McLuhan's distinction between "cool" and "hot" media, on the other hand, is especially salutary for a reading of "The Courtyard." According to McLuhan as cited by Ryan, cool media are " 'high in participation or completion by the audience' " (348), whereas hot media foster " 'the state of being well filled with data' " (347). As Ryan elaborates, "A hot medium facilitates immersion through the richness of sensory offerings, while a cold medium opens its world only after the user has made a significant intellectual and imaginative investment," and "the type of involvement that McLuhan associates with cool media is much closer to the interactive than to the immersive dimension of virtual reality" (348). With this understanding of hot and cool registers in mind, the extensive deixis of the courtyard narrative appears medially hot. Readers are " 'well filled' " with spatial data in particular, and temporal indicators are likewise abundant. Here it is important to distinguish between temporal and historical markers. In contrast to most of Özdamar's work, which references diverse historical and national contexts in rich detail, "The Courtyard" is strikingly spare in its historical references. In this connection the text is medially cool, and readerly effort is required to situate the narrative historically. This coolness is linked to the even greater chill that emanates from the emotional register of the story. Narrator and readers repeatedly encounter rupture events, the interpersonal and emotional significance of which can only begin to be imagined but not resolved. "The Courtyard" thus operates in terms of both a hot and a cold medium as it continually prompts readers to negotiate the here and now on the cusp of a new age. This explains why gestures of intimacy and structures of connectivity are literal pivot points in this text, which relies on and elicits the warmth of the strangers who read it.

A medial function accrues to affect in this connection too. The text alerts us to this when we read that Mr. Volker's young lover used to sew suits for the two men. "The rattling of the sewing machine made Mr. Volker's wooden floor tremble, and my ceiling trembled along with it" (11). This shared trembling is no anthropomorphic projection onto things of feelings that the neighbors in contiguous apartments might have, for the moment described represents the untroubled norm from which the rupture event involving Mr. Volker stands out. This particular trembling is a physical form that might connote feeling, but the text presents this trembling as an act only (and an act of things at that), not yet something that could be called an emotional response or a sustained feeling. The courtyard neighborhood is likewise not yet a "community of sentiment," which Appadurai defines as "a group that begins to imagine and feel things together" (1996: 8). The keen attention paid to routine behaviors in the neighborhood and significant departures from them involves the narrator's labor of imagination and demands the concomitant labor of imaginative readers too. The ethnoscape of the courtyard occupies a here and now where the process of imagining a shared life world begins, but where the phenomenon of feeling things together has not yet taken hold. The text's emphasis on affect (as a function of narrative) underscores this distinction. In relation to the history and theory of psychoanalysis André Green discusses several meanings of the French verb *affecter*, two of which are especially apt for capturing the function of affect in the courtyard tale.[69] Generally the word means "to tend to take on this or that form" (6). Another relevant usage involves "performing an action, causing an impression on the organism" (6). The first definition cited applies in crucial ways, some of which are only hinted at when the

Turkish neighbor calls Mr. Volker to tell him, " 'your telephone is taking a little pity on you after all' " (17). The narrator's call takes on the form of an expression of sympathy with the man who had been crying, while the subjective significance of their exchange is open to speculative interpretation. The next section of this chapter elaborates how the taking on of this or that form advances the narrative in more central ways. Particular forms to be discussed include counterfactual speculation, dialogic exchange, and synecdochic configurations. More broadly, the taking on of this or that form in the narrative signals an act of imagination from which newly intimate bonds might be forged on the labyrinthine path to a postnational world.[70]

Key moments entailing the taking on of this or that form revolve around the old nun across the way. For example, the scene in which she directs her observant neighbor's attention to birds in the garden is a rupture event in more ways than one. This is the first time that the Turkish woman sees the nun's face in the mirror rather than just her crumb-dispensing hand. The manner in which the nun leans her head against the dusty curtain in her room leads the Turkish woman in a different apartment to wonder why fear attends the older neighbor. After endowing the woman in the mirror with a fur coat that makes her resemble Garbo, the narrator takes the rare step of going to the balcony and looking directly across the courtyard. "Now she saw me too" (29), she says of the nun. This triply heightened rupture event yields the moment when the nun points to the birds. "Then she drew my attention to the birds, which were picking at their bread crumbs down on the ground, as if I were her child, and she showed me how nicely the birds ate together. We both watched until the birds flew away" (29). This behavioral composite of drawing attention, showing, and watching foregrounds a gesture of sharing and a sharing of gesture. In and of itself the mundane social act in which the two neighbors engage has no relational substance, and yet some intimacy seems to take shape here. The use of the adverb "nicely" and the shared act of watching until the birds fly away speak to this, however tentatively.

Most striking is the phrase "as if I were her child," which initially suggests a counterintuitive bond. The older neighbor is after all a nun (the text draws our attention to her virginal status), and the younger neighbor hails from a predominantly Islamic country. If the narrator speculated that the nun drew her attention to the birds as if the Turkish woman were "a child" rather than the nun's child, the gesture would appear condescending. Because we later learn that the migrant persona decisively resists the proselytizing efforts of Jehovah's Witnesses and another nun, it is also clear that the old nun is not figured in terms of religious conflict. No civilizations or cultures clash here. On the contrary, the scene takes on the form of mundane intimacy and social warmth. At the same time the relational substance of interpersonal exchange is tagged as an imaginative speculation by the focalizing voice of narration. The "as if" construction is itself a grammatical form indexing a taking on of form that seems counterintuitive, an act of imagination bridging the gap between the real and the counterfactual. In Özdamar's diction "as if"—which figures frequently—more precisely bridges the gap between the real and the not-yet-real. The Turk in this story will not become the nun's child, but the "as if" clause marks a moment when the narrator begins to imagine having a relationship with the old nun that could be intimate in substance, not form alone. By the same token, the "as if" prompts readers to launch their own speculations about ties that could bind strangers and neighbors to each other in some degree of shared feeling.

Something reminiscent of dialogic exchange constitutes another central venue for the taking on of form in Özdamar's narrative. This claim does not speak to the many passages that represent conversational interaction merely to reflect diverse functions that dialogue can serve or variable registers that dialogue can deploy. For example, one extended telephone conversation includes excerpts from several Yücel poems, a tagged reading of the Mock Turtle's song from "The Lobster Quadrille" of *Alice in Wonderland* (a song that itself narrates dialogic exchange), and various questions, answers, requests, and declarations in addition to embedded narration.[71] Another recounted interaction includes a recipe for eggplant. While one might surmise that dialogic variety is most evident in exchanges between Turks, or that information is more smoothly exchanged among migrants than with Germans, the text defies any presumption that dialogic fault lines rigidly separate migrant interlocutors and German neighbors as distinct groups. The crossover is dramatically apparent in pivotal exchanges involving the narrator and Hartmut in the first instance to be discussed and the narrator and the old nun in the second. These scenes foreground the taking on of this or that form, and the form taken on is that of dialogue.

Hartmut is introduced as "a new tenant" across the way, "an elderly gentleman with thick sacks of tears under his eyes" (36). His Turkish neighbor first observes his emphatic restlessness. "His shadows wandered in all three mirrors back and forth, back and forth." The unspecified relationship that develops between them is characterized by far greater reciprocity than any of the other actual or imagined relationships between the Turkish narrator and her German interlocutors to which attention is drawn. Hartmut is the only neighbor invited into the narrator's apartment, where she cooks for him and converses with him. The dinner invitation stems from a heightened sense of interpersonal engagement, which ensues from a propositional attitude adopted by the narrator with regard to her agitated neighbor. Noting his restive movements, she speculates, "Maybe it is cold for him there" (36).[72] This prompts her to offer him bedding, to which he responds, " 'I haven't sunk that low yet' " (36). This exchange gives rise to what the narrator cognitively labels her feeling of shame, and this perception of shame segues syntactically into an invitation to dinner. According to Silvan Tomkins, the affect of shame (as distinguished from cognitive awareness of shame) "operates ordinarily only after interest or enjoyment has been activated" and is itself activated when one encounters a barrier to pursuing that interest (Sedgwick and Frank 134, 149).[73] The spark of interest the Turkish neighbor feels for Hartmut finds its discursive echo when Can speculates as to why Hartmut leaves a false forwarding address in the wake of his eviction. " 'Then the man has no apartment at all. He probably was ashamed, that's why he gave you his old address' " (39). Whether Hartmut actually felt shame is secondary. The invocation of shame as a vector of relationality marks the two neighbors textually as conjoined by an affect of reciprocal interest. This is much more the case with Hartmut than the old nun, who never visits or converses with her Turkish neighbor. Most significantly, the "elderly gentleman with thick sacks of tears under his eyes" is the only courtyard figure to stand directly in front of his neighbor's kitchen mirror and look at the Turkish woman in it. She not only sees this object of her observations looking at her in her mirror from the vantage of her own kitchen; she also sees the two of them dancing together in multiple mirrors. "The old man, whom I had seen and observed through the mirror for days, suddenly stood next to me and invited me in the mirror to dance. We danced the tango through all the rooms, and I saw us appear briefly in all three mirrors" (37). Because the narrator explicitly remarks the congruence of observational perspectives, what Tomkins calls "interocular intimacy" (Sedgwick and Frank 148) appears intensified in form.[74]

Some degree of reciprocity is generally associated with conversation. Herman and Kacandes recapitulate for narrative inquiry some basic features that sociolinguists have identified in "the logic of conversation" (Herman 184). These include "adjacency pairs," which are "typically defined as paired utterances issued by alternating speakers." Embedded in this definition is another basic feature, whereby "participants take turns" according to variable procedures for knowing when it is appropriate to do so (Kacandes 3). Herman's analysis of notoriously "anti-communicative" exchange in *Finnegan's Wake* draws on scholarship by Paul Grice, Gillian Brown, and George Yule to demonstrate "the extent to which the cognitive frame 'dialogue' (or 'conversation') guides comprehension of narrative discourse," even in literary fiction (174). This involves another basic feature of dialogue in any venue, the "presumption of coherence that interlocutors and readers bring to the utterances comprised by texts, discourses, and conversations" (179).[75]

Contiguity and turn-taking characterize the conversation between Hartmut and his Turkish neighbor, so much so that the presumption of coherence extends to other features of their exchange when contiguity and turn-taking are not necessarily given. Notably this concerns excerpts from Baudelaire's *Les Fleurs du mal*, cited in the French original. While visiting his neighbor, Hartmut intersperses couplets from the first verse of "The Balcony" (James McGowan 72–75) with remarks about a back injury and the dinner's seasoning. The passage in which this interspersal is embedded begins with the narrator's shame and ends in tango, but the Turkish figure says nothing. Anything she might have said to Hartmut is not represented as speech of any kind, but left to readers' imagination. The older dancer's citation of symbolist poetry alters the conversational register considerably, but the presumption of coherence prompts readers to imagine that Hartmut is using poetry to communicate something to his Turkish addressee, even if his meaning is not readily intelligible. Baudelaire's "flowers of evil" figure again in the urination scene, which precedes Hartmut's eviction. Before leaving, he stands beneath his dance partner's balcony and calls up additional excerpts from "The Balcony." In contrast to the dinner scene these lyric excerpts are not embedded in anything resembling conversation.

Or are they? Readers are not privy to anything that the remaining neighbor might have said in direct response to Hartmut's recitation. Only a few narrative lines and some time later, however, she awakes to see Hartmut's light still burning in her mirror. This prompts her to recite the third verse of another poem from *Les Fleurs du mal*, which takes on the form of a dialogic rejoinder to Hartmut's balcony recitation, precisely because these poetic excerpts are nearly contiguous and because the conversational markers of the neighbors' earlier exchange call for her continued response. The response that does come takes the form of an excerpt from Baudelaire's "Obsession," which pays lyric homage to acts of pleasing, speaking, and seeking. The narration of the woman's unsuccessful quest to visit Hartmut at his new address follows immediately on the heels of this quotation. The fact that the narrator's poetic rejoinder cites another poem from the Baudelaire collection underscores the sense that these two figures are engaged in something characterized by dialogic coherence. The fact that her rejoinder leaves both "The Balcony" and her balcony behind in favor of something resembling obsession speaks to the intensified and untethered affect of interest that attends these two figures in the courtyard ethnoscape. The taking on of dialogic form rather than the exchange of communicative content lends additional heft to the textual emphasis noted earlier in reference to the kitchen mirror. In the medial economy of the courtyard there are apparently many ways to lengthen the ties that bind.

More than with any other figure, the taking on of dialogic form with Hartmut connotes something akin to interpersonal intimacy. The function of dialogic form shifts to more abstract dimensions of social intimacy when this form is activated in reference to the old nun, with whom the Turkish neighbor never has an actual conversation. Although they see each other and communicate some sense of shared feeling in the bird-watching scene, anything that the old nun might say or feel is only imagined by her observant neighbor, never subject to emendation by the nun. When the dying woman responds to her younger neighbor by struggling to express joy and drawing attention to garden birds, readers witness the only active expression of the nun's interest in the Turk across the way. This weak expression of interest contrasts with the attention paid by Hartmut (who compliments his Turkish neighbor on her cooking, recites poetry to her, dances with her, gives her things, and observes her use of electric light), and yet the courtyard narrative is structurally organized around pivotal references to the old nun. The singular moment in which dialogic form attaches to this courtyard figure thus warrants scrutiny.

This moment immediately follows the shared act of bird-watching, with the transition marked by a change in posture and position for both women. The old nun leans her forehead against her window frame, and the narrator steps away from the shared space of watching into the interior of her apartment. This passage is cited in full to facilitate discussion of its dialogic form:

> I walked from the balcony back to the mirror, leaned my forehead
> in the mirror against her forehead and cited from Heinrich Heine:
>> Lone I wander on the shore
>> Where the white waves break and leap,
>> And I hear a voice so sweet,
>> Voice so sweet upon the deep . . .
> And the old nun said:
>> Ah, my heart cannot be still,
>> And the night is far too long—
>> Lovely nymphs, oh come to me,
>> Dance and sing a magic song!
> In the mirror the face of the old nun had now disappeared. I said,
> my forehead still against the mirror,
>> It drives you fair, now here, now there—
>> You know not even why;
>> A tender word rings in the air—
>> You stare with wondering eye. (29–30)[76]

This exchange simulates dialogue. Both before and after the nun's face disappears from the mirror, the narrator only imagines herself in dialogue with her neighbor. Any sense of physical proximity associated with shared bird-watching is doubly dissipated, first when the narrator retreats to her mirror and again when the nun's face disappears altogether. And yet the presumption of coherence that readers bring to this passage is mediated by the formal contiguity of the utterances attributed to the old nun and her Turkish neighbor. Turn-taking procedures too are formally upheld as the younger woman ventriloquizes the nun. Mediating phrases such as "I . . . cited from Heinrich Heine," "the old nun said," and "I said" additionally tag the utterances as direct discourse or quoted speech, even though what is said consists solely of poetic excerpts from Heine. In contrast to Hartmut's recitation of Baudelaire's "The Balcony" in close proximity to an actual balcony in the textual world, the Heine excerpts effect greater distance from any immediate world of reference. There are no ocean waves or lovely nymphs in the courtyard. Reference is nonetheless made to elusive qualities that do circulate in the courtyard narrative: loneliness, tenderness, and an indeterminate source of restlessness and wonderment. One might imagine that the aura of death surrounding the nun resonates with the grief and restlessness the narrator will soon face when her mother dies. But why should dialogic form be pointedly exercised in this passage if no interpersonal relationship with the nun is intended? The forehead-to-forehead posture mediated by the kitchen mirror recalls the nose-to-nose aesthetic associated in the text with "the Orient" and in this chapter with a stretching of the ties that bind. Who is meant here, if not the nun? The answer lies in multiple references indexed by the "you" of the final stanza cited. The second-person address in this stanza underscores the dialogic form of the mirror transaction, but the narrator could be directing this "you" just as easily to herself as the now-absent nun. Beyond this, the poetic "you" embedded in this simulated dialogue positions the reader as an addressee, one whose own looking around in wonderment is given in the indicative, not the subjunctive.[77] Here readers are more than summoned to the affective project of lengthening the ties that bind. By virtue of reading "The Courtyard," they are already figured as active participants in this project. The taking on of dialogic form in reference to the old nun highlights, above all, the imaginative labor of reading.

The third example of affect similarly stresses acts of imagination that revolve around reading. References to the reading of a particular book, *Alice in Wonderland*, dovetail tightly with implied strategies for reading "The Courtyard" and imagining postnational forms of intimacy. This linkage pivots on the reading of synecdochic configurations, as an analysis of one especially concentrated mirroring sequence demonstrates. When the television repairmen first inform their neighbor that the old nun is reading *Alice in Wonderland*, the Turkish woman replies, "I love *Alice in Wonderland*" (22), in a dialogic rejoinder that ties loving to reading.

> Once I knew what the old nun was reading just now, I stood in front of the kitchen mirror, in which I saw the old nun's light, grinned like the Grin Cat

from *Alice in Wonderland* and turned the light off. The Grin Cat disappeared as in *Alice in Wonderland*. Then I turned the light on again, grinned again like the Grin Cat and imagined the old nun. Both her hands were holding the book in front of her face.... (22)

The Cheshire Cat appears as the Edamer Cat in Christian Enzensberger's German translation of *Alice in Wonderland* (the one that Özdamar lists as her source), but Özdamar opts for a designation centering on the inclination to grin. Invoking a physical gesture capable of expressing a broad spectrum of interest, the repeated acts of grinning here inhabit the realm of affect as a form of representation and relation. Both are tied in this passage to acts of reading and imagining. The narrator explicitly imagines the old nun reading *Alice in Wonderland*, and she envisions herself grinning first like and then as the Grin Cat from Carroll's tale. She imagines the nun reading and herself a figure being read by the nun. Another way of saying this is that the narrator inserts herself as a figural image into the narrative being enjoyed and interpreted by the nun. The younger woman does not figure herself, however, as a self in the mirror. While the narrator imagines the nun having a face, she narrates her own mirror image only in terms of a grin.[78] In something like reverse prosopopoeia the Grin Cat passage draws attention only to those parts of the narrator's face that would be involved in the act of grinning. The proposed reading of this passage pivots on the famously synecdochic figure of the Cheshire Cat's grin.

Beyond drawing attention to repeated acts of grinning, Özdamar activates a reading of partial signs in two key ways. First, the description of the nun reading commingles synecdoche and metonymy:

> ... she had on her long white nightgown with the long sleeves, but in this nightgown she had no body. A long nightgown is reading *Alice in Wonderland* with a head and two hands, and as the Grin Cat I grinned at the nightgown in the mirror. (22)

Here one partial figure reads another in a scene marked by reciprocal interest and imagined reciprocity. This emphasis on a relational reading of partial signs echoes throughout the narrative in ways that bear on a critical understanding of interactive contexts in a postnational world. For the moment, we turn to the second key means by which the Grin Cat passage activates a reading of partial signs. When the narrator reports that she grinned like the Grin Cat, this provides information that readers unfamiliar with *Alice in Wonderland* can easily assimilate, for the nominative designation already imparts the information that grinning is what this cat does. The epistemic perspective shifts when we read that the Grin Cat "disappeared as in *Alice in Wonderland*," for only readers familiar with Alice's story will know, not merely that the fictional cat disappears, but in what manner the Cheshire Cat disappears. Those familiar with Carroll recall that the Cheshire Cat "vanished quite slowly, beginning with the end of the tail, and ending with the grin, which remained some time after the rest of it had gone" (56). Alice can only marvel at " 'a grin without a cat'," for this is " 'the most curious thing' " she has ever seen. In the courtyard context the figural image of something remaining after the rest of it has disappeared from view suggests interlaced themes of transnational migration and personal grief. But the reading of partial signs is not configured as a recuperation of losses from national, cultural, or familial archives. The bits and pieces of interpretive matter circulating in the courtyard activate new modes of reading instead, which reconfigure the very relationships among the bits and pieces that remain when familiar referential contexts slowly vanish from view. Because no universal perspective attaches to the focalizing "I" or its implied readers, acts of reading enabled by the courtyard narrative foreground multiplicity, reciprocity, and curiosity in addition to affective innovation. The fact that the nun expresses less interest in her Turkish neighbor than the other way around is less significant than the abstract functions inhering in the figuration of the nun as a partial sign that both reads and is read. In this she is rendered like the migrant subject that reads her.

7

Tracking the bits and pieces of figural matter in this narrative also means revisiting the birds. In the passage first linking birds and love the narrator describes her grieving father. "Like a bird blinded by longing, in a closed room, he had butted his head against all the walls, sought all the voices from his past by telephone, laid his feathers onto the table, one by one, with each telephone conversation, and then he was gone" (16). This laying down of feathers as a cipher of death triggers associations with a profound sense of longing and affinity, associations that reverberate more abstractly in reference to the old nun, who also leaves a bird feather behind when she dies. The narrator finds this feather in the nun's copy of *Alice in Wonderland*. As she informs readers, "The feather lay on page 103" (43). This indicative assertion is repeated when the narrator tells Can that the old nun is dead, had read as far as page 103, and a bird feather marked the page. Like matching bookends, the narrator's indicative claims about the feather in the nun's book frame other pieces of information that she imparts. First comes the speculation that "the old nun had probably used it as a book mark" (43). This speculation underwrites the narrator's indicative claim that the nun had read as far as page 103, for the surviving neighbor cannot know whether the nun used the feather to mark the last page she read or a favorite page instead. The speculative and propositional attitudes cultivated by the Turkish "I" vis-à-vis the old nun throughout the narrative are in one sense resolved when the nun's death is twice confirmed in the indicative (first by the television repairmen and then by the narrator talking to Can). This is significant because the text's inaugural speculation is epistemically resolved in this passage. Yet the speculative habits of the focalizing "I" appear as a kind of grammatical residue in the "probably" directing our attention to the feather as a bookmark. Herman counts "probably" among the "grammatical markers of doubt" (320).

One might speak more appropriately of a courtyard grammar of imagination. The German word for bookmark is *Lesezeichen*, literally, a sign of reading or a sign to be read. Once the narrator ascertains that the feather lay on page 103, readers encounter a tagged act of reading in which the narrator reads what she imagines to be the last passages from *Alice in Wonderland* to have been read by the dying nun. (Structurally this recalls the shared scene of paying attention to garden birds, except that the nun is not physically present for this shared scene. In that regard the "shared" scene of reading is more like the final segment of dialogic exchange involving Heine quotations.) "I read in the book" is the tag phrase announcing an excerpt from the Mock Turtle's song in "The Lobster Quadrille," in which various animals speak and sing of relational movements, proximate shores, and a shared dance (Carroll 1965: 84). The narrator skips a bit and then highlights the "last sentences" on the page.[79] Here the German translation deviates from the source text. For Carroll,

> There is another shore, you know, upon the other side.
> The further off from England the nearer is to France—(1965: 85).

The German version cited reads instead:

> Wir kommen auf der drübern Seit' ja auch an einem Ufer an!
> Und je weiter wir hier weg sind, desto näher liegt Peru. (Carroll 1963: 103; Özdamar 2001: 44)

A translation of this back into English might read: " 'On the other side we'll arrive on another shore, not to fret! And the farther away from here we are, the closer lies Peru.' " Whereas the geographical coordinates of Carroll's song are confined to Europe, the German translation in Özdamar's prose serves a broader imaginative project of deictic localization, one to which the courtyard story is dedicated. The internal rhyme of the "u" in *Ufer* and *Peru* also resonates with courtyard themes of transubstantiation (death as the other side, the other shore) and transnational migration, even though no one from the courtyard ethnoscape actually comes from or visits Peru. The deceased nun continues to be an object of imaginative speculation by the Turkish narrator, her indicative claims to the contrary. But when she repeats for Can what she has already imparted to readers—a bird feather lay on page 103—the burden of interpreting this remainder falls to readers of the courtyard narrative. The narrator's emphatic resolution of the inaugural speculation may be a partial deception, but it serves an imaginative purpose. The feather that the nun leaves behind summons readers of the courtyard narrative to the labor of reading the material signs of relationality in newly creative ways.

Partial remains and perspectives infuse the courtyard narrative in spite of its singular focalizing agent, who reads not only books but a neighborhood. This rhetoric also links the two female figures in whom the narrator invests the greatest interest, the mother she mourns and the nun who acts as if her Turkish neighbor were her child. Because this linkage culminates in a figure of reading, as will be argued, we may well ask what role gender plays in envisioning new ties that could bind courtyard strangers and neighbors to each other in some degree of shared feeling. The intensity of the narrator's interest in Hartmut and her apparent closeness to Can indicate that any affects involved in extending the ties that bind are not reserved for one gender or another.[80] This is underscored by the fact that all the literature cited stems from male authors. As one scholar notes in reference to other works by the author of the courtyard narrative, however, mother-and-daughter pairs figure indispensably in much of Özdamar's prose (Konuk 1999: 65).[81] This is also true of "The Courtyard," which revolves around an imagined relationship to the old nun as the Turkish migrant interacts with and then mourns her actual mother. The narrator's mother also appears as a sad orphan in the mirror, a butcher mother mourns her young, and a Kurdish mother cries in the rain. The intertextual spirit of Heine in Parisian exile suggests the image of another mother if we recall these lines from "Night Thoughts," a poem that Özdamar does not cite:

> I would not yearn for Germany so
> Were not my mother there, I know.
> The fatherland will live forever—
> That dear old woman may die, however. (Draper 408; Heine II 129)

The "old woman" in the courtyard is likewise a cipher of longing that national frameworks are ill equipped to capture.

In Özdamar's text "the old woman" (*die alte Frau* in Heine's diction) does die, more than once, and the narrator's partial perspective on what remains yields the sign of a book released from one reader's grasp and subject to another's interpretation. The narrator's description of her mother's funeral in Turkey is crucial to this connection.

> When she died, I stood at the cemetery, not under the tree where the men let her into the earth, but under the next tree, for the girls were not allowed to stand at the open grave of the dead, only the sons. The men took her out of the coffin, grabbed her shroud at the four corners, suddenly I saw her heels peeking out from the shroud. She is swinging, I thought, here is a garden, she is swinging in a swing that someone has attached to the two trees, I'm standing down below and seeing her heels. (12)

Gender marks social difference here decisively and the narrator perspectivally; the daughter is not allowed to stand in the inner circle with the men. But the "suddenly" marks a radical shift in perspective for narrator and readers alike. Reconstituting the partial signs of her mother's heels in a constellation that departs from the graveside assemblage, the "I" of narration leaps into imaginative action, thus modeling an act of reading for readers of the courtyard text. The phrase "here is a garden" reverberates rhetorically with the imaginative deixis of the courtyard, especially in conjunction with the old nun's fondness for feeding crumbs to garden birds. More important, the narrator's dream of transubstantiation casts her in virtually the same perspectival position vis-à-vis the older woman in the courtyard who so captured her imagination. Holding *Alice in Wonderland* in her own hand (as she imagined the nun doing in the Grin Cat scene), the narrator dreams of the old nun following the flight path that leads her Turkish parents and grandmother into heaven. In this dream sequence "the old nun stood there in her nightgown and looked up at the sky" (45). Prior to ascension the old nun stands on the same plane as the narrator and looks upward. When she flies off into the sky, she does so while "reading" the book that the narrator in her waking life has come to possess. Because the book falls out of the nun's hands and embarks on its own flight trajectory, the narrator looks up and sees the book as what remains of the nun, much as she looked up and saw her mother's heels as if from below a swing. Deixis situates readers imagining themselves in the same position. A triple cry of a woman's name—"'Alice, Alice, Alice . . .'"—is the prelude to waking. Generally taken to be a woman's name in English, "Alice" harbors the implied Turkish pun of "Ali-ce," encoding male and female alike in the name as Özdamar deploys it. More to the point, the Turkish suffix draws attention to the manner or habit in which something is done, in this instance, the taking on of this or that form as a preliminary step in forging newly intimate bonds. Here and elsewhere, a woman's eye view is the favored lens of narration for Özdamar. The graveside scene reproduces this first literally in the sense of social exclusion and then figuratively in a flight of imagination. The gender of mothers and daughters functions more as a cipher for avant-garde modes of reading than as a representation of arrière-garde norms of socialization stereotypically attributed to Turkish and Islamic cultures. Like affect, gender here serves a medial rather than a representational function in the rupture event that imagining a postnational world would be.

The figure of a woman reading is indispensable to the medial economy of the courtyard narrative. To the extent that this figure is cast in the mold of partial perspectives rooted in social marginalization rather than outright exclusion, it resonates with the migrant status of the most central woman who reads, which is equally indispensable to the affect of tracking rupture events in the urban neighborhood. Manifold political histories of marginalization also attach to the three male poets whose lyrics enable an affect of dialogue in this story. Notoriously subject to censorship in Prussia and France in the nineteenth century, Heine and Baudelaire stand in a highly problematic relationship to national norms, contexts, and states that suppressed their work and views, as does Yücel in the twentieth century in Turkey. These diverse figures of marginalization (women, migrants, leftists, artists) conspire to draw our attention again to the problem of contextual reference in the courtyard narrative, which transcends national constraints without abandoning national ground altogether. How then does the text's mobilization of partial signs and perspectives relate to the boundary work of contextual anchoring? Is the figure of reading partially only an abstract function in this tale, or does some contextual residue linger like a feather that must be laid down before transubstantiation can be imagined? These questions implicitly converge in the story's conclusion, which echoes the speculative gesture with which the text began in some ways while radically shifting the locus of speculation in others. How this culminates in Yücel's "Casting Net," with which the story releases its readers from their attentive encounter with the courtyard narrator, is the subject of this chapter's conclusion.

8

To recall Herman's operative terms, boundary work consists of those means whereby stories both "rely on and challenge the border between text and context" (332), and contextual anchoring is "the process whereby a narrative, in a more or less explicit and reflexive way, asks its interpreters to search for analogies" between textual and contextual worlds (331). Explicit and implicit means by which the courtyard narrative calls attention to such boundary work and contextual anchoring have been elaborated above.

Those who respond to this call with the warmth of their interpretive ardor are interpellated as partial readers in every sense—reading partial signs, from necessarily partial perspectives, with quickened interest in an imaginative reconfiguration of the ties that bind. Some textual details interpellating readers with second-person address have also been discussed. At other key moments the interpellation proceeds more subtly when attentive readers are likely to feel the contextual ground of their reading shift beneath them. This is best characterized in scalar rather than binary terms, and movement along the scale does not necessarily proceed in linear fashion. Let us recall the supermarket exchange between the compassionate narrator and the German cashier, whose eyes remind the Turkish woman of an industrial chicken. The description of the cashier's eyes is immediately followed by this exchange:

> "Ruth, is something troubling you?"
> "My brother is dying in the hospital, cancer."
> "Mother, the cashier's brother is dying in the hospital."
> "Yes, my daughter, people die, that's what they do." (34–35)

The transition between two conversational contexts within the story world is nearly completely unmarked; the diacritical markers of direct discourse with no explanatory tag clauses foster the impression that these utterances belong to the same conversation. Readers may infer from the address directed to the narrator's mother that the center of dialogic gravity has shifted, but the transnational ethnoscape in which these utterances belong to the same conversation is textually instantiated in this segment. Something more radical occurs when readers imagine themselves entering the butcher shop along with the Turkish woman who has no need of meat. The narrator explicitly remarks her entry into the shop, such that the phrases that follow—"Kling, kling. The door opened and shut" (19)—are superfluous in informational terms. They serve rather to highlight the moment of entry as an intensified moment of boundary work for readers, who enter the world of the story, as the narrator enters the butcher shop, when the bell on the door rings non-diegetically for them. Equally important is the fact that readers are never released from the butcher shop. No "kling, kling" signals our departure from this shared space where something elusive and significant has transpired in the story world. Which world or worlds do readers inhabit at the oscillating boundary between text and context? This is a question that readers engaged in the boundary work of contextual anchoring implicitly confront with a heightened degree of intensity in the butcher shop stretch of narration.

Readers experience a radical contextual turn when "The Courtyard" concludes with Hallaç's German adaptation of Yücel's "Casting Net." The only poem not cited in bits and pieces in the courtyard narrative, this verse literally has the last word:

> A sky, thoroughly soaked
> Had been caught in the nets
> Sky-blue now all
> Anglers (46)

The disorienting referentiality of a pivotal pun reverberates in the words *Himmel* and *himmelblau*, and in the lyrical theme of reorientation as well. The word *Himmel* also forms a bridge between the poem and the narrative segment that immediately precedes it, for the narrator has just described birds she sees in the mirror, now looking for crumbs in vain and flying off into the sky. Partial readings and affective extensions converge here in ways that the German version of the poem strengthens vis-à-vis the Turkish. For example, Yücel uses *gökyüzü*—the sky one can see—rather than the more versatile *gök*—which could mean sky, heaven, or heavens—and his *masmavi* means deep blue or very blue rather than sky-blue. The Hallaç translation also adds the key word "now" (*nun*), which recalls all the deictic strategies of localization that advance the courtyard narrative. In all these senses the text's final poetic citation builds on what has come before. But some features of this citation signal a rupture event that calls now for interpretation by someone other than the courtyard narrator. "Casting Net" is the only poem or song cited that is not explicitly tagged or identified as a recitation, and no punctuation marks the end of the poem or the conclusion of the story.[82] The concluding citation is not embedded in courtyard narration. Rather than marking a conclusion, it forms a kind of textual residue that takes flight from the courtyard locale but still functions as a sign to be read in newly constituted contexts of interaction.[83] The last dialogic segment reported by the courtyard narrator (just prior to the sky-blue verse) involves Can asking his Turkish friend when she plans to come visit, since his days are also numbered. To this final question she replies, " 'Tomorrow' " (46). Called to deixis once again, readers are directed to thoughts of the future. This is the moment when "Casting Net" floats like a feather on currents and in contexts that only readers of the courtyard narrative can track. No longer a focalizing agent, the courtyard narrator frees her readers to negotiate their own contextual moorings as they track significant rupture events in the here and now. If the butcher shop scene held readers in the world of the text, the extradiegetic scene of the casting net releases them into the interactive contextual worlds of their lives. All anglers now, readers of the courtyard narrative are prompted to ask themselves what future-oriented worlds and ethnoscapes they already inhabit or could cultivate. Tracking the interactive contours of the here and now, Özdamar's courtyard technologies of localization entail an imaginative engagement with possible postnational futures to which partial readers are affectively summoned.

Yet frames of reference that are at least in part national linger like a poetic refrain. As discussed, aesthetic extensions associated with living "nose to nose together" in the courtyard are cast as a social gesture actively imported by the Turkish "I" into her German neighborhood, and most of the narrator's affective curiosity is directed toward her German neighbors. The unique status of Yücel's poetry in "The Courtyard" is striking along similar lines of differentiation. Of the three poets whose verse fuels the motor of dialogic exchange, Yücel is the only one whose work is rendered as requiring translation.[84] Reasons for this appear self-evident if one assumes that the story is intended for German-speaking readers more likely to be schooled in French rather than Turkish, but this seemingly apparent need for translation warrants critical remarking. The Heine poems need not be translated for the simple reason that German is the default language of the courtyard narrative. Readers fluent in German are its intended audience. This could also include many German Turks (or Turks otherwise educated in German schools, for example, in Turkey) who are fluent in both German and Turkish. But the contrastive choice between leaving the Baudelaire citations in French and translating the Yücel citations into the default language of the narrative suggests that the text's intended readers possess either greater familiarity with the French literary canon or merely more tolerance for French as a foreign language. Even if readers are not fully conversant with poetic usage of French, the text implies, a seemingly intolerable difference might attach to Turkish-language citations, by contrast, from the vantage point of those German-speaking readers interpellated by the text. The Yücel translations thus mediate an unmarked sense of difference associated in the text with the Turkish language and modern Turkish history.[85] This sense of difference is not specified as having national parameters alone, though national formations are integral to it. At most one can say that the choice to translate Yücel but not Baudelaire highlights a line of differentiation between a preponderance of things that appear somehow "German" and those that appear somehow "Turkish." The use of German translations foregrounds a courtyard boundary that the text actively reworks, traverses, and occasionally effaces. Just as the narrator extends her spatial perspectives and social affects to refashion the ties that bind, the translations signal an extensional affect without negating cultural differences that might make a difference. If the act of translation seems too great a concession to the world of parrot-shop proprietors and drunken bar patrons, we would do well to remember that the narrator's tracking routines are the default routines in the world of the courtyard, to which only Hartmut and the text's readers pay focused attention. On the one hand, this indicates a skewed sense of reciprocity among the courtyard neighbors. On the other hand, this also means that German-speaking readers are subtly but emphatically interpellated as perceiving both routine behaviors and rupture events from the partial vantage point of a migrant subject. To the extent that one can speak of distinctly German and Turkish perspectives at all in "The Courtyard," one can speak of them only as already approximating each other. The boundary work of contextual anchoring proceeds in terms of partial rather than absolute differences, as this discussion of the text's affective extensions has shown. Whatever figures interact here, mutually exclusive categories of self and other do not apply.

Observing that a "competitive mediaverse" was "already in place at the turn of the [last] century," the editors of *Reading Matters* begin their introduction by describing Anselm Kiefer's sculpture *Das Buch* [The Book], a book with huge leaden wings (Tabbi and Wutz 8). They read the image as suggesting "a phenomenon that is passing" in "the so-called late age of print" (1), a suggestion that their anthology defies. The innovative medial economy of "The Courtyard in the Mirror" yields a dynamic ethnoscape in which reading literally takes place. The copy of *Alice in Wonderland* that the departing nun carries with her into the heavens, reading all the while, falls from her hands, a victim of gravity, only to take flight again in a turn of phrase that situates us reading the newly configured sign of the book to which the story refers. Partial readers all, we are summoned to inhabit forms of intimacy that notions of communicative dialogue, group cohesion, and political membership alone cannot grasp. What lies beyond the reproduction of established communities? This is one of the many questions that Özdamar's tale of a courtyard implicitly asks. Interrogating the production of locality in the here and now of the 1990s, this is a fundamentally curious narrative. The affect of interest that it models for its readers probes possibilities for intimacy in an increasingly postnational world. "The Courtyard in the Mirror" neither retrieves a Turkish national archive nor seeks admission to a German archive in any familiar national sense. The Turkish neighbor is already an established resident in the German courtyard, where vectors of relationality are being newly forged. Imagining the future emerges as a shared enterprise, in which national affects may vanish like the Cheshire Cat, "quite slowly, beginning with the end of the tail, and ending with the grin, which remained some time after the rest of it had gone." The medial chill of the courtyard narrative elicits the laborious warmth of the strangers who read it, but the labor of imagination figured as an act of reading is not shared equally by migrant subjects and their German neighbors. In this the courtyard narrator is like the migrant laborers who preceded her, with one significant difference. The weight under which she labors is as light—and as material—as a feather.

Chapter Two
Genocide and Taboo

1

The year 1990 marked the national unification of German territories and communities divided by the victors of World War II and the dictates of the Cold War that followed. Erected in August 1961, the Berlin Wall could be seen as a belated manifestation of the metaphorical Iron Curtain that Winston Churchill famously coined as a historical referent in 1945. When the Wall fell no less famously in 1989, the concrete holes chiseled out of it paved the way to a unified free Germany, which the West German state had claimed in its constitutional preamble as its provisional reason for being and its ultimate reason not to be.[1] But this Germany was not free of the drag of historical narrative, and every story about the national turn takes recourse to figural language of some sort. What tales of German metamorphosis does the literature of Turkish migration weave at century's end? What does the Turkish touch effect in the cultural archive of the 1990s? This chapter delineates partial answers to these questions by contrasting two innovative texts in which Turks, Germans, and Jews figure in surprising ways, Feridun Zaimoğlu's *Kanak Sprak: 24 Mißtöne vom Rande der Gesellschaft* [Kanak Speak: 24 Discordant Notes from Society's Edge] (1995) and Zafer Şenocak's *Gefährliche Verwandtschaft* [*Perilous Kinship*] (1998).[2] Because no direct path leads from there and then to here and now, the line of analysis wends a circuitous path toward the configuration of genocide and taboo in the literature of Turkish migration.

No German tale alone, the story of the 1990s features "memory without borders" (Huyssen 2003b: 4) or even a global "cosmopolitanism of memory" (Levy and Sznaider 2001: 10; see also Levy and Sznaider 2002). By Huyssen's account, "North Atlantic societies since the late 1970s" have evidenced a growing loss of faith in the capacity of historical knowledge to sustain national traditions or generate desirable futures (2–5, 11–15). Coupled with the proliferation of new mass media "as carriers of all forms of memory" (18), this crisis of historical consciousness coincides uneasily with a widespread "culture of memory" (14 and passim). In the wake of 1989, Huyssen contends, political concerns about what will be remembered or forgotten in countries throughout Europe, the Middle East, Africa, Australia, Asia, and Latin America yield a highly mediated memory culture of unprecedented proportions (2003a: 147–148; 2003b: 15). Toward their ideal of "a global social cosmos" unfettered by nation-based modernity, on the other hand, Levy and Sznaider pursue "a sociology of globalization" by evaluating changing cultures of memory in Germany, the United States, and Israel (2001: 10). Although they posit that global and national cultures of memory necessarily coexist, they too identify the 1990s as a historic moment when cultures of memory undergo a radical shift.[3] Two important differences between Huyssen's claims and those advanced by Levy and Sznaider warrant immediate summary. First, for Levy and Sznaider, this is the moment when the culture of memory becomes more "cosmopolitan" than ever before. Huyssen suggests instead that there is "no such thing as a postnational or a global memory" (2003a: 148). Second, Levy and Sznaider contend that "global media" foster cosmopolitan memory through "the visualization of culture" (48–49). For Huyssen, medial effects are complex facets of memory culture meriting neither vilification nor celebration on medial grounds alone. But for both accounts, unprecedented shifts in the transnational culture of memory hinge on "a globalization of Holocaust discourse" (Huyssen 2000: 23; 2003b: 13).

With this Huyssen means something different from what Levy and Sznaider have in mind when they speak of "the cosmopolitan significance of Holocaust memory" (56). Recalling other long-distance theories of "imagined communities" (Benedict Anderson; see also chapter one), Levy and Sznaider posit Holocaust memory as "the key" to modernity beyond nationalism.[4] As "the point of departure for a new solidarity beyond borders," Holocaust memory becomes "a measure for humanist and universalist identifications" in an era of ideological disorientation and "the basis for a global politics of human rights" (9–11). When they speak of Holocaust memory, they mean the ability of victims in different contexts to identify with Jewish victims of the Holocaust, "to recognize themselves in the Jewish victims" (56). Global media facilitate this process of identification, Levy and Sznaider assert, by circulating images of murdered Jews; people then " 'work' " with these images in the contexts of their lives (48–49).[5] In Levy and Sznaider's unduly optimistic view, this mediated identification with Jewish victims of Nazi genocide promotes cosmopolitan solidarity with human suffering and human rights campaigns. This goes hand in hand with what these global sociologists call "the lifting of the taboo of the Holocaust," by which they mean a widespread shift from ritualized usage of the historical referent to its generalized invocations in profane realms of public life (60–63). Despite Germany's pivotal status in their study, Levy and Sznaider mention migration only briefly, in connection with Yasemin Soysal's scholarship on legal concepts of universal personhood and new incorporation regimes in Europe (240–241). Virtually none of Levy and Sznaider's claims about transnational shifts in the culture of memory applies to the German literature of Turkish migration. This literature does not generally revolve around normative rights claims. Turkish figures in this literature rarely appear as victims in their own eyes or identify themselves with dead Jews. Furthermore, touching tales of Turks, Germans, and Jews in this literature are infused with the stuff of taboo. Levy and Sznaider are correct only in noting that taboos reflect something that beats at society's core (61). The literature of migration examined in this chapter draws its figures and lines of thought from cultures of memory riddled with taboo. What sorts of taboos are at stake here?

Huyssen helps us understand possible linkages between Turkish migration and German taboos, first, by highlighting a longstanding aversion to national identifications in the wake of the Third Reich and, second, by stressing the acknowledgment of *de facto* immigration as one crucial component of any national identity that Germans could understand as fully democratic rather than merely post-fascist (1995: 67–84; see also Herf 2002: 292). For Huyssen, imagining a democratic future in collective cognizance of a murderous past is a task to which Germans and migrants among them should feel summoned. The present study underscores an orientation toward a shared future history already evident in the literature of Turkish migration. But as Huyssen observes, the labor of migration in this sense may be stymied if "this national host culture is intensely oriented toward memory and traumatic history," as German culture clearly is (2003a:162).[6]

Like Levy and Sznaider's account of cosmopolitan memory, Huyssen's remarks on a global discourse of Holocaust memory rest on the observation that "the Holocaust as a universal trope of traumatic history has migrated" into social contexts other than those in which the historical event occurred or continues to leave its mark (2003b: 14–16).[7] Where the sociologists celebrate global cosmopolitanism, the cultural theorist cautions us to consider "the globalization paradox" (13), whereby the Holocaust, as a mnemonic trope, mobilizes universal claims and local contexts simultaneously.

> It is precisely the emergence of the Holocaust as a universal trope that allows Holocaust memory to latch on to specific local situations that are historically distant and politically distinct from the original event. In the transnational movement of memory discourses, the Holocaust loses its quality as an index of the specific historical event and begins to function as metaphor for other traumatic histories and memories. (13–14)[8]

What happens rhetorically when figures of Holocaust memory retain (in however mediated a fashion) their quality "as an index of the specific historical event" and when they do so in the democratic successor state to both the Third Reich and a divided Germany? In Huyssen's formulation the Holocaust is a trope that migrates outward from Germany. This chapter explores instead cultural effects of Turkish migration to the country where anti-Semitic policies and practices ending in genocide first took shape.[9] This country was then heir to a convoluted legacy of guilt, shame, and atonement.

Huyssen rightly admonishes us "to recognize that although memory discourses may appear to be global in one register, at their core they remain tied to the histories of specific nations and states" (16; 2003a: 148). There are few facets to the configuration of genocide and taboo in the literature of Turkish migration that could rightly be considered englobing. A landmark event in many ways, Şenocak's novel of 1998 is unique in its commingling of narrative strands about the Armenian genocide of 1915 and Turkish migration to Germany decades later. Even here, the novel intervenes predominantly in a German culture of memory amidst accelerated transformation in transnational cultures of memory more generally. As Huyssen observes, memory in any form "is always more than only the prison house of the past," and an analytic lens that perceives all memory functions in terms of trauma will be blind to other functions of memory that pertain at the end of a uniquely genocidal century (2003b: 8–9, 25). As an epochal sense of disorientation gradually gives way to new modes of mnemonic orientation, what role falls to migrant "memories" of a genocidal past in Germany? In her contribution to a book on historical obsessions and memory lapses in German culture since 1945, Aleida Assmann notes that most people living in Germany today have no living memory of the Nazi past. Partly for this reason, she observes, social milieux have changed dramatically since the Mitscherlichs wrote of a collective German neurosis or "inability to mourn" in 1967. In this connection Assmann only hints at "multicultural" implications for rethinking the premises of a culture of memory in Germany (Assmann and Frevert 25). To the extent that figural constellations of Turks, Germans, and Jews circulate in mnemonic narratives of the 1990s, the literature of migration is neither quaint nor odd. It participates in German and transnational cultures of memory as both undergo broad change. Yet it would be misleading to elide the German dimensions of these interventions in a rush to embrace the transnational.

Many German taboos appeared to lift in the wake of unification, first among them the political taboo against any desire for national unity. Public contestations over "the claims of memory" (Wiedmer) flourished in the decade that followed, as controversies over the National Monument for the Murdered Jews of Europe to be built in the heart of Berlin or the then newly available files of the East German secret police attest. In 1998 a prominent author from the West unleashed a maelstrom of protest and applause when he publicly decried the ritualized invocation of Auschwitz in Germany as a routinized means of moral intimidation and taboo enforcement (Walser 1998: 20).[10] Around the same time W. G. Sebald's widely received lecture and essay on the air war against Germans in the 1940s opened the door further to public and private narratives of German rather than Jewish suffering during World War II and its aftermath. More than ever before, talk of suffering experienced by Germans in the firestorms of saturation bombing and forced expulsion from eastern territories fills the air.[11] (Books by Günter Grass and Jörg Friedrich were major catalysts for discussion of German losses related to Allied bombing campaigns.)[12] This is compelling evidence that some internalized injunctions against certain figures of speech (notably, the figure of German suffering) have begun to be lifted in public life. This is not to say that deeply ingrained taboos surrounding the figure of Jewish suffering at German hands no longer hold.

If the figure of Jewish suffering has acquired the status of the sacrosanct in Germany (more as an icon of national atonement and state legitimacy than an index of Jewish experience and loss), this mnemonic figure functions in public life as a ritual object in two conflicting senses. As something sacrosanct, it is revered and held apart from what is profane. But as a ritual object in public life, it is also used, managed, and touched in many different ways and settings. The national tradition of memorialization demands and proscribes this touch at the same time. A constitutive ambivalence additionally inheres in the notion of taboo. As Gertrud Koch observes in remarks on Germany of the 1990s, taboos regulating German relations to murdered Jews are jointly fueled by desire and fear (2003).[13] According to Koch, these taboos have intensified in the wake of unification, and German culture of the 1990s must be understood in part along these lines. This heightened sense of taboo is perhaps another facet of the broad epochal disorientation discussed in the introduction. The touch of ambivalence adhering to figures of Jewish suffering in contemporary German culture in any event reverberates in tales of Turks, Germans, and Jews that touch in the literature of migration. Even if one may speak of "the lifting of the taboo of the Holocaust" in some global sense, those taboos that continue to regulate relations to the dead and murdered cannot be grasped with recourse to globalization. Oskar Negt and Alexander Kluge once characterized history as a set of relationships resulting from the labor of "long-distance senses" (1981: 597; Adelson 1993: 10–11). To the degree that the history of genocide remains palpably present in unified Germany, taboos generated by that history operate most forcefully along short-distance lines of affinity.

In this vein the literature of Turkish migration becomes part of an evolving national tradition of Holocaust memory in Germany.[14]

2

Initial euphoria over unification quickly gave way to heated debates about the "competing narratives" of twentieth-century German history, the legitimacy with which they apportion guilt and adjudicate truth, and representational modes on which they rely to render various pasts, contested presents, and possible futures intelligible to interlocutors today.[15] The Third Reich and the Holocaust remain key points of reference in wide-ranging assessments of German unification, antifascist totalitarianism, and ongoing cultural attempts to come to terms with German histories, hopes, and accountabilities. This is an interpretive landscape in which one customarily expects representational figures of Germans and Jews to meet in ghastly and ghostly ways. But Germany's resident Turks have tended to figure only indirectly in this fraught landscape of national recollection. Throughout the 1990s political tensions between East and West were recounted in narratives peopled largely by Germans alone, with German Turks appearing only at the margins of newly national narration. Scholars make passing reference to a causal link between the raising of the Berlin Wall in August 1961 and the signing, in October 1961 (Şen and Goldberg 10), of the agreement between Germany and Turkey to recruit migrant labor in response to German need (e.g., Bade 393; Barbieri 28; Chapin 280; Chin 46).[16] Despite the fact that ensuing migrations and births have made Turks the largest minority in unified Germany, they are rarely seen as intervening meaningfully in the narrative of postwar German history. (See Georgi on migrants' "borrowed memory" of German history.)

Figural references to Turks nonetheless acquire a pivotal function in German debates about twentieth-century history, especially when commentators measure the degree to which West German society could be deemed civilized, democratic, and European. Throughout the 1980s and 1990s controversies raged over German citizenship law and the political status denied most Turkish residents. The early years after unification saw a surge in violent attacks on Turks and other "foreigners," real or perceived. This elicited public outcry at home and abroad, as many wondered what values the newly unified and powerful German nation would represent. In roughly the same decade that spanned the German Historians' Debate of the mid-1980s and extended debates about Berlin's National Monument for the Murdered Jews of Europe, German public figures repeatedly opposed full membership for Turkey in the European Community and subsequently the European Union. This debate continues in Germany and internationally, and political arguments on many sides of the issue are genuinely complex rather than merely ideological. Since the 1980s German opposition to Turkish membership, however, has frequently been voiced in discursive terms alleging incompatible cultural values. According to the predominant version of this argument, the Turkish Republic is insufficiently committed to human rights and hence not civilized enough to be fully welcomed into Europe's warm embrace, unlike a fully western, democratic Germany.[17] The more the Federal Republic chastised Turkey for its "civilizational" deficiency before and after 1990, the more robust Germany's own civilizing commitment to European identity appeared. Since Turkish residents in Germany are often presumed to embody Turkish national culture, as if they had swallowed it whole, longstanding German rejection of Turkey with regard to EU-membership has not infrequently dovetailed with the rejection of Turks as fellow citizens. Overarching historical narratives of barbarism and civilization circulate in such public contestations. These are the teleological touchstones on which evaluative accounts of the Third Reich and its place in modernity rely (see, e.g., Bauman and Weitz), as do those of the Islamic "Orient" and its place in Europe. In this broad narratological sense, twentieth-century tales of Germans and Jews are not so much analogous to those of Germans and Turks as they are proximate. They "touch."[18] They do so by means of figural reference and developmental narrative, but the touch of these tales has an unsettling effect on referential functions beyond the one inhering in figural language as such. To what exactly is reference made when one speaks of a Turkish presence in German stories of genocidal legacies and cultural divides? This is a contemporary riddle of referentiality.

During the 1970s a commonplace held that "the Turks are the Jews of today." This leftist slogan criticized a perceived continuity of fascist attitudes in West German society with a rhetorical gesture substituting Turkish guest workers for Jewish victims of the Nazi past.[19] For decades, comparisons and analogies between living Turks and dead Jews were more likely to be drawn in political and anthropological arenas where discrimination and assimilation were at stake, rather than in literary sectors.[20] German literature that began to emerge from the Turkish migrant experience in the early 1980s did not make much of Turkish–Jewish comparisons or juxtapositions. This has changed since national unification.[21] Works discussed in this chapter are haunted by some linkage between "things Jewish" and "things Turkish" as they negotiate the German present of the 1990s. One sophisticated immigrant author from Turkey has even been touted as "the Woody Allen of Berlin."[22] This figural invocation of one of the world's "funniest" Jews seems out of sync with a pivotal marker of time in Turkish–German relations of the 1990s. For some, lethal firebombing attacks on Turkish residences in the West German towns of Mölln and Solingen in 1992 and 1993 have definitively riven the telling of time. As a Turkish woman living in Germany puts it, "we say here: the time before the fire and time after it" (Zaimoğlu 1998b: 82).[23] In this rhetoric of deadly fires that cleave time, tales of Turks and Jews in Germany are also made to "touch."

When figural Turks and Jews make contact in German narratives alluding to stories of victimization and genocide, these narratives become "touching tales" of Turks, Germans, and Jews. They function as such, in part, because they evoke a culturally residual, referentially nonspecific sense of guilt, blame, shame, and danger.[24] If Turkish and Jewish figures meet in German literary narratives of the recent past and do not merely stand in for each other, however, what does the representational touch effect? Dominick LaCapra's insights into the return of the repressed in historiographical narratives of National Socialism index more or less known events in a traumatic past and the ongoing renegotiation of their meaning. The question put here to the literature of migration in the 1990s has a somewhat different focus. What happens when "the Holocaust" or things vaguely "Jewish" become a kind of language through which something happening in the present—as yet undefined—is rendered intelligible as something happening in the present?[25] This clearly has something to do with the Nazi past too, but the nature of this relationship is not pre-given. Neither should we presuppose that this undefined something in the present is traumatic. What then is the structural function of "Jewish" references in the literature of Turkish migration? How does this literature render contemporary historical experience intelligible? What can it tell us that we do not already presume to know before we take this literature in hand?

3

Still wending a circuitous path to the configuration of genocide and taboo in the literature of migration, the argument now turns to seminal discussions of history and narration by Dominick LaCapra (1998) in the field of Holocaust historiography and Homi K. Bhabha (1990a) in the field of postcolonial theory. Both scholars advance methodological claims about ways in which pasts and presents are locked in a constitutive if disquieting embrace in the narration of modern time. LaCapra's remarks on "history and memory after Auschwitz" are relevant to Germany's cultural history as it turns toward a new marking of time, and Bhabha mobilizes "the Turkish *Gastarbeiter*" as an icon for "the radical incommensurability of translation" in modern national narratives of Europe (317).[26] Against temporal models of linear progression whereby "after" is distinct from what comes "before," both scholars stress a constitutive cleft in time inhering in structures of narration. Both offer insights that promise greater purchase on riddles of referentiality in touching tales of Turks, Germans, and Jews. Yet neither scholar offers a model that lends itself unproblematically to an analysis of the literature of migration. Acknowledging the stumbling blocks to such application helps us refine our critical grasp of the cultural contexts in which this literature intervenes.

Relationships posited between barbarism and civilization (as teleological points of reference in narratives of European modernity) entail assumptions about time and history. Writing on transferential practices in Holocaust historiography and cultural analysis, LaCapra addresses a phobic sacrificialism in the Third Reich that "seems utterly out of place and appears, deceptively, as a regression to barbarism" in a historical context otherwise construed as that of "advanced 'modernity' " (3). Rather than seeing barbarism and modernity as mutually exclusive temporal modes, LaCapra argues forcefully that scholars of the Holocaust, and of subsequent cultural attempts to come to terms with that past, must account for an "uncanny return of the repressed."[27] His remarks on the time of history shed light on how figures of reference circulate in German historical and cultural narratives.

> The concept of a regression to barbarism rests on an indiscriminate and self-serving view of other societies to which modern, presumably advanced societies are compared. It also frequently assumes an idea of progress leading from "them" to "us." Neither of these assumptions is required by a notion of the return of the repressed. Indeed the latter is related to a very different understanding of temporality in which any features deemed desirable must be recurrently rewon, and less desirable ones pose a continual threat that reappears in different guises over time. (3)

LaCapra's focus is the historiography of trauma and, more specifically, the historiography of the Holocaust and its aftermath. In this connection he criticizes accounts of the Third Reich that categorize Nazi atrocities in terms of a temporal "regression to barbarism" and post-Holocaust societies in terms of a straightforward temporal advance or reclamation of civilization. LaCapra thus sketches one relevant context in which touching tales of Turks, Germans, and Jews in the literature of migration may be situated.

LaCapra makes only brief reference to the troubled status of Germany's guest workers in his chapter on the Historians' Debate that took center stage in Germany in the 1980s.[28] This makes *History and Memory after Auschwitz* less useful for our purposes than it would be if Turks in Germany or the literature of migration were focal subjects of LaCapra's analysis. Yet his comments on temporal structures of historical narrative and the heightened indirection of reference after Auschwitz suggest one crucial frame of reference for understanding German debates about victims, civilization, and modernity since 1945. Turks have figured significantly in such debates since the early 1970s, as demonstrated above. Yet a cautionary note is in order. While there are some good reasons for understanding the referential status of Turkish figures in Germany today against the background of the ongoing traumatic history of the Holocaust, it is not at all clear in any given instance what it might mean to do so, or even whose traumatic history is most palpably present in the warp and woof of any given narrative. References to Turkish figures in German culture of the 1990s at times bear traumatic traces of a genocidal history in Germany, but Turkish figures do not merely stand in for Jewish ones. To say that something about the past is being negotiated in the present does not yet tell us what it means for reorientation in the 1990s or beyond. Several interactive contexts vie for analysis as we interrogate the proximity of Turks, Germans, and Jews in contemporary literature. This is an arena in which the touch of historical narrative and the configuration of cultural contact are readily felt, if poorly grasped. Contemplating the riddle of referentiality allows us to hone our analytical skills in this regard.

4

A Turkish riddle of referentiality figures centrally in what has become a standard text of postcolonial thought. The trope of the incoherent Turk in Germany makes its little remarked entry into the narratological history of postcolonial theory and transnational cultural studies in Bhabha's otherwise seminal essay on "DissemiNation: time, narrative, and the margins of the modern nation," first published in 1990.[29] This is a treatise on the uncanny time of cultural modernity, about the uncanny *temporal* hybridity of modern national narratives in Europe.[30] In the wake of mass migrations beginning in the nineteenth century, Bhabha argues, the modern nation "fills the void left in the uprooting of communities and kin and turns that loss into the language of metaphor." By this account, the metaphor of home underwrites "the imagined community of the nation-people" across geographic distances and cultural differences alike (291). Near the end of the essay, Bhabha turns "to the desolate silences of the wandering people; to that 'oral void' that emerges when the Turk abandons the metaphor of a *heimlich* national culture" to the degree that "the Turkish immigrant" longs for his Turkish home but imagines his return only as a mythic goal, never to be achieved " 'as imagined' " (316).[31]

Two things must be said about this. First, Bhabha links his narrative of nineteenth-century migrations within Europe to his story of transcontinental labor migration, diasporic exile, and postcolonial ambivalence in the latter half of the twentieth century. The linkage he posits between nineteenth-century tales of national belonging and twentieth-century tales of transnational displacement becomes squarely anchored in the figure of "the Turkish *Gastarbeiter*" in a subsequent turn of argument. Second, Bhabha cites decisively but elliptically from John Berger's impressionist account of migrant laborers from many nations who were working in Europe in the early to mid-1970s (Berger 1975).[32] Bhabha's "Turkish" composite is a figural hinge on which some doors open to insightful vistas and others slam shut. Whatever oral void this Turk is made to represent, its figurality reflects a particular and early moment in the history of Turkish labor migration. The phantasm of the Turkish guest worker continues to circulate in the 1990s—this too bespeaks a present past—but it would be misleading to interpret this figure as if it were frozen in time, to understand it in terms of a historical void.

For Bhabha, the "lost object" of home in its national configuration comes to be "repeated in the void that at once prefigures and pre-empts the 'unisonant', which makes it *unheimlich*" (315). In this postcolonial narrative about the modern story of national belonging in Europe, Bhabha posits a constitutive disjunction in the latter. By this he means a constitutive disjunction between the actual loss of home for many migrants in the nineteenth century and the imagined restitution of home through the metaphor of home on which the modern nation-state in Europe relies. And this is where the figure of the Turk acquires strategic centrality. For in Bhabha's view, the body of a Turkish laborer in Germany "prefigures and pre-empts the 'unisonant,'" thereby becoming the sign of the uncanny heartbeat at the core of the national narrative. The Turkish guest worker "prefigures" the unity of national belonging because—it is assumed—Turkish migrants long to go "home." And the Turkish guest worker "pre-empts the 'unisonant' " because the Turkish body doomed to "gesture and failed speech" (316) serves as a constant reminder that the modern European nation is not and can never be one. This Turk, again according to Bhabha, "leads the life of the double, the automaton." This figure of a Turk is not incapable of speech, but the speech he utters in Germany is thwarted and thwarts understanding in turn, because such speech remains "eerily untranslated in the racist site of its enunciation" (316). Bhabha ultimately claims that "the experience of the Turkish *Gastarbeiter* represents the radical incommensurability of translation" in the modern national narratives of Europe, whereas "Salman Rushdie's *The Satanic Verses* attempts to redefine the boundaries of the western nation, so that the 'foreignness of languages' becomes the inescapable cultural condition for the enunciation of the mother-tongue" (317). Rushdie becomes the privileged migrant voice of narration, for his literary art crafts what Bhabha considers "the articulation *through* incommensurability" that structures cultural modernity (319). The figure of the Turkish laborer serves Bhabha as the necessary companion piece to the figure of the postcolonial writer. For in Bhabha's oddly ahistorical account of historical structures of narration, Rushdie articulates the disjunctive structure of modernity that the incoherent *Gastarbeiter* can only represent or embody. Understanding the conjunction of figuration and narration in the literature of Turkish migration written two decades after Berger gathered his haunting impressions—and in the land where Turkish migrants live, speak, and write—is going to take much more than this. The literature of Turkish migration is a historical formation in its own right, and it contributes significantly to the evolving story of the German nation.

As LaCapra does with reference to historical narrative, Bhabha stresses the uncanny temporality of cultural narrative. Unlike LaCapra, Bhabha ascribes pivotal representational significance to the Turkish "automaton" in Germany. He does so without establishing any German context for his remarks. "DissemiNation" puts forward a sophisticated analysis of the uncanny antimetaphoricity of national cultures in Europe, yet one may reasonably wonder whether the figure of the incoherent Turk does not function metaphorically in this account, as a generic postcolonial cipher for "the radical incommensurability of translation." This renders Bhabha's strategic figure of limited value in assessing Turkish configurations of German culture in the historically disjunctive time of the 1990s. In another venue Deniz Göktürk avers, "[e]ven Homi Bhabha, the great propagator of hybridity . . ., imagines the Turkish migrant worker in Germany as an incommensurable, alienated, speechless victim without any voice" (1999b: 4). Göktürk decries the linked paradigms of victimology and authenticity that continue to inform cultural discourses of migration and diaspora.[33] The "social worker's perspective" that she associates with this generally is one that she ascribes to Bhabha's dire portrait of a Turkish *Gastarbeiter* as adapted from Berger (1, 14). My methodological concern is somewhat different from the important one articulated by Göktürk.[34] Touching tales of genocide and taboo do not lend themselves easily to celebratory hybridity. If we reject the premise that Turkish figures in postwar German culture merely stand in for some other phenomenon (such as migrant minorities in a global arena, national cultures in a transnational age, or post-Wall specters of the Nazi past), then how can we read the literary "touch" of Turks, Germans, and Jews? How should we delineate our objects of analysis? What stories should we tell about the contexts in which these objects pulse with meaning for the historical present?

5

A German riddle of referentiality precedes the literature of migration, in which it reverberates. The difficulty of delineating a discrete object of commentary—and narrating a historical development that takes that object as its point of reference—has been a core issue for studies of German culture since 1945. The date itself stands in for a kind of referential suspension, especially regarding representations of "the past," much invoked in literary studies but less seldom delineated as a discrete structure, entity, or even as a problem. For what specific past is referenced in public discourses and literary manifestations of *Vergangenheitsbewältigung*?[35] This is not always as clear as many presume, and the ambiguity exceeds what inheres in any palimpsest or the figural language of literary representation generally. While official discourses of reparations and atonement in the West have formally acknowledged the Holocaust since the decisive days of Konrad Adenauer, the conservative politician who served as Federal Chancellor from 1949 to 1963, West German literature often muddied the referential waters approaching and retreating from a past that somehow encompasses the Holocaust as well as the Third Reich and World War II.[36] To mention two of the best-known representatives of *Vergangenheitsbewältigung* in German literature from 1959, Jews and the Holocaust barely figure in *The Tin Drum* by Günter Grass or *Billiards at Half-Past Nine* by Heinrich Böll. This observation is as innovative today as it is to remark that absence, silence, and unspeakability have been contested staples of German and Jewish discourses about the Holocaust for over fifty years. Countless examples revolve around the referential status of Auschwitz and the narrative functions that accrue to the name on the basis of this referentiality.[37]

Ongoing debates about irrational and rational features of this past, about its proper or improper place in a narrative of modernity, are not at issue here. This context of referential tensions and historical narrative is mentioned only to suggest that touching tales of Turks, Germans, and Jews in the 1990s be read both with and against the grain of a cultural context in which Turks are presumed to have no place at all. LaCapra refuses to see representational language and reverent silence as mutually exclusive responses to the Holocaust. "Auschwitz . . . may reduce one to silence. Silence that is not a sign of utter defeat, however, is itself a potentially ritual attitude; but in this sense it is a *silence survenu* intricately bound up with certain uses of language" (1992: 126). LaCapra's attention to "a relation between language and silence that is in some sense ritualized" provides a useful provocation here. For if proximate narratives of Turks, Germans, and Jews have been unsettling a ritualized configuration of historical phenomena and cultural contact in German literature since unification, the cultural labor signaled by the literature of migration in Germany is hardly a minor concern.[38]

One now canonical author whose tormented relationship to things German and Jewish was characterized by exile, displacement, guilt, and transference was Peter Weiss, best known in German Studies for

The Investigation.[39] This play premiered in fifteen different theaters in West and East Germany in October 1965. Weiss himself had attended "the Auschwitz trial," which took place from 1963 to 1965, marking the first major court proceedings against Nazi perpetrators initiated by the Federal Republic. The play draws heavily on documentation from the trial and other sources about Auschwitz, in addition to Dante's *Inferno*. This is well known, as is the pointed analogy that Weiss posits between fascism of the 1940s and capitalism of the 1960s.[40] This logic informed much leftist discourse from the student movement of the 1960s into the 1980s.[41]

Analogies hinged on the referential significance of Auschwitz swing in one of two directions. As in *The Investigation*, Auschwitz is sometimes cast as analogous to something else lending it greater meaning than it would have without the analogue. In *The Investigation* ruthless capitalism looms much larger than genocidal anti-Semitism, which appears in the play as an instantiation of the former. Or Auschwitz functions as the historical referent bestowing weightier significance to something else drawn in analogy to it. One graphic example of this from the left-liberal milieu of 1974 was a provocative poster by Klaus Staeck, a popular political artist of the period, who photographed two foreign sanitation workers collecting and emptying German trash (Staeck and Adelmann 166–167). The image is in black and white except for a Star of David superimposed on a guest worker's shirt pocket. This six-pointed star is not yellow but striped in the colors of the Italian flag. Staeck titled his image, which was distributed and exhibited in poster and postcard format, "*Fremdarbeiter*," a term normally shunned in the postwar era because of its associations with forced foreign labor in the Third Reich. Italy had been the first country to sign a labor recruitment agreement with the Federal Republic in 1955, and Staeck was not alone among German leftists in dramatizing the plight of migrant laborers in the 1970s by depicting them virtually as "the Jews of today."[42] This substitution rests on a structural analogy posited between the political realities of the past and those presumed to hold for the 1970s.

No such analogies lend themselves to a reading of the dramatic text that Weiss had written one year prior to *The Investigation*. The play that jolted theater internationally with its explosive combination of epic and absurd effects catapulted Weiss to stardom in and beyond Germany. To this day it remains the work for which he is best known outside German Studies. Weiss's imagined encounter between the extreme individualism of the Marquis de Sade and the revolutionary zeal of Jean Paul Marat defies both dogma and dialectic (Weiss 1964).[43] Staged by de Sade for the ostensible edification of unruly patients in the insane asylum where the Marquis is a political prisoner, the play within the play circles masochistically around Marat's murder at the hands of Charlotte Corday.[44] Set in 1808, the framing play bespeaks historical consciousness of things that cannot be undone. Corday assassinated Marat, and the French Revolution violently betrayed its rational ideals. This knowledge proves just as unruly as the asylum's patients and inmates, an unruliness agitated and underscored by the dynamism of Weiss's rhymes and syntax. *Marat/Sade* is less about the French Revolution as an inspirational and cautionary tale than it is about a crisis of historical consciousness. Known outcomes are continually interrupted and deferred in the play, such that historical progress as a concept is radically at stake. The burning question that seems to crackle throughout is whether the French Revolution lies behind or ahead of participants and spectators involved in the play.[45] What relationship prevails, the play seems to ask obsessively, between the historical past and present history? What ethical and political responsibilities to the past accrue to individuals and societies in the present?

While one might speculate that the play of 1964 prefigures political questions about historical consciousness that will occupy the playwright more directly in *The Investigation*, this is not a case to be stressed unduly here. What prompts the mention of Weiss in this discussion of migration is a moment in *Marat/Sade* when a postwar German riddle of referentiality seems very nearly to have been posed. We know that Weiss inverts ritualized language at times, for example, when one patient turns the Our Father on its head and prays to Satan to "forgive us our innocence" (Weiss 1964: 43).[46] While most names, events, and issues invoked in the play revolve referentially around the French Revolution, the Holocaust seems close at hand in Scene 22 of Act I.[47] Calling for quill and ink so that he may address the nation, the ailing and persecuted Marat is almost blinded by a darkness that comes over him. His attendant reassures him, "Es war nur eine Wolke, die vorbeiging / oder Rauch / Man verbrennt jetzt die Leichen" (Weiss 1964: 74). The published translation omits the deictic *jetzt* [now] of this last line: "That was only a cloud over the sun / or perhaps smoke / They are burning the corpses" (Weiss 1965b: 59). (A literal translation would yield, "They are burning the corpses now.") The scene concludes with sung commentary on Marat's revolutionary status. "Armer Marat wir wolln an dich glauben / doch kann all deine gesammelte Weisheit noch taugen / Jetzt wo du da in der Wanne sitzt / und in Wundbrand und Atemnot schwitzt" (Weiss 1964: 75). The Skelton translation does not translate this passage at all but transforms it into the now familiar rhyme: "Marat we're poor and the poor stay poor / Marat don't make us wait any more / We want our rights and we don't care how / We want our Revolution NOW" (Weiss 1965b: 59). A literal translation of the verses so transformed would read unrhythmically, "Poor Marat we want to believe in you / But can all the wisdom you've gathered still be true / Now that you sit there in your tub / And sweat, with festering wounds and short of breath." What are we to make of this "Atemnot schwitzt" (literally: shortness of breath / [you] sweat)? Since the string of syllables appears in such proximity to a constative reference to corpses being burned and smoke darkening the air, are we justified in detecting a partial echo of "Auschwitz" in the German original? Or is this merely a filament of a readerly imagination?[48] At most we might speak of an affective shiver of cognitive uncertainty. We might derive from this paroxysm of suspended recognition, not a historical reference, but a question about referential excitability. If German references to Auschwitz and the Holocaust have never been stabilized, if considerable excitation attaches to them because of their heightened referential ambiguity in literary texts, then how and with what effects does the literature of Turkish migration appropriate and adapt this central feature of postwar culture?

Speaking of referential excitability in these contexts may conjure loose associations with Judith Butler's incisive work on "excitable speech" in U.S.-American politics and rhetoric, but some distinctions apply. "In the law," Butler explains, " 'excitable' utterances are those made under duress, usually confessions that cannot be used in court because they do not reflect the balanced mental state of the utterer" (1997: 15). Arguing instead that "speech is always in some ways out of our control" (15) and hence excitable, Butler assesses hate speech in terms of linguistic conventions by which humans are interpellated as social subjects.[49] Because "to be addressed is to be interpellated" (2) in this sense, hate speech may wound and subordinate those to whom it is addressed. But because even hate speech exceeds the control of those who hate, Butler elaborates, injurious "name-calling may be the initiating moment of a counter-mobilization" (163) by subjects whom the conventions of hate otherwise render abject and subordinate. In contemporary contexts centered in Germany, one might well concur with Manuela Günter that Zaimoğlu's *Kanak Sprak* of 1995 fits Butler's model of "counter-mobilization."[50] After all, "Kanak Speak" sparked a broad antiracist coalition called "Kanak Attak," emphatically defies the derogatory usage of "Kanake" in German parlance (in reference to Turks), and appropriates the term as a badge of honor.[51] And when a German woman addresses a Turkish figure in *Kanak Sprak* as "you my beautiful Jew" (70), the latter is literally addressed and interpellated. But all acknowledgment of genocide and discrimination levied at Jews or Turks in Germany notwithstanding, "you my beautiful Jew" hardly qualifies as hate speech or excitable speech as Butler defines them. If anything, the phrase constitutes a kind of problematic love speech, albeit one that cannot be grasped in conventional terms of postwar philosemitism in Germany (Stern 1991, 1992), precisely because the phrase is addressed to a Turkish figure imagined to be Jewish by a German figure who knows that the Turk is not a Jew. Something is subject to excitation in such figural acrobatics, but what that something might be is not self-evident. The texts by Zaimoğlu and Şenocak to which this chapter now turns thematize and parody ways in which many German conventions interpellate Turkish migrants and their progeny. Beyond this, however, these groundbreaking examples drawn from the literature of Turkish migration enter into a murky realm of German excitability around Auschwitz as both a historical signifier and a literary allusion. What happens when this German riddle of referentiality encounters the ostensible "thingliness" of Turkish figures in reference to which a story of migration might be told? Zaimoğlu and Şenocak approach this question by rather different stylistic means, and this too tells a tale of the 1990s.

6

Despite his actual age, Zaimoğlu reigns in German print, performance, and television media as beloved *enfant terrible*, cult author, and entertaining *Kanak* spokesperson for the critical disaffection of migrant youth.[52] A film version of the author's 1997 book on drug addiction and "scum" (*Abschaum*) appeared under the title *Kanak Attack!* in 2000 (dir. Lars Becker). According to Cheesman:

> By then, Zaimoglu's work had been adapted for the stage in a dozen cities, adapted for radio and marketed on CD. He had become a regular contributor to *Die Zeit* [a major weekly German newspaper read by the highly educated], and articles or interviews had made him known to readers of many other publications (including *Newsweek*), and to viewers of several talk shows. He is a superb performer of his own material, capable of bringing both male and female characters sharply to life; in interviews, he often improvises dazzlingly in the stylized slang of his books. (2004: 85–86; see also Cheesman 2002: 185)

As Cheesman further observes, "In 1996 one of Germany's Turkish papers dubbed him 'the Turks' Malcolm X': the comparison cannot be sustained, yet no German writer of color has conquered so much cultural space for himself and others" (2004: 84).[53] In 2003 Zaimoğlu was among a select group of writers invited to compete with unpublished literary material for the prestigious Bachmann Prize. For a short, unsentimental story called "Häute" [Skins] depicting village life outside Europe, he was awarded the second-place "Prize of the Jury" by the Austria-based organization that administers the competition, broadcast live via different media. This piece was subsequently published in a collection of stories on the vagaries of "happiness" (Zaimoğlu 2004).

All this has transpired since Zaimoğlu erupted onto the German radar screen in 1995 with the publication of *Kanak Sprak*, the author's first book, which was shepherded into the limelight by one of Germany's major presses. Other books in its wake include a far less fiery "female" version of *Kanak Sprak* (1998b), a masculinist migrant take on the epistolary novel of the eighteenth century (2000), and a pseudo-artsy novelistic romp through Berlin and its eastern environs after the demise of the GDR (2002; see also 2003b). While Zaimoğlu has indicted the commercial success and liberal appeal of early guest worker literature and the defanged "Kanak" hipness his own publications have inspired (1996, 1997b, 1998a)—with "Kanak-Chic" (Steyerl) having enjoyed far more commercial success in the 1990s than guest worker literature ever did in the 1980s—the author has been decried as an all too reputable Turk for show-and-tell (Droste) and praised for promoting a "language of the uprising" (Tuschik 2000a: 107; 2000b: 283). By one account, "commercial popular culture has overtaken Zaimoğlu's project and is building up a huge body of worthless but lucrative work, which ensures that 'Kanak' generally still signifies what it always did—a derogatory term of racist abuse—with the difference that it is no longer taboo in public discourse" (Cheesman 2002: 193; see also Cheesman 2004: 99).[54] Three years younger than Şenocak, Zaimoğlu had been born in Anatolia in 1964 before moving with his mother in 1965 to the Federal Republic, where his parents reunited the family under official auspices of labor migration.[55] The desire to study medicine led him years later to Kiel, where Zaimoğlu eventually "concentrated on painting and writing, taking jobs as a 'street worker' in drugs projects" instead (Cheesman 2002: 181). This familiarity with street life on the fringes of German society clearly informs the rhetoric of *Kanak Sprak*, but what kind of book is this? How does it weave a genocidal legacy and ongoing cultural taboos surrounding the Holocaust into a story of Turkish migration?[56]

Allusions to the Holocaust play a crucial role in *Kanak Sprak* without taking center stage. Whether this text is literary or ethnographic is subject to debate. The expository prose of the author's preface informs readers that Zaimoğlu had spent eighteen months interviewing male representatives of the "Generation X" resulting from Turkish migration, those who do not recognize themselves "in the supermarket of identities" (12–13). These are young men occupying a slangy netherworld "on society's edge." Asked what is it like to live "as a *Kanake* in Germany" (9), they have a lot to say. At agitated odds with middle-class values and ideals (German and Turkish), Zaimoğlu's subjects include a thief, a pimp, male prostitutes, a junkie in the process of shooting up, a psychiatric patient, a transsexual, an Islamist, a trash collector, and several unemployed, in addition to a trucker, a sociologist, a poet, and others.[57] Although only two interviewees are designated as actual rappers, most of the interview " 'protocols' "—Zaimoğlu uses the word in quotation marks (15)—read like rapid-fire, rap-like bursts of transgressive linguistic material, much of it involving scatology, criminality, and sexuality. Defiantly rejecting the xenophilic myth of the loveable oppressed Turk, the author and his subjects dismissively reserve the word "Turk" for those deemed "socially acceptable" (8) and desiring integration. Zaimoğlu's celebratory attention goes instead to the downtrodden but unvanquished *Kanaken* of the book's rebellious title, those for whom bourgeois society and even liberal multiculturalists reserve no space but down: "Here only the *Kanake* has the say" (18).[58] In this sense, *Kanak Sprak* challenges the cultural icon of the Turkish migrant whose powers of speech fail him in Germany. As Cheesman recounts, the book's multiple provocations were "widely welcomed as bringing fresh sparkle into the literary scene, although Zaimoğlu's work was no less widely regarded as not being literature at all: many reviewers assumed Zaimoğlu had merely transcribed real 'ghetto talk' literally" (2002: 184–185).

As ethnographic transcriptions, the " 'protocols' " are not especially reliable. Zaimoğlu claims in the preface to present an " 'authentic' image of [Kanak] speech" as a visible whole, while he simultaneously claims to have helped the creation of this image along with his own stylistic after-effects (18). Explaining that his creative reworking of the interview material was necessary to avoid the false folkloristic impression of a "flowery language of Orientals" (14), Zaimoğlu indicates that some of the interviews were originally conducted in Turkish. Yet readers encounter in *Kanak Sprak* "a highly original literary German bearing a strong authorial stamp, featuring rap rhythms and rich in vernacular metaphors" (Cheesman 2002: 184).[59] While Petra Fachinger notes only that *Kanak Sprak* does not consist of "unrehearsed first-person chronicles" (2001: 102), Moray McGowan speaks of "one voice, one performative delivery style" with which the so-called protocols are presented (2001: 303–304; see also Karakuş 2001: 275–277). Although readers can easily identify different personalities and opinions, I too understand the text as consistently bespeaking a creative product made in Germany by Zaimoğlu.[60]

Against "the state-sanctioned dialogue between 'Germans' and 'Turks' " (Cheesman 2004: 83), against the "intercultural paradigm of understanding" (Günter 27), *Kanak Sprak* gives voice to what Cheesman dubs the "pseudo-ethnicity" (2004: 83) and parodic identity (2002: 187) of the *Kanak* brotherhood.[61] The rhetorical figure through which this voice speaks exudes anger, scorn, and feistiness, but denotes a site of wounding too. Zaimoğlu explains this in the expository preface by indexing emotional despair and psychosomatic illnesses to which second-generation *Kanaken* fall prey when Germans dismiss them as inferior or invisible, but also when Turkish families migrating back to Turkey impose "forced assimilation" in a foreign country to which these young *Kanaken* from Germany have no real linguistic, emotional, or cultural affinity (10–11). If Zaimoğlu calls a pseudo-ethnic identity into being, he does so to indict the normative presumption that identities and communities are ethnic formations in the mosaic sense of multiculturalism.[62] What is often lost in discussions of the critical and commercial projects crystallizing around Zaimoğlu is the recognition that *Kanak Sprak*, for all its fierce rhetoric of alienated insubordination, draws a picture of an ethnoscape that Turks and Germans co-inhabit in Germany. This is an image drawn in words to give voice to disenfranchised migrant youth, but the image is also designed to render *Kanaken* visible in this shared landscape of worlds in flux.[63] The presumed "thingliness" of Turkish figures in German media is thus countered by something else otherwise obscured from view. "I show and produce presence," Zaimoğlu insists (14).

The "presence" to which *Kanak Sprak* lends voice and visibility can be understood in at least two ways. Both converge in powers of speech that Zaimoğlu ascribes to his *Kanak* protocols. On the one hand, the author explicitly links "the rich gestural language of the *Kanak*" to a "basic pose," described in physical detail as signaling the expectation of "a lively conversation" (13). Moray McGowan aptly characterizes this position as "half soapbox orator, half raging bull" (2001: 303), thus underscoring the "word power" conjured by Zaimoğlu in terms of a visual repertoire that does not necessarily yield or connote informational content, let alone real political power. The author's preface encourages readers to visualize his defiant young Turks, but what exactly are they saying with such bravado? Even more than the physical presence of these *Kanaken* in Germany, Zaimoğlu oddly enough articulates the significance of their presence in terms of incoherence at the crossroads of affect and speech. "The word power of the *Kanak* expresses itself in a hybrid babble, expulsed and breathless, without punctuation, with arbitrary pauses and improvised turns" (13). Is this an updated version of "the Turkish *Gastarbeiter*" whose failed powers of speech led Bhabha to enshrine him as an icon of incommensurability and alienation? This is hardly the case, for Zaimoğlu regards the incoherence of "Kanak speak" as powerful rather than powerless. When he decries the "'garbageman-prose' that pins the *Kanak* down in the role of victim," moreover, he rejects both the guest worker literature of the 1980s and a liberal proclivity to feel pity for Turkish victims of German circumstance (12). Zaimoğlu comments retrospectively on his first major publication by characterizing the language of his *Kanaken* as a "flood of images" drawn from street life and migration history "to unleash fireworks of cultural excitation" (2001: 15). Waxing epic, he avows, from the first generation into the fourth, "hundreds and hundreds" of migration experiences flow together to form the story of migration as "the great narrative stream" (21).

But in *Kanak Sprak* very few stories actually get told. Beyond the summative preface, the " 'protocols' " more often than not depict an unruly state of mind, stirring up a sense of "cultural excitation" instead. This may explain in part why the text has been deemed "effectively untranslatable" (Cheesman 2002: 183). The figural "presence" of Zaimoğlu's *Kanaken* is largely one of intensified affect and attitudinal posturing. The powers of incoherence lie in this realm, where a pose of power is imagined to trump the exercise of power by the nation-state and its cultural norms. The affects at stake in this figural presence do not belong to the Turks in the text alone.

Pointing the way to a "new realism" (17), Zaimoğlu presents his cast of characters as an underworld of affect, a substratum of reality reflecting a deeper truth about German society in the 1990s. Yet the figure of "Kanak" speech often comments on such deep structures critically, rather than merely mirroring an irritating state of affairs. Inverting the disdainful ethnographic gaze that the bourgeoisie otherwise directs at migrant youth (Cheesman 2004: 86), those made to feel like society's dregs assert their self-worth and castigate German behaviors from a self-ascribed position of moral superiority. (This migrant perspective and affective interest in German behaviors differ from those at stake in Özamar's courtyard ethnoscape.) The masculinist voices of *Kanak Sprak* recast life at the bottom into a view from the top. The sense of overview is sometimes articulated in referential terms only vaguely indexing tough choices on mean streets, rather than life in Germany as such. One eighteen-year-old expounds on what rap culture means to him:

> Be a lamb, they eat you alive, be a little fish, they eat you, you got no code, they eat you, and because the shittiest rules apply, 'cause what counts is: eat or die, because only the very few keep a cool head, you've got to say: here with us, with the breakers and rappers, with the brothers and sisters, it's over with the clover, we're not swimming with the current, we make our own strict stream, where everyone's a river and stops being a lousy trickle that god shat out. (41–42)

More commonly, the under-class view from the top is mediated through an appeal to cleanliness and purity. This entails generic connotations of street life, as when one rapper vows to help "the kids" get free of drugs and "stay clean" (29–30), or when the pimp insists on "the purity law" to protect his prostitutes from sexually transmitted disease (54). The pimp's use of *Reinheitsgebot* is also a pun invoking the proud tradition of cleanliness and purity in the making of German beer. When the rapper maligns servile Turks who stoop too low for German approval, he describes them as emerging from debasement with "cocoa coating as a kind of identity" (32). In these examples Zaimoğlu's *Kanaken* lay claim to standards of purity otherwise associated with German precepts, and ostensibly deeper truths about social relations are figured in terms of dirt, filth, excrement, and disease. One of the unemployed confesses his fears of being infected by German crises: "The *alemanne*, brother, devours crisis, craps crisis, and infects you with a brooding microbe, so there's crisis inside you too and it rattles till judgment day" (83).[64] If the mainstream relegates these *Kanaken* to the fringes of social life in contemporary Germany, their defiant rhetoric of abjection bespeaks something unsettled within German culture. This exceeds German prejudices vis-à-vis young Turkish men on the edge.

The Third Reich is sometimes invoked explicitly. A trucking apprentice who knows he has been consigned to "the league of the damned" situates Germans ("this little aryan *volk*," as he calls them) on a lower level of this league. "What is all this pomade shit with german-is-number-one-there-is, the ones who get their workers' mug out of joint and howl *über-alles*-in-the-world, where everyone clearly sees that even the lowest and clumsiest guy from the asiatic realm has more manners and memories" (84–85). More commonly, the genocidal legacy of the Third Reich shadows speech in more ambiguous ways. One of several Yiddishisms in the text (also common in German parlance), *kosher* literally refers to rabbinical laws meant to distinguish between foods safe to consume and those that are not. Orthodox Judaism considers pork unclean and hence unsafe for consumption; adherence to the dietary taboo in turn serves as a sign of Jewish piety.[65] Colloquial usage of the term connotes standards of proper behavior and integrity. One of Zaimoğlu's *Kanaken* speaks of his powerful "kosher will," which allows him to keep his "skin clean" in a hostile German environment. "For brother," he says, "all I have are my clean morals, which are firmly planted here in this cadaver" (22). Referring to his body as a "cadaver," this interlocutor impeaches German attitudes consigning *Kanaken* to abjection, and the mere use of "kosher" here hardly offers strong evidence of "cadaver" serving as a palimpsest for other histories of abjection. When a psychiatric patient imagines being forced by "danger" to devour "thousands of hollow-headed maggots" that stick in his throat and render him mute, however, one begins to wonder. For the one who senses unspecified danger feels compelled, "like a pig," to stuff "unkosher *dreck*" into his insides, where it becomes literally incorporated, because "there is so much room in the stomach" (57). Given that *dreck* can mean dirt, trash, or shit in German and Yiddish, "unkosher *dreck*" is a tautology compounded by the porcine simile. In this heightened rhetoric of filth and danger, some touching tale of Turks, Germans, and Jews is subject to excitation, but it would be difficult to say what kind of story or whose this might properly be. This changes when the gigolo speaks in one of the few sections of *Kanak Sprak* where a story of Turks, Germans, and Jews is told.

Zaimoğlu's topography of above and below is animated by transgressive bodies and unruly *dreck*. Fachinger reads the embodied figure of *Kanak* men marking the site of transgression as "self-affirmation" (2001: 110). This makes partial sense, especially if we recall the Turkish Power Boy who justified his criminal behavior to an ethnographer by saying that Germans refer to all Turks, regardless of behavior, as " 'shitty Turks' " (Tertilt 233).[66] Tertilt theorized that gang members had molded themselves into the indecent Turks Germans presumed them to be.[67] But Zaimoğlu's *Kanaken* emphatically assert their decency and integrity in contradistinction to what they perceive as German indecency and self-deception. Although *dreck* refers throughout the text to gross physical matter (especially shit and corpses), the " 'protocols' " also resonate with trace effects linking flesh, filth, dirt, shit, and German history.[68] This is a familiar strain in postwar German literature. A once youthful soldier in the German *Wehrmacht*, whose novels later garnered him a reputation as the moral conscience of a post-fascist nation and the Nobel Prize for Literature, Heinrich Böll is well known as a "scatologist of high degree" (Durzak 2004: 111). And in Günter Grass's *Crabwalk*, a novel about German suffering in World War II, German taboos in the postwar era, and neofascist dangers in our electronic age, twentieth-century German history is rendered figurally in scatological terms. "History . . . is a clogged toilet. We flush and flush, but the shit keeps rising" (122). In *Kanak Sprak* the rhetoric of *dreck* linking flesh, filth, dirt, and German history is intensified when sexual touch between a German "christ lady" and her Turkish gigolo is mediated through the imagined figure of a Jew. Here a well-read German woman insists on calling the gigolo "you my beautiful Jew" while performing fellatio, and this "Kanak" commentator attributes his surplus value in the sex trade to his circumcised penis. In the mind of the "christ lady" this marks him phantasmatically as a Jew.[69] The gigolo asserts that those Germans whom he services see him only as an embodied thing, "an order of meat." He indexes their fantasies about his flesh as a kind of *dreck* that he must keep from clinging to his soul (69–71).

As a "connoisseur" of German sex practices (69), the *Kanak* figure whom readers are made to visualize as a desirable body also describes in detail his sexual encounter with the "christ lady." But the physical touch of sexual commerce quickly yields in this narration to a touching tale of Turks, Germans, and Jews, as a Turkish proxy spins a story of proximate narratives instead. In an exchange of words that is not entirely dialogic, the gigolo reports what the woman said to him as tagged speech, and his theoretical reflections on her erotic fantasies are recounted as a *Kanak* protocol. On both narrative levels the affective charge of words outweighs reference. Initially interpellated by his client as "you my beautiful Jew," the object of desire speaks to dispel the illusion, only to discover that this infuriates the lady, who admonishes him not to "destroy" her (the German verb *zerstören* stems from *stören*, which means only to disturb or interrupt), "to keep [his] mouth shut and let her do what she wants" (69–70). Speculating that this cultured German woman is playing a "forbidden game" in which she can take "false for true," the gigolo conjectures that the knowledge she has gleaned from reading "a slew of smart-books" heightens her sexual excitation in their physical encounter (71). The gigolo implies that the woman's excitation stems from extensive knowledge about the Holocaust, not ignorance of it. When they part ways, the satisfied customer interpellates the young Turkish man again, this time with a linguistic twist: "my bad jew diddle (*judenschniddel*)" (71). The beautiful Jew of German desire becomes the bad but now nonthreatening penis in this heterosexual fantasy, with the slang word *Schniddel* connoting penis, diminution, and things that have been cut or severed. Characterizing himself as taking distance from these projections in critical thought, the gigolo reworks the linguistic material of forbidden fantasy when he reflects: "what all a christ lady like that stammers together, when the whole world knows that the ol' *alemanne* was top-dog barbarian in cutting up jews for filets [*judenschnitzeln*] and driving gas into them their lungs" (71). Here the *Kanak* gigolo refashions the lady's *judenschniddel* as *judenschnitzeln*, a pun that also operates in a diminutive register compared with the enormity of genocide. The gigolo's narrative deployment of the pun additionally identifies his customer's fantasy as both an evasion of historical accountability and active engagement with a German taboo surrounding the image of murdered Jews as objects of desire and fear.[70] This attests to the *Kanak* power of speech in a German context where the national discourse of ritualized atonement leaves many things unsaid about the affective residue of genocide. In their discussion of globalized Holocaust memory, Levy and Sznaider distinguish between taboo and prohibition by claiming that taboos are not subject to discussion (62). The excited speech of *Kanak Sprak* is riddled with the affect of taboo, even unthinkable without it.[71]

When the gigolo expounds on his theory about German fantasies and the Jewish undead, he reclaims powers of speech that German stereotypes of Turkish incoherence deny him. He analyzes a German fantasy projected onto him as a pseudo-Jewish body, and he asserts himself as a figural presence that cannot be reduced to German fantasies of Jews and genocidal legacies. The rhetoric of abjection fueled by references to dirt, filth, shit, and tainted flesh (living and dead) reverberates here too:

> . . . down to the last speck of dirt this land is soaked with dead jew-innocent-meat that the ass-horny violins killed and quick threw rude in the ditch or switched to ash and swept away. So the meat dumped on the sly gets even and clumps as ghost and lots of ghosts in the living, so they crack or get a complex

or a rash on their soul, so my theory tells me that a lady like that, once she fucked me, picked something up, only she doesn't know it, caught something from the corpse deep down in the mud bad blood. (71–72)

Other interlocutors similarly present themselves as having the inside scoop on dirty business in Germany. With a keen *Kanak* "eye for what goes on behind the scenes" (110), the poet proclaims: "As long as this land denies us real entrance, we will suck up the anomalies and perversions of this land like a sponge and spit out the shit" (113–114). The sociologist deems himself "a typical child of the east" because he has always been driven to muck with "subterranean" matter, "the stuff that has drifted off into the depths, into the chasms that no gaze can penetrate" (100). More pointedly than any other "Kanak" speaker, however, the gigolo emerges rhetorically as a figural presence occupying the same murky ground shared by postwar Germans and their Jewish ghosts in the 1990s, when so many cultures of memory seem unmoored by globalization. Zaimoğlu's *Kanaken* do not occupy this ground in the same way as Germans and Jews, and the author never introduces a living Jewish figure in his ethnoscape of excitation.[72] To recollect Culler's essay on puns, "the call of the phoneme" is hard at work in the gigolo's critical reflections on the figure he cuts in Germany. Serious echoes resounding in real or implied word pairs such as *judenschniddel-judenschnitzel* and others unsettle the referential determinacy of Zaimoğlu's "Kanak speak" and effectively prevent any one figure from standing in for a discrete self or distinct other. Yet *Kanak Sprak* is explicitly devoted to the task of rendering visible within German culture an immigrant presence that a rhetoric of Turkish thingliness only obscures; the text bespeaks a deeply felt desire for one kind of visibility as a curative for another. In the erotic fantasy of the "christ lady," a Turk is made to represent the scene of abjection in twentieth-century German history, while the gigolo theorizes the cultural space he is made to occupy. This complicates any simple notion of social hierarchies, but it ultimately reasserts the image of a *Kanak* speaker whom readers can easily visualize as a referential figure whom one might conceivably meet on the mean streets of Germany.

This tension between a type of figural representation that comes to rest in the physical icon of the *Kanak* male and the referential indeterminacy of historical affect is never resolved in Zaimoğlu's text, as one last example demonstrates. Whereas the gigolo complains that Germans see his eroticized body only as "an order of meat," the interviewee from the flea market disco protests that he cannot get Germans to see him as a fully embodied presence at all. To describe this impasse, he draws a figure—or is it a line?

> The numbers just don't add up, you feel as if you were a piece of meat or better yet stinky garbage or an old tin can that gets kicked away and rattles

like hell. The bad thing is that the alemannen don't see you, not even for a tired mark, you're just not there, you can tap them on the shoulder and say: man, I've been around forever, grab a hold, get a grip, here's flesh and bones, to them you're nothin', air and less than fairy air, you ain't got no sector where they could place you, so it looks like when an ol' corpse is lying around, and they make an outline with a piece of chalk. In the outline there's nothin' when they cart the cadaver away, you see a little stick man out of carpet. (118–119)

The diminutive compound used to depict a stick figure (*strichmänneken*) relies on *Strich*, a line drawn but also an area of prostitution. In this we recognize themes and rhetoric familiar from other passages. More important, the "little stick man" we are made to imagine as what remains when a corpse has been removed conjures a figure that is missing and a line demarcating its absence. This could apply to Jewish and Turkish figures from a *Kanak* perspective. To recall Brodsky Lacour's discussion of Descartes, the discourse of European modernity begins with "writing which conceals its own status as line in its intelligibility as representation." By this account, modern lines of thought appear figurally to the extent that they can be thought and represented *as lines*, but a modern line of thought by this definition is fundamentally iconoclastic because it "commits an unprecedented form to being." This allows for "discourse with no worldly analogue" (1996: 7–8). *Kanak Sprak* presents a cast of iconoclastic underdogs on top in a creative attempt to render visible something most Germans had not thought possible before. The text teeters between a figural representation of iconoclastic Turks that occasionally reinforces stereotypes of migrant youth and a more iconoclastic mode of representation that excitedly gestures toward new ways of imagining a Turkish presence in Germany.

7

Competing registers of figuration also play a key role in Şenocak's *Perilous Kinship*, where readers encounter many representational duds in a maze of lines. Turks in Germany have long borne the burden of an optical illusion whereby Turkish figures appear *as* and *on* the face of things in public life. Despite Zaimoğlu's iconoclastic intentions, *Kanak Sprak* extends this illusion by foregrounding the anthropomorphic figure of migration as an iconoclastic pose. The figures and lines of thought drawn in Şenocak's first novel yield a tale of iconoclastic narration instead.[73] This too is a touching tale of Turks, Germans, and Jews in the Berlin Republic, compounded by an Armenian story as well. Genocidal histories of the twentieth century touch literally and phantasmatically in the fictional autobiography of Sascha Muhteschem, a German writer of Jewish and Turkish descent whose family history bespeaks multigenerational entanglements in "the murderous side of the modern world" (Gellately and Kiernan 4).[74] Compared with the rhetoric of excitation and excavation in *Kanak Sprak*, the tenor of narration in *Perilous Kinship* seems laconic and flat. This also stands in stark contrast to the narrative fullness of Franz Werfel's *The Forty Days of Musa Dagh* (1933) and Edgar Hilsenrath's *The Story of the Last Thought* (1989), the epic novels of German literary history that preceded Şenocak's tale of "dangerous affinity" in telling a German story of the Armenian genocide.[75] *Perilous Kinship* is only the second German literary text since the Nazi genocide of the Jews to configure the Armenian massacres early in the century as somehow related, as the book's title suggests. Told as an especially brutal "fairy tale" with the caustic humor of the damned, *The Story of the Last Thought* predated *Perilous Kinship* by just nine years. A Holocaust survivor who has lived in Berlin since 1975 and a notorious breaker of literary taboos, Hilsenrath is surely no stranger to German scenes of Turkish migration. But the rhetorical figure of migration appears in tandem with other Turkish, German, Jewish, and Armenian figures drawn from twentieth-century histories of genocide only in *Perilous Kinship*. Unlike Werfel, Hilsenrath, and Zaimoğlu, for whom embodied figures of brutality, sexuality, and prejudice are indispensable to narration, Şenocak structures his touching tale around figural references that seem oddly disembodied, some so lifeless that they conjure cardboard rather than flesh, living or dead. What "Turkish" lines of thought are drawn in this story drawing breath from the long reach of history without giving it much of a pulse? Delineating a historic transnational landscape of the visible and the phantasmatic, *Perilous Kinship* defies various taboos and unsettles multiple cultures of memory from the vantage point of Turkish migration to Germany.

By the time this touching tale of genocide and migration had appeared, Şenocak was well established as Germany's first public intellectual of note from the field of Turkish migration, and his literary career was well underway.[76] Having moved to Munich as a nine-year-old with his adventurous and well-educated parents in 1970, Şenocak pursued a classical education in Bavaria through 1987. University studies in German literature, politics, and philosophy coincided with initial publications of lyric poetry and literary translations, notably of Yunus Emre, Pir Sultan Abdal, and Aras Ören, whose *Gündoğduların Yükselişi* [The Rise of the Gündoğdus] opens a novelistic series "in search of the present" following a prototype discussed in chapter three.[77] Recognized for his literary talents by the City of Munich, the Bavarian Academy of Fine Arts, and the Berlin Senate, Şenocak received an Adelbert von Chamisso Prize (for foreign-born authors of German literature just starting out) in 1988, the same year in which he cofounded the international literary journal *Sirene* [Siren]. Since moving to Berlin in 1989, he has published in a broad range of German newspapers, appeared frequently on German television and radio (even cohosting a talk show from 1991 to 1992), and lectured throughout Europe, the United States, and in other parts of the world. Collections of essays on German politics and culture in the era of globalization have appeared with such provocative titles as *Atlas des tropischen Deutschland* [Atlas of a Tropical Germany] (1992), *War Hitler Araber? IrreFührungen an den Rand Europas* [Was Hitler an Arab? A Crazy Guide to the Edge of Europe] (1994), and *Zungenentfernung: Berichte aus der Quarantänestation* [Tongue Removal/Tongue Distance: Reports from the Quarantine Station] (2001).[78] Together with Claus Leggewie, Şenocak coedited a bilingual collection of responses to the public crisis signaled by Turkish deaths in Mölln and Solingen. In mid-decade he edited the multicultural page for Berlin's leading alternative newspaper, a regular feature originally designed to commemorate the fall of the Wall.

Between 1995 and 1999 a tetralogy of literary prose appeared as *Der Mann im Unterhemd* [The Man in the Undershirt], *Die Prärie* [The Prairie], *Gefährliche Verwandtschaft* [Perilous Kinship], and *Der Erottomane* [The Erottoman].[79] In undocumented conversation Şenocak once remarked that the figure of Sascha, who appears in various guises in the disjunctive vignettes of *Mann*, does not become a character until *Prärie* and acquires a story only in *Perilous Kinship*. More recently, collaborations with Berkan Karpat, an installation artist in Munich, have resulted in lyric scenarios cast as a transnational "futurist epilogue" and a German "speech labyrinth" involving Nâzim Hikmet, Kemal Atatürk, Mevlana Jalal al-Din Rumi, and outer space (Karpat and Şenocak 1998, 1999, and 2000).[80] A growing body of translations into French, Turkish, Italian, English, Spanish, Catalan, Dutch, Danish, Hebrew, Urdu, and Greek has garnered Şenocak an international following as he continues to publish literary work as well as journalistic pieces on the international war on terrorism and Turkey's ongoing quest for admission to the European Union.[81] In spite of his obvious presence in German media, Şenocak enjoys nothing like the recognition or success that falls to Zaimoğlu or Özdamar in Germany. Sometimes he seems oddly invisible to the readers to whom his work is largely addressed. When a major newspaper known for serious journalism published a full-page article in 2003 explaining how "German Turks can save not only our economy, but also our culture" and celebrating the "energy" that Turks bring to German life (Diez), Şenocak was not even mentioned. The editors of a British anthology devoted to the writer's work note that Şenocak is both "widely regarded as the foremost writer and intellectual of the Turkish diaspora in Germany" and "increasingly neglected in Germany" (Cheesman and Yeşilada ix–x). There are undoubtedly many reasons for this state of affairs. The fact that Şenocak's literary prose offers no Turkish figures that lend themselves to easy consumption, imitation, or "edutainment" (Zaimoğlu as cited in Tuschick 2000a: 112) may be one of them.[82] In journalistic essays Şenocak often writes about cultural contact between "Orient" and "Occident" in terms of an entangled history of touch rather than encounter.[83] Public appeals for a dialogue of civilizations in the strong sense of multiculturalism conjure such dialogue as an encounter of talking heads. When Şenocak appeals to an entangled history of touch, he challenges the commonplace that "Orient" and "Occident" exist as discrete cultural entities or historical phenomena encountering each other as "seamless wholes," to recall Benhabib's account of the problem. More than this, touch conjures a dual figure of intimacy, for to be touched is to exist in embodied form and also to be moved. *Mann*, with which Şenocak opened his tetralogy in 1995, repeatedly presents this doubly intimate figure in short disjointed scenarios of desire, humiliation, torture, murder, and lust, from an underground city of sadists to the bridges and canals of Berlin, where "even rats cannot expunge the history" written on faces of desperation mirrored in murderous waters (36). Despite this insistent rhetoric of embodiment and affect, neither the voices nor figures of narration in this text subtend identification. They are not characters but elusive personae—"just an image" (48). These images are often hypersexualized, yet bodies dissolve into less tangible though visceral components. "It begins in the disorientation of night—the transformation of time into flesh, the dissolution of flesh into its components, fear and desire" (74). In this textual economy neither bodies nor selves cohere. Living spaces in Berlin and Istanbul are likewise subject to phantasmatic disorientation. Rooms are "blind" (133), and a "burned house" in a writer's head (78) makes any house of residence suspect.[84] Emphasizing the difference that ostensibly prevails between one figure thought to be referential and another thought to exist only in the imagination, the text effectively agitates this distinction, endowing it with so much energy that presumptions of referentiality are unsettled. The boundary between literal and figurative frames of reference is made to oscillate. Something similar happens in *Perilous Kinship*, a fictional autobiography where affects and genealogies otherwise congeal into characters and histories. What can be said to oscillate when all that is fluid seems almost welded for ware?

The boundary work of contextual anchoring in *Perilous Kinship* differs significantly from the imaginative labor of Özdamar's courtyard. Because Şenocak's novel includes numerous references to really existing persons, places, and organizations (especially in Germany and Turkey, but also in Eastern Europe and "America") by name, it initially seems to have an anchoring effect similar to the courtyard production of a here and now in which text and context are conjoined. But *Perilous Kinship* gives readers no deictic purchase on presence, and the novel is saturated with historical references, especially to twentieth-century phenomena such as the Third Reich, German–Jewish exile and Nazi sympathizers in Turkey, the Holocaust, German unification, World War I, the Turkish war of liberation, the Russian revolution, Stalinism, the Internet, and others. While Sascha Muhteschem occasionally recounts the grand sweep of history in first-person summation, most of the transnational developments he invokes are reflected in his family history, which he does not fully know or understand. The son of a bourgeois Turkish father and a German mother whose Jewish family had found refuge from the Nazis in Istanbul in 1934, Sascha is conceived in Turkey, born in Germany in 1954, and naturalized as a German citizen in 1972. The acquisition of German citizenship is linked by narration with the Munich Olympics of 1972, when Arab terrorists murdered Israeli athletes, thus bringing the international legacy of the Holocaust uncomfortably home to roost for many in Germany at the time.[85] Blond-haired and blue-eyed, Sascha speaks no Turkish, Yiddish, Hebrew, or Arabic. As an adult he engenders so much comfort in Nazi widows that they entrust their private documents and personal mementos from the Hitler years to his collection of the "unused up side" of history (51).[86] Fluent in Armenian and Russian, the young Turk who was to become Sascha's grandfather fights alongside Germans in World War I and then with Mustafa Kemal, later the best man at his wedding, against the Allied occupation. (The German–Jewish grandfather also claims to have fought in the same military unit with the man who would come to be known as Atatürk, "father of all Turks" by this designation. In the novel Kemal is a figure cited as the " 'Great Saviour' " instead [30].) Sascha's Turkish *pater familias* is described as nineteen years old in 1915, "the year of corpses" (39). The explicit reference is to World War I, when the Ottoman and German empires were brothers in arms. The text never explicitly indexes the Armenian genocide of 1915. Yet this relative whom Sascha never met is no revolutionary hero alone. For in 1921, as the voice of narration reveals soon after "the year of corpses" is mentioned, this "hero of the east" is "the first to draw up a deportation list of Armenian names" (40).[87] Years later, on the eve of his scheduled participation in the Berlin Olympics as a member of the Turkish delegation, the Turkish grandfather commits suicide. The storytelling riddle around which the novel revolves is a why posed by the grandson only in the wake of German unification. Although Sascha declares himself "a grandchild of victims and perpetrators" (40), his quest is not cast as an evidentiary pursuit of truth, but as languid musings on script.[88] In contrast to Özdamar's courtyard narrative, which has an emotionally "cool" register but is rich in affect as the taking on of this or that form, *Perilous Kinship* is narrated with virtually no affect other than lassitude. How does the boundary between text and context come alive in such first-person narration, when some of the most moving histories of the twentieth century are at stake? Writing appears in the novel as a theme and additionally as a figure drawn by the lines of the text.[89] Thematic allusions to writing are often tied to the life history of the first-person narrator and various houses that he inhabits, uses, or observes. Between 1989 and 1992 Sascha's minimal talents as a novelist earn him a visiting position in the United States as "writer in residence" (19). This fixed designation connotes figural reference or house arrest with a touch of irony, since Sascha often changes his place of residence, describes his home as whatever place of residence he has just left behind, and observes how houses and people are swallowed up by the winter fog in Berlin, the city to which he and his German lover return from their sojourn in the American prairie in 1992. This transpires well after the historic fall of the Wall, but it coincides with a manifold legacy involving a house that does not appear foggy at all and more writing yet. When Sascha's estranged parents die in an accident after years of separation, they leave behind "no gaps" in his life (36), we are told, but the family home in Munich. The progeny of persecution grew up in this house, which had belonged to Sascha's German–Jewish grandfather before being used a meeting place for the Hitler Youth. This house is not accorded much attention in the novel, its referential solidity never questioned. Yet an anecdote from Sascha's childhood implicitly locates the scene of taboo in this house. Forced to play "in the storage room" up in the attic because of possible land mines in the yard, the young boy discovers old photographs of Hitler, whom he does not recognize. "They all showed a man with a funny moustache. When I showed the photos to my parents, they were immediately burned in the fireplace" (9).[90] No additional dialogue, recollection, or description is devoted to this episode or the historical palimpsest its fiery reference so coolly suggests. But when Sascha develops a passion in adulthood for collecting German handwriting samples from the 1930s, he deposits his collection in this family home, which he no longer inhabits and does not plan to rent out. "There should be a place in my life," the narrator explains, "where my past is preserved and remains accessible to me" (66). Sascha does not visit this house again. If it appears to readers as a kind of archive, it is not one that Sascha accesses in any direct way. From the vantage point of this literary author and handwriting collector, "history always has a used up side and an unused up side." The archival work and reconstructive narratives of historians tend to the former, he asserts. As a novelist, he seeks active engagement with the side of history that has not yet been used up. "What did I need the archives for?" (51), he asks.[91]

Sascha's transnational family legacy bespeaks the theme of writing in other ways, too. The object of inheritance to which the narrative repeatedly returns is not a building but a box containing diaries written by the Turkish grandfather in extraordinarily clear handwriting between 1916 and his suicide in 1936. Because these diaries are penned in Arabic and Cyrillic script, however, Sascha cannot decipher them.[92] Readers are privy to a lethargy that overtakes him as he contemplates what he perceives as inscrutable script. "It is always tiring to look for any length of time at a script one cannot read" (38). But Sascha is not the least bit eager to have the diaries translated. In a rare display of excitement near the end of this touching tale, Sascha imagines that he can keep the secrets of the diaries at bay by having a Slavist translate only those segments that appear to be literary quotations from Russian masterpieces.[93] Learning that his grandfather was " 'a charlatan' " of script and directed to a translator who " 'speaks seven languages and understands a few more besides,' " Sascha feels trapped (116). Compelled by circumstance to commission the translation, he hurriedly flees the multilinguist's apartment, and results of the long-term project are indefinitely deferred. Throughout the first-person novel narrated by Sascha, the grandson desires to solve nothing, "to invent" rather than "reconstruct" the life of his grandfather (15, 38). On the one hand, this desire conflicts with Sascha's later realization that the Turkish grandfather is "the secret" standing between Sascha and his lineage. "I had to reveal his secret in order to reach myself," the voice of narration declares (118). On the other hand, Sascha's desire to invent his relative pointedly entails the invention of a literary figure as well, since the Turkish grandfather is the "central figure" in the text that Sascha as a novelist struggles to write. The Turkish veteran does not merely harbor a secret but is drawn as the figure of a secret: "concealed," "mysterious," "left in the dark" (*unaufgeklärt*) (51).[94] Sascha's ruminations on his grandfather's suicide result in a snippet of writing characterized by omniscient narration. This is the imagined segment of his novel, with which *Perilous Kinship* concludes. As Sascha either recounts or imagines in the frame novel, his Turkish grandfather had struck the name of one woman alone from the list of 500 Armenians he had scheduled for deportation in 1921. At the end of *Perilous Kinship* a Turkish man who might or might not be Sascha's grandfather receives a letter from Paris, "a sign of life" twenty years in coming, from an Armenian woman whom he recalls as the love of his life in rapacious times. Omniscient narration seems to clarify what no suicide note in either novel reveals. Understanding the short angry letter as a reminder of a long-ago promise (*Versprechen*) to end his life should the two lovers ever be separated, the man "knows what he has to do" and dies (136–137). In this imagined conclusion the suicidal impulse stems from a lover's promise rather than a perpetrator's guilt, and this too seems incommensurate with the novel's theme of documented genocide. In the frame novel Sascha once characterizes his Turkish grandfather as belonging to a generation of powerful men. In a coinage recalling the German "rubble women" who cleared the ruins for reconstruction following World War II, the grandfather's Turkish cohort of the 1920s is described as *Trümmermänner*, "the men of the ruins who built a new house out of the building stones of a collapsing empire." Sascha's response to the embattled history of the twentieth century, he announces sardonically, is characteristic of his power-shy generation. "For my part I have decided to write" (39, 40).

The multifaceted scene of writing in *Perilous Kinship* hinges on extensional references to the genocidal history of the twentieth century and intensional references to the textual world of figural representation. Parodic riffs on migrant monologues, the German reception of migrants' literature, and the representation of Turkish Muslims in German media similarly hinge on extensional references to a German history of labor migration and intensional references to the world of text.[95] The figure through which such contextual anchoring is made to speak is the first-person narrator in two different senses. First, in his characterological function, Sascha is born of a transnational history of genocide but is often mistaken in Germany for a product of labor migration. (Here Şenocak presents a very different sort of "Turkish" figure from the foreign imports we encounter in texts by Nadolny, Özdamar, and others, for Sascha's very existence is unthinkable without the German history of National Socialism.) This linkage between twentieth-century histories of genocide and migration in the character of Sascha is not cast as a political analogy between Turks and Jews, but as a language problem in Germany. As a character, Sascha sometimes comments critically on German rituals of speech, gesture, and atonement that connote mourning without grief or counter catastrophe with caricature. "The mourning keeps the reason for mourning secret from those who mourn. This phenomenon is called being moved (*Betroffenheit*)" (61).[96] The novel's explicit reference to this culture of atonement additionally evokes the "literature of being moved" (Biondi and Schami), as the guest worker literature of the 1980s was both conceived and received. As Christian Begemann observes, this "literature of being moved" was not meant only to mirror the social experiences of migrant laborers, but also to interpellate German readers as empathetic interlocutors, and the frequency of first-person narration in early migration stories was deemed to foster this (213–214).[97] In the Berlin Republic Sascha experiences the lingering effects of this phenomenon when, despite his biography, he becomes "visible" as a writer only to German readers who want "to see the foreigners" (129, 130). But *Perilous Kinship* is curiously devoid of thick description. Like the momentous histories he recounts in summative fashion, Sascha appears flatly drawn rather than richly dimensional, and the stories he tells have a similar quality. "I have stories but no details," he observes regarding his way of being in the world. "Without details stories have no voice" (93). To explore why a touching tale of such profoundly historical dimensions hinges on an oddly laconic narrator with no apparent depth perception, we must turn to abstract functions of Şenocak's first-person narration that exceed Sascha's role as a character. This concerns the second sense in which the "I" of the text bespeaks the boundary work of contextual anchoring.

As an abstract function, the first-person narrator is a figure of speech. We know from Paul de Man that the rhetorical trope of prosopopeia enables autobiography by rendering one's name "as intelligible and memorable as a face" (1984: 76) and that it does so by producing "the illusion of reference" (69). As a fictional autobiographer, Sascha Muhteschem is doubly illusory, yet the one who speaks in this name voices decided interest in his own identity at times, and the narrative repeatedly seems to ground his autobiographical lineage in the grand sweep of historical references that are anything but illusory. This may explain why so many scholars stress the theme of identity as a personal attribute in *Perilous Kinship* (e.g., Dollinger 2002; Jordan; Hall; and Eigler 2005).[98] References to identity and history in the novel should not be taken at face value, nor should they be read only as ironic allusions to German preconceptions about migrant identities. If we take the rhetoric of narration seriously, Sascha is an abstraction in search of texture and depth. Pains occasioned by memory "give life sharper contours" (47), this figure remarks, but Sascha never acquires such contours. "I live in the void where my threads, the ones that grow thinner and thinner, the ones that are supposed to connect me to the three parts of myself, have nothing to hold on to" (90).[99] If the Turkish grandfather is rhetorically crafted as the figure of a secret, the German–Jewish–Turkish grandson manifests rhetorically as the bloodless figure of a history drenched in blood.[100] Compared with the Turkish narrator in "The Courtyard in the Mirror," Sascha, a mirage of reference, is historically informed and visually uninterested in the German world around him. He writes in the murky state of being "half asleep" (79), and according to his lover, his stories appear " 'blurred' " (23).[101] Memory appears to him "as a great big hole," reality as "a dark hole" with no dimensions he can gauge. Speaking from within that dark reality, the "I" of narration hears "others breathe" but cannot see them (87, 90).[102] This figure of others breathing in the dark is where the novel comes to life, so to speak, and a capitalist entrepreneur in the novel even complains about the long breath of Sascha's prose.[103] Why does the figure of history who speaks so knowledgably about historical events falter in the world of dimensions?

It would be tempting to attribute the "dark hole" of the narrator's reality to the incommensurability or aporia of representation in the face of genocide and its traumatic residue. Tropes of incommensurability and unspeakability have ironically acquired iconic status in genocide studies, especially in reference to the Holocaust, even as words and images indexing the historical phenomenon have proliferated in various media.[104] Striking contrasts between Sascha's literary riddle and his lover's documentary film, both under construction throughout the novel, would seem to support such a reading. After the accidental death of his parents in the 1990s, Sascha is the only surviving member of a German–Jewish family that had otherwise been annihilated in the Holocaust, a family history about which his mother had steadfastly refused to speak. While the writer lethargically contemplates the (to him) inscrutable script of his Turkish grandfather, Marie energetically shoots footage for her filmic biography of Talât Pasha, one of the major "architects" of the Armenian genocide (Melson 152; Dadrian 1995: 287).[105] A prominent leader among the Young Turks who governed the Ottoman Empire before and during the war, Talât Pasha decisively shaped governmental policy as Minister of the Interior and later Grand Vizier. Fleeing to Germany in 1918, he evaded criminal proceedings that would soon be brought against him by a vanquished empire. His death sentence was never executed, partly because Germany refused to extradite the decorated war hero (Dadrian 1996: 216–217). But in 1921 he was assassinated by a young Armenian on the streets of Berlin. In the 1990s Sascha's lover travels to those places she deems important for Talât's biography to trace and depict as authentically as possible what the text calls the Young Turk's development from an "enlightened politician" to a "mass murderer" (72). On rare occasions the clear-thinking Marie wonders about the interchangeability of locations she films and the historical narratives that such footage is intended to represent. Without living witnesses, she notes with passing irritation, her camera work yields only " 'silent pictures' " (15). The footage she shoots in the " 'dull place' " on Hardenberg Street, where the assassination occurred, could just as easily have been " 'footage for a film about Berlin after the Wall' " (15). These observations notwithstanding, Marie is undeterred in her documentary pursuit. While she ultimately relies on what can be rendered visible as having three dimensions, Sascha contemplates lines on a page and lines in his head that never form a coherent image at all. In the end he leaves his decisive lover and imagines one possible conclusion to his novel. This suggests that Sascha and Marie denote opposite ends of a representational spectrum, perhaps even that Sascha's dark breathy hole is somehow more befitting of a genocidal legacy than Marie's illuminated images where nary a human sound is heard. But perhaps these characters have more in common than initially meets the eye. The touching tale that unfolds in *Perilous Kinship* clearly requires both figures. Marie's devotion to filmic documentation and historical accuracy is echoed in Sascha's frequent metanarratives of European and Ottoman history, if not in his demeanor or activities. Finally, the image of reality as a hole in which others can be heard breathing but not seen is also an image, a rhetorical figure of speech that readers are asked to imagine and perhaps even inhabit. One might say that the hole is haunted by unseen forces, but the darkness of indiscernible dimensions is also where breath becomes possible, according to the economy of the text. If Sascha is a figure of history that cannot be understood as strictly anti-representational in the unspeakable shadow of genocide, how else might we read the trope of the abyss?

In what follows I argue that Sascha steps into a particular historical moment by inhabiting and bespeaking (literally, giving voice to) this breathy abyss. The dark hole of his reality neither pays homage to unspeakable horrors in any generic sense, nor does it connote the mute despair of those who know too much about a century of genocide. The particular historical moment Sascha inhabits in the 1990s has both German and transnational contours, albeit of distinctly asymmetrical dimensions. What this means is tied to the figure of belatedness, which shadows Sascha's biography and speech. Away in America from 1989 to 1992, the writer-protagonist takes possession of his German–Jewish inheritance and Turkish legacy only after he returns to Berlin. Having missed the historic fall of the Berlin Wall, Sascha wonders: "So I had missed the historic event. Did I still belong here?" (121).[106] The explicit event in question at this juncture is the fall of the Wall, but deictic indicators of place, time, and person soon conjure another historic event when Sascha twice indexes the "community of fate" in Germany, to which he is not terribly eager to belong. "I feel as if I'm spared some responsibility. Who expects anything of someone like me? Who can trust me? I don't have to apologise for anything. I came along later" (121).[107] We might say that Sascha comes either too late or simply "later" to everything that matters in this story. Growing up in Germany, he learns volumes about the history of National Socialism but nothing about his murdered relatives. The story of his Turkish grandfather's involvement in the Armenian genocide is a mystery to him, one that he ponders only once his parents are gone. The defining German moment of unification is an event that he seems metaphorically to have overslept.[108] All these historic phenomena to which Sascha comes belatedly are also tinged with taboo. Unlike the silver box containing his grandfather's diaries, for example, the "Pandora's box" of German desires for national identity after the Third Reich had been "kept locked shut" prior to unification (34). A multivalent legacy of genocide and taboo is thus inscribed in the belated and benighted voice of narration. As a figure of history, Sascha may be likened to abstract features of temporality that LaCapra ascribes to historical narratives and Bhabha to cultural narratives of European modernity. The "before" and "after" of Sascha's characterological timeline yield a discernible progression, but the distinction crumbles if we focus on Sascha as an abstract function of first-person narration.

The trope of belatedness inhering in the voice of narration is especially resonant when Sascha distinguishes his quest for his grandfather from Marie's quest for Talât, which leads her at one point to travel to Greece.

> I do not travel after my figures. Talât Pasha is not my concern. He is Marie's project. He does not lead me to grandfather, I can find him nowhere. My parents left their country a long time ago. No things are being kept for me there any longer, the value of which for the present would be visible at first glance. Architects of forgetting build their pompous structures into the drafty gaps in memory. When I look into the history of this country, I see nothing. (74)[109]

One telling phrase is the programmatic statement, "I do not travel after my figures" (*Ich reise meinen Figuren nicht nach*). On the one hand, this echoes what we already know about Sascha's literary endeavor, namely, that he wants to invent rather than reconstruct the figure of his grandfather. On the other hand, this statement does more than convey information about a character that happens to be speaking. Beyond this, Sascha speaks as a figure of speech, and what this figure "says" is that the "I" of narration does not come "after" at all. That is to say, the figural references of Sascha's narration, historical facts from the past and dark holes in the present alike, are jointly constitutive of the voice that speaks. Additionally, the deictic indicator "there" in clear reference to Turkey is followed by the highly ambiguous reference to "the history of this country" in which Sascha sees "nothing." Is he speaking of Turkey or Germany? If a "then" inheres in the "now" of narration, a Turkish "there" would seem intrinsic in the German "here" of narration as well. One might read "this country" as referring literally to a given nation or figuratively to a shared past. (Tony Judt's "The Past Is Another Country" comes to mind.) In either case the rhetorical conceit of seeing "nothing" can only index an optical illusion. For what Sascha sees is a "dark hole" of plenitude where "no things" can be discerned with a contemplative eye.

How does the here and now of *Perilous Kinship* delineate or engage a predominantly German context rather than one we might simply call transnational? After all, this chapter began with a discussion of the "globalization of Holocaust discourse," and the growing field of genocide studies situates the Armenian genocide and the Holocaust in the broadly transnational history of twentieth-century warfare and radical nationalism (e.g., Gellately and Kiernan; Melson; Helmut Smith; Weitz). The evolving culture of German memory exists in this frame of reference too, and it would be misleading to speak of the culture of memory in postwar Germany as ever having been a national formation alone. *Perilous Kinship*, however, anchors Sascha's imaginative endeavors in the Berlin Republic of the 1990s. His affect of lassitude in the face of a genocidal legacy responds to what the text depicts as a German landscape of public memory in which ritualized speech and monumental commemorations of Jewish suffering and German guilt promote a sense of historical accountability, on the one hand, and an affect of *Betroffenheit* obscuring the reasons for being moved, on the other.[110] If Sascha speaks as a figure of history, the figure he enlivens (however lethargically) is not always one of remembrance rather than forgetfulness or even inattention, for Sascha is also born of the landscape of memory to which he responds. This is why he knows so much and discerns so little. This may also explain why some figures seem so disproportionately banal in relation to murderous modernity. Dreaming of violent death, Sascha wakes up "instead of dying" and discovers a pimple, "only a little inflamed," marking the spot where the bullet had struck him (7–8).

Lines drawn in blood on a map appear less vivid than a line drawn in chalk on a bench by a schoolboy. Sascha's "dark hole" of reality is hardly "the darkness [that] does not lift but becomes yet heavier" for W. G. Sebald (2001: 24), an acclaimed expatriate German author who lived in England until his death in 2001. Sebald's haunting literary reflections on the visible and invisible traces of a traumatic history are elegiac and ponderous, not banal or laconic, in tone.[111] (In this sense one might really imagine Sascha—rather than Şenocak—as "the Woody Allen of Berlin.") Alerting us to an "aesthetics of description" tied to a "refusal of realism" in Sebald's oeuvre, Julia Hell identifies a cultural crisis of "post-Holocaust authorship" more generally, one that manifests in a simultaneous disturbance of vision and masculinity (2003: 28–29 and passim). For a male coterie of non-Jewish German authors in particular, Hell argues, the compulsion to look at a genocidal legacy commingles with the spectral taint of "the fathers' crime" and shocking "after-images of piles of dead bodies and emaciated survivors captured in photographs and films made at the opening of the concentration camps in 1945" (14, 15). Exacerbated by national unification, this scopic crisis of German authorship yields a literary culture that has revolved "obsessively around that which cannot be seen, can no longer be seen, could never be seen, but which still determines both German culture and its subjects" (36).[112] Şenocak's author-narrator is not driven by this obsession, though his field of vision might be said to encompass it. Sascha too is an artist who looks into history, albeit from the perspective of a different lineage. He is not compelled either to look or to avert his gaze—to see "nothing"—for the reasons that Hell attributes to Sebald, Walser, and others. When Sascha inhabits the figural abyss of his textual world, he steps into a historical moment in German culture in order to revive remembrance, to restore the deep breathing of historical memory otherwise stifled or frozen in a culture of *Betroffenheit*. There is a dual moment of irony in this. *Perilous Kinship* responds to a German culture of memory that has expanded exponentially since the Historians' Debate of the 1980s. And in the year of the novel's publication, an explosive public debate featured a major author insisting on the innocence of his autobiographical configuration of a German childhood.[113] Child of a transnational history in which his German–Jewish family was essentially annihilated, Sascha "came along later" without coming "after."[114] No one bothers to expect anything from him as a person in Germany, he tells us, yet as a figure of history, Sascha is neither ignorant nor innocent, but accountable to the multivalent claims of transnational memory. Looking into the history of "this country" and seeing "nothing," he in effect sees something that neither graphic images nor archival documentation reveals. Does he appear accountable because he spends so much time in the dark or in spite of it?

Sascha might write stories that appear blurred to Marie, but *Perilous Kinship* blurs no boundaries between Nazi perpetrators and their Jewish victims or Young Turk murderers and their Armenian prey.[115] The story line involving the Turkish grandfather and his Armenian lover never absolves the former of his culpability in genocide, and some might interpret his suicide in 1936 as delayed punishment for his involvement in the deportations of 1921. To the degree that various historical facts and truth claims about the history of genocide circulate in the novel, *Perilous Kinship* could be said to revolve in some way around normative precepts of identity politics that do not generally play a major role in the literature of Turkish migration. But what are we to make of the novel's Armenian leitmotif? Explicit references to Talât Pasha as a "mass murderer" felled by an Armenian bullet in Berlin render the Armenian genocide and its legacy figurally as a German scene of sorts, in addition to whatever else it might be, though it would be misleading to assert that the novel advances any claims about German military complicity in the Armenian genocide or German missionary activities in documenting the atrocities.[116] (These topics do not figure in the novel at all.) Published in 1998 and configuring the 1990s as a historic moment, *Perilous Kinship* might be said to reflect truth claims advanced by the Armenian diaspora with increasing success in the international arena since the late 1980s. These truth claims have had to contend with competing truth claims made equally vociferously by Turkish officials. Founded in 1923 as the modern successor state to the Ottoman Empire, the Republic of Turkey has consistently and fiercely denied that mass deportations, rapes, and murders of Armenians between 1915 and 1923 constituted genocide.[117] Taner Akçam has taken the international lead among Turkish scholars in calling for dialogue beyond denial (1993, 2001, 2002).[118] In their jointly authored foreword to Akçam's English-language essays on the Armenian genocide and Turkish taboos, Kevork Bardakjian and Fatma Müge Göçek state the problem baldly. "The Turkish state has developed a master story that aims to deny and erase the genocide from Turkish collective memory" (2001: vi).[119] "While the Turkish diaspora seems to adhere to this official state line," they continue, "the people of Turkey often do indeed have their own alternative narratives. These narratives circulate informally among groups and individuals, but are never brought into the public arena, for fear of retribution from the state" (vi). The Armenian diaspora in the United States, Canada, and France has long struggled to achieve international recognition of the Armenian genocide in spite of official objections and interventions by the Republic of Turkey.[120] In the mid-1980s such attempts resulted in the formation of a Human Rights Subcommittee in the United Nations, and the European Council formally recognized the genocide in 1987 (Chaliand and Rageau 91). Official records of the U.S. Congress from the 1980s on document debates on the subject, as various resolutions in favor of recognizing the genocide or deferring recognition have been passed.[121] In 1995 a French court made international headlines when it ruled that a professor of Middle Eastern Studies from Princeton University, interviewed by *Le Monde* in 1993, had failed in his duties as a historian by suggesting that Armenian claims of genocide had no basis in fact. Such international contestations in the 1990s and since have coincided with growing attention to universal rights of personhood and community in supranational bodies of adjudication and legitimation (see introduction for a limited discussion of this in relation to changing structures of incorporation in Europe). So-called ethnic cleansing in the Balkans and Rwanda in the early and mid-1990s shattered lived communities and international complacency with more genocide as the century closed. Partly as a result of this, "the sustained study of genocide and other forms of mass murder," Gellately and Kiernan observe, "accelerated in the 1990s" (4). A touching tale of Turkish taboos, the Armenian genocide, and more, *Perilous Kinship* is a German text that must surely be situated in this broadly transnational ethnoscape of the dead with whom the living must contend.[122] The novel clearly participates in the explosion of cultural memory in the 1990s. By depicting Sascha's Turkish grandfather as both a beloved hero of national liberation and a powerful agent in the Armenian genocide, "the first to draw up a deportation list of Armenian names," *Perilous Kinship* defies a deep-seated Turkish taboo from the vantage point of contemporary Germany. Şenocak's configuration of genocide and taboo is decidedly transnational in this sense.[123] The figure of historical accountability that speaks to us from a dark hole where breath resonates unseen begins to address some Armenian claims of genocidal memory.

At the same time, it would be misleading to suggest that the voice of narration speaks in the normative register of truth, acknowledgment, adjudication, or reparation.[124] Basic Armenian demands for representation are clearly not met by the text in the dual sense that it neither provides a metanarrative of the Armenian genocide nor presents an image of Armenian experience in any gripping detail.[125] The Armenian genocide does not emerge as something Sascha sees or readers could visualize on the basis of this text. *Perilous Kinship* differs dramatically from Atom Egoyan's *Ararat* (2002), a Canadian film that graphically portrays the raw violence of the Armenian genocide and lovingly depicts a present-day diaspora in rich visual detail, even as it interrogates the medium of the visual with a critical eye. In *Perilous Kinship* we encounter a novel within the novel. In *Ararat* we see a film about the events of 1915 being made within the film about the Armenian diaspora in North America today. When the filmmaker within the film hires an art historian as a consultant, the latter objects to an oversized image of Mount Ararat used as a backdrop for scenes set in the city of Van, since the mountain is not in reality visible from the location depicted. The director justifies his choice by appealing to "poetic license," whereby a symbolic Armenian landscape trumps geography. Not quite persuaded by this argument, the art historian inverts the metaphor of "poetic license" by reestablishing its literal register, which indexes institutional processes of adjudication and legitimation: "Where do you get one of those?" Such quips notwithstanding, *Ararat* is an intensely visual reflection on the Armenian genocide and its diasporic legacy, and this cannot be explained by its status as a film rather than a novel. Compared with the history of the Holocaust, the history of the Armenian genocide is not widely known or well represented in international archives of visual culture. If Sascha steps into a figural abyss to revive remembrance amidst a German culture of *Betroffenheit* and a longstanding discourse of national atonement in Germany, this is a dark German hole that does not speak very effectively to an Armenian need for visibility.

The imagined conclusion to Sascha's novel hinges on a figure of speech rather than an image. We know that Sascha's grandfather commits suicide on the eve of his scheduled participation in the Olympic games held in Berlin under the auspices of the Third Reich. The grandson's emphatically literary reflections on possible reasons for this suicide yield the figure of a letter from an Armenian woman, presumably the one whose name had been removed from the list of those scheduled for deportation. In this sense the historically and geographically disparate scenes of genocide are linked in narration. Yet the surviving lover who writes from France speaks of separation, flight, rape, and brutality, not love. Her letter carries a stamp depicting Louis Pasteur at a microscope but no return address. Not knowing the married name of his former lover, the addressee is unable to reply. Whatever response he articulates must therefore be directed, the text implies, to the future. Unless they are purely rhetorical, questions call for answers. The only question posed by the letter-writer that seems answered in Sascha's novel also invokes a matter of speech: " 'Had you not said that you would put an end to your life if we could no longer be together?' " (136). Interpreting this question "only" as a reminder of his "promise" (*Versprechen*), the Turkish addressee of the Armenian question in this German story is effectively interpellated when he keeps this promise, however belatedly. In this imagined scene of a letter and a promise ending in death, the grandfather's complicity in genocide is strikingly absent as a figure of reference.

A figure of history that speaks from within a dark hole, Sascha also writes. In the novel fragment he writes we see the Turkish grandfather, who otherwise appears as the figure of a secret, transformed into the figure of a promise that must be kept. That this should be cast in terms of a love story may seem trivializing or sentimental given the enormity of genocide. Other factors countermand this impression. For one thing, as discussed, Sascha is a child of the landscape of memory to which he responds, and nothing in the text suggests that readers are meant to imagine him as an especially gifted writer. The ending he conjures is also characterized as an experiment, so readers are implicitly called upon to imagine other endings too. Second, the lover's address can be read figuratively as a call to rejoin in speech-effects what had been sundered in the violence of genocide. This yields a narrative fragment in which Turkish and Armenian voices "touch" as figural elements involved in the same story. One might also say that the Turkish lover's promise is an illocutionary speech act in that he commits himself in the act of speaking to subsequent fulfillment, while the Armenian lover's perlocutionary reminder brings about the fulfillment of the promise by an act of speech (Austin 109–132). These Turkish and Armenian figures are thus articulated as bound to each other in a language of consequence and commitment. Finally, the indirection of the lover's promise hinges on the German word *Versprechen*, which means "promise" and connotes the act of misspeaking as well. Committed to speech rather than silence, *Perilous Kinship* reflects the knowledge that words are necessary but also treacherous partners in the culture of memory. Decisively shaped by a postwar culture of being moved in West Germany, this knowledge became all the more acute in the 1990s, when transnational news of genocide and entangled visions of the past commanded the world's attention in dramatically concentrated ways.

Şenocak's touching tale of "perilous kinship" marks a distinctive moment in the configuration of cultural contact and historical narrative in the literature of Turkish migration and contemporary German literature more generally. Unlike *Kanak Sprak*, the novel does not counter the ostensible thingliness of Turkish figures in German life with an easily envisioned alternative or an embodied affect of agitation. Neither does it restore a voice or face of authenticity to any Turkish figure at all. When Sascha enters into the resonant abyss of a complex German and transnational history, he does so as an abstract line of thought in the guise of an "I" who speaks.[126] One crucial passage pivots precariously on this distinction. Reflecting on the history of Jewish assimilation and German anti-Semitism, Sascha muses on present-day Germany as well, where "Jews and Germans no longer face one another alone."

> In Germany now, a trialogue is developing among Germans, Jews, and Turks, among Christians, Jews, and Moslems. The undoing of the German-Jewish dichotomy might release both parties, Germans and Jews, from the burden of their traumatic experiences. But for this to succeed they would have to admit the Turks into their domain. And for their part, the Turks in Germany would have to discover the Jews, not just as part of the German past in which they cannot share, but as part of the present in which they live. Without the Jews the Turks stand in a dichotomous relation to the Germans. They tread in the footprints of the Jews of the past. (89–90)[127]

Sascha immediately characterizes such "fantasies" as the optimistic product of "a good mood" and then segues into the "dark hole" with no discernible dimensions, where he detects the breathing of those he cannot see. Readers are thus virtually instructed to consider the optimistic vision of a trialogue involving Turks, Germans, and Jews as highly suspect. This is a suspicion I want to underscore, but not because we should agree with Sascha's characterological opinion or because readers might be independently skeptical about the real-life efficacy of multicultural dialogue. The trialogic vision is suspect instead because of the way it relies on a referential language of representation. When Sascha envisions a trialogue, he conjures a triangulated image of talking heads that promises to release Germans and Jews from the traumatic embrace of victims and perpetrators.[128] This figural image of a trialogue is only a slightly modified version of the dialogic paradigm that underwrites a mosaic sense of multiculturalism. As such, it makes representational claims that are repeatedly undermined by the lines of narration in the novel overall.[129] The visual image of immigrant Turks stepping into the footsteps of German Jews reiterates the claims of representation by means of an iconic metaphor and warrants suspicion for the same reason. Finally, the figure of Armenian history is literally effaced in this trialogic fantasy, which may partly explain why a dark hole with no clearly discernible dimensions appears more promising as a figure of history than geometric calculations.[130] Speaking from a resonant void where the "threads" in his head yield the story lines of a novel and the Turkish–German–Jewish "threads" of his lineage grow ever thinner (51, 90), the "I" in which these threads converge speaks only as a trickster when Sascha quips, "triangular relationships are the most complicated" (90).[131] Much like borders drawn in blood and chalk, handwriting drawn on paper, or even names entered onto a fateful list, these threads appear figurally as something that looks like a line, which then functions abstractly as lines of thought that "touch" in the voice of narration. The configuration of genocide, taboo, and migration in *Perilous Kinship* neither bespeaks a trialogue nor depicts a triangle at all. Such figures of speech are representational decoys in an anti-representational story of Turkish migration, German transformation, and transnational interpellation. To recall Brodsky Lacour, writing becomes iconoclastic when a line drawn in thought "conceals its own status as line in its intelligibility as representation." The fictional autobiography of Sascha Muhteschem may be described this way, and I submit that it "commits an unprecedented form to being." The intensely refracted figure of Turkish migration that draws breath in *Perilous Kinship* is an iconoclastic line that Zafer Şenocak draws in the imaginative landscape of contemporary German narrative.

Chapter Three
Capital and Labor

1

Agonal forces of capital and labor are inscribed in the story of Turkish migration, as economic conditions prevailing from the 1950s on attest. The Cold War closely shadows this tale of human need and industrial demand, especially after 1961, when the Berlin Wall sundered the German populace overnight and formal recruitment of Turkish laborers began. Because of government-sanctioned policies regulating the flow of international labor into a divided Germany, and because the Federal Republic long had the most liberal laws in Europe pertaining to political asylum, Turkish migrants have been interpellated for four decades in Germany as subjects, if far less frequently as citizens, of a capitalist state committed to certain forms of historical memory. For Saskia Sassen, migrant laborers in the late twentieth century become "emblematic subjects" (2000: 216; 1998: 55–76) of a global economy dating to the 1970s. This economy is "characterized by a rapid growth of transactions and institutions that are outside the framework of interstate relations" (1998: 100, n. 2), and migrant laborers acquire emblematic status at "frontier zones" of capitalist development where national domains and a global economy interact (Sassen 2000: 216). As K. Anthony Appiah aptly observes in his foreword to *Globalization and Its Discontents: Essays on the New Mobility of People and Money*, the political economist conjoins "a discourse about global capital and the discourse of migration" by reconceiving the latter "as the globalization of labor" (Sassen 1998: xiv). What is at stake for Sassen in this conceptual shift from migration to labor, especially since she does not understand globalization to mean the utter erasure of national domains? By emphasizing labor rather than migration in studies of global capital and demographic mobility, Sassen pointedly highlights structural processes and strategic networks of economic transformation that "the language of immigration and ethnicity" obscures (1998: 87 and passim). She hardly treats immigration and ethnicity as wholly inoperative terms, but her mode of analysis exceeds any experiential perspective on migration and ethnicity as social frames of reference.[1]

The Turkish Turn emphatically retains the category of a literature of migration. By addressing the conjunction of capital and labor as a nodal point where touching tales converge and interpretive dilemmas arise, this final chapter does not displace the phenomenon of migration with the category of labor. Like Sassen in the realm of economic analysis, however, I pursue a mode of analysis that exceeds any understanding of labor as an experiential property of migrant actors that could be identified as characters or authors. Recalling Appadurai's emphasis on the social practice of imagination as a pivotal "form of work" in "the new global order" (1996: 31), this chapter asks what forms of imaginative labor fall to literary texts when the story of Turkish migration turns on entanglements with capitalist reconstruction, Cold War antagonisms, and German unification under the triumphal sign of capital.[2] This figural coupling of capital and labor indexes, not a political agon of predictable Marxian contours, but a relational nexus that warrants interpretive scrutiny.[3] Much as Benhabib stresses the need for a "disaggregated" approach to changing social practices of citizenship in Europe, I argue for a disaggregated approach to the imaginative labor signaled by the literature of migration. To the degree that much of this work in a broadly imaginative sense is enabled by some figure of ethnic labor in a more narrow thematic sense, it behooves us to turn a disaggregated eye to this figure, which proves more protean than proletarian. This is not at all to suggest that the literature of migration produces hybrid identities as a cultural innovation. The literature of Turkish migration reconfigures the sign of ethnicity instead. As this chapter demonstrates, this sign functions in the literature of migration as a construction zone where national and transnational ethnoscapes are so transformed that they become newly intelligible. The thingliness of Turkish figures in German public life yields here to abstract forms of imaginative labor and cultural capital that no rhetoric of experience, identity, or authenticity can delineate. Beyond this analytical impasse, touching tales and "Turkish" lines of thought in this arena beckon. How are we to follow?

"A small master folk sees itself in danger: one has summoned forces of labor, and human beings are coming" (Frisch 374). The axiomatic status of Max Frisch's dictum of 1965 seems only to grow over time. Sooner or later, most commentaries on migration cite what follows the colon, not always accurately, usually without bibliographical reference, and customarily without any contextualization.[4] One would not know from such commentary that Frisch indicts Swiss resistance to envisioning a national future that would reflect rather than deny the reality of Italian labor migration. The fact that Frisch was speaking about Italians in Switzerland in 1965, not

Turks in Germany, is less significant for present purposes than the axiomatic authority that has come to inhere in the categorical assertion. When Kien Nghi Ha invokes Frisch in a study of Turkish migration and postcolonial ethnicity, he does so in a manner characteristic of scholarly and journalistic deployments of the observation generally: "By pinning these people down . . . as a flexible 'industrial reserve army,' these human beings were dehumanized" (20).[5] At times German xenophobia rather than industrialization or capitalism is faulted for casting migrants as something less than human, the "lowest of the low" (Wallraff 1988).[6] Beyond political or sentimental presumptions that usually attend citations of Frisch's adage, what circulates in repetitive distinctions between "forces of labor" and "human beings" is the continual reminder that competing regimes of incorporation are at play in the social scene of migration and cultural narratives ensuing from it.[7] Frisch's ghost cues us to recall that structural tensions in the process of incorporation form the crux of stories about transnational migration to and in Europe since the 1950s. The cultural fable of migrants suspended "between two worlds" obscures rather than illuminates such tensions. Yasemin Soysal and others alert us to changing and interlocking systems of political "incorporation" or membership for migrants and nation-states in Europe. Without doing so exclusively, such systems often revolve around citizenship, denizenship, human rights, and labor functions. Even sentimental invocations of Frisch index, perhaps unwittingly, related preoccupations and contestations in an era of accelerated social transformation.

If the globalization of labor proves a richer structural grid for Sassen than a personalized discourse of migration allows, Frisch and those who cite his pronouncement as if its import were self-evident regard the category of "human beings" as having both broader scope and greater value than "forces of labor." This is not a tension the present chapter intends to resolve. Literary analyses here foreground abstract forms of imaginative labor and cultural capital that matter in text, and certain conceits of human personhood enable these abstractions in pivotal ways. These conceits revolve around ethnicity and gender, rhetorical figures of social deixis without which the story of Turkish migration cannot seem to function.[8] The relevance of these figures for migration narratives is neither self-evident nor self-explanatory. On the one hand, it would be counterintuitive to propose that references to ethnicity and gender are immaterial to stories of migration. The argument unfolded here does not entail such an extreme proposition. On the other hand, more analytical curiosity about these social referents as strategic nexes of narration is warranted if historical and cultural innovations in the literature of migration are to become intelligible. The thingliness of Turkish figures in Germany is often enmeshed in fables of migration in which ethnicity and gender are presupposed as figural categories of personal identity and organizational frames of social reference. What labor functions actually accrue to such figures and frames of reference? What types of cultural capital do they underwrite?[9]

Lambasting migration studies that recast the story of postwar demographics from a sociology of labor to cultures of identity, Levent Soysal cites Frisch's emphasis on personhood and Wallraff's reliance on "experiential narrative" as representative of this broad shift in epistemological perspectives on migration (2003a: 496–497). Soysal's larger point is that "an elementary story of exclusion and inclusion" predicated on categorical frameworks of ethnic identity and cultural difference overlooks "processes of incorporation" where migration is concerned (499). For this reason, the anthropologist considers the recurring figure of the *Gastarbeiter* in migration studies a referential anachronism that reproduces the ethnocultural paradigm rather than attending to newly transnational labors of incorporation. Levent Soysal cites Yasemin Soysal in this vein, for as the latter observes, "Guestworkers become *symbolic* foreigners" (Y. Soysal 1994: 135; L. Soysal 2003a: 500). Two clarifications are in order. First, the claim that figures of guest workers are symbolic has a very different analytical thrust from Sassen's designation of migrant laborers as "emblematic subjects" of economic globalization. By Sassen's account, migrant laborers at the end of the twentieth century participate in structural transformations that the discursive figure of migrant labor indexes. According to both Levent Soysal and Yasemin Soysal, guest workers become symbolic figures precisely because the ethnocultural paradigm attaching to them cannot index the changing sociality of migration. A subsequent section of this chapter revisits this argument, which in some ways echoes claims made in the introduction but in other ways requires further differentiation to be compatible with them. Second, jettisoning the figure of ethnicity altogether is an exaggerated response to the analytical blind spots of a focus on identities cohering or conflicting as cultural blocs. The same caution applies to the figure of gender, which often appears twinned with ethnicity as a determining social referent in stories of migration. The discourse of incorporation is not diametrically opposed to all possible discourses of ethnicity, only to those relegating all cultural formations to the straitjacket of anthropomorphic identity and inherited cultures. Instead of considering ethnicity and gender through an experiential or even an ideological lens, this chapter refocuses critical attention on these figural markers as strategic sites where imaginative labor and cultural capital in the literature of migration conspire to transform the meaning of *ethnos* rather than delineating the content of any particular ethnic identity. Elaboration of these claims entails some discussion of Rey Chow's concept of "ethnicity as alienated labor" (33) and John Guillory's understanding of "cultural capital." Before proceeding to more theoretical terrain, readers may appreciate a brief sketch of those fables of Turkish migration in which figures of labor, capital, ethnicity, and gender are persistently interlaced.

2

As Ruth Mandel observes, Turks in Germany are subjected to "processes of ethnicization" (2003, 2006) and perceived as an ethnic minority regardless of citizenship.[10] Liberal critiques of stereotypes casting ethnic minorities as forever strange are so ingrained in multiculturalism that one could forget to notice that the reverse does not necessarily apply, even when figures of ethnicity are at stake. Tropes of strangeness do not necessarily translate into categories of ethnicity as strong multiculturalism construes them. Cultural nexes of difference and ethnicity are sometimes configured in ways that exceed models of inclusion and exclusion calibrated to prevalent concepts of ethnic cohesion, identity, and community. Literary analyses of work by Aras Ören, Emine Sevgi Özdamar, and Zafer Şenocak illuminate interpretive alternatives that emerge when the critical eye allows for this possibility. The figural coupling of capital and labor in these authors' texts, however, routinely competes with other couples and laborers with a much firmer hold on the popular imagination. Even if Levent Soysal is correct in regarding the Turkish *Gastarbeiter* as an anachronistic social referent in the age of globalization around 2000, the figure of ethnic labor associated with Turks in Germany continues to exert a spectral force in cultural rhetoric in Germany well into the 1990s and beyond.[11] In this sense the Turkish *Gastarbeiter* is not merely an outdated stereotype, but also a stock figure in the cultural fable of migrants suspended "between two worlds." This fable marks an imagined encounter with the material history of modern migrations. Yet this central figure never stands alone on that drafty bridge of migration lore.

Although most migrants recruited under official auspices between 1961 and 1973 found jobs in German industry, the anthropomorphic figures of Turkish migration that circulate most widely in the popular imagination are coded in gendered terms that do not necessarily index industrialized labor: the trash man and the cleaning woman.[12] Some degree of abjection inheres in these icons, which locate Turks attending to the detritus of German life and render their presence easily visualized. This iconography of social experience reinforces the thingliness of Turkish figures in contemporary German culture and their heterosocial normativity too. Özdamar once remarked, the image assigned to Turks in German theater is "the role of the poor man" (Wierschke 1996: 258), and Özdamar herself mobilizes the stock figure of the Turkish cleaning woman for dramatic parody (1991).[13] A postcard bearing the Turkish title "Münih'in yakışıklı çöpçüsü" (Munich's Beautiful

Trash Man), one of three produced by German media specialists in 2003 on behalf of the Bavarian capital, attests to the continued spectral presence of the trash man as a cipher of abjection to be countered, for this "beautiful" Turk sports a spiffy orange uniform and is everything that migrant laborers depicted by Klaus Staeck in the 1970s and Günter Wallraff in the 1980s are not: happy, confident, clean, and at rest though gainfully employed (Edgar Medien).[14] While a masculinized trope of Turkish abjection overshadows its feminized counterpart, both images underscore the social capital that German culture generally withholds from Turkish migrants.[15] If one thinks of these images as infused with cultural capital, however (as opposed to merely indexing the absence of social capital), one notices three things.[16] First, the gendered division of labor in the iconography of migration splits again as tropes of female emancipation and male criminality vie with the cleaning woman and the trash man for public attention. Second, this multiply bifurcated division of labor along axes of gender takes on new meaning in the 1990s. Third, the cultural capital accruing to feminized tropes of emancipation and masculinized figures of criminality depends for its symbolic value on the imaginative labor they perform in public.

If icons of migrant labor mediate cultural values and social capital, the value mediated by images denying social capital to Turkish men and women is a cultural sense of German superiority. This perception rests on the conceit that Turkish migrants are at bottom dispensable features of German life, much like the refuse they make disappear. This is important because the conceit falls away when public discourse shifts attention to equally iconic images of Turkish women reaping the benefits of emancipation from Turkish and Islamic patriarchy in Germany or even Turkish men cast as delinquents or thugs. With these gendered tropes, the woman divested of her headscarf and the man wielding aggression like a knife, the figure of migration becomes integral to German self-perceptions tethered to standards of civilization and security.[17] While these archetypes circulated in the 1980s too, they acquire greater force and signal heightened disorientation in the 1990s. In 1988 *Yasemin*, a commercial film directed by Hark Bohm, which Deniz Göktürk describes as having enjoyed more success with German audiences than any other film dealing with migration in the 1980s (2000: 335), captured both images on screen. In one crucial scene the seventeen-year-old heroine, rebellious daughter of Turkish migrants in Germany, appears dressed in white and surrounded by swarthy men trying to abduct her to Turkey, where her father imagines she will be safe from the corruption of German freedom. The "night and fog" action (Göktürk 2000: 336) is thwarted when Yasemin's boyfriend appears on his motorcycle like a Teutonic *deus ex machina* to rescue the damsel in distress.[18] Since the 1970s Alice Schwarzer has been the most vocal and visible representative of

German feminism in the public sphere, with countless publications and television appearances. Editor of *Emma: The Magazine by Women for Human Beings*, the longest-lived feminist magazine in Germany, Schwarzer responded with outrage to the murders of Turkish women and girls in Solingen in an essay targeting patriarchy as the root cause of such violence. Turkish men are made to bear the burden of German history in an odd twist of rhetoric in 1993. Although it was German men who killed Turkish women in Solingen, Schwarzer uses the occasion to equate Islamic fundamentalism and German fascism. "Both are men's domain"(35).[19] It is hardly a coincidence that this issue of *Emma* features an article decrying German tolerance for Muslim headscarves with the words, "A Turkish Woman: I Am a Human Being Like You," or that it includes a vivid photograph of dark-haired men slaughtering sheep whose blood runs red from one page onto another. Schwarzer's grossly undifferentiated rhetoric of 1993 situates the icon of the headscarf in a broad narrative about German civilization battling cultural barbarism. The fault lines of such a narrative are encoded as stories of symbolic women in relation to communities of men.[20] The symbolic value ascribed to Turkish women perceived as liberated from Islamic strictures thanks to civilizing interventions in Germany yields what circulates as the cultural capital of German superiority.[21]

This changes radically over the course of the 1990s. Women wearing Islamic headscarves in European spaces have increasingly claimed their right to do so in the commingled language of cultural particularism and universal personhood (Benhabib 2002b: 94–100; Yasemin Soysal 2002: 144–145).[22] This alters the symbolic stakes of the headscarf, for the civilizing effect of personhood is now claimed by avowedly secular states and demonstratively religious minorities in Europe alike. This transpires in competing but interactive regimes of sovereignty and incorporation. In Germany these tensions have crystallized since 1998 around the case of Fereshta Ludin, a German citizen (originally from Afghanistan), practicing Muslim, and public schoolteacher who sought legal redress from the Federal Constitutional Court when authorities refused to allow her to wear a headscarf in her classroom.[23] In this case Schwarzer aligns herself with the state rather than feminism as the ostensible guarantor of secularism (2003).[24] Her fervent views in this regard are similar to those of Bassam Tibi, a practicing Muslim and German citizen who considers the headscarf an "emblem of political Islam" and a threat to women's rights, European civilization, and what the international relations expert terms Euro-Islam (1998a: 320–339; 2001; 2002).[25] My point here is to highlight the changed centrality of gender in Germany as a fulcrum for thinking about the cultural capital of Turkish migration.[26] According to Nilüfer Göle, "Islam has acquired new forms of visibility over the last two decades as it has made its way in the public avenues of both Muslim and European societies" (2002: 173).[27] Such changes challenge, as she puts it, "the borders and the meanings of the secular public sphere." They do so, I submit, in ways that earlier debates about gender and ethnicity in Germany no longer capture. The cultural capital accruing to the newly configured icon of the headscarf in Germany is no longer a sense of German superiority, the self-confident largesse of a civilized nation with rights it is eager to bestow on migrant women, but a heightened sense of German insecurity. It may seem odd to speak of insecurity as a form of cultural capital, yet this is fitting because many narratives about Turkish migration and the German future gain public momentum and social weight by invoking precisely this frame of reference.[28]

The figural counterpart to the newly emboldened woman in a headscarf is that of defiantly aggressive Turkish men, especially young ones. Zaimoğlu's iconic *Kanaken* are interpellated by this figure, though they are not generally represented as Muslims. Tertilt's study of "Turkish Power Boys" aims a critical lance at deep-seated perceptions of cultural conflict associating gang violence with ethnic identity.[29] With a widely cited book on "seductive fundamentalism," Wilhelm Heitmeyer and other social scientists drew dramatic attention in 1997 to stark dangers posed to civil society in Germany when migrant youth express a willingness to resort to violence in the name of Islam.[30] "The stereotypical male Turk in the German popular imaginary is . . . armed for street fighting and mugging . . . . Reports of knives and knifings are legion where 'Turks' are present, or more precisely, the fear of them" (Cheesman 2003: 149). According to Christopher Clark, the "stereotype of young Turkish males as delinquents or gangsters has succeeded earlier stereotypes of the *Gastarbeiter*" in German popular media including television and film (231). The argument advanced here is that the spectral figure of abject male laborers coexists with more recent icons of male criminality, but that such figures underwrite competing forms of cultural capital in reference to migration. If the trash man and the cleaning woman were long denied social capital (in terms of status or legitimacy), the image of a Turkish woman who could be liberated from "Oriental" patriarchy by embracing German personhood yielded the cultural capital of German superiority. In this scenario Turkish women represented the possibility of cultural gains, from which Turkish men were iconographically excluded. In the 1990s additional labor functions accrue to the conjoined and changing figures of ethnicity and gender. The woman who claims an Islamic headscarf as a sign of personhood in German courts unsettles the cultural economy of German civilization. In this sense both newer icons of migrant ethnicity, male and female, provide crucial figures of reference for German narratives of heightened insecurity and cultural disorientation. Masculinist paradigms in the literature of migration have gained prominence at a historical moment when the gendered iconography of an earlier phase ceases to have the public purchase it once exercised.[31]

According to some, the literature of migration by or about women emerged either significantly later or more slowly than the literature of migration associated with men (Ackermann 2002: 147; Zierau 147).[32] Considering the favorable reception of literary works by Özdamar and other foreign-born writers such as Libuše Moníková (Czechoslovakia) and Yoko Tawada (Japan), Zierau concludes that the 1990s saw women writers in the field of migration catch up with and finally surpass male writers in public recognition (148). Other scholars paint a picture at odds with this chronology. For Carmine Chiellino, an Italian-born writer who cofounded and coedited the two main publishing projects devoted to "guest worker literature" in the early 1980s, "women's literature" by migrant authors attracted considerably more attention from German readers in the 1980s than the largely male-oriented literature about the international solidarity of migrant labor (2000: 390–391). From the mid-1980s until the mid-1990s Turkish women writing in Germany (such as Saliha Scheinhardt, Aysel Özakın, Renan Demirkan, and Alev Tekinay) attracted far more public attention as a group than male writers such as Güney Dal and Aras Ören.[33] This was a time when Turkish-related themes were forcefully present in German news media and political debates concerning NATO, the European Community and later the European Union, the Gulf War, citizenship laws and asylum policies, violent xenophobia, Kurdish terrorism, and human rights (Adelson 1997b: 305). As Sigrid Weigel and Heike Henderson observe, women writers who enjoyed the lion's share of what interest there was in the literature of migration during this period were commonly understood as highlighting gender as a special hallmark of conflict between national cultures and civilizational values (Weigel 1992: 222; Henderson 1997: 226).[34] Most starkly, Scheinhardt's name stands in emblematically for once popular interest in gruesome stories about Turkish women oppressed by a backward national culture, Islamic norms, or both (Göktürk 1999a: 520).[35] According to B. Venkat Mani, women writers such as Scheinhardt and Özakın were long "hailed as the voices of their communities," interpellated in Germany as privileged "native informants" attesting to cultural divides (2003: 33).

The widespread tendency in the early 1990s to celebrate the conceit of naïveté in Özdamar's prose as a mark of authenticity reflects this representational paradigm without doing justice to gender functions in literary texts or a changing cultural terrain. The sustained coupling of prostitution and storytelling in *Life is a Caravanserai*, for example, articulates a transnational economy of fictionality in which gender and ethnicity serve as strategic nexes of historical narration rather than literal signposts of embodied identities.[36] This is easy to overlook if one concentrates on female characters, collectives, and motifs in this novel about Turkish life in the 1950s and 1960s (including bathhouses, menstruation, lesbianism, and prostitution).[37] The interpretive focus shifts when the author of *Madame Bovary* or *Robinson Crusoe* appears as the most inspirational prostitute or "mouth whore" (Özdamar 2000b: 82–87) in the novel. The "lies" of storytelling are the tools of the trade to which the first-person narrator of the caravanserai novel aspires, and Flaubert and Defoe are explicitly conjured as her muses. No persona of authenticity speaks here. Similar cautionary notes could be struck in reference to earlier examples from the literature of Turkish migration. When a cruel German manager treats a foreign janitor's ulcers with estrogen, the hapless laborer in Dal's tale of a wildcat strike grows breasts that disfigure and confound him with disastrous results (1979). This character is "literally unmanned by the indignities of migrant labour" (Moray McGowan 2001: 301; see also Wise 88–89). This narrative constellation may also be read as a figural nexus of epochal disorientation that bespeaks the labor of migration in ways exceeding the anthropomorphic voice of migrant experience.[38] No absolute historical divide distinguishes literary registers of migration in the 1990s from an earlier phase. In scalar terms, however, shifting configurations of ethnicity and gender in the literature of the 1990s coincide temporally with a destabilizing moment in public perceptions of the cultural capital of migration. The figure of the Turkish woman ceases to be a liberal *cause célèbre* and begins to trigger national insecurities instead. Not coincidentally, this is also a moment when the masculinist iconicity of Zaimoğlu's *Kanaken* enjoys its widest commercial appeal. At the same time, German culture reflects a heightened crisis of male authorship and historical consciousness entangled in crises of vision and visibility (Hell 2003). Whether directly related or not, these phenomena indicate that representational and narrative codes of gender and ethnicity were beginning to be fundamentally reforged as the century neared its end. The literature of migration is one of many sites where the imaginative labor and cultural capital of such codes call for disaggregated analysis. Returning to Berlin after having missed the fall of the Wall, Sascha Muhteschem of *Perilous Kinship* recalls "that unreal things are worth just as much in Germany as real ones" (19). Here the German word *irreal* does not connote the opposite of real so much as something both intangible and material, much like currency and commodities, which enable and exceed exchange. Figures of ethnicity and gender in the literature of migration function as such intangible yet material "things." The labor of imagination is often concentrated in and around these figures when the volatile cultural capital of transnational migration is at stake.

3

Turning to Rey Chow's treatment of "ethnicity as alienated labor" (33) and John Guillory's approach to "cultural capital," this section elaborates key premises on which subsequent readings of Turkish figures and narrative structures in the literature of migration rely. While neither Chow nor Guillory addresses German contexts, their work is conceptually instructive where literary cultures of migration are concerned. Chow takes liberal manifestations of multiculturalism and feminism to task for subscribing, sometimes unwittingly, to "the philosophical foundation of individualism" (154). By her account, this foundation favors the conceit of "an inviolable human subject" (32), thereby obscuring abstract structures of labor and commodification that call ethnic and gendered subjects into being as social forms of alienation rather than personhood.[39] This conceit inheres, not only in universal paradigms of ethnicity as cultural heritage to be passed on as embodied identity, but also in oppositional paradigms of ethnicity as political resistance to be articulated as a critical voice. Attending instead to the capitalist production of ethnicity as an ambivalent index of social relations, Chow situates "our contemporary culture of protest . . . within the framework of a prevalent work principle" (viii). With Weber as her muse, Chow argues that "the protestant ethnic"—the ethnic subject whose calling is to protest injustice—is called forth as an event intrinsic to rather than outside capitalist modes of interpellation and circulation (43 and passim).[40] On these grounds she faults ethnic studies (especially in the United States) for presupposing that "protestant" ethnics represent a kind of Lukácsian proletarian consciousness necessarily "engaged in a struggle toward liberation" (40–41). On the same grounds she chastises scholars who approach the migrant or minoritarian experience of otherness as a positivist fetish, for they presuppose "that ethnics are, indeed, aliens from *elsewhere*" (34). For Chow, the "experience of migration" should more properly be discussed as "the *ethnicization of labor*." Ethnicity becomes, according to Chow, a flexible social mechanism for producing an internal boundary between what is considered proper and valuable, on the one hand, and "foreign and inferior," on the other (34–35; 137).

Regarding the literature of Turkish migration in Germany, I submit that figures of ethnicity mark the site of many forms of imaginative labor, not a few of which bedevil the internal boundary concerning Chow. Figures of ethnicity in tales of migration sometimes enable new modes of affiliation rather than reproducing familiar patterns of differentiation. Protest may or may not be a central feature of this configuration. Chow's refusal to treat "ethnicity as a thematic concern" (51) is nonetheless compatible with the more structural approach to Turkish figures presented here. A scalar model of contextualization also characterizes the literature of Turkish migration by and large as intervening in German culture from within rather than from "elsewhere."[41] Like Sassen, Chow assesses anthropomorphic constellations of ethnicity and gender as emblematic subjects of social transformation involving the labor of migration. These are neither the symbolic subjects of migration studies decried by Yasemin Soysal and Levent Soysal nor individuated human subjects of any make, though human beings are interpellated by them. Unlike Sassen, however, Chow is especially interested in cultural narratives in which "the turn toward the self, especially the ethnic self" functions "as a form of production" rather than representation (111). This leads her to identify a form of contemporary mimicry overlooked in postcolonial theory associated with Bhabha, namely, "the level at which the ethnic person is expected to come to resemble what is recognizably ethnic" (Chow 107). By this account, the protestant ethnic "must both be seen to own her ethnicity and to exhibit it repeatedly" in a problematic process of "*self-mimicry*" (112) or "coercive mimeticism" (107). Noting "the overwhelming popularity of self-referential genres, such as autobiographies, memoirs, journals, and diaries, in contemporary cultural politics," Chow radically questions the presumption of liberatory consequences attaching to such genres where ethnic subjects are concerned (112–113).[42]

These criticisms of ethnic mimeticism in capitalist production resonate with my own critique of the thingliness ascribed to Turkish figures in German culture and literature. Most of the texts addressed here are also written as first-person narratives, from which one might conclude that the self takes center stage. Yet two basic precepts of *The Turkish Turn* point to phenomena for which *The Protestant Ethnic* cannot account. First, the Turkish figures at stake, with the notable exception of Zaimoğlu's *Kanaken*, are not protestant ethnics as Chow defines them.[43] The German literature of Turkish migration does not revolve around the identity politics that Chow targets for critique in the United States and Great Britain. Minority subjects often resort to self-referential modes, Chow observes, as if they were "performing a confession in the criminal as well as noncriminal sense." Socially interpellated as inferior, they proclaim their selfhood almost religiously, "as if it were a crime with which one has been charged" (115). In the German literature of migration (including the Ören novella to be discussed in the next section) one often encounters migrant characters who feel they are about to be accused or actually are accused of a crime. Thematically this is frequently tied to fears of deportation.[44] Even when this motif comes into play, conceits of selfhood do not necessarily serve the self-referential or confessional functions that Chow ascribes to them in other contexts.[45] As chapters one and two demonstrate, first-person narratives in the literature of migration can be dramatically at odds with presumptions of selfhood in an ethnic or humanist vein. When fears of illegitimacy circulate in this literature, the figure of ethnicity sometimes operates as a relay station where imaginative work on illicit affairs central to German culture is enabled. The Turkish gigolo's encounter with the German "christ lady" in *Kanak Sprak* is one example of this. Ören's *Please, No Police* provides another. Such a configuration of ethnicity exceeds the confessional reproduction of an ethnic self. Second, for all her insights into ethnicity as a form of labor, Chow does not interrogate the production of "ethnic community," though she sometimes uses the term casually.[46] By contrast, this study argues that literary narratives of Turkish migration imaginatively labor to reconfigure tropes of ethnicity and gender underwriting the cultural capital of migration in Germany. To be sure, this approach to labor also exceeds the thematic emphasis on industrial labor that prevailed in guest worker literature prior to the 1990s. Attending to a less familiar form of labor allows us to recognize how literary cultures of migration begin to reimagine what it might mean to belong to an ethnoscape (as distinguished from an ethnicity) in the rapidly changing worlds of our day. To recall Appadurai, an ethnoscape is "the landscape of persons who constitute the shifting world in which we live," not a cultural heritage that can be embodied.

Until now I have used the term cultural capital loosely for values, beliefs, predispositions, and affects that lend greater purchase to some public stories of migration as compared with others. For example, the fable of migrants suspended "between two worlds" has far more cultural capital today than the iconoclastic stories of migration that this book seeks to tell.[47] By contrast, John Guillory engages post-Marxist theories of value to illuminate institutional aspects of U.S.–American debates regarding canon formation that an ideological emphasis on minority representation obscures. Transnational migration and German contexts are far removed from Guillory's purview, where cultural capital denotes first and foremost "a problem of access to the means of literary production and consumption" (ix). According to Guillory, turf wars over the literary canon in terms of inclusion *versus* exclusion fail to grasp deep structures of school curricula and their effects on social life. The contents of the canon are not the real issue in such battles, he contends. "The canon debate signifies nothing less than a crisis in the form of cultural capital we call 'literature' " (viii). Guillory aims to clarify the nature of this crisis, in dialogue with canon debates in the United States and post-Marxist theorists such as Bourdieu, by rethinking how economics, aesthetics, and social relations are entangled in institutional processes regulating judgment and access. I foreground only limited aspects of Guillory's argument that shed light on a relevant problem of representation. Notably this concerns cultural capital, a term that Guillory wields with greater conceptual precision than I have done thus far.[48]

At the heart of "the liberal pluralist critique of the canon" Guillory identifies "a confusion between representation in the political sense—the relation of a representative to a constituency—and representation in the rather different sense of the relation between an image and what the image represents" (vii–viii). One can readily argue that the experience of Turkish migration has enjoyed little social capital in Germany and that German readers usually expect literature by authors identified as Turks to represent the experience of migration. Guillory's approach to the conceptual relationship between commodities and works of art indicates that such observations are ill equipped to grasp the deeper cultural significance that the literature of migration does have. Defending Bourdieu's sociology against the charge "that it reduces the cultural field to a reflection of the economic" in spite of its post-Marxist critique of " 'economism,' " Guillory nonetheless finds that Bourdieu's distinction between " 'an economic logic' " within the cultural field and " 'narrowly economic interests' " of the market is insufficient to address the nature of cultural capital (326–327). This always entails an illogical "remainder," which Guillory identifies as "aesthetic experience" (327). His understanding of this remainder stems from his argument that no object, "not even the commodity," can be reduced to exchange value as a universal measure of equivalence (325). From this perspective, the common distinction in political economy between commodities and works of art is singularly misleading, for commercial value and cultural value are as inseparable in social reality as they are distinct. Inspired by Bourdieu, Guillory's rhetoric turns these " 'two faces' of reality" back toward each other where political economy has them facing in opposite directions (326). The crux of the matter, for Guillory, is an ineluctable tension between use value and exchange value.

> The double discourse of value emerged as a way of assimilating the fact that exchange in the market really does function as an epitome of social relations, . . . , but as the site of the objective disharmony of these relations, as the site of the commensuration of the incommensurable values objectified in every object. The "logic of equivalence," according to which every exchange is supposed to be an *equal* exchange, denies the crucial fact revealed in the market, that social relations do not *make sense*. (326)

This brief foray into Guillory's terrain reminds us that the relationship between labor and capital in the literature of migration cannot simply mirror agonal forces of production in a transnational economy late in the twentieth century. For Chow, ethnicity becomes a form of alienated labor, a commodity. If the thingliness of Turkish figures in German life is traded like a commodity indexing equivalence where none exists, then the aesthetic effects of Turkish figures in literary texts yield "a remainder," something out of step with the logic of representation to which cultures of migration are often held. The figural image of migration and what such images represent are not bound to each other by equivalence. This reminder proves especially helpful when we consider Ören's depiction of Ali Itir, a would-be guest worker in Germany who emerges in text as neither a person nor a thing, but a remainder where cultural capital resides.[49]

In those cases where the cultural capital of Turkish migration touches on Cold War scenarios in Germany, as in work by Özdamar and Şenocak yet to be discussed, the reminder is also worth bearing in mind. David Bathrick and Julia Hell argue forcefully that cultural production in East and West Germany cannot be adequately mapped along the agonal axes of "a Cold War mirror logic" (Hell 1997: 6), whereby the socialist East appears as the mirror opposite of the capitalist West.[50] More popular attempts to deal with German–German relations of the Cold War era or their legacy (e.g., Schneider 1983; Drawert) wrestle with and defy this logic as well. Looking beyond German horizons as such, Susan Buck-Morss concludes that the mirror logic of the Cold War elides the latter's reality as "a story of similarities." *Dreamworld and Catastrophe* "interprets cultural developments of the twentieth century within opposed political regimes as variations of a common theme, the utopian dream that industrial modernity could and would provide happiness for the masses" (xiii–xiv).[51] It may seem counterintuitive to turn to "a story of similarities" to avoid the pitfalls of mirror logic where labor and capital are concerned, but such a turn helps us appreciate the cultural capital of migration in a new light, too.

If East and West German cultures were never mirror opposites, then what "remainders" of representation come into play when Turkish figures enter German scenes of a Cold War divide and its aftermath? Many anecdotes circulate about Turks appearing on the periphery of the German–German drama of unification. Petra Fachinger alerts us to a novel by Kerstin Jentzsch, for example, one of the more successful writers in the 1990s to have come from the former GDR. When the protagonist crosses the newly opened border to receive her western "welcome" money, she realizes that the only warm welcome from the West emanates from Turkish "guardian angels" (Fachinger 2001: 41). As one anthropologist notes, "Turks cornered the market on Soviet and East German government and military paraphernalia, which they hawked with great bazaar professionalism . . . on the east side of the Brandenburg Gate, formerly the central symbolic locus of the city's Cold War division" (Jenny White 1997: 766–767, n. 12). By focusing on touching tales of Turkish migration and German scenarios of capitalist reconstruction, Cold War divisions, and national unification under the triumphal sign of capital, the textual commentary here aims beyond the anecdotal to reassess what passes as representation of and on the periphery of German life and culture. To recall another key term adapted from Appadurai, this literature of migration functions as one technology of localization among many in a time of great transition. The labor of imagination it enables reconfigures the cultural capital of migration. Conceits of ethnicity and gender remain central to this enterprise, albeit in surprising ways.

The rest of this chapter turns a disaggregated eye to creative texts published in 1981, 1990, and 1991/1995 by Ören, Özdamar, and Şenocak, respectively. The commentary brings to light isolated aspects of four relatively modest texts, all of which spur critical reflection on the diversified embrace of labor, capital, ethnicity, and gender. By drawing attention to these dimensions of narrative prose by these three authors (among the most important to emerge from the phenomenon of Turkish migration), I hope to demonstrate from yet another perspective how the concept of touching tales opens up interpretive horizons foreclosed by the cultural fable of two worlds. The disaggregated effects of national and transnational frames of reference will likewise be considered. A comparison of gender effects in Özdamar's "Grandfather Tongue," one of the short stories included in her debut volume of 1990, and two essays written by Şenocak in response to German unification and later the fiftieth anniversary of World War II's end in Europe lends itself emblematically to such consideration. By some standards, juxtaposition of these authors reveals a straightforward division of labor or at least orientation. As Özdamar's biography and much of her creative writing indicate, this author is intimately familiar with life and culture in the GDR in ways that no other writer from the realm of Turkish migration can claim. In an interview with Cheesman, on the other hand, Şenocak indicates that his virtually complete lack of attention to the GDR prior to 1989 was characteristic of "the absolute majority" in West Germany (Cheesman and Yeşilada 29). To the extent that the literature of Turkish migration reworks postwar cultures of German memory, one might expect Özdamar and Şenocak to represent the ongoing bifurcation of German interests along a Cold War divide, after the fall of the Wall and through the filter of migration. Because so much of Özdamar's work revolves around women characters and matrilineal motifs, and because so much of Şenocak's work pivots on male figures and patrilineal motifs, it would also be tempting to conclude that these authors represent opposing paradigms or mirror opposites on more than one score.[52] Even a cursory comparison of ethnicity and gender in their work demonstrates that the relationship between labor and capital in the literature of migration is never so clear-cut. No logic of equivalence applies. Despite this study's overall focus on the 1990s, the discussion at this juncture requires a retrospective turn, which revisits the luckless Turkish laborer who figures so centrally in *Please, No Police*.

4

Bitte nix Polizei (1981, or *Please, No Police* in English translation) is an anomaly here, partly because the novella concerning Ali Itir was originally written in Turkish before being translated for German publication.[53] Unlike Nadolny, Özdamar, Şenocak, and Zaimoğlu (but like Dal), Ören does most of his literary writing in Turkish, even when the texts seem aimed primarily at an audience in Germany. As the prototype for a series of novels that Ören subsequently authored under the near Proustian rubric of being "in search of the present," the German version of *Please, No Police* marked the tale's original publication.[54] Additionally, *The Turkish Turn* focuses on transfigurative dimensions of the literature of migration in the 1990s to clarify the historical significance of this cultural turn. Why should *Please, No Police*, first published in 1981, matter here? Answering this question entails recalling the distinction between emblematic subjects, which index structural transformations afoot in the labor of migration, and symbolic figures, which have lost their ability to index the changing sociality of migration and hence acquire the status of anachronism. Earlier I argued that the figure of migrant Turks suspended "between two worlds" is an anachronistic social referent. This is closely related to Levent Soysal's argument about the endless figural reproduction of the *Gastarbeiter* in migration studies (2003). As observed above, the Turkish *Gastarbeiter* is an outdated stereotype and a stock figure in a cultural fable out of sync with an era that nonetheless clings to figure and fable alike. Recalling that the fable of "two worlds" marks an imagined encounter with the material history of migration, one wonders why the male figure of ethnic labor associated with Turks in Germany continues to exert such spectral force in spite of its anachronistic status. Perhaps the popular imagination is simply resistant to change, especially when change comes so rapidly and stereotypes are held so dear. Perhaps figures of the Turkish *Gastarbeiter* hold a place open for unfinished business with an earlier phase of migration history. Or perhaps this ghostly icon performs some other kind of labor than what we have customarily attributed to it as a cipher for capitalist exploitation or ethnic anomie. Reading *Please, No Police* with this third possibility in mind proves worthwhile, for this early text begins to recast in literary form the imaginative terms of cultural labor and capital forged by migration. Such efforts intensify in the 1990s, but Ören's touching tale of Ali Itir and capitalist reconstruction in Germany indicates that there was more to the labor of migration than meets the eye well before unification and globalization loomed large on public horizons. Some critics will object that the proposed reading of *Please, No Police*, which focuses on the original publication in German translation, elides the linguistic subtleties and cultural identity of an author who composes his manuscripts in Turkish. Like Chiellino, I prefer to probe the structures of the literary text as published rather than be guided by categorical presumptions of identity (2000: 391). In scalar terms favored throughout this study, the woeful story of Ali Itir reworks largely German frames of reference as it crafts a tale of postwar reconstruction on the anvil of Turkish migration.

Born in Istanbul in 1939, Ören represents a different generational encounter with national polities, Cold War antagonisms, and transnational migration from younger writers such as Şenocak and Zaimoğlu without representing the guest worker experience. Although the author characterizes his life in Germany as a "private exile" (a volume of poetry published in 1977 and lectures on aesthetics in 1999 bear this title), his decision to move to West Berlin in 1969 predates the military coups d'état of 1971 and 1980, which devastated the Turkish left and prompted many intellectuals to seek refuge in Germany.[55] Ören cites the provincialization of Istanbul resulting from domestic migration in the 1950s and 1960s as one motivation for his move (1999a: 9–11, 17–20, 34–35; Loentz 104). Between 1959 and 1969 the fledgling author concentrated on acting and dramaturgy, mostly in Istanbul, but also in Frankfurt on the Main and West Berlin. Here Ören participated in ultimately unsuccessful efforts to establish a theatrical troupe for Turkish laborers in the mid-1960s after having performed compulsory military service in Ankara (Hohoff and Ackermann 1; Chin 59; Suhr 1990: 228). Renewed theatrical work in Istanbul as of 1966 and marriage to a German in West Berlin made for frequent sojourns in both cities. The permanent change of residence in 1969 brought occasional stints as an industrial laborer in addition to scattered jobs in restaurants and theater. Associated with a German group promoting workers' literature in the early 1970s, Ören enjoyed some success as a literary author in Germany in 1973, when the first prose poem of his "Berlin Trilogy" was published.[56] This "mosaic of working-class experience" (Moray McGowan 2000a) depicting the entangled lives of Turkish migrants and German laborers in the Berlin neighborhood of Kreuzberg, known as Little Istanbul, was so well received that a major media station adapted it for television. According to Chin, this led the same station (*Sender Freies Berlin*) to hire Ören in 1974 to edit "a thirty-minute daily news and cultural radio program, the first Turkish-language broadcast of any kind in the Federal Republic" (63).[57] Since 1996 Ören has served as the editor-in-chief of this station's expanded Turkish program (Hohoff and Ackermann 1).[58] His novels, short stories, and poems are now published mostly in German and Turkish, with some translations available in English and Dutch (Chiellino 2000: 466). Known as "a German author," "a Turkish writer in Germany," and "a German writer who lives in Berlin and writes in the Turkish language" (Hohoff and Ackermann 2; Loentz 99; Ören 1999a: 51–52), Ören was the first recipient, in 1985, of the Adelbert von Chamisso Prize for German literature. Never involved in publishing enterprises that formally gave rise to "guest worker literature" in the 1980s (Biondi and Schami; Taufiq), this author is publicly perceived in Germany as the emblematic "protagonist" of that phenomenon (Hohoff and Ackermann 2–6; Suhr 1990: 226; Heinze 62). This has something to do with the thingliness ascribed to Turkish figures in the public sphere, but it also has something to do with how one understands the relationship between labor and ethnicity in Ören's touching tales of class history.

Scholars find that an "essentially Marxist perspective" (Moray McGowan 2001: 297) early on gradually yields to emphasis on ethnic identity and multiculturalism (Gott 174–201; Chin 2002: 45–46).[59] By some accounts, the novels "in search of the present" signal "the exhaustion" of Ören's original political project (Moray McGowan 2000a) or an abandonment of realism in favor of fantastically fluid identities (Ackermann 1997; Hohoff and Ackermann 10). Most scholars resort to anthropomorphic conceits of identity to argue for one interpretation or another regarding a given text or the writer's oeuvre. Remarks on *Please, No Police* and its pitiful protagonist sometimes stand in for an evaluation of Ören's contributions to the interpersonal culture of migration at large. For Yüksel Pazarkaya, "the identity question" is central to Ören's depiction of life "between two worlds," and Ali Itir occupies the "no-man's-land" dividing them (1986: 19–20). Ackermann echoes this view when she calls Ali Itir a typical victim of labor migration and the novella "exemplary" in its "realist depiction of a migrant's fate" (1997: 21). Susan C. Anderson wisely points instead to "the need for more creative ways of imagining group identities in multicultural German society" (155), but still focuses on identity debates to argue that *Please, No Police* undermines absolute precepts of difference or similarity where Germans and Turks are concerned.[60] According to Mani, the novella seeks "to render transparent the economic factors that . . . dominate the ideology of xenophobia," whereas the novel *Berlin Savignyplatz* (1993/1995) looks back critically at the earlier text to underscore "the ephemeral and phantasmagoric nature of identity" (2002: 118, 120). By Chin's reckoning, Ören's labors from the early 1970s into the early 1980s "demonstrated a fundamental rethinking of what constituted German identity" (46). Others are inclined to see a search for personal identity as central to the writer's work whether the writing is considered subjectively authentic or radically antirealist (see Hohoff and Ackermann 5, 10 for both views in one article). Several scholars make the important observation that stories of Turkish and German laborers converge in *Please, No Police* (Susan Anderson 149; Şölçün 1992: 25; Hohoff and Ackermann 6; Mani 2002: 116). But when one reads the touch of these tales through an anthropomorphic filter alone, the novella is reduced to "the pyschogram of a neighborhood that has lost its humanity" (Hohoff and Ackermann 7; see also Anderson 149) and Ali Itir to a human victim of social circumstance: "homeless, isolated, and lost" (Suhr 1990: 232; see also Şölçün 1992: 29; Ackermann 1997: 19; Mani 2002: 119). In these approaches we recognize shades of Frisch's conundrum. Competing regimes of incorporation are clearly at stake in the novella and its reception, but conceptual confusion prevails when one tries to read Ali Itir as a human being subjected to the cruel constraints of economic migration. How else might we read this literary figure of ethnic labor as an emblematic subject—and specter—of late-twentieth-century migration?[61]

In many ways, Ali Itir fits the male mold of Turkish abjection discussed above. Driven by economic need to migrate to Istanbul and then Berlin, the central character in *Please, No Police* is desperate for work in December 1973 after a week of fruitless searching. Unable to communicate effectively with Germans or even other Turks, including the married relatives who shelter him in their kitchen, he is emotionally bereft. Ever fearful of German police and their dogs, he wants only to work so that he may realize his dream of personhood in Germany. When he lands an odd job shoveling snow off a factory courtyard, he ecstatically envisions extended employment, if only the weather cooperates. Laid low by human interventions, this migrant laborer is accused of causing the death of a German man and raping a German woman in the course of the story, which concludes with the Turk's disappearance. Although the time of narration is otherwise confined to a single day, the final chapter is set eleven days later and describes police attempts to identify a corpse found in one of Berlin's more famous canals.[62] Driving through Kreuzberg with a loudspeaker, the police display a " 'phantom image' " of the person found and a mannequin dressed in the clothes of the dead man, " 'presumably a Turk' " and possibly the " 'victim of a crime' " (1983: 87; 1992: 128–129). The young woman who had filed rape charges against an unidentified Turkish assailant claims to recognize the man in the "display dummy," but no one believes her (1992: 128).[63] Though Ali Itir resurfaces in various guises in Ören's novel series, his sudden erasure is left unclarified by the novella. This notwithstanding, scholars are in striking disagreement as to whether the story's ending is open (Rösch 107; Şölçün 1992: 28; Susan C. Anderson 156, n. 11; Mani 2002: 117) or closed (Ackermann 1997: 21; Suhr 1990: 232). For some inclined to read Ali Itir as a pathetic cipher of abjection, a migrant laborer trapped in a downward spiral of bad luck and inhuman conditions, suicide seems a self-evident conclusion (Suhr 1990: 232; Hohoff and Ackermann 7).[64] The abject effects of labor migration come full circle here. What is wrong with this picture?

Economic motifs are key to *Please, No Police* (Mani 2002: 118). Ali Itir wants desperately to earn hard cash as a means to acquire personhood, to leave behind his status as "a nobody" (Ören 1992: 25; Ackermann 1997: 19;

Loentz 100). This is another way of saying that this figure, as a character, lacks capital in any form except for the small amount of money he earns shoveling snow. Peppered with words from a semantic field linking "non-person," "person," "personality," "personnel office," and "personal identity card," the text underscores this thematic link between money, personhood, and the symbolic legitimacy accruing to those who possess them.[65] Brigitte Gramke is the young German who accuses the unidentified foreigner of raping her, and she too is driven by a desire for symbolic capital. Although she earns something as a hairdresser's apprentice, she imagines she could earn more by prostituting herself on the sly, as her older sister does, and thus gain the personal stature her parents and boyfriend deny her. Humiliated by an unsuccessful attempt to be accepted as a sex worker at a brothel, Brigitte tries her luck with Ali, whom she approaches on the street and persuades to take her to his relatives' apartment, where the rape occurs and no money changes hands. Unlike this act, later documented in police protocols in spite of "a few things that don't match up" in the telling (1983: 79; 1992: 118), another rape of pivotal importance to this story of migration goes unreported, and this rape too is narrated in reference to an economy of labor. During the Allied occupation following World War II, Brigitte's mother had belonged to those legendary "women of rubble" whose raw physical labor cleared the ruins of war to make way for reconstruction. This was paid work, which she and other women needed to survive. Events that transpire in December 1973 prompt Mrs. Gramke to recall, but only to herself through flashbacks, how the German man who had been appointed the women's crew boss traded sugar and cigarettes for sexual favors and sometimes raped members of his crew in dark cellar ruins too. Never a willing trader in this economy, Mrs. Gramke recalls her rape at Ernst Kutte's hands. "I wanted to scream, but I couldn't get a sound out. Defending myself was senseless anyway, he was stronger and I needed work and vouchers for food rations" (1983: 57; 1992: 84).

All these economies of labor, violence, and legitimacy converge in the figure of Kutte in 1973. Now Mrs. Gramke's elderly neighbor, the former crew boss walks his dog on a snowy street early in the morning. When he slips and falls, unable to right himself, Mrs. Gramke recognizes his plight but "in a strange mood of revenge" leaves him be, hoping that " 'the swine' " will freeze to death (1983: 11; 1992: 10). By the time Ali Itir happens upon the injured man, Kutte is "a whining heap of misery out of fear and pain," his tears "like frozen chickpeas" (1983: 37; 1992: 53). Although the foreign laborer wants to help, fear overwhelms him when he hears "police" from Kutte's lips and other people starting to gather around. (The title of the novella derives from this.) Able to flee the belated scene of a crime he did not commit, the Turk is nonetheless perceived by German bystanders and gossips as having beaten up an old man, who dies as a result of whatever transpired, a "murder" victim of sorts.[66] These converging story lines of material need and ethical ambiguity may highlight, as Mani and Anderson propose, a bedrock of shared humanity binding Germans and Turks together more than any differences drive them apart.[67] Such readings are compatible with indictments of capitalism and xenophobia as social systems depriving individuals of their basic humanity. In a different analytic register I argue instead that the textual economy of *Please, No Police* hinges on abstract functions accruing to Ali Itir as a "non-person."[68] Some will see his fate as tragic because this migrant laborer remains "a nobody" without any form of capital. This perception shifts once we recognize that Ali Itir—as a literary figure of ethnic labor—may best be understood as a commodity. This figure's capacity to index the cultural capital of migration pivots on this distinction.

To the degree that ethnicity becomes a form of alienated labor under capitalist conditions late in the twentieth century, ethnicity is a commodity indexing abstract social relations, as Chow demonstrates. But not even commodities, Guillory tells us, can be reduced to exchange value as a universal measure of equivalence, for something illogical remains. Cultural capital is Guillory's term for this remainder, which points to ways in which the commensurability of economic value is befuddled by the incommensurability of social relations. The aesthetic effects of Turkish figures in literature at times yield such a remainder, something out of step with the logic of representation to which cultures of migration are usually held. No text lends itself more emphatically to such a contrapuntal reading than *Please, No Police*, which many readers find unquestionably realist in its representation of working-class history and labor migration. There are numerous allusions in the text to human beings performing various types of labor. Mrs. Gramke and a Turkish woman clean office buildings for a living, and Mr. Gramke went from lucrative tailoring to " 'rationalized' " ironing before being replaced by unskilled laborers (1983: 60; 1992: 88). Vegetable vendors, street cleaners, trash collectors, and sex workers people this story in lesser roles as well. What labor falls to the ethnic figure of Ali Itir as a functional commodity rather than a would-be person and guest worker? As a character, this figure portrays his labors as anything but alienating, for he sees an immediate relationship between money to be earned and dreams to be realized. On a thematic level this underscores market principles and ideologies of personhood, though the migrant's dreams dissolve predictably into nightmares instead. Yet this figure of ethnicity falls between the cracks on at least three additional levels.

First, Ali Itir is not actually a guest worker at all. Deemed medically unfit to participate in the recruitment program, he has entered the Federal

Republic on a tourist visa and resides there, precariously, as an illegal alien. His presence in Germany is both elicited and proscribed by government policy.[69] Holder of a valid Turkish passport, he can claim personhood on grounds of citizenship. This is important because his figural role in the narrative turns on the uncertain status of the labor Ali Itir performs, not the personhood he desires.[70] Second, because of his illegal status, Ali Itir circulates in the novella as no mere commodity but as contraband. He is explicitly interpellated as such when a Turkish leftist tries to explain how legally traded goods become " 'contraband' " (*Schmuggelware*) when " 'individual persons' " attempt to deal in commerce otherwise handled by the state. " 'You are contraband (*Schwarzmarktware*),' " the orator declares with more ardor than efficacy (1983: 23; 1992: 30–31).[71] Disappointed that this educated person has not really helped him, Ali Itir nonetheless receives his proper designation in this scene. Dipesh Chakrabarty's assessment of the sublation of difference in commodities is helpful here. "Commodity exchange is about exchanging things that are different in their histories, material properties, and uses. Yet the commodity form, intrinsically, is supposed to make differences—however material they may be—immaterial for the purpose of exchange. The commodity form does not as such negate difference but holds it in suspension so that we can exchange things as different from one another as beds and houses" (2000b: 655; see also 2000a: 51). Difference is neither "external to capital" nor "subsumed" by it (2000b: 671; see also 2000a: 70). In Guillory's terms something illogical is suspended in cultural capital, which cannot be grasped in terms of equivalence. The figure of Ali Itir indexes this remainder, a network of relations that are not subject to open trade or direct representation precisely because no equivalence applies. Despite decoy exchanges in *Please, No Police*—Ali Itir receives day wages and buys socks, for example—the touching tales at issue in the novella are not narrated in a register of exchange. (Ali Itir and Brigitte Gramke's central attempt to engage in exchange also fails miserably.) There are no mirror opposites here. As an indexical figure in reference to which stories that don't quite "match up" can nonetheless be articulated, Ali Itir falls between the cracks of representation on yet a third level.

Unlike the self-confessional genres that Chow targets for critique, and unlike most of the texts addressed here, *Please, No Police* proceeds mostly by third-person narration, multiple focalization, interior monologues, and reported discourse. The sole exception occurs almost immediately, when the voice of narration speaks as an "I" to propose of a flower in a dream: "I do not believe that the shape and species of flower are so important" (1983: 5; 1992: 1). This seems only a teaser, since the narrator never speaks as an "I" again. This "I" is neither omniscient by grand abstraction nor identifiable by anthropomorphic attributes. Though provided with many anthropomorphic features by contrast, Ali Itir teeters precariously between the first-person medium of interior monologues and the third-person status of objectified narration.[72] The precariousness of his role as person or thing is exacerbated when he disappears altogether, only to be resurrected (and this only perhaps) as a " 'phantom image,' " a "display dummy" with which police hope to reconstruct lived circumstances resulting in death. The text's central conceit of lived histories brought to a standstill—frozen or suspended in matter—effectively culminates in this phantom image, which literally displaces Ali Itir as an individualized character from the narrative. It is *as if* he had disappeared. Other rhetorical figures drawn in keeping with this central conceit include the still ambulatory Kutte as a wooden marionette, Brigitte's boyfriend as a built monument, Mrs. Gramke as a "woman of rubble" in a group photo with her crew boss, and "a huge plastic doll in a wedding gown" in the bedroom where the disastrous encounter with Ali Itir occurs (1983: 10, 18, 68, 77; 1992: 9, 22, 101, 114).[73] Lived histories that crystallize into frozen images in this winter landscape are suspended in tears that look to Ali "like frozen chickpeas" and the ice "frozen solid" that brings Kutte to ruin (1983: 37, 9; 1992: 53, 7). "It looked as though the entire neighborhood had frozen and held its breath from so much cold" (1983: 25; 1992: 33).[74]

Amidst so many frozen and suspended histories of desire, shame, fear, rage, and transgression, one crucial image of life brought to a standstill nearly leaps off the page with renewed vitality. Mrs. Gramke recalls being raped by her crew boss in the ruined cellar through the medium of interior monologue. Where we might expect a forceful image of something frozen, we read, "Together we fell onto something soft." The woman's interior monologue opens up into an external perspective on this scene by means of indirect discourse and reported speech. Only from this external perspective can we identify this "something soft" and understand how it can be simultaneously dead and alive.

> Suddenly a few kids were standing at the entrance, I heard a boy with a deep voice say that he knew where the dead horse was, and another boy screamed: "There it is, up ahead, it's even moving." The kids ran out of the cellar screaming, and the boy with the deep voice called after them: "You dummies, you know a dead horse doesn't move!" (1983: 57; 1992: 84)

As a genre the novella famously "flourished in Germany more than anywhere else," and J. W. v. Goethe's definition of its structural cornerstone still holds, for a novella turns on a mysterious event that is " 'unheard of' " but takes place nonetheless, something that takes the reader by surprise but follows from what has been recounted (Cuddon 641–642). The dead horse that moves qualifies as such an event, and Ören's novella pointedly draws our attention to the illogical status of something that has nonetheless transpired. Other mysterious events (e.g., Ali Itir's disappearance and Kutte's demise) are weighted more heavily in terms of plot, but the dead horse that moves is emblematic of the indexical economy on which *Please, No Police* hinges. The equine figure of life in death does not represent the rape but gestures toward it, and only a disaggregated voice of narration alerts us to the gesture at all. The story of this primal violation under the guise of capitalist reconstruction is not recounted as authentic experience, but as a relational nexus of illogical remainders. If Kutte and his victim fall onto something soft in a bombed-out cellar, things have apparently hardened considerably by the time Ali Itir enters the scene. No equine corpse points to social relations that don't quite add up in 1973. This indexical labor falls instead to Ali Itir as an ethnic commodity, a phantom image alerting us early on to the cultural capital of Turkish migration.

As Sargut Şölçün observes, the main story lines involving Ali Itir and the Gramke family converge in two pivotal scenes, Kutte lying on the street and Brigitte lying on a bed (Şölçün 1992: 26–27). How are these scenes and story lines related? Do they converge in equivalence after all, or do these tales of Turkish migration and German reconstruction touch in some other way? Much speaks for convergence in the first sense, since histories of economic need and sexual transgression appear encoded in street and bedroom alike. Both women are raped and both men portrayed as rapists. Mrs. Gramke is partly responsible for Kutte's death, and her daughter is partly responsible for Ali Itir's disappearance. Both women conceal the truth about their relationships with these men from others, Brigitte by lying to the police, and her mother by purchasing a funeral wreath for Kutte, for which she plans to prepare a nice ribbon that reads: "*To our dear neighbor, a final farewell*" (1983: 86; 1992: 127). As the actual turning point in the novella, the violent transaction between the hairdresser's apprentice and the illegal alien stems initially from a reversal of fortune for both. Ali Itir can respond to Brigitte's proposition only because he has just been paid and envisions himself en route to personhood, and the young woman approaches him only because her efforts to achieve personhood have been spurned by organized sex workers. Most important, Ali Itir utters the title phrase when he tries to silence both the fallen man and the frightened woman. What then speaks to anything but a mirroring of equivalent experiences?

The answer lies in the relationship between events that are narrated and figures in reference to which such narration becomes possible. Ali Itir's role as a phantom image is crucial here too. As the narrator predicts, the young woman will remain ill at ease, even after reporting her assault to the police, "because even the recording of an event (*Tathergang*) is not enough to produce an offender (*Täter*)" (1983: 81; 1992: 121).[75] Yet Ali Itir's situation is not to be envied, the narrator elaborates. "Although he had a passport and thus officially existed, he did not exist after all, on the other hand, because as an illegal, he did not officially exist. He existed only in the police report: as an unidentified offender" (1983: 83; 1992: 123). The illegal alien's status as a nonentity is underscored earlier in the text when his relatives and their building manager confirm for police that only registered residents in fact live in the Turks' apartment. This refrain denoting a course of action with no identifiable agent is a bit like the "little stick man" in *Kanak Sprak*, circumscribing a presence where a body used to be. Whereas Zaimoğlu relies on an anthropomorphic iconography of presence, Ören favors an indexical phantom instead. If Brigitte's police report yields an event without an agent, her mother's story has an offending agent who goes undetected because the rape is never reported. The case of the daughter seems, nearly exactly, the mirror opposite of the mother's. Yet Mrs. Gramke's story goes unreported only to legal authorities and those with whom she cultivates social relations in the textual world. Readers are privy to what transpires in the darkness of cellar ruins. Our access to this course of events is enabled in the first instance by an equine figure that draws our attention to something beside itself. At greater remove from the event, the phantom figure of migrant labor assumes this structural function in the narrative overall.

In a chain of indirect references this phantom figure keeps pointing elsewhere, to events and relations that never resolve into equivalent images. Ören's configuration of a would-be guest worker indexes frozen histories of crime, shame, exploitation, fear, anger, and revenge and restores movement to them. Not unlike Nadolny's Selim in this regard, Ali Itir functions as a rhetorical figure in reference to which an untellable German story of capitalist reconstruction can be told, all logical expectations to the contrary. This is the cultural capital of Turkish migration to which Ören draws our attention as early as 1981. While conceits of ethnicity, gender, and sexuality enable the telling of this tale, Ali Itir is best understood as a strategic nexus where imaginative effects of migration only appear to congeal into something resembling a person. This emblematic conjunction manifests as a specter of capitalism, which haunts a national history and a globalized economy in disaggregated ways. Writing on "post-fascist authorship" in Germany, Hell observes that the "spectral histories" of West and East Germany pivot on an obsession with the masculinity and crimes of German fathers, especially regarding the Holocaust (2003: 15). Cut from a different cloth, *Please, No Police* weaves a spectral tale of complex social histories that only appear tailor-made for the men and women compelled to wear them. Male and female, German and Turk, such characters are display dummies in which the hopes and fears of a changing transnational economy of *ethnos* are suspended, as if on ice.

5

In her contribution to *The Postnational Self* Benhabib draws attention to a geopolitical rhetoric that made communism appear "Oriental."

> Whereas once the term *east*, or the *Orient*, would have been reserved for that border which separated Europe from the Ottoman Empire, after 1945 and the division of Germany, the line separating "east" from "west" ran through the heart of Europe, that is, the city of Berlin. The communist regimes of Europe became, oddly enough, part of the Orient; "Eastern Europe" designated differences in types of political regime by making communism appear as part of "them," the East, as opposed to "us," "the free West." (2002a: 89)

While capitalist and communist discourses of "Oriental" and "Asiatic" modes of social production have a long and checkered history, Benhabib's apt synopsis of European halves conjured by Cold War rhetoric sets any ostensible mirror logic, once again, spinning. This chapter concludes with a discussion of Özdamar's "Grandfather Tongue"—a short story set in Berlin just prior to unification—and two essays by Şenocak—one reflecting lyrically on the effects of unification in 1991 and one commemorating the end of World War II from a migrant's viewpoint in 1995—to highlight the variegated means by which the literature of migration reconfigures the cultural capital of a Turkish presence in Germany in the 1990s. If such labors revolve around displays of affect by the foreign woman who narrates Özdamar's tongue story in the first person, and around patrilineal legacies or masculinist affinities in Şenocak's essays, they are not enabled by conceits of gender and ethnicity that could readily be resolved into flip sides of a coin or two faces in a mirror where opposites converge. Touching tales of Turkish migration yield some surprising "remainders" here too.

Huyssen remarks "the affinity of diasporic memory to the structure of memory itself"—"always based on temporal displacement between the act of remembrance and the content of that which is remembered, an act of *recherche* rather than recuperation" (2003a: 152).[76] To the degree that diaspora studies focus one-sidedly "on loss rather than on renewal," however, they are ill equipped in Huyssen's view to grasp how a diasporic culture actively engages "the majority culture within which it operates" (153–154). This caution is especially warranted if we consider that literatures of migration are not necessarily diasporic. Enabled by the unanticipated collapse of the Cold War, German unification did not inaugurate a literary commingling of Turkish and German remembrances, as early texts by Ören and Dal demonstrate, but such entanglements intensified in the wake of geopolitical upheaval in 1989. Even here, however, we are mistaken if we imagine that acts of recollection in the literature of migration are always or only about the past. If lived histories suspended in figural matter are brought to life by the narration of touching tales in *Please, No Police*, such literary "re-collections" also labor to imagine a post-ethnic future shared by Germans and Turks among them.[77] This too marks a scalar enterprise delineating the here and now of transnational migration against the grain of predominantly national frames of reference.

The intergenerational tongue stories included in Özdamar's debut publication of 1990 ("Mother Tongue" and "Grandfather Tongue") have been discussed by other scholars in some detail (see especially Wierschke 1996, 1997; Breger 1999; Seyhan 2001; Konuk 2001; Boa; Neubert; Begemann; Bayazitoğlu; Littler; Bird; and Brandt 2003, 2004).[78] The discussion here makes no pretense of doing even partial justice to the work of these scholars but aims to illuminate some facets of "Grandfather Tongue" that have received virtually no critical attention to date, facets that bear nonetheless on the labor and capital of migration. By and large, analyses of the tongue stories have focused on identity, embodiment, language, and tradition as leitmotifs and cornerstones of narrative reflections on national histories or ethnic paradigms.[79] Seyhan cites Benedict Anderson on the function of mother tongues. " 'Through that language, encountered at mother's knee and parted with only at the grave,' as Anderson writes in *Imagined Communities*, 'pasts are restored, fellowships are imagined, and futures dreamed' " (Seyhan 2001: 144; Anderson 1991: 154). The post-ethnic future toward which much of the literature of migration gestures cannot be dreamed in the mother tongue as Anderson conceives it. Likening Özdamar to "many a bilingual writer," Seyhan remarks on splits and chasms that the language of migration crosses when Özdamar, who writes in German, "re-members the mother tongue in translation" (144). Geopolitical fissures inscribed in a still divided Berlin mark the setting for the tongue stories so transparently that the mirror logic of the Cold War appears readily at hand. The Turkish woman who narrates "Grandfather Tongue" lives in East Berlin, repeatedly crossing the border into West Berlin to make contact with a pre-republican Turkish past that Atatürk's sweeping language reforms of the 1920s, directed largely against Arabic, Persian, Muslim, and Ottoman influences, had effectively obliterated.[80] Although these reforms played a key role in establishing the national identity of modern Turkey, as is well known, they might also be situated in a transnational context of alphabet reform. This broader frame of reference encompasses not only the capitalist west, which Turkey under Atatürk sought to emulate culturally, but also the communist east, to which many Turks had a political aversion and an ethnic affinity. Various alphabet reforms in the Soviet Union in the 1920s and 1930s likewise involved the adoption of a Latin script to minimize Muslim influence in the Turkic republics of the Soviet Union and subsequently, at Stalin's behest, the adoption of Cyrillic script to weaken Turkey's potential influence on Turkic peoples living under communist rule (Zürcher 196–197; Frantz; Michael G. Smith 125; Grenoble 54). The contact that Özdamar's narrator establishes in West Berlin with the Turkish nation's pre-republican past takes the form of a heterosexual romance with Ibni Abdullah, a love story cast as lessons in the forbidden language of Arabic.[81] Myriad splits and couplings, anthropomorphic and otherwise, are thematically explicit and narratologically manifest in "Grandfather Tongue."[82] Yet no agonal pairs resolve into equivalence in Özdamar's prose.

Frequent references to a divided Berlin in the tongue stories can be read as an exilic background for weightier tensions informing Turkish memories of national trauma. Speaking concurrently of Özdamar and Gloria Anzaldúa as writers giving voice to life in the borderlands of contemporary culture, Seyhan astutely assesses the aesthetic innovations of "Grandfather Tongue" in this vein.

> Image, metaphor, and metonymy re-member bodies of language, culture and their inhabitants dismembered by imperialism, war, conquest, colonization, poverty, and violence. They not only restore them . . . to memory but also invest them with a kind of material reality. Names, identities, and histories that expired along with passports and visas can now be brought back to life only through the potent medicines of memory: language, image, script. (121)

When the script of history lies "forgotten" in Turkey, Seyhan continues, Özdamar configures "easier access to the study of Arabic in Germany" as an agent of healing; in Turkey the narrator's "desire to reclaim her 'grandfather tongue' could be construed as a reactionary gesture" out of step with the national ideology of laicism (121–122). Like Seyhan, Kader Konuk argues that Özdamar articulates a Turkish "countermemory" in Germany, unsettling fixed concepts of German identity as well (Seyhan 1996c, 2001; Konuk 1999, 2001; see also Wierschke 1996; Frölich). The woman who narrates "Grandfather Tongue" seeks refuge in East Berlin and Arabic lessons in West Berlin after having been treated like a communist in Turkey, (Konuk 2001: 87), so multiple counter-narratives are evidently at stake. At odds with Seyhan and closer to Konuk, Margaret Littler suggests that "Grandfather Tongue" entails, "not a restoration of plenitude, but an acceptance of ambivalent and provisional identifications" vis-à-vis narratives of national belonging in Turkey and Germany alike (230).[83] Stephanie Bird contends that both tongue stories "insist upon the radical reappraisal of tradition through its decontextualization" (158).

For many readers, an apparent aversion to polar opposites in Özdamar's prose is tied to constructs of identity as necessarily performative, hybrid, fluid, contingent, multiple, and the like (see Wierschke 1997: 188; Konuk 2001; Bayazitoğlu 111–112; Littler 226; and Bird 158). Bird observes how critics agree "that the relationship established between identity and language in these stories is such that neither Turkish nor German identity is privileged," but draws our attention to "Özdamar's active exploration of specific subject positions" as an analytical corrective to too much fluidity (161). Bird makes the important observation that something German inheres in the Turkish voice of narration, but the conclusion she draws regarding ethnicity sounds a familiar note: "the unavoidable implication is that German identity itself is unstable, incoherent and *ethnic*," that is to say, not merely a neutral value against which ethnicity could be "measured" (163). Littler and Bird favor the trope of palimpsests of identity where I would stress touching tales of labor and capital instead.[84] Ahmet Bayazitoğlu emphasizes hybrid constellations of identity in Özdamar's prose overall but alerts us to Arabic, in Turkey and this literary context, as at once "a ubiquitous presence and a locus of estrangement" (109). This phrasing is fortuitous in a discussion of ethnicity as commodity, a form of alienated labor, to recall Chow. To the degree that social relations and lived histories appear suspended in capitalist commodities—and to the extent that cultural capital indexes social relations that do not add up, as Guillory clarifies—identity is an illusion, an anthropomorphic display dummy. Rather than focusing on the use of Arabic and Turkish in "Grandfather Tongue" to highlight the text's interventions into national narratives and ethnic paradigms of identity, as others have done, I shall discuss only two aspects of Özdamar's literary diction in this tongue story: an untagged invocation of Friedrich Hölderlin, a German *Dichter* if ever there was one, and a colorful pun involving Islam, communism, and illogical remainders.[85] Attending to such details reveals how the imaginative labor and cultural capital of "Grandfather Tongue" exceed national categories of identity and even transnational frames of reference generally brought to bear on literatures of migration presumed to represent the experience of ethnicity.

A counterintuitive focus on a citational allusion to the high canon of German poetry demonstrates how a decidedly national frame of reference—in this case, German rather than Turkish—continues to matter in the literature of migration and is at the same time reconfigured. Özdamar's literary configuration of divided sites and split acts of remembrance in the tongue stories can be read as a complex locus of suspended German memory brought to life. If "Grandfather Tongue" incorporates the divided scene of modern Germany's most emblematic city into splintered recollections of a taboo Turkish past, what additional labors of imagination does the voice of migrant narration perform? The refracted perspective of the Turkish "I" is articulated as a form of German memory work, in this instance, through affect rather than reflection in either sense of the term. This is partly a question of evolving literary traditions. Özdamar's fascination with Brecht is well known, and many of her texts explicitly conjure the legendary German and Marxist playwright as a kind of Turkish muse. In "Grandfather Tongue" he figures as a statue, which the narrator visits in a little park outside East Berlin's premier theater, which Brecht, having returned from exile in 1948, directed until his death in 1956. Though never named in the textual world, by contrast, Hölderlin haunts the text like a faint but distinct sound or breath of air. Friends of the narrating persona watch film clips from 1936 depicting two young couples at play. Craig Thomas's English translation reads: "they are on vacation on the banks of a river, flags of the period are hanging in the small city, crackling at the City Hall. There are no other people in the streets, the four of them eat, drink, throw each other into the river. My friends said, 'Oh, those 1930s aluminium [sic] cups'" (1994: 23). This obscures an important verb ascribed to the Nazi flags hanging from the town hall. In the Thomas translation these flags can be heard "crackling." In Özdamar's German the Nazi flags in the film "clatter" or "clash" rather than "crackle." The verb used is *klirren*, which connotes the acoustic effects of something that shatters, such as glass, or something metallic that clashes, such as arms of opponents on the battlefield. The young couples, the film scenes, and the friends' responses to these images thus have a different valence in the original (1990: 18).

The narrating persona hears the voice bespeaking nostalgia for aluminum cups from the 1930s "as an echo" (1990: 18; 1994: 23). This echo reverberates in her consciousness, followed by pains and fever that wrack the Turkish spectator's body. While her friends respond to what they see with speech, her responses to this multifaceted scene are registered with other senses. Split subjectivities and refracted memories converge and diverge in this Turkish persona, positioned narratologically as a locus of German remembrance nonidentical with itself. The Nazi past is recollected or "re-incorporated" in this scene, together with its nostalgic erasure in the German present of a divided Berlin. Remembrance and erasure both are inscribed in the figural image of the migrant narrator, who implicitly becomes a kind of "room in which script takes place" (*Schriftzimmer*), a designation that the text otherwise reserves for Ibni Abdullah's study, where lessons in love and Arabic take place. Claudia Breger observes that this scene of inscription marks precisely the moment when the Turkish lover realizes that Ibni Abdullah has virtually entered her body as well. The voice of narration then tells us, "I walked around for a month with Ibni Abdullah inside my body, in both Berlins" (1990: 24; 1994: 19). In narrative terms the figure by means of which the migrant woman hopes to re-collect her Turkish past, beyond taboo, is thus "tied" to German scenes of postfascist remembrance (Breger 1999: 38). How does the unmarked Hölderlin citation figure into this?

The reference to *Fahnen* that *klirren* in Özdamar's German wording can only be an allusion to Hölderlin's "Hälfte des Lebens" (Hölderlin 236). The famous title of the great poet's hymn from circa 1800 has alternately been translated as "The Middle of Life" (Hamburger) or "Half of Life" (Constantine). The *Fahnen* that *klirren* or shatter with "clatter" are customarily rendered as metal "[w]eathercocks" (Hamburger) or "weathervanes" (Constantine), that is, as the *Wetterfahnen* (literally: weather flags or indicators) that the abbreviated *Fahnen* would have implied colloquially.[86] In Özdamar's appropriation of Hölderlin's diction, the Turkish narrator describes what she sees while observing her friends watch German home movies from 1936. Two young men and two young women, two couples of some sort, vacation by a river, "flags of the period are hanging in the small city, crackling at the City Hall"—"in der kleinen Stadt hängen Fahnen von damals, klirren am Rathaus." These *Fahnen* that hang from the town hall in 1936 are clearly not metal weathervanes but Nazi flags that "clatter" in the wind. The subtle transposition of a canonical semantic coupling (*Fahnen* and *klirren*) yields a jarring impression for the informed reader, perhaps akin to the echo that wracks the narrator's figural body with affect.[87] The meaning of *klirren* heightens this impression, and the Turkish character also appears subjectively split, emotionally divided. What I want to stress, however, are more abstract functions of the Turkish narrator, who syntactically re-members the Nazi past and re-marks its erasure in the nostalgic scene of a divided Berlin, all the while re-membering the German literary canon as well. This is a strategic nexus of affect where newly commemorative labors are enabled. The friends watching film clips from the Third Reich express only nostalgia for the aluminum cups of the time. This nostalgia marks the friends as German. It is the Turkish body that registers this German nostalgia "as an echo," registering its incorporated presence with fever and pain. Özdamar's transposition of Hölderlin's distinctive coupling of *Fahnen* and *klirren* thus marks a translation from German into German, so to speak, via the figure of migration.[88] But affective form and poetic language conspire to animate the illogical remainders of histories suspended in things—oh, those aluminum cups! This is no longer about capitalist or even ethnic commodities as such. Beyond this, the text draws breath from what shimmers and resounds intangibly in the Cold War as a lived phenomenon rather than an ideological matrix. The affective labors of the Turkish woman who narrates "Grandfather Tongue" are anything but naïve. If one associates subjectivity with identity formation, they are possibly not even subjective attributes at all.[89] Abstract patterns and literary conceits of halving, dividing, coupling, and re-membering in this touching tale are filtered through enlivening affects not properly divisible by two. Ascribed to an adult female as a figural person, they effectively demarcate a hyperactive relay where national remainders circulate in newly intelligible and interactive frames of reference.

Uncharacteristically for the literature of Turkish migration, "Grandfather Tongue" explicitly establishes Islam and the Qur'an as pivotal figures of reference in the narrative. Sacred script becomes the means by which the Turkish woman in Germany learns her Arabic letters and articulates her intense longing, for a Turkish history beyond taboo and an Arab lover. As Bayazitoğlu observes, Arabic has both a political and religious valence in the text. "By evincing interest in the language of the past that is the rhetorical enemy of Kemalism, the Turkish woman breaks the covenant of the republican daughter with the Kemalist father," and Arabic simultaneously appears as "the language of the literal word of God in the Islamic tradition" (119). When spiritual longing is voiced in the language of erotic desire, however, as it is in Islamic mysticism and many other mystic traditions, the indexical words and letters of the tongue story appear anything but literal.[90] Despite their differences, both Littler and Bird pin their analyses of gender and ethnicity on the narrator's kinship, not with her male relative (who barely figures at all), but with the animated letters of Arabic script, which at times take wing or look angry, for example, in Özdamar's diction (1990: 16–17; 1994: 20–22). Taking issue with feminist objections that the text subordinates a woman's identity and desire "to the greater ideological concern with ethnicity," Bird concludes that the unruly vitality ascribed to the Arabic alphabet accounts in part for the Turkish woman's ability to "incorporate the Arabic of the Koranic verses . . . without accepting the female role which both she and her teacher associate with the scriptures" (164, 172). Inspired by Bhabha's account of modernity and migration, Littler finds that Özdamar's letters of the Arabic alphabet "liberate themselves" from scriptural doctrine and "symbolic reference" altogether (223–225). No personal, cultural, or national identity can be fixed, according to this analytical framework (see also Bayazitoğlu 120). Various scholars thus point in important ways to the inadequacy of dichotomous paradigms for grasping the cultural capital of Özdamar's literary prose. Leaving identity behind as an organizational frame of reference, however, allows us to address other textual functions that accrue to the figure of Islam in "Grandfather Tongue." How does this tale, where so many lived histories are made to touch, incorporate Islam as a Cold War phenomenon?

A partial answer lies in Özdamar's thematic and rhetorical use of the German language. In this tongue story German is initially identified as the only language that the Turkish pupil and her Arabic teacher share.

The voice of narration records this as a sign of lamentably rough-hewn relations, and German is marked as a language of crude exchange.[91] Allusions to capitalist principles of exchange may be closer in this inaugural scene than they first appear. As Ibni Abdullah and the protagonist introduce themselves, a structural equivalence seems to emerge between the political experiences resulting in German exile for each. Speaking out " 'rather loudly against the government' " after his seven brothers had been killed and Ibni Abdullah wounded in war, the Arab is accused by his government " 'of being a member of the fanatical Islamic brotherhood' " (1990: 13–14; 1994: 18). In another country, where so many friends were dead and teenagers hanged, the Turkish woman reveals that her government considered her " 'a Communist' " (1990: 14; 1994: 18). Littler stresses a structural parallel when she claims of the two interlocutors, "their iterative assurances of the proximity of death provide a cultural bond which differentiates them from their western European environment" (226). Yet the narrative repeatedly belies whatever logic of equivalence is implied in dialogic exchange. While both characters are reviled as enemies of the state by their governments in the 1970s, only the Turkish woman is described as having an identifiable state. On the basis of allusions to a fanatic Muslim "brotherhood" and Arab–Israeli wars, one might surmise that Ibni Abdullah is Egyptian, but in textual terms he is stateless and hence structurally unlike his pupil.[92] More to the point, the conversation opens with formulaic exchange in Arabic, where greeting and reply are nearly mirror opposites: " 'Selamünaleyküm' " (peace upon you) and " 'Aleykümselam' " (upon you peace). The text likewise closes with tagged dialogue and chiastic exchange, this time between the Turkish protagonist and a young German woman whose lover has committed suicide: " '*Ruh* means soul,' I said to the girl. / 'Soul means *Ruh*,' she said" (1990: 46; 1994: 57). As others note, the discrepancy between the Turkish *ruh* (soul) and the German *Ruh* (a shortened form of *Ruhe*, meaning peace, calm, quiet) defies any notion of translation or exchange as a structure of equivalence.[93] Acts of translation and lists of translated words, between Arabic and Turkish through the medium of German, liberally pepper the text. In one extended exchange the pupil asks her teacher what one Arabic word after another means. Upon hearing the reply, she repeatedly says, " 'The same for us' " (1990: 39; 1994: 48), before moving on to another question. Here a dialogic structure of repetition feigns equivalence on the subject of translation. Another key utterance, this time regarding politics, links Islam and communism to a mode of intralingual translation where, once again, no equivalence applies.

Arabic is conjured, mostly by means of German words, as an eroticized language of Islamic mysticism. Because "Grandfather Tongue" weaves a tale of the Cold War as a lived phenomenon, we would do well to recall that

Marxism too, meant to reveal the mystification of social relations under capitalism, entails a language of mysticism in a different key. To the degree that poetic language thrives on tensions between pragmatic significations and indexical mysteries, even utterances not tagged as poetic may operate in a mystical register of sorts. Poetic language masquerades as a logical definition in an emblematic exchange between the Turkish woman and her Arab lover, to which the argument now turns. Upon entering Ibni Abdullah's study one day, the pupil notices it smells "of people." The teacher explains that many of his students are " 'Germans, specialists in Middle Eastern studies, men and women,' " many of whom " 'vote green' " (1990: 15; 1994: 20). He asks the student before him if she knows what that means, to which she replies, " 'Green is anything that is not red' " (in German: *Grün ist, was nicht rot ist*). Tagged neither as a translation nor as a pun, this seemingly straightforward definition is both.[94] In German politics "green" is the color (and name) of the environmentalists, in contradistinction to "red," the color code for communists throughout the twentieth century and social democrats in the postwar era. In Middle Eastern and now European contexts "green" is the color of Islam, while "red" indexes the godlessness of communism. This puts us in the "world of yoking," where "the surprising coupling" of disparate elements sets meaning spinning (Culler 1988). Thematic content and rhetorical form are conjoined in this world of surprisingly productive remainders.

The same may be said of the narrator-protagonist, who continually "crosses" the two parts of Berlin divided by the Iron Curtain, figurally embodying a moving point of intersection and the fulcrum of chiasmus. Whereas chiastic or "crossing" structures in rhetoric are usually associated with opposition (Cuddon 138; Ueding and Steinbrink 308), Özdamar deploys them in ways that subtly but steadily undermine presumptions of absolute antithesis. The Turkish pupil's definition of "green" *per negationem* mobilizes opposition as a logical structure, which the intralingual pun of this chiastic utterance defies. This yoking world of definition likewise recalls the sorites paradox of vagueness, discussed earlier in reference to scalar rather than absolute modes of contextualization.[95] Though Islam and communism are often cast as polar opposites in political debates, and both are considered mirror opposites of capitalist Europe, "Grandfather Tongue" tells a touching tale of Cold War histories that yield many "illogical" remainders, in Guillory's terms. Pivoting on a Turkish figure that appears in the guise of a woman with desires unbound, the labor of affect and the exchange of words in this tale produce incoherence that is not the opposite of coherence. Beyond introducing a new migrant subject of national recollection (German as well as Turkish) on the cusp of the Cold War's end, Özdamar's extended tongue story mobilizes newly interactive transnational frames of reference for understanding the cultural capital of migration. In a Cold War setting un-equivalent but enmeshed histories are brought surprisingly to thaw.

As much an essayist as a novelist and poet, Şenocak reflects critically on the meaning of Nazi and Cold War pasts for a Germany reconfigured by unification and migration when capitalism emerged victorious from twentieth-century conflicts.[96] Cheesman suggests that "essay-fiction" is the author's "most distinctive literary form" (2003: 147). The essay as a literary form is an aesthetic medium operating in "the tradition of the incomplete," its only reliable feature a resistance to stasis (Şölçün 1998: 13, 15). Although Sargut Şölçün does not include Şenocak in his historical assessment of "deconstructive turns" in the German tradition, some of the qualities he ascribes to the genre apply to Şenocak's essayistic labors.[97] These include the constitutive function of the essayistic "I" as an "existential and epistemological" nexus where subject and object worlds meet (10, 13). Bespeaking critical consciousness of social norms, the "process-oriented thought" of the essay as form seeks other conditions of relationality (10, 243). Relying on a schematic distinction between the individual and the social at times, Şölçün nonetheless clarifies that the aesthetics of the essay hinge on the always divided "identity" or consciousness of the essayistic form, not any personal identity inhering in the author as an individual. Opening his discussion of German essay-writing about Europe after 1945 with Hans Egon Holthusen's query, "What is Occidental?" Şölçün subsequently situates a concern with freedom at the essayistic heart of German writing about Europe after the defeat of the Third Reich. In this body of writing, Şölçün contends, the antithesis to freedom is not tyranny, which essayists considered "European and provisional in nature," but despotism, which they deemed an unchangeable attribute of "non-European peoples" (238, 241).[98] Given these formal, thematic, and historical emphases in the German tradition, Şenocak's essays from the 1990s—when the orientation of a newly unified German nation and its treatment of "non-European peoples" were widely debated, often in tandem—warrant consideration as more than journalistic responses to current events. How does this body of work articulate an essayistic "I" at the crossroads of German national history and Turkish migration? Comparison of the two essays featured here marks one point of entry for reflecting on this question. Chow addresses the "personal essay" so common in immigrant writing "as a second-order autobiography," that is to say, autobiographical writing centered on personhood that is "always already blocked and silenced" (144). This is writing "about trauma and injustice under Western eyes," which tends to stress group histories (rather than individual lives) and, above all, "the question of heritage" (144). Şenocak's essayistic "I," varying from text to text, is no protestant ethnic as Chow defines the term, though it bespeaks critical thought. The question of heritage is crucially posed in "The Island: A Travelogue" and "Thoughts on May 8, 1995" (Şenocak 2000: 20–24, 58–61), but this is not an ethnic heritage in any predictably multicultural sense.[99] This heritage bears the stamp of German histories involving fascism, genocide, and the Cold War in decisive but hardly overdetermined ways.

If the narrator of the tongue story "articulates her desire to learn Arabic in terms of family structure and gender" (Bird 166), the critical voice with which Şenocak delineates the touch of German legacies and Turkish migration in the 1990s is likewise articulated in terms of genealogical structures and gendered conceits.[100] Where Özdamar mobilizes affective labors and illogical exchanges that cross in the figure of a Turkish woman, however, Şenocak foregrounds critical reflection and genealogical legacies passed on from fathers to sons. But what kind of son is the essayistic subject of migration? Roland Dollinger characterizes Sascha Muhteschem of *Perilous Kinship* as an "heir to a history of perpetrators," by which he means the history of the Armenian genocide, and the grandfather's secret in that novel as a "translation" from Turkish history into the German language (2002: 67–68). The history of perpetrators at issue in Şenocak's essays is a history of German perpetrators instead. Together with Bülent Tulay, the author asked his Turkish and German compatriots in January 1990: "Doesn't immigrating to Germany also mean immigrating to, entering into the arena of Germany's recent past?" (Şenocak 1992: 16; 2000: 6). What this might mean is explored in an expository essay written in 1995 to commemorate the historic significance of May 8, 1945, and a lyrical essay written in August 1991 to navigate the Baltic Sea island of Hiddensee as "a historical place that has become an imaginary site" (2000: 24). While the later essay focuses on decidedly West German genealogies, the earlier piece attempts to traverse the ghostly ground of a divided Germany.

Lending his voice to public reflections on the fiftieth anniversary of "1945," Şenocak begins his "Thoughts on May 8, 1995" with a highly mediated image of historical experience. "My father experienced World War II on the radio." The ensuing description effects estrangement, at least for a liberal German audience. Fearing a Soviet invasion in the summer of 1941, Turks around the village radio reacted with surprised relief when Hitler invaded the Soviet Union, thus preventing the Russian invasion of Turkey. "Hitler was highly rated." The essay then broadens the historical framework and extends the trope of patrilineal generations. We read that the essayist's grandfather and great-grandfather were captured on the Turco-Russian front in World War I, when Germans and Turks were "brothers in arms"; his forefathers experienced the end of the tsarist era as prisoners of war. The patrilineal chronicle segues into a metacommentary on national narratives and new beginnings on an international scale. "A new world arose on Russian soil. Whoever sympathized with this new world was considered in Turkey as godless. Although even modern Turkey was a godless republic, it persecuted these godless others" (2000: 58). Sigrid Weigel addresses the symbolic weight of gendered "generational" discourses of historical time and new beginnings in the West German culture of coming to terms with the Nazi past, especially as promoted by the nation's most influential literary group, founded in 1947 and known as Group 47, which once included Martin Walser, Alfred Andersch, Günter Grass, Heinrich Böll, and others who rose to prominence among the literary elite, often for attitudes that garnered them the status of a democratic nation's moral conscience. One might consider Şenocak's "generational" essays in light of Weigel's analysis (2002).[101]

According to Weigel, "the German understanding of history since 1945 has been based mainly on a temporal paradigm of what makes a generation" (264). Critically unraveling this paradigm by targeting " 'generation' as a symbolic form," Weigel speaks instead of a cultural code that negotiates historical guilt and establishes "a hierarchy of memories," which appears on the surface as the supersession of one counting of time by another (265). This is a crosshatched cultural code relying on gendered discourses of natural reproduction and the filial innocence of German boys in what Alexander Mitscherlich once dubbed the "fatherless society" of postwar Germany (Mitscherlich 1963, 1969; Weigel 2002: 268).

> Before 1945, during the Third Reich, only children, but at the end of the war, men—the earlier Hitler Youth Generation is not only excluded from discussion of guilt but represents the political and cultural elite in the Federal Republic of Germany. As founder generation of the new state, this is the concealed first generation whose roots in the Nazi period are negated due to their age at the time. This generation came to see itself still as the innocent child . . . . (Weigel 2002: 273)[102]

Many of the authors Weigel has in mind were children in the Hitler Youth and soldiers in the Third Reich. In probing the masculinist myth of successive generations as a deceptively linear account of cultural history, Weigel uncovers traces of divided historical memories of National Socialism that cultural histories of the Federal Republic, often organized around temporal concepts of generation and renewal, obscure. "The contrast of young and older generations is a cover for memory . . . , through which a heroic soldier collective tries to escape from historical responsibility for Nazism" (275). Not to be confused with a thesis of collective German guilt, Weigel's argument about the "divided knowledge" and experience of the Third Reich goes to the need for critical concepts of historical memory as a cultural code "that crosses and links generations" rather than merely replacing one with another (265, 275).[103] Referring here and elsewhere to the West German "project of *Wiedergutmachung*, the ultimately impossible attempt to exchange historical guilt (*Schuld*) with money debts (*Schulden*)," Weigel notes, the frequency with which "money symbols" circulate in postwar culture "is not so much a question of inherited debt as . . . a question of the continued effect of the remnants left over after guilt has been converted to debt" (2002: 269; Weigel 1996). This points to a cultural heritage that cannot be grasped in economic terms of equivalence. For Weigel, the "secret" or "concealed first generation" of the Federal Republic consists of those founding fathers of cultural codes and ethical imperatives who cast themselves "as a generation born from an immaculate birth made possible by catastrophe" (274). Sons of a tainted generation, they were encoded as untainted by contrast. In "Thoughts on May 8" Şenocak presents a patrilineal chronicle of successive generations initially, but his essayistic persona rapidly becomes a narrative problem in this historical account. "What access does someone whose father experienced World War II on the radio, far from the battlefields, have to this event?" (58). This is not cast as a traumatic problem in any psychological sense, but as a cultural problem exceeding prevalent discursive categories for the experience of Turkish migration, the experience of German unification, and the divided West German culture of "coming to terms" with a traumatic past. Şenocak articulates the nature of this problem by pinpointing his historical position. Rhetorically this is enabled by distanciation and negation. "In 1945 my father experienced neither a liberation nor a collapse. He was neither victim nor perpetrator. This vantage point allows me to raise a few questions" (58–59). The position that allows speech here is precisely that of a question. The essayistic subject is in effect a question that tries to speak itself. It does so by interrogating the cultural nexus of Germany past, present, and future at the extended historic moment of national transformation.

The rest of the essay turns to dichotomies that do not hold as German contexts are reconfigured. As Şenocak notes, the collapse of the Third Reich led to Germany's bifurcation "not only into East and West but also into victims and perpetrators" (59). Casting a critical eye on the West German cult and culture of *Vergangenheitsbewältigung*—"the preoccupation with the victims led above all to attention being distracted away from the perpetrators"— he argues that "the overcoming of the German division," not the fiftieth anniversary of war's end, "has stirred up questions" about the way that "Germans deal with their difficult history" (59). If the equation never added up in the sum of historical experience under the shadow of the Third Reich, the figure of Turkish migration throws yet another monkey wrench into German works of recollection by undoing the mirror logic of guilt and innocence, perpetrators and victims, from an unprecedented perspective. It is striking at this juncture that the essayistic subject of migration activates, not just a soldierly rhetoric of patrilineal legacies and ruptures, which at first glance appears to mimic the founding cultural code of generation that Weigel illuminates, but a more subtly encoded rhetoric of historical divides vis-à-vis the Third Reich and its immediate aftermath. This rhetoric bespeaks cures and calculations. "Without a doubt," Şenocak writes, "all those peoples who were occupied, persecuted, and subjugated by Nazi Germany were liberated in 1945" (59). "But what," he asks, "happened in Germany?" Did the Allied forces defeat "only a regime" or "an entire people"? Remarking "the hugely civilizing accomplishment" of these forces, which did not wreak vengeance on an enemy guilty of horrific crimes but granted Germany new life as a nation, the essayist speaks of a pragmatic "curing." This figure of healing the German body politic, on the one hand, links the period around 1945 rhetorically to a heightened German desire for "normalcy" once national sovereignty was restored in 1990 (59). "No longer does the nation lie half anesthetized on its sickbed, hoping for recovery. The patient assumes that he has been successfully cured and is free to go. One knows how newly recovered patients can be" (60). On the other hand, this longer medicinal riff distinctly echoes what is known in Germany as "the great controversy" of 1945–1946. Marking heated public exchange among German *literati* who had survived the Third Reich in political exile or endured in "inner emigration"—as Frank Thieß termed it in August 1945 (Grosser 23)—this controversy retained "undeniable topicality" as late as 1963 and was recently described as "the decisive signal event" to shape literary relations in the western zones of occupation (Grosser 7; Braese 2001a: 8, 33).

The central figure in this conflict was Thomas Mann, the Nobel Prize–winning novelist and essayist who had loudly decried the Nazi regime from political exile in the United States, often in speeches broadcast internationally by radio, and in mid-May of 1945 published an essay in occupied Germany on the profound shame and disgrace that Germans had brought on themselves. Mann encouraged the Germans to regard the Allied forces of occupation as liberators rather than enemy victors. The first to respond in an "open letter" was Walter von Molo, a prominent novelist prior to 1933 who remained in Germany throughout the Third Reich in spite of his differences with the regime. Pleading with Mann to return to Germany "like a good doctor" who could cure the illness that has befallen their people, von Molo pits the curative possibility of the exiled author's return against the potentially devastating humiliation of occupation (Grosser 20).[104] When Mann's refusal appeared the following October (Grosser 27–36), he appeared to deliver the devastating blow himself. Pleased that Germany desired his return as well as his books, he still considered himself "a German writer" but found something "unsettling" in such appeals (27, 33). Mann refers to a "naïve" presumption that one could pick up in 1945 where one had left off in 1933, in unmediated fashion, "as if these twelve years had never happened" (31). But in Mann's rhetoric the "something unsettling" that keeps him away emerges as a calculation that cannot be made. His compatriots' appeals bespeak "something illogical" (27). Smelling of "blood and disgrace," books published in Germany between 1933 and 1945 are, in another turn of phrase indexing what no structure of equivalence can capture, "less than worthless" (31). When Şenocak's "thoughts" revisit the national scene of Allied liberation and occupation in a rhetorical key of illness and cure, the essayistic subject invokes the remainder of that fraught divide between antifascist exiles and authors of "inner emigration" without identifying with the historical position of one group or the other. To the degree that "Thoughts on May 8, 1995" conjures two masculinist legacies that have been pivotal for the articulation of postwar literary history and the national culture of West Germany, one soldierly and the other medicinal, the essay weaves the multiply divided knowledge of the German past into the very fabric of the "I" articulating itself as a subject of Turkish migration.

No straightforward account of the author's family history or a mere presentation of views on current events, the essay assays to take on a difficult German legacy, not by identifying with historical roles played by others, but by crafting a critical relationship to them from the vantage of the 1990s.[105] Adoptive sons and sons of disputed paternity are hardly new or peripheral to West German literary culture. Recalling the long-suffering hotel boy of Heinrich Böll's *Billiards at Half-Past Nine*, deemed suitable for adoption because he embodies the soul of a lamb in a den of beasts, or the indeterminate lineage of Oskar Matzerath in Günter Grass's *The Tin Drum*, we might even say that uncertain affinities between fathers and sons have been central to the development of this culture. Rather than waiting passively to be adopted by German fathers, however, the essayistic "I" of Şenocak's "Thoughts on May 8" actively claims a German legacy of historical responsibility by means of critical reflection. Here a Turkish subject writes itself into German history, not by asserting or "confessing" an ethnic self, but by adopting German history critically as its own. This is not the only arena in which Şenocak tackles fraught and divided legacies among men. As Karin Yeşilada notes in an essay on the author's poetry, the "futurist epilogue," on which Şenocak and Berkan Karpat collaborated, revolves around patrilineal conflicts regarding Atatürk, whose moniker means "father of all Turks" (2003a: 117).[106] In other poems, she finds, "the men are heroes no longer" (124). The tripartite futurist project includes a "speech labyrinth" bearing the primary title "how not to kill the father," which begins with an "I" dreaming of a violent Atatürk and growing up doubly "fatherless" (Karpat and Şenocak 2000). If the figurative father of the Turkish republic has been enshrined in Turkey as a national soldier-hero *par excellence*, the first collaborative production in the futurist trilogy is devoted to the working man's hero, poet, and playwright, Nâzim Hikmet (1902–1963), a beleaguered communist who spent many years in Turkish prison—his poetry banned but hardly forgotten—and later Soviet exile (Karpat and Şenocak 1998). Yeşilada underscores a literary legacy as familial genealogy when she writes of Karpat and Şenocak, "Nâzim Hikmet's grandchildren write, and they are writing in German" (2002: 182).[107] The prose work that completes Şenocak's tetralogy puns on more than erotomania (1999). As others note, the masculinist pun of the title operates in German and Turkish registers; the " 'He-Ottoman' " in German yields, in Turkish, an Ottoman configured as a "militant, aggressive man" (McGowan 2003: 68; Carbe 80). And the subtitle—"a foundling book"—plays on a linkage between literary writing and "the abandoned child" of unknown parentage (McGowan 2003: 68).[108]

In "Thoughts on May 8, 1995," however, the adopting agent is focused on an emphatically national German heritage, under the sign of transnational migration. The essay calls prescriptively for "paths of remembrance . . . that lead into the present" (61). Three things must be said about the writer's project. First, the present in question decidedly follows unification. Second, it is a commonplace that the German present must confront its national past. Şenocak inverts the customary formula by arguing that history must be confronted with its present. Otherwise remembrance becomes ritualized to the point of being rote or lacking genuine effect. Such remembrance appears only "as a calculation" (60). Insisting on the continued importance of commemorating the victims of genocide, Şenocak nonetheless opines that formulaic calculations fail to grasp the cultural significance of either the German past or Turkish migration. Third, the nonsymbolic mode of remembrance he has in mind requires an imaginative rethinking of relationships between the Nazi past and a present that reflects the changing ethnoscape wrought by unification as well as migration. The essayist directs this requirement at multiple addressees. The question posed in January 1990 reverberates as a lament and a critique in May 1995 when Şenocak writes, "The foreigners in Germany . . . barely bother to reflect on the history of the Germans" (60).[109]

East German cultural politics posited a socially progressive heritage of "the other Germany" leading from premodern times to the establishment of the German Democratic Republic in 1949. (This is partly why the GDR long held that atoning for Nazi crimes was solely the responsibility of capitalist Germany.) As Hell deftly details, this heritage was commonly framed in terms of family narratives and "post-fascist fantasies" of communist paternity (1997). When Şenocak turns his essayistic eye to the scene of German division shortly after its formal erasure, he neither seizes on this East German rhetoric of heritage nor applies a West German concept of legacy to the "imaginary site" located where the GDR used to be. "Thoughts on May 8, 1995" couples Germany's divided pasts and a unified present in imaginative but nonsymbolic ways, by means of critical reflection. By contrast, the essay written in August 1991 conveys a heightened sense of both affect and abstraction. In this constellation the coupling of mirror logic rapidly yields to illogical remainders of a Cold War divide. "The Island: A Travelogue" is a lyrical essay that literally thematizes trajectories of movement and rhetorically enacts paths of remembrance. The writing persona undertakes a journey from Berlin to the island of Hiddensee, where the great exemplar of German Naturalism, Gerhart Hauptmann, is buried. But the essay's nebulous atmosphere of playful dejection is anything but naturalist.

> From the landing dock everyone moves backward. The larks trill. A look scrutinizes the neighbor. While the travelers move backward from the landing dock to mingle among the lives that the dead have laid down—only in this manner do they as strangers reach the village—they run, the island's inhabitants, forward, run ahead of their own lives, with glances fixed on the future. They load their thoughts and dreams onto kites that they let fly along the main thoroughfares of the island. (2000: 21)

Metanarratives of historical development are invoked when the owner of the bicycle shop calls capitalism "the dessert of socialism" (21), which prompts the writing persona to reflect, "According to this view, fascism was the appetizer to the main course—for forty years the brothers and sisters sat at the table and no one got really full" (22). This miming of German national narratives and ideological paradigms for the twentieth century, which figures male and female siblings more than fathers and sons, takes place in a rarified setting for historical reflection.

Formerly in the GDR, the island is imaginatively conjured as a phantasmatic *lieu de mémoire* by the subject of the essay, who pointedly asks what many people wanted to know about unified Germany in the early 1990s. Was it moving forward or backward in time?[110] Şenocak's travelogue casts this question in terms of abstract patterns of movement, encounter, direction, and filiation. Paths are described:

> that split whoever walks on them into two parts (or doubles them, depending on one's point of view). One part strives forward, the other backward; one comes with a stomach full from the meal, picking his teeth, the other is

a gap in himself between tables set and cleared, a dog without a master. Groups dissolve, couples split, individuals lose their thoughts and dreams. All of them are looking for the path not yet blocked by the department stores' delivery trucks, beyond the main traffic routes. Does this path lead to the future or to the past? (23)

This is clearly an essay on the imaginative highways and byways of East and West German unification. But who is the essayistic subject tracing these paths of remembrance in and between the lines of the essay? In stark contrast to Şenocak's "Thoughts on May 8," the island travelogue makes no reference whatsoever to Turkish persons, families, histories, or contexts, and only initially draws attention to an embodied voice of narration. The essayistic "I" wears no cloak of identity at all. Is there a "Turkish" subject in this text? If so, it can only be traced as a migrating line of thought in a time of historical disorientation. The essay of 1991 begins with a puzzler—"Where had Hauptmann buried his box of notes?"—and segues into an assertion: "This question preoccupied me when I went to the island" (20).[111] Here we see the emergence of a new subject in historical formation, as the essayistic persona is constituted initially as the transitive object of a question that preoccupies him. The imaginative engagement with the question allows the subject of the essay to articulate as an "I," the contemplative vantage point from which the rest of the essay unfolds. Yet this is a strikingly wistful essay full of affect: "dejection," "aggression," "suspicion," "forced gaiety," "weeping," and more. What type of memory work does the subject of such an essay perform?

"Turkish" paths of German remembrance cannot follow historically prescribed lines of inquiry. For no German pasts come to the essayistic subject as family lore, affective chain, or cultural inheritance that social convention deems to be properly its own. Concentrating on "second-generation memories" of children of Holocaust survivors, Marianne Hirsch defines even "postmemory" in a way that could not apply to Şenocak's essayistic subjects and the cultural work of imagination they perform:

> postmemory is distinguished from memory by generational distance and from history by deep personal connection. Postmemory is a powerful and very particular form of memory precisely because its connection to its object or source is mediated not through recollection but through an imaginative investment and creation. . . . Postmemory characterizes the experience of those who grow up dominated by narratives that preceded their birth, whose own belated stories are evacuated by the stories of the previous generation shaped by traumatic events that can be neither understood nor recreated. (22)[112]

The "sense of belatedness and disconnection" that Hirsch associates with postmemory (244) might apply to the literature of migration written by any generation. This work entails "an imaginative investment" with the German past, and even migrants deemed "second-generation" have grown up in a German culture "dominated by narratives" of the German past. But Hirsch's insistence on the deep ties of family relations renders her term inadequate to memory work performed by Turkish lines of thought in unified Germany. Şenocak's essays delineate a German future in which Turks have a proper place, in part, because of the commemorative work they perform. This memory work also differs from the critical memory work performed by some texts written in the GDR about the communist past. A brief comparison between Şenocak's "Island" essay and Christoph Hein's acclaimed novella of 1982, *The Distant Lover*, makes this point. Stunning parallels between these texts draw our attention to unequal remainders of personhood as a strategic nexus of sociality.

Şenocak's reflections on May 8 prescriptively call for a new form of memory work by Germany's immigrants, and the "Island" essay enacts such labor lyrically. The latter weaves a stylized web of abstract movements through historical time. Travelers proceed in opposite directions with different affects but along the same spectral route, always out of sync. In this, Şenocak's essay on "Comrade Hauptmann" (22) is reminiscent of the dream-like sequence that introduces an especially haunting portrayal of alienation under GDR communism. Hein's novella originally appeared as *Der fremde Freund* [The Strange Friend] in East Germany, as *Drachenblut* [Dragon Blood] in the West in 1983, and as *The Distant Lover* in Krishna Winston's translation of 1989.[113] Hovering over the ensuing narrative in suspended animation, the eerie prologue establishes the narrating persona as a question. "I, or this person who may be me, hesitate. I—let's say it is me—look around" (2). This tentative "I" steps into an originary landscape and espies a jagged ruin bridging an abyss: "Two beams spanning a bottomless deep" (2). Two fearful companions undertake this crossing, the dangers of which seem ominously and infinitely evident. "We've only started, and the beam seems to stretch on interminably." This rhetoric of a starting point and directional movement echoes the novella's opening line: "In the beginning was a landscape" (1), which echoes a Biblical sense of genesis and recalls " 'generation' as a symbolic form." But this landscape is hardly the Garden of Eden, and pale lieutenants of a collective history burst mechanistically onto the scene.

The precarious position of the questioning subject is spotlighted by the sudden approach of five male runners, all dressed in athletic uniforms with a "rune-like" insignia and all bearing an uncanny resemblance to each other. They race rhythmically toward the fearful pair and effortlessly past them across the broken bridge, which quivers in their wake. The two frozen figures know that they must still cross to the other side without any hope of knowing how. The terror of this sylvan encounter lingers: "A dream. Or a distant remembering" (4). From there the novella proper begins. Noting that the narrative overall "produces an irresistible pressure to read that which is *not* said," Hell stresses the GDR-specific implications of a gendered utopia in Hein's seemingly "a-utopian text" (309). For the female protagonist exhibits a subjective despair at odds with a paternalistic state that claims to have realized the conditions for human happiness. For David Roberts, the inaugural dream "signals the need to distinguish between the manifest and the latent content of the first-person narrative" (480–481). One would be hard pressed not to read the tonal affects and movement patterns of the bridge scene in terms of the reluctant protagonist's personal history, which is desperately entwined with GDR history, including a popular uprising quashed by Soviet tanks in 1953. For the protagonist, this entails her childhood betrayal of a beloved friend and the state's betrayal of its communist ideals.

Both the Hein prologue and the "Island" essay posit an originary but highly mediated landscape where human movements through space are figuratively coupled with historical developments in time. Progress is undermined by physical stasis or directional looping. Island residents traveling forward in time and visitors traveling back in time move in a circle where "[t]hey will not meet" (23). Hein's terror-stricken duo and athletic runners briefly cross paths in a space of precarious transition, but what remains is a cipher of nonsynchronicity. Both texts render historical trajectories and their lived effects as something that cannot be seen, beyond the reach of reference. Yet this bridge over an abyss and the island all abustle beg to be read as figural markers indexing a site or a moment where something intangible is afoot.

If both texts circumnavigate historical remainders of social relations that do not make sense as calculations of equivalence, the conditions for their insistence on what appears illogically in the landscape of memory differ.[114] Hein probes the conditions of living as a historical subject in the GDR from the 1950s into the1970s. Şenocak reflects on remembrance from the vantage point of a new German subject, the likes of which did not exist prior to the large-scale migration of recent decades. Hein conjures a landscape in which an "I" can exist only asynchronically, out of step and out of time with official GDR narratives. This persona bears the scars of a particular subjectivity in time. The relationship between affective amplitudes and historical scenes is reversed for Şenocak. The reluctant persona of *The Distant Lover* projects her fractured interiority onto a seemingly originary landscape. "The Island" presents us instead with an external splintering, a Germany divided before and after unification, which then becomes constitutive for the essayistic subject. This persona of German memory work goes unrecognized by the ethnic categories that strong multiculturalism makes available to us. The fact that Şenocak was born in Turkey or even that he once traveled to Hiddensee is hardly sufficient grounds to regard the subject of this essay as an ethnic Turk. This writerly persona does not reside outside German time but enters it in thoughtful contemplation, that is to say, enters it *by means of* thoughtful contemplation coupled with affective remainders. This is a persona of migration as historical formation, not of ethnicity as anthropological ascription.

The stark asceticism of the northern German landscape sunders, this persona pronounces, "the most intense couples" (20). This is not the anthropomorphic figure of heterosexual coupling common in accounts of unification and its residue (see Keim and Dollinger; Schneider 1990: 156; 1991: x). Şenocak's essays approximate instead a conceptual reconfiguration of the divisions and pairings that have most intensively shaped the way one tends to think about German scenes of remembrance. East/West, past/present, victim/perpetrator, self/other: these scenes do not customarily allow for "Turkish" inflections of German memory because Germany's resident Turks did not live the German pasts that are meant. Studies of immigrant cultures often stress an obsessive longing for the lived pasts and familiar locales left behind. The lines of thought featured in Şenocak's essays are iconoclastic. They engage more pointedly with a highly mediated German past en route to a future that Germans and the Turks among them will certainly share, albeit not as ethnic blocs presumed to mirror each other as East and West Germany were once thought to do. If structures of remembrance and forgetting are undergoing significant changes in our time (Huyssen 2000), Şenocak too writes a new subject of German remembrance into being with his essays of the 1990s. This is less about the dangers of forgetting the past than it is about new conditions for re-membering twentieth-century Germany in a shared republic. The future of Germany lies ahead no less than its past, and the literature of Turkish migration labors to articulate newly intelligible relationships between them. Şenocak's rhetoric ultimately unravels those conceptual processes that rely on a familiar logic of coupling to grasp either national unification or the Cold War. Conceits of gender and ethnicity in these essays and many other literary works of migration, too, are best understood in emblematic rather than self-confessional terms.

The collaborative effect of these figural conceits marks a strategic nexus where the imaginative labor and cultural capital of migration are actively being reconceived. Rather than representing ethnic characters articulated as men and women, the literary figures designated as "Turkish" throughout this study thus index the disaggregated phenomenon of transnational migration on the cusp of the twenty-first century. In this light "difference" is the cultural difference that migration makes as a historical formation, not the bloc difference ascribed to ethnicity as an inherited category of belonging. The gendered division of labor one initially associates with Şenocak and Özdamar—one body of writing predominantly western, masculinist, and reflective, the other seemingly eastern, feminist, and naïve—also gives way to messier stylistic relations and cultural remainders. If "Grandfather Tongue" foregrounds an affective register that mediates illogical histories in highly sophisticated ways, Şenocak's essays combine reflection and affect to similar ends, and texts by both authors engage East and West German legacies across a Cold War divide. As an analytical alternative to a familiar and familial logic of coupling, however, the concept of hybridity is too invested in the paradigm of identity to account for the nature of this engagement. By probing the conjoined effect of figuration and narration in prose works by Ören, Özdamar, and Şenocak where the sign of capital and its ostensible "other" are key, this chapter demonstrates how the concept of touching tales sheds more differentiated light on literary labors of migration. Not sparked by economic forces alone, these disaggregated works of imagination reforge the suspended residue of national and transnational histories to yield the changing cultural capital of migration. No mirror logic of equivalence or opposition holds. In a period of heightened dis- and re-orientation, east is no longer east, west is no longer west, and neither the nation nor its pasts are exactly what they used to be either. Perhaps we may take one final cue from an imaginary island and a quivering bridge, landscapes that anthropomorphic figures traverse in variously interactive constellations but do not embody. If an ethnoscape is "the landscape of persons who constitute the shifting world in which we live," this is a variegated landscape of emblematic relations. The German literature of Turkish migration draws such a landscape in iconoclastic lines of thought.

Postscript

When Molly Bloom says yes to an embeetled charmer named Gregor Samsa, readers are invited to delight in an unholy coupling of sorts.[1] Inspired by Jorge Luis Borges in 1941 and millennial fervor at the century's end, Kemal Kurt (1947–2002) crafts a fanciful novel in which over 180 fictional characters drawn from literatures around the world vie for survival. (Ali Itir from Ören's *Please, No Police* resurfaces among them.) Unlike Borges, who entertains the possibility that the library of the universe is " 'total'—perfect, complete, and whole," with room to house "all that is able to be expressed, in every language" (23), Kurt casts the "*conditio protagonista*" (131) as a bloodthirsty and anxious affair. Assassinations abound as storied figures poison, shoot, bomb, or otherwise do away with each other in response to reports that only one fictional work of modernity will endure beyond 2000 in the Library of Babel, where shelf space is at a premium and new rules of storage will soon prevail. Molly and Gregor's erotic pastiche provides the contrapuntal backdrop to this cutthroat competition, which reflects tongue-in-cheek on the twinned specters of globalization and digitalization.[2] According to Jerome McGann, who predicts a radical transformation of cultural archives with considerably more enthusiasm than Kurt's beleaguered protagonists can muster, advances in digital technology that have accelerated since the early 1990s have initially had their "greatest impact on the library" itself (3).

The narrative prose of print literature, however, continues to comprise a "virtual meeting space" (Tabbi and Wutz 23), one where the touch of texts and archives is now being newly imagined. This touch appears literal in the *tête-à-bête* that Kurt stages between Molly and Gregor, and multiple story lines in the classical narratological sense clearly converge in this German novel born of Turkish migration as well. Yet *Ja, sagt Molly* [Yes, Says Molly] additionally mobilizes the improper proximity of figural abstractions that *The Turkish Turn* has sought to capture under the rubric of touching tales. Best known in Germany for his children's literature and critical essays on the phenomenology of multiculturalism, Kurt bequeathes to his readers a millennial novel that is not merely about the angst of survival attending one literary medium and many inherited cultures around 2000. More than this, the immigrant author's dialogue with Borges speaks to fundamentally new possibilities for contemplating the order of things. If a romantic tryst between Molly Bloom and Gregor Samsa prompts readers to delight in an unholy coupling, it must be stressed that no literary or cultural narratives are invoked here as "seamless wholes."[3] The critical study that concludes with this postscript similarly offers, not a comprehensive picture of cultural migration, but partial perspectives on referential riddles, interactive contexts, and lines of thought most often obscured, either by those nation-centered paradigms of analysis that have prevailed since 1945 or by a facile reach for transnational and global frameworks today. Once we step outside the cultural fable that doggedly confines cultures of migration to a third space "between two worlds," untold interpretive vistas begin to appear. What began with transnational labor migration fifty years ago now summons us to read literatures of migration and the labors of invention they entail in newly imaginative ways. Only the curious need apply.

Notes

Introduction

1. This anecdote is recounted with an appreciative nod to Keith Ashley.
2. Seyhan offers a more sustained comparison between Turkish–German and Chicana literatures at real and metaphoric borders (2001: 99–124); see also Sieg 240. See Faist for a comparison of social contexts (1995). For a sophisticated critique of comparative methodologies, see Melas (1995, 2006). A special issue of *Diacritics* addresses shifting conditions of comparison (Cheah and Robbins).
3. The phrasing reappears in Appadurai 2000. In *Modernity at Large* Appadurai stresses "the *work of the imagination*" in social life (3 and passim). This emphasis is important for my discussion of literary work in the 1990s. Appadurai has also contributed to an interdisciplinary project on public spheres and "new imaginaries" associated with the Center for Transcultural Studies (Gaonkar and Lee). My study engages more directly with Appadurai's earlier book, which makes more pointed claims about the nexus of migration, mediation, and imagination.
4. This proposal intends only to loosen up scar tissue that has thickened intractably around rhetorical worlds that migrants are thought to inhabit. Philosophies of worldliness are not addressed.
5. The performance artist defines the Fourth World as "a conceptual place where the indigenous inhabitants of the Americas meet with the deterritorialized peoples, the immigrants, and the exiles" (1996: 7) and the Fifth World as virtual space mediated by new electronic technologies.
6. Some also note the "historical amnesia" that attends contemporary discussions of transnationalism and globalization (Cohen and Dever 27).
7. Many individuals feel caught "between two worlds." The rhetorical conceit is always within easy reach, shorthand for complex subjective and social processes in flux. The claim of historical obsolescence applies to the analytical purchase of the conceit.
8. Rimmon-Kenan explains that the "deep structure" of a story is paradigmatic, while the "surface structure" is syntagmatic (10).
9. See Appadurai on degrees of fluidity between premodern and modern approaches to ethnic cohesion (1996: 139–157). See also Gaonkar on "alternative modernities" (2001).
10. Benhabib aptly criticizes two "faulty epistemic premises" in contemporary politics: "(1) that cultures are clearly delineable wholes; (2) that cultures are congruent with population groups" (2002b: 4).

11. Compare Cohen and Dever's geometrical definition of a "zone" as "a structure produced through the intersection of other structures that are coherent formations in their own right" (2).
12. Irzık and Güzeldere address the rhetorical tenacity and analytical impoverishment of understanding Turkey as a bridge "between two worlds."
13. See Levent Soysal for additional evidence of this fable's forceful presence in studies of migration and globalization. As he critically observes, "Despite the changes occurring in [the] *trans*national geography and the imaginary of migrancy, and almost four decades after its arrival in our scientific and everyday lexicons, the term *Gastarbeiter* continues to captivate our scholarly and popular imagination. . . . In our narratives, migrants, and Turks in particular, appear as perpetual guest workers, arrested in a state of cultural and social liminality" (2003: 493). Analytically indebted to Yasemin Soysal's scholarship on political membership, Levent Soysal stresses the need for a new critical approach to "the migration story" (494). By his account, the sociology of labor that once attached to the international figure of the guest worker has yielded to a widely accepted narrative positing migration as a story about cultural identities instead (498).
14. Leggewie decries excessive celebration of hybridity as a weak antidote to the "social pathology" ascribed to immigrants " 'between the cultures' " (2000: 882). See the introduction to Bronfen, Marius, and Steffen for one example. For critical approaches to hybridity in Germany, see Faist 2000a: 44–45, Wägenbaur, Umut Erel in Gelbin, Konuk, and Piesche (172–194), Terkessidis 1999, and Encarnación Gutiérrez Rodríguez in Hess and Lenz (36–55). Chow criticizes theoretical models that confuse hybridity with freedom. For relevant migration histories, see Bade; Hochstadt; Bade and Weiner; Castles, Booth, and Wallace; Castles and Miller; Sassen 1996, 1999; Sackmann, Peters, and Faist. See also Şen and Goldberg for publications by the Center for Turkish Studies in Essen. In 2003 an association calling for a "migration museum in Germany" was founded in Cologne to address the lapse of memory that prevails in Germany about migration history (Migrationsmuseum). Yalçın-Heckmann speaks of the 1990s as a period of heightened interest in that history, as reflected in new associations, exhibits, and film projects.
15. The legal category of "minority" was long reserved in Germany for autochthonous groups such as Sorbs, Friesians, and Danes (Schmalz-Jacobsen and Hansen 341). Turks without German citizenship are technically "foreigners." A lexicon of ethnic minorities reflects a terminological shift by including a section on "the Turkish minority" (Schmalz-Jacobsen and Hansen 511–528).
16. As Levent Soysal observes, the figure of "the Turk" in Germany also acquires symbolic status in migration studies generally (2003: 500). If 80 percent of Turks in Europe resided in Germany prior to unification (Ardagh 241), casual references to Turkish migrants "in Europe" also indicate the symbolic status of Turks in Germany. More concretely, Turks bore the brunt of racism in West Germany long before the surge of attacks following national unification (Castles, Booth, and Wallace 100). See Kurthen et al. on post-unification developments.
17. Benhabib offers a sophisticated variation on this theme by arguing forcefully for deliberatively "democratic dialogue" as distinguished from multiculturalist dialogue (2002b: ix and passim). By her account, "intercultural justice between

human groups should be defended in the name of justice and freedom and not an elusive preservation of cultures" (8). Benhabib's understanding of dialogic complexity derives from her critique of models and movements that treat cultures as "seamless wholes" (25).
18. On "bridge" rhetoric, see especially Moray McGowan 1997, 2000b, and 2004 in literary studies or Waldhoff et al. in social sciences. Adelson 2001 is also relevant.
19. As Ausländer demonstrates, "Christian" and "secular" are sometimes deployed as complementary rather than contradictory terms in debates about religion and immigration.
20. The 1950s marked "the onset of large-scale labor migration" in transnational markets (Yasemin Soysal 1994: 145), and the 1960s marked crucial change involving "global foreign investment flows" and "massive new migrations" (Sassen 1988: 3). Lee and LiPuma trace new developments in capitalism to 1973.
21. For medium-specific alternatives, see Göktürk and Mennel in film studies or Asu Aksoy and Robins in television studies.
22. See, e.g., Senders. For broader perspectives; see Barbieri; Brubaker. Yasemin Soysal posits a postnational model of civic membership, "the main thrust of which is that individual rights, historically defined on the basis of nationality, are increasingly codified into a different scheme that emphasizes universal personhood" (1998: 189; see also Sassen 1998; Jacobson). Rejecting nation-based models of citizenship and territorial models of denizenship, Soysal argues, "the incorporation of guestworkers . . . reveals a profound transformation in the institution of citizenship, both in its institutional logic and in the way it is legitimated" (191). Benhabib also discusses changing infrastructures of citizenship in Europe (2002b: 147–177).
23. "Sociologically, the practice and institution of 'citizenship' can be disaggregated into three components: collective identity, privileges of political membership, and social rights and claims" (162). Benhabib's disaggregated theory of citizenship, which accounts for institutional and ethical tensions between national sovereignty and human rights in Europe, reflects this disaggregation of citizenship in social practice. Regarding the tense simultaneity of universalist and particularist claims, see Benhabib 2002b: 153; Soysal 2002: 142. According to Benhabib, recent political developments unsettle the philosophical category of citizenship (160). Considering the German past "with 2000 as its pivot rather than 1945," Jarausch and Geyer observe, "for all the attention to exile and diasporas, the lengthy processes of cultural transformation involved in becoming or unbecoming 'German' still remain largely in the dark" (ix, 199).
24. See Leggewie for a related polemic (2000: 883).
25. Tarrow coins the term "rooted cosmopolitans" for his analysis of new forms of transnational activism (2002, 2005).
26. Sassen emphasizes corporate strategies, financial markets, legal infrastructures, and labor systems of globalization, whereas Soysal and Benhabib concentrate on systems of political membership in Europe.
27. As chapter one elaborates, I adapt *technology of localization* from Appadurai (1996: 180).
28. Benhabib engages in dialogue with Arendt and Taylor, from whom she borrows " 'web of narratives' " and adapts " 'webs of interlocution' " (7, 56). Benhabib otherwise faults Taylor for treating culture as analogous to language (55).

29. It also sets them apart from "postpositivist realism" (Mohanty 1993, 2003; Moya and Hames-García; see also Mohanty's contributions to Elliott et al. as well as Mohanty et al.). Sommer articulates a "rhetoric of particularism" to counter the rhetoric of universalism in literary analysis and political theory (1999: 1–31). As Soysal and Benhabib indicate, however, universalism and particularism are thoroughly interlaced in the cultural effects of transnational migration.

30. Apter distinguishes between transnational literature and the "nation-neutral" Euro-fiction of the future (Cohen and Dever 287). Very few German examples wrought by Turkish migration could be described as nation-neutral.

31. This argument is compatible with but different from Mandel's discussion of "processes of ethnicization" concerning German Turks and Russian Germans as ethnic categories managed by the state (2003, 2006). See Hollinger on ethnicization in the United States.

32. Citing Modarressi, Konuk discusses Turkish women writers in three countries (2001). In Latin American Studies Mignolo approaches interdependent contexts by forging the postcolonial concept of "border gnosis," with the border understood "as threshold and liminality, as two sides connected by a bridge, as a geographical and epistemological location" (309). Despite Mignolo's attempt to capture complex networks of interdependence, his phrasing comes precariously close to the conflation of geography, history, epistemology, and *ethnos* that underwrites the cultural fable of migrants suspended "between two worlds." The occasional reach for postcolonial terminology in some scholarship on German literature of Turkish migration is no less problematic. First, a metaphorical invocation of postcoloniality as an oppositional cipher in debates about inclusion appears to broaden the analytic framework without challenging blind spots created by simplistic models of membership discussed above. (Fachinger's book has several qualities to recommend it but evidences this weakness.) Second, I am wary of scholarship that wants to grasp the literature of migration in decidedly postcolonial terms without more than a nod (and sometimes not even that) to the complex history of German colonialism. (Invoking Fanon, Tertilt's social ethnography of a Turkish street gang points without clarification to a "structural relationship between colonialism and the societal disregard for ethnic minorities" [245]. Ha discusses Turkish migrants in Germany in postcolonial terms of oppositional hybridity; indexing Auschwitz and slavery [20], the political scientist never mentions German colonialism. Littler acknowledges that Turkey was never colonized by Germany but cites Özdamar on the Turkish migrant experience as "a kind of 'inner' colonialism." According to the literary scholar, "postcolonial theory forces us to challenge notions of homogeneous cultural identity which still prevail in Germany" [221]. See also Bird [162]. Fennell makes the extreme claim that "Germany has no history of colonialism," concluding that "a kind of belated, internal, economic colonialism" prevails for immigrants in Germany today [137].) To say that Turks were not subjects of German colonialism is not to say that issues concerning Turks in Germany today have nothing to do with the history, legacy, or cultural memory of German colonialism. In this sense I share Seyhan's skepticism about hasty social analogies (2001: 12–13) and invite more reflection on the cultural and affective nexus that pertains. (Huyssen 2003a: 155 points in this direction, too.)

See also Steyerl and Gutiérrez Rodríguez.) One of the most widely cited essays in postcolonial theory introduces the rhetorical figure of "the Turkish *Gastarbeiter*" as an icon for uncanny dimensions in the modern national narrative writ large (Bhabha 1990a: 317). Could it be that the figure of Turks in Germany, who do not come to the Federal Republic by way of colonial history, appears to lend itself to discussions of the uncanny *because* the figure lends itself to an effacement of German colonialism in popular and scholarly narratives? Spivak's remark about the migrant as a "figure of the effacement of the native informant" may be especially pertinent. To be clear, I am not suggesting that discussion of Turks detracts attention from German colonialism and its legacy as more important objects of analysis. Whatever linkage applies between Turkish migration and German colonialism needs to be addressed with far greater methodological rigor than phrases borrowed loosely from postcolonial theory can provide. (Sieg also offers critical thoughts in this regard.) Some scholarship additionally treats national unification as a "process of colonization" by the Federal Republic (Dümcke and Vilmar 13; Fachinger 12, 35). Here too one must ask which legacies are acknowledged and obscured in the name of oppositional "postcolonialism."

33. Chapter two revisits Bhabha's influential configuration of the Turk. For related critical commentary, see Göktürk (1999b: 4–5) and Levent Soysal (2003a: 500–501). Soysal is only partially correct in noting that "[s]ilence becomes the story" of migration that Bhabha tells, for Bhabha's story of migration additionally revolves around Rushdie as a figural counterpoint to "the Turkish *Gastarbeiter*." Benhabib discusses Bhabha's account of pedagogical and performative operations in national narratives without mentioning his Turkish trope. Her discussion immediately segues into "a paradigmatic example of civic nationalism" drawn from Atatürk's reforms (2002b: 8–10).

34. Leggewie suggests that Turkish–German life in general clearly revolves around Germany rather than Turkey (2005: 83). Keyder discusses what the 1990s have meant for Turkish society. Another political scientist fuses *Deutschland* and *Türkei* to yield *Deutschkei*, which she literally considers "Turkey in Germany" (Argun). Faist offers a far more differentiated account of the "transnational social spaces" of migration (2000a, 2000b), but his incisive approach to newly interactive frameworks in migration studies, which favors social networks of relationality over container models of territoriality, also ignores the role of literature. Faist construes the social spaces in question as pointedly *transstaatlich* rather than *transnational* in the German usage (2000a: 13–14), with both words meaning "transnational" in English. Faist's distinction thus stresses varying relations to multiple nation-states as such rather than the reconfigurations of *ethnos* discussed here in chapters one and three.

35. Seyhan and I emphasize different facets of this literature. Even when one may speak of " 'diasporic narratives' " (2001: 12–13), these narratives may not be exclusively diasporic. (By contrast, Littler insists on reading this literature as diasporic but rejects Seyhan's emphasis on restorative qualities of literary remembrance.) For a historical overview of the Turkish diaspora that does exist in Germany, see Chapin. For more speculative discussion of Turkish Muslims in Germany from a diasporic perspective, see Ewing. For a range of approaches to institutions involving Turkish Muslims in Germany, see entries in Horrocks

and Kolinsky or Vertovec and Peach on the 1990s, in addition to Goldberg (2002); Henkel (2004a, 2004b); Shore; and Tibi (1998a: 242–319; 2000) on more recent developments. Stoll notes a problem with German demographics, which "do not always take religious membership into account so one is left to infer such membership on the basis of nationality" (266).

36. This literature does not revolve around ethnic categories of discrimination, enfranchisement, or identity, though public discourses informed by such categories sometimes appear as objects of ridicule in this literature. Anthropologists who also see something beyond conventional identity politics "between two worlds" in the German-based cultures of Turkish migration include Mandel; Levent Soysal; Jenny White; Römhild; and Henkel. Compare also Faist (2000b, 2000a: 44–45) and Leggewie (2005). Even *Kanak Attak!*, the antiracist movement sparked in the late 1990s by the publication of Zaimoğlu's *Kanak Sprak* in 1995, cannot be grasped in terms of Turkish identity politics, since the constituency is broadly diverse. The movement's political manifesto explicitly abandons categories predicated on ethnic or national identity, which also leads explicitly to a rejection of the "culture of dialogue" (Kanak Attak). See Cheesman (2002, 2004) and Yıldız (2004, 2005) on *Kanak Sprak*, Zaimoğlu's formulation of "KanakAttack" (2001: 8–21), and the broader movement called *Kanak Attak!*. Identity politics in liberal democracies today mark a historical shift in the sense that groups claiming distinctive cultural identities "demand legal recognition and resource allocations from the state and its agencies to preserve and protect their cultural specificities" (Benhabib 2002b: 1). In her studies of Turkish migrants during the 1990s, Kolinsky retains a focus on identity but argues, "the only feature common to the population designated as 'Turks' in Germany is their country of origin" (2002: 205; 2000). See also Rudiger on migrant organizations.

37. See Tertilt for a critical ethnography of a street gang called Turkish Power Boys, e.g. Tertilt challenges cultural-conflict theory in the social sciences, which he faults for overemphasizing cultural difference and underestimating social, economic, and legal factors. (Ha also comments on this [53–57].) According to Tertilt, this imbalance recycles static cultural models of migrant and host populations alike, failing to grasp the normative values these populations share (219). A former German parliamentarian of Turkish descent suggests that Turks in Germany organize themselves politically as Latinos have done in the United States (Özdemir 2003). This call to engage in identity politics demonstrates that the phenomenon is not pre-given for minorities in Germany.

38. Stoll's examples attest to a weakly developed motif indexing a generic sense of cultural difference or Islamic mysticism. Allusions to Islamic mysticism play varying roles in work by some of the authors taken up here; chapter three addresses some of them. Frischmuth links the motif of Islamic mysticism in one novel to transnational migration and technological surveillance in contemporary Austria (1998a). Özdamar and Şenocak's references to Islam are usually embedded in complex narratives about Turkey's commitment to national secularization, notably under Atatürk. Other scholars address Özdamar's rewriting of the Turkish national narrative (see especially Seyhan 2001; Konuk 2001; Frölich; Bayazitoğlu; Littler). As Seyhan notes, a love story in *Mother Tongue* "also tells a veiled political history" of national Westernization, a history

that entailed "the collective forgetting of Turkey's cultural past" and the erasure of its "Islamic Ottoman heritage" (122). I focus on aspects of the literature of migration for which scholarship has not yet accounted. For broad perspectives on Islam in Germany, see Tibi 2000. See Tibi 1998b, 2001, and 2002 on "Euro-Islam," a term coined by the political scientist and international relations expert. Tibi's rejection of strong multiculturalism and defense of reasoned dialogue are similar to Benhabib's position on equality and diversity in the age of globalization. (For a different approach to Euro-Islam, see Ramadan, who focuses on France and Britain. For additional commentary on Islam in Europe and the European Union, see relevant entries in Hunter and books in progress by both Max Pensky and Peter Katzenstein on European integration.) Benhabib briefly discusses the Kemalist language reform of 1928 as an example of Bhabha's concept of national pedagogy. In creating a Turkish alphabet based on Latin rather than Arabic script, "Ataturk simply chose the West, expressing this most dramatically by abolishing the cultural and literary medium in which the Muslim elite of the empire had expressed itself" (2002b: 10).
39. Neither do the tools of historiography unlock the secrets of literature. Yet schematic models of cultural difference have obscured the historical dimensions of this literature. The present study speaks to this lacuna.
40. I take issue with Johnson's notion that literary structures and social contexts can be separated (1997a: 261; 1997b: 153). Johnson also has trouble sustaining this notion (1997a, 1997b, 2001). Bayer calls for but does not deliver literary analysis of "migrants' literature" beyond cultural studies.
41. Literature of migration need not be authored by migrants. This is why I now speak of a literature of migration rather than "migrants' literature." See Heinze; Teraoka 1987; Suhr 1989; Adelson 1990; Gökberk 1991; Rösch; Şölçün 1992; Weigel 1992; Taufıq; Grünefeld; Amodeo; Fischer and McGowan 1996; Esselborn 1997; Chiellino 2000: 389–390; and Bayer for a sampling of references and debates indexing "guest worker literature," "foreigners' literature," "migrants' literature," "literature in Germany," and "intercultural literature."
42. Short- and long-distance modes of affiliation are not mutually exclusive. The short-distance intimacy discussed in chapter one, e.g., is predicated both on the sociability of a courtyard (short-distance) and the print medium of literature (long-distance).
43. See Kuruyazıcı 1995 for a partially anecdotal account of one book's reception in Germany and Turkey. Social effects sparked by Zaimoğlu are the exception to the rule. See Cheesman 1998, 2002, and 2004 on *Kanak Sprak*'s reception.
44. The archival metaphor appears literal in one novel when East German theater directors desire notes and drawings by the Turkish protagonist " 'for the archive' " (Özdamar 2003: 129). While the novel may contribute to a transnational German archive of cultural affairs, it does not constitute a historiographical archive. My archival claim thus differs from the more casual one made by Mani, who characterizes Özdamar's novels as "an archive where the documents of Europe's recent history are written by a woman worker" (2003: 30). If the literature of migration functions as a cultural archive then, its function differs radically from "the archive as counterweight to the ever-increasing pace of change" in the 1990s (Huyssen 2003b: 26). Archival functions accruing to the literature of migration are also too context-dependent for Agamben's definition

to apply: "the system of relations between the unsaid and the said in every act of speech" (144). Derrida's remarks on archival operations of "house arrest" and "consignation" are more apt (2–5).
For one historian, "historiography serves a function of cultural orientation" (Rüsen 256). I argue instead that the literature of migration speaks to a broad shift in historical orientation. Rüsen's understanding of historiography speaks rather to what Huyssen describes as the "pedagogical and philosophical mission" associated with historical continuity and national tradition (2003b: 2–5). To the degree that matters of orientation figure centrally in the literature of migration, it lacks postmodern features that Lützeler otherwise identifies in German literary encounters between past and present around 1990 (1993). Yet the literature of Turkish migration celebrates no grand narratives of any sort.

45. Mattson refers to the stereotype casting guest workers as "forlorn and disoriented" (73). Tertilt notes the sociological presumption that migrants suffer from normative disorientation predisposing them to delinquency (219).
46. "Federal Republic of Germany" refers to both West Germany and unified Germany; "Berlin Republic" refers to the latter. Santner describes the late 1980s as a period of "great disorientation" in Germany (1990: 150).
47. Benhabib lists phenomena broadly altering the terms of multiculturalism since 1989 (2002b: 113–114). To Benhabib's list one could add civil, inter-, and transnational wars as well as humanitarian crises exacerbating a widespread sense of urgency coupled with disorientation between 1990 and 2003. Gaonkar describes "a radically different . . . milieu signaled by the cataclysmic events of 1989 and their aftermath" (Gaonkar and Lee 1).
48. No comprehensive overview of either the literature of Turkish migration or scholarly publications on Turkish-born authors of German literature will be provided.
49. This passage from "Through the Looking-Glass" is not cited in Özdamar's story.
50. Analysis here emphasizes narrative, especially novels, short stories, and some essays. For insights into theatrical and lyrical works of migration, see Sieg (233–253); Clark (222–249); Sven Sappelt and Mark Terkessidis's contributions to Chiellino (2000), and Yeşilada's trailblazing dissertation in progress on lyric poetry.
51. Levent Soysal explains, "migrations are less and less about origins and destinations" (2003: 492). I speak of a literature of migration rather than immigration for two reasons. First, Germany has only recently begun to understand itself as a country of immigration. Second, even though Turks may be German citizens or permanent residents, the literature does not turn on normative claims to admission.
52. Heidenreich underscores the centrality of visual perceptions of difference (31). While visible difference is often associated with Turkish threats to German life, Brady demonstrates, discourses of threat function "not only as a language of exclusion but also as a part of the process of inclusion" (208).
53. Contrast this with anti-Semitic discourses of visibility and disguise in German culture (Gilman 1985, 1991; Sieg 29–71).
54. My approach is more beholden to flexible theories of narratology such as those articulated by Herman and Marie-Laure Ryan. See also Rimmon-Kenan on postclassical narratology in the revised edition of *Narrative Fiction*.
55. Santner offers nuanced reflections on elegiac structures in the late writings of de Man (1990: 15–30), especially regarding cultures of mourning in postwar Germany.

56. Herman reviews relevant scholarship and clarifying distinctions between the intensionality and extensionality of literary texts (324–325).
57. LaCapra faults White for ignoring affective dimensions of historical narrative (2004a), while Rothberg argues, "White ultimately removes the discourse of realism from 'real events'" (101–102).
58. Sieg modifies Roach's concept of surrogation for her German context (13).
59. The distinction is between historical narratives positing an analogy between one minority group and another (say, Turks and Jews in Germany) and fictional narratives in which disparate histories are made to bump up against each other by circulating in the same narrative (Adelson 1998). Oral remarks to this effect in various venues introduced earlier versions of work presented here in chapter two. The distinction between *proximate historical narratives* and *historical narrative by proxy* also informs my understanding of "touching tales," as elaborated below.
60. The title of the novel could also be translated as "dangerous relations" or "dangerous affinity." For intertextual allusions in the German, see Gerstenberger (238) and Huyssen 2003a (157).
61. Sieg observes, "Özdamar avoids positivist notions of migrant identity" (251). At the same time, she considers Özdamar's play one example of "what happens when the referent takes the stage . . . for political purposes of her own" (222).
62. Konuk similarly rejects the "fetishization of alterity" (2001: 191; see also Sieg 245).
63. Gökberk makes a related observation (146). My emphasis is not on minority writing in Germany generally but on "touching tales" as a distinct literary phenomenon, which may also be found in texts considered minority writing.
64. *Lines of Thought* is also a critique of Foucault on the historical relationship between words and things.
65. I thank Jeffrey Librett for dotting this i in discussion at Stanford University in April 2001.
66. Shafi focuses on German-language encounters between white Europeans and what they consider the Third World. Noting the tendency to speak of "intercultural literature" arising out of migration, Kuruyazıcı assigns this literature to a "third space" between national cultures (2001: 10). Sometimes citing Bhabha (1994: 37), other scholars suggest much the same (e.g., Göktürk 1999a: 519; Waldhoff; Bachmann-Medick 1996c: 278–280; Veteto-Conrad; Milz). This gesture tends to reproduce the cultural fable of "two worlds." Faist rejects hybridity and thirdness as sociological concepts (2000a: 44–45). Kramsch's insights into "thirdness" regarding intercultural linguistic competence are of limited value for literary analysis. Karakuş speaks of a third "language of literature" between Turkish and German (1994: 232–233).
67. Rüsen identifies intercultural communication and comparison as cornerstones of "a renewed historicism" that could address the worldwide "crisis of orientation" since 1989 (194, 209, 229). Rieger, Schahadat, and Weinberg stress intercultural performance but reject anthropological concepts of cultures as seamless wholes. The archive of their subtitle is an archive of fissures within culture construed as always already intercultural.
68. Citing Gadamer favorably, Benhabib speaks of more differentiated functions of understanding (2002b: 5, 34–35). Like Sommer, Bachmann-Medick stresses the importance of "(mis-)understanding" as a corrective to the erasure of difference that universalism can entail (1987; 1996c: 280).

69. For commentary on Şenocak as a public intellectual, see Adelson 2000a; Konzett 2003a; and Bullivant 2004.
70. Sommer; Seyhan; and Gökberk do not account for the full range of hermeneutic thought or even Gadamer's philosophy.
71. Reasons for this displeasure diverge. Şenocak argues for recognition of what Kocka would call "entangled histories." Sommer suggests that bilingualism wields a dual political advantage, first, by demanding "respectful distance" among interlocutors and, second, by promoting a democratic taste for ambiguity (2003: 10–11). Sommer later stresses playful aspects of this relationship (2004).
72. Committed to classicial humanism, Pazarkaya began writing stories and poems about Turkish migration in the 1970s. Having moved to West Germany in 1958 to study, this author is respected in German and Turkish circles alike for essays and translations promoting cross-cultural dialogue on humanist grounds. Section head for Turkish affairs in a major radio concern, Pazarkaya has played an important role in German news media.
73. Gökberk's account of intercultural hermeneutics is indebted to "intercultural Germanistics" associated with the Society for Intercultural Germanistics, founded in 1984 and conceived in terms of "comparative cultural anthropology" (Wierlacher 1994: 40). First president of the Society, Wierlacher locates the field "between the cultures," its mission to contribute to the "dialogue of cultures" in an era of growing interdependence (42–45). (See entries by Krusche; Mecklenburg; Phipps; and Zimmermann.) Chiellino faults German universities for twenty years of "monocultural" discussions about the need for intercultural approaches to literature (389).
74. Gökberk's example is an Özdamar novel set entirely in Turkey, in which Turkish idioms rendered into German lend a whimsical effect to the German narrative, which evaporates in the Turkish translation. For divergent approaches to the use of language in this novel, see Aytaç 1997; Boa 1997; Konuk 1997; and Kuruyazıcı 1997. For an alternative approach to spatial configurations in the literature of migration, see Adelson 2001. (This article deals with texts by Şenocak and Zaimoğlu that chapter two analyzes in terms of historical figuration rather than spatial conceits.)
75. Taylor speaks favorably of hermeneutics in "the politics of recognition" (1992: 25–73). This endorsement rests on Taylor's paraphrase of Gadamer's key term, whereby "a fused horizon of standards" forecloses erasure of difference (70).
76. Huyssen 2003a and Leggewie 2002 (2005: 94) echo this question, which Şenocak first posed in 1992.
77. Leggewie explicitly states that his remarks are not meant to be comprehensive (2005: 81). On the general issue of immigrants' relationship to Germany's genocidal past, see Klopp (188–193) and Georgi.

Chapter One: Dialogue and Storytelling

1. Excluded here are both journalistic exposés that rely on strategic fictions of "Turkish" identity and ethnographic narratives of Turkish life in Germany (see Sieg; Teraoka 1989, 1996b).
2. See publisher's front matter (n.p.). West German history from 1965 to 1989 is meant.

3. Şölçün calls Ören the only author belonging to the Turkish minority to be "recognized as a German author, even though he does not write in the German language" (Chiellino 2000: 146).
4. Levent Soysal criticizes both tropes in social studies and cultural studies of migration (2003a).
5. The present study focuses on transformations in a national context shaped by the history of West Germany, which differs significantly from other countries where German-language literature is the norm. Novels by Frischmuth and Rabinovici warrant special mention in the Austrian context. Turks do not figure significantly in East German literature, though "third world" figures do. Teraoka compares such figures in East and West German literature (1996a).
6. See also Taufiq. Schmalz-Jacobsen refers to migrants as "the blind spot" in German schoolbooks.
7. Hielscher reviews "a new pleasure in storytelling" in German literature of the 1990s (321). See Bullivant and Briegleb on "the crisis of narration" associated with 1968.
8. Kuruyazıcı additionally criticizes the presumption that readers' responses are predetermined by their culture of origin. Hoffmann speaks of "independent cultures" and distinct "life worlds" (98, 132).
9. Mani defines "narraphasia" as "a kind of narrative aphasia," whereby narrators' inability to know their subjects and subalterns' inability to make themselves known are reflected in a narrator's "self-interrogation" (24–25). For Mani, *Selim* represents something new because an ethnically German author writes "guest worker literature" (31). This may be another way of saying that *Selim* is the first mainstream novel to take labor migration seriously (Durzak 1993: 294), but the category of "guest worker literature" is too narrow to account for the novel's significance.
10. Gökberk especially targets my earlier analysis of *Selim* (1994). See Adelson 1997c for my response. Gökberk elsewhere analyzes dialogic scenes in a novel by a Turkish author living in Germany in the 1980s (1997b).
11. Primarily concerned with the ambivalence of national identities, for which Bhabha's terms were key, and only secondarily with the "emblematic" function of the train encounter (1994: 312), my earlier analysis failed to make this argument clearly. The train scene marks the moment when the main characters' lives first intersect, not the novel's beginning.
12. Durzak notes the novel was the first to recognize "a cultural symbiosis" exceeding "social co-existence" (1993: 294), but the relationship he means is one of mutual respect for national identities.
13. Bosse observes that Alexander is preoccupied with his newspaper without commenting on the news Alexander reads (198).
14. *Selim* could be added to Braese's list of postwar literature in which the Auschwitz trials play a central role, a "slim" subfield (2001b: 224).
15. Alexander's reflections here largely concern his disappointment with the antifascist student movement of 1968, which he deems a "catastrophe of communication" (273).
16. Because this concerns a German national narrative, the novel still reflects basic premises of the postwar era. See Huyssen 2003a on changing tensions between national and postnational memory cultures of the 1990s. Cornerstone events in

Turkish history are indexed in the novel only occasionally. Scholars emphasizing its intercultural features highlight disagreement between Alexander and Selim about Atatürk's legacy and the role of the military in Turkey. While this exchange, like the chapter "In Turkey," is key to intercultural interpretations advanced by Durzak and others, it does not have the sustained heft of far more numerous dialogues indexing the Nazi legacy in West Germany.
17. Schlant's title reflects a paradigm often invoked to understand West German culture. See Stern (1991, 1992) and Braese (2001a) for important challenges to it. Geyer speaks of "the myth of a German amnesia" about the Nazi past (169).
18. In 1982 the narrator retains interest in the oppositional potential of storytelling but bemoans the "blabber about resistance, the basis of which no longer comprises decisions, but feigned or borrowed conditions of excitation instead" (361).
19. Alexander imagines Selim as "something like a natural teacher for rhetoric" (8).
20. Bude discusses 1968 as a mythological German *lieu de mémoire* "between 1945 and 1989" (122), but like most others writing about the German significance of 1968, he never mentions Turkish migration. Leggewie makes the broader point that the anthology on German *lieux de mémoire* includes no example from a Turkish–German milieu (2002, 2005: 73). Huyssen lodges a similar complaint against scholarship on German and French *lieux de mémoire*, which fails to allow for "diasporic phenomena" (2003a: 152). The "tremendous subjective forces unleashed" for young Germans in the late 1960s (Schmid 128) combined with transgenerational guilt and loss in the democratic successor state to the Third Reich (Bude, Lepsius). Nadolny situates the story of Selim and Alexander in this morass.
21. Gökberk notes the predominance of references to "German national discourse" in *Selim*, but explains it by saying that "everything is narrated from the European perspective" (1997a: 106–107).
22. "Minor" is meant here in its prosaic sense. On literature of Turkish migration as both minority literature and "minor literature" in the sense articulated by Deleuze and Guattari, see Teraoka 1987; Suhr 1989; Gökberk 1991; Weigel 1992; Seyhan 1996b; Boa 1997; Frölich 1997; Mattson 1997; Ghaussy 1999; Begemann 1999; Konuk 2001; Seyhan 2001; and Chin 2003.
23. Charging minority literatures with elitism, Weidauer polemically asserts, "Turkish Germans do not read Emine Özdamar's books" (21). The subject of intended readership is addressed below. On Özdamar's life and oeuvre see Wierschke 1996; Horrocks and Kolinsky 1996; Konuk 2001; Seyhan 2001; and Sieg. According to her publisher (as reported by Özdamar), the author had given a record-breaking number of public readings by 1993 alone (Wierschke 1996: 268).
24. Nadolny had received the Bachmann Prize in 1980. On controversies surrounding the competition of 1991, see Wierschke (209) and Jankowsky.
25. Özdamar also acted in German films, notably Hark Bohm's *Yasemin* (1988) and Doris Dörrie's *Happy Birthday, Türke!* (1992).
26. Poetry by Else Lasker-Schüler (1869–1945) provides the title for the later novel.
27. Named after a French aristocrat who found Prussian refuge from the French Revolution and contributed to German Romanticism, this annual prize was

established in 1984 to recognize talented writers for whom German is not a first language. (See Esselborn 1995 for details.)
28. To date this text is available only in the German original.
29. References to the first-person narrator as a Turkish woman rely on textual indications that the narrator was born and raised in Turkey as a Turkish citizen. This applies to Özdamar too, though the author's ethnic background is Kurdish and her citizenship German. There are no explicit references to citizenship in the story, and the only mention of Kurds features a woman whose crying resembles that of the narrator's mother. The equivocal narratological relationship between the nameless "I" of the story and the author is discussed below.
30. Özdamar mobilizes interest in crosscultural intimacy without pandering to the kind of universalism that Sommer indicts along with the "conspiratorial intimacy" of understanding (1994: 526–527). See introduction for related remarks.
31. On the imagination as a social category and political phenomenon, Appadurai cites Weber, Anderson, Castoriadis, Lefort, Laclau and Mouffe, Gramsci, Williams, and others. To this list one could add contributors to the issue of *Public Culture* devoted to "New Imaginaries" (Gaonkar and Lee 2002).
32. Appadurai defines *mediascapes* in a way that seems to exclude literature. Özdamar's approach to figural mediation might nonetheless be considered in terms of a mediascape of sorts.
33. Indebted to Appadurai, Jenny White could be clearer on this important distinction when referring to "interactive ethnoscapes" (1997: 755). She generally does not presume the primacy of a Turkish national context for Turks in Germany, and she too stresses "a grammar for future community" (765).
34. Weidauer misreads Appadurai differently when he ascribes a nation-centered concept of diaspora to the anthropologist's account of "modernity at large."
35. Anderson discusses "long-distance nationalism" (1998: 58–74) as a modern phenomenon involving decisive affinities among persons with no "face-to-face contact" (1991: 6). He also addresses the changing "grammar" of nationalism "as a consequence of contemporary mass migrations and revolutions in communications and transportation" (1998: 26). This "disjunction" represents only one historical form of "long-distance nationalism" as Anderson defines it. For other seminal discussions of long-distance affiliation in public spheres and social imaginaries, see Habermas, Gaonkar and Lee.
36. Besides the author's father, the book is dedicated to the poet Can Yücel and the writer John Berger. The courtyard story evokes the latter in its attention to modes of seeing and experiences of migration.
37. Özdamar's riff on this "long-distance-viewing news service" might also be a spoof of sociological stereotypes of migrants' television viewing habits in Europe. See Robins as well as Aksoy and Robins for critical alternatives.
38. In linguistics, "*deixis* refers to all the resources of language that anchor it to essential points in context" (Herman 332). Kacandes applies the concept "to any literary strategy that can be interpreted as signaling a text's orientation to an answering" (30).
39. If the telephone is "inhabited by new modalities of being-called" (Ronell 3), courtyard use of this medium mostly serves conventional communicative purposes.
40. This distinguishes the courtyard narrative from *Rear Window* (1954). As Eric Santner recalled in discussion at the University of Chicago in May 2003,

the Hitchcock classic and Özdamar story revolve around fantasies of community. The German title of the former may be echoed in the title of the latter. Özdamar additionally conjures cornerstone films indexing migrant subjects in Germany, one by Fassbinder in 1973 and another by Başer in 1986. Mirrors, windows, and doors are especially important in the latter, in which an isolated Turkish woman looks longingly into an apartment courtyard but establishes no real contact with her neighbors.

41. Breger notes that the "art of the indirect gaze" in Özdamar's *Life* undermines the mirror as a means of imaging the self (1999: 39). Neighbors in and around the courtyard are often unaware that they are being watched.
42. Cohn critically cites Lejeune's account of first-person indeterminacy in autobiographical prose to advance her "separatist thesis," positing that literary fiction "is not a matter of degree but of kind." Lejeune considers an autobiographical voice "indeterminate" when the narrating "I" bears no name and the text evidences no other formal signs of autobiography. For Cohn, first-person narration that is not unequivocally non-referential cannot be read as literary fiction (32). Özdamar's narrator would be referential in kind—and the text non-fictional—by Cohn's account. My reading of the story is incompatible with Cohn's absolute demands.
43. Cohn cites "presentation of the inner life" of characters as a necessary condition of fiction (16).
44. Those with less power and fewer rights often pay keen attention to the habits of the powerful. More is at stake in "The Courtyard."
45. See Corngold on the "literary tension" arising when "what sentences say and what they do" diverge. In literature such tension becomes "concentrated to elicit new forms of feeling" (xii–xiii).
46. Özdamar uses a modified German translation of a two-line Turkish poem called "Voli" or "Casting Net" by Can Yücel (1926–1999), acclaimed in Turkey for literary translations of Anglophone masterpieces (Fergar 21). Fergar includes the Turkish original and his English translation (66–67). Özdamar credits Recai Hallaç with the German translation.
47. The most striking pun tagged as such is identified as a line from Baudelaire when an impoverished neighbor is evicted for not paying rent and urinating into the nuns' flower pots while screaming " 'Les fleurs du mal—Blumen des Bösen' " [flowers of evil] (38).
48. While colloquial use of "blue" in English connotes sadness, the Turkish word for the color connotes no affect. The disorientation of relationality warrants emphasis in Özdamar's German appropriation.
49. Wise reflects this punning combination in her dissertation title.
50. Referring to social activities studied by anthropologists, Appadurai speaks of "moments in a general technology (and teleology) of localization" (180). While this reference to technology is especially apt for literature of migration, no teleology of localization applies.
51. See introduction. The only courtyard reference to an actual border involves a chicken and an egg.
52. Characteristics ascribed to the narrator might encourage readers to interpret her voice as the author's. This feature in Özdamar's prose generally fuels references to her work as autobiographical. Breger pointedly rejects the presumption of

autobiography in her reading of *Life* (1999). Others challenge presumptions of "authenticity" regarding this novel (Wierschke 1996: 162; Göktürk 1999a: 532).
53. Yücel's translations of Shakespeare, Yeats, Eliot, and others garnered him much acclaim in Turkey; for his translations of Che Guevara and Mao Zedong he reaped a prison sentence (Fergar 21; Halman 1982: 451). Özdamar once likened Yücel to Joyce in stature (Wierschke 1996: 253).
54. Source notes incorrectly identify the Brecht song cited as the "Alabama Song."
55. Ryan notes, "even when fiction uses names that have currency in the real world, it does not refer to real-world objects, but to their counterparts inside its own textual world" (2002: 359). She characterizes this as "more akin to self-reference" than non-referentiality (358).
56. Breger analyzes Özdamar's strategic use of mimicry as a critical rejoinder to German Orientalism (1999). Konuk discusses Orientalist tropes in Özdamar's early German reception (1997, 1999).
57. In a gesture that similarly challenges distinctions between real and virtual worlds, the narrator tickles a young nun in her mirror, warms the old nun in the mirror with a fur coat, and kisses the mirrored priest.
58. As discussed in the introduction and chapter two, Bhabha figures Turkish guest workers in Germany as a trope for "the radical incommensurability of translation" (1990a: 317).
59. A parrot also figures in Özdamar's novel of 1998. On stereotypes in other migration stories, see Mattson and Durzak 2004. On Turkish–German satire, see especially Yeşilada 1997b. Chow discusses stereotyping as a structurally necessary site where historical relations between ethnicity and representation are negotiated (50–94).
60. Reading the parrot as a cipher of mimicry would thus not exhaust its figural function.
61. Although the narrator communicates with various individuals by telephone, the lone reference to telegraph poles conjures a different medium.
62. See Fergar for a slightly different English translation. Mine derives from Hallaç's German rendition. The second Yücel poem featuring "love" that Can cites is "Baharla Ölüm Konuşmaları" [Death Conversations with Spring]. The relevant excerpt appears in Fergar as "Dust-Bath/IV" (96–97). For the longer Turkish text see Yücel (9–38).
63. This is in addition to emotional attachments that she has to her parents and Can. These figures never travel to Düsseldorf, though they too belong to the courtyard ethnoscape.
64. The bus driver conjures romantic love as well.
65. This text paradoxically lengthens the ties that bind by foregrounding short- rather than long-distance modes of affiliation.
66. The urban German tradition of apartment buildings organized around a shared courtyard—across which neighbors can see into each other's units—might also be captured by reference to neighbors waking up "nose to nose." Housing represents one technology of localization discussed by Appadurai.
67. Benhabib elaborates a related critique (2002b: 24–48). "Philosophical theories of strong incommensurability," she suggests, "produce bad historiography" (39).
68. Like Sommer, who stresses romance in literary contributions to national intimacy in Latin America, Zantop discusses romance in pre- and transnational

colonial fantasies in German culture (1997). No emphasis on romance holds for the courtyard. Margaret Cohen distinguishes between romance and "sentimental codes" in fiction of an earlier era (Cohen and Dever 123, n. 2). Sommer calls for a "new sentimental education" adequate to the present (2003: 4; 2004).
69. Green's refined account of views of affect that prevail in psychoanalysis is invoked here in a very limited way. For Silvan Tomkins, whose theory challenges a Freudian emphasis on drives, the affect of interest–excitement is physically indicated by tracking, looking, and listening (Sedgwick and Frank 74). The courtyard narrator's observational habits signal the affect of interest.
70. This taking-on-of-form differs from structures of mimicry, performativity, theatricality, or drag in earlier works by Özdamar evaluated by Breger (1999); Konuk (1999); Sieg; and Mani (2001, 2003). To varying degrees, these scholars engage critically with the notion that mimicry harbors oppositional potential for history's oppressed (see especially Bhabha 1994: 85–92).
71. See Kacandes for insights into "talk fiction" and "secondary orality" in today's medial economy.
72. Propositional attitudes are signaled by particles of speech "denoting belief, doubt, intention, etc." (Lyons 190). Herman argues, "ways of focalizing a story can be redescribed as the narrative representation of propositional attitudes" (310).
73. For Tomkins, shame always involves intersubjective relationships as "an actual or potential source of positive affect." Broad social significance accrues to shame as distinguished from contempt for this reason (156–157).
74. Hartmut is also the only neighbor to track the tracker's habits.
75. Herman cites Grice's "Cooperative Principle," whereby conversational partners assume that responses are nonrandom (176), and Brown and Yule's principle of contiguity, whereby contiguous utterances are interpreted as connected (224).
76. The first two Heine verses cited are contiguous in "The Homecoming" (*Die Heimkehr* in Heine I.1 488). The final verse cited is from Heine's "Abroad" (*In der Fremde* in Heine II 71). Cited here, Draper's English translations are not entirely felicitous (173, 362). For courtyard purposes, the final verb should be "look around" rather than "stare."
77. See Kacandes for extended discussion of narrative "you."
78. Tomkins calls the face "the prime organ of affect" (204).
79. The sentences cited are not actually the last sentences on p. 103 of the Enzensberger translation.
80. Neither are they reserved for any particular sexual orientation, though gay and lesbian figures have relatively minor roles in Özdamar's prose.
81. Despite their differing interpretations of a mother–daughter configuration in *Life*, Konuk (1999) and Breger (1999) both reject the presumption of naïve or authentic voices there. Şölçün stresses Özdamar's performance of naïveté in *Brücke* (2002); Mani also rejects any "fetishization of authenticity" in readings of that novel (2003: 32). See also Göktürk (1999a: 532). Although Özdamar generally privileges women as focalizing agents, a feminist perspective is not necessarily given in her work. Sieg identifies "a masculine discourse on migration" in *Keloglan* (251).
82. The original Turkish poem includes no punctuation marks either (Fergar 67). Deviating from Fergar's English translation (66), my English translation is from Özdamar's usage of Hallaç's otherwise unpublished German adaptation.

83. In this it is like the falling book in the dream of transubstantiation, except the dream book is embedded in narration.
84. Translated excerpts from Carroll and Conrad do not play the same role in courtyard exchange that accrues to poetry by Heine, Baudelaire, and Yücel.
85. If we assume that Turkish interlocutors would normally conduct their telephone conversations in Turkish, these conversations comprise another set of implied translations unmarked as such.

Chapter Two: Genocide and Taboo

1. "The entire German people are called upon to achieve [*vollenden*] in free self-determination the unity and freedom of Germany" (Karpen 226). The revised preamble of 1990 announces the completion of this task. West German culture was largely characterized, however, by "a strong anti-nationalism" and everyday acceptance of the national divide (Huyssen 1995: 68).
2. With the translator's kind permission I rely mostly on Tom Cheesman's English version of the novel; exceptions will be noted. First published in Adelson 2000b, the Zaimoğlu translations used are mine.
3. Levy and Sznaider stress the late 1990s as the moment when transnational memory culture begins to shape-change decisively (29).
4. Like Beck, they speak of a "second age of modernity." Compare this with Appadurai's "global modern" (1996: 9–11). Intending no linear model, Levy and Sznaider nonetheless propose modernity's "second age" as a normative ideal.
5. Contrast this approach to visual culture with the sophistication of Koch (1992, 1999b). For analytical reflections on the interplay between "defining enemies" and "making victims" in representational culture and historical research, see Bartov (1998).
6. "Perhaps nowhere else have issues of memory and forgetting played such a key role in the delineation of the national self-image as in the two Germanys after 1945 and in Germany since 1989–90" (Herf 2002: 275; see also Herf 1997; Fox). Citing Huyssen on the "memory boom" (1995: 8) of the 1980s and 1990s, Neumann notes a concomitant "boom in memorial criticism" (2).
7. Assmann notes that symbolic invocations of Holocaust memory have intensified since the mid-1980s in Germany and that Auschwitz has simultaneously come to function as a universal symbol for twentieth-century crimes against humanity (Assmann and Frevert 144–147). Echoing Diner (1999, 2003a, 2003b), Huyssen writes, " 'Auschwitz' has become something like a civic religion in Germany, and for better or for worse, it may by now have become a foundational myth of the new Europe" (2003b: 143). Reference to a "myth" in this context merely highlights symbolic functions of the word in the 1990s. See also Borneman 1992.
8. Huyssen notes that this decentered rhetoric of Holocaust memory may "serve as a screen memory" for or obscure unrelated local histories. Levy and Sznaider do not allow for this.
9. This formulation stresses the centrality of anti-Semitism in Nazi ideology and the pivotal function of "Jewish" figures in the literature of migration discussed.

Huyssen focuses on Şenocak's novel precisely because it explores how German Turks "can migrate into German history" (2003a: 158).
10. Hell discusses the speech in terms of a post-Wall crisis of "post-Holocaust authorship" (2003: 19–21); see also Eshel.
11. This is a scalar claim. Talk of German suffering is "the oldest component of a long tradition in talking about National Socialism, World War II, and annihilation of the Jews," claims one historian (Berg).
12. New public narratives of Germans being bombed coincided with widespread German resistance to the Iraq war launched by the United States in 2003. "To speak about the air war seemed inescapably tied to [an older] discourse of German victimization and thus to a relativization or denial of the Holocaust," Huyssen explains (2003b: 147). "Today this taboo has lost its force." On competing memory claims in the early Federal Republic, see Barnouw. Langenbacher addresses the growing field of "memory regimes" competing for public attention in Germany today.
13. Her historical analysis is centrally informed by Freud's structural account of taboo.
14. This Turkish novum entails a partial turn rather than a "new beginning." See Huyssen on "new beginning as a key myth of postwar German literature" (2003b: 144).
15. Santner speaks of "competing narratives" regarding the representation of trauma in German history (1992: 143). On "the limits of representation" in this regard, see Friedlander; LaCapra (1998); and Rothberg. For less than euphoric remarks on unification from a minority viewpoint, see Ayim.
16. See Eryılmaz and Jamin for additional factors influencing Turkish migration to Germany in the 1960s.
17. This discourse often links "democratic," "European," and "Christian" explicitly. See Wehler for a recent example. Şenocak took pointed issue with this discourse of incompatibility in 1991 (2000: 13–19).
18. For Hayden White, metonymy "presupposes the spatial or temporal contiguity of the objects conflated in a reductive metaphor" (104). Such contiguity cannot account for the proximity I have in mind, partly because of the pragmatic associations that metonymy connotes.
19. This figural role did not originally fall to Turks, as a political poster from the early 1970s (discussed later) demonstrates.
20. See Axel Vahldiek's problematic entry in Waldhoff et al. Brumlik rejects glib comparisons of Turks and Jews circulating around 1990. For related remarks see Linke; Peck; Şenocak 2000: 53–57. A chapter in Peck's book in progress on "new Jews in a new Germany" will also be relevant. So-called Turkish jokes and violent electronic games hinge on explicit linkages between Turks and Jews (Linke 57–58). This phenomenon predates unification (Milich). "Kanak jokes" of recent vintage were partly sparked by Zaimoğlu's celebration in German media.
21. This is not to say that no such juxtapositions may be found earlier, but that the frequency and intensity of the linkage are qualitatively new.
22. This characterization is attributed to Grünefeld, as cited on the dust jacket for Şenocak 1997.
23. Remarking on Mölln and Solingen, one political scientist observes: "Instead of 'integrating' in the manner the German government and the majority of the

German population appear to desire, that is, by becoming invisible as Turks, these young Turks insist upon visibility and upon an acceptance of their Turkish identity" (Kolinsky 2002: 14). Jenny White cites a survey taken in 1994 indicating that 83 percent of Turks surveyed had no plans to leave Germany in spite of the attacks (1997: 755; Goldberg 1996: 3).

24. The narrator of *Perilous Kinship* reflects critically on the German culture of ritualized *Betroffenheit*, a state of being moved and, through this movement, interpellated. "Grief hides from the mourners their reason for mourning. This phenomenon is called 'feeling deeply affected.' . . . It is the birth of farce from the spirit of tragedy" (61–62). Compare this with "narrative fetishism," which Santner defines as "the construction and deployment of a narrative consciously or unconsciously designed to expunge the traces of the trauma or loss that called that narrative into being in the first place" (1992: 144). See also Morris on "fetishized reverence" (303) and Hell on a scopic "structure of fetishism" (2003: 25).

25. This coincides temporally with the globalization of Holocaust discourse, but Germany's resident Turks have not appropriated a universal rhetoric of victimization or pursued a victim-based politics of identity. The literature of migration responds instead to German discourses that construe Turkish migrants as stand-ins for Jewish victims of the Nazi genocide.

26. Chow overlooks something important when she characterizes Bhabha's work as "iconophobic" (106).

27. LaCapra's reliance on psychoanalytic terms is subject to challenge by both historians who reject psychoanalytic emphases and scholars who favor keener engagement with psychoanalysis. LaCapra does not adhere to any particular psychoanalytic school of thought, and he characterizes his approach to psychoanalysis as "nontechnical" (1998: 6).

28. LaCapra's overall project articulates methodological alternatives to the binarisms that often prevail in the writing of cultural history (e.g., victims and perpetrators, past and present). See also Perry Anderson's distinction between juxtaposition and comparison (Friedlander 54–65).

29. See Adelson 1994; Göktürk 1999; and Levent Soysal 2003a on this conjunction as an analytical problem.

30. I underscore Bhabha's temporal emphasis, since his work is cited by many who stress hybrid identities instead.

31. The German word *heimlich* can mean "having the quality of home" or also "secret." Key to Bhabha's argument is the fact that *unheimlich* is the German word for "uncanny." Like LaCapra, Bhabha relies pivotally on Freud. The work of Abraham and Torok influences both scholars too. Loosely appropriating their psychoanalytic terms for his story of migration, Bhabha posits the loss of home as the point of departure for national narrative and "the Turkish *Gastarbeiter*" as a figural icon for the nullification of metaphor.

32. This probably explains why the Turkish guest worker appears so clearly male to Bhabha.

33. Sieg similarly resists melancholic notions of "migrant identity . . . in a twilight zone of 'in-betweenness' " (239). Göktürk notes elsewhere that Bhabha borrows from Berger to arrive at the "figure of the speechless Turk in Europe" (Chiellino 2000: 330). Levent Soysal criticizes Bhabha for rendering the story of migration as a story of silence (2003a: 500–501). See n. 33 of introduction.

34. Hybridity is a leitmotif in the reception of literary works by Özdamar (Boa 1997; Konuk 1997) and other minority writers (Arens). See n. 14 of introduction for related references.
35. In West Germany this has been the standard term for mastering, overcoming, or otherwise coming to terms with the past. Usually the Nazi past is meant. Scholarship on this subject is vast. See Judith Ryan and Maier for important points of entry in different disciplines.
36. Literature has no monopoly on this ambiguity. See Herf's discussion of politicians' competing approaches to memory and democracy in the early years of the Federal Republic (1997: 267).
37. Schlant's study received widespread media coverage in the United States. Other relevant titles include Angress; Briegleb and Weigel; Judith Ryan; Steiner; Stern 1991; Friedlander; Braese 2001a; and Briegleb 2003. See also Braese 1998, in which Dan Diner systematically addresses the referential omission of the Holocaust from one historian's account of modern Europe. Distinguishing between "the absence of representation" and "the representation of absence," Bartov contends, "the representation of absence is arguably one of the most crucial tropes in German literary, cinematic, and scholarly representations of recent German history" (1997: 211). Indicting the most influential literary circle in West Germany, Briegleb links an absence of Holocaust representation in literary texts by former soldiers of the *Wehrmacht* to what he considers the group's disdain for Jewish authors. Briegleb challenges the foundational myth of the *Gruppe 47* as the moral conscience of the West German nation. See Braese 2001a on "the other memory" in German literature written by Jewish survivors.
38. The disruption of a ritualized approach to the Holocaust is not the only significant feature of this literature.
39. Teraoka argues that Weiss's world theater, which cultivates solidarity with oppressed peoples of the so-called Third World, "performs the missing act of resistance against fascism" that Weiss himself did not perform (1996a: 37). See Judith Ryan on the missing figure of Hercules in Weiss's *Ästhetik des Widerstands* (Ryan 30–31).
40. Weiss and *The Investigation* warrant two articles in Gilman and Zipes. See Robert Holub, "The Premiere of Peter Weiss's *The Investigation*," 729–735, and Robert Cohen, "Peter Weiss Attends the Frankfurt Auschwitz Trial," 722–728.
41. Robert Cohen discusses "scandalized" reactions to the absence of the word "Jew" in *The Investigation* (1998: 53–59). Compare this with Weiss's essay on Auschwitz as a place for which he had been "destined" because the Nazis classified him as Jewish in spite of his German Protestant upbringing, but which he had "managed to avoid" through exile (1967: 20).
42. See Wise for a vibrant analysis of German representations of "guest workers." Chin's synopsis addresses government policy and literary phenomena in tandem (2002). Prowe argues that the new radical right in Germany targets immigrants rather than Jews for vilification in an essay on "the power of (false) equation." Tibi argues that parallels drawn between anti-Semitism and xenophobia in Germany are "based on a false footing" (1996: 85).
43. I shall cite both the German original and the English translation by Skelton published in 1965 (Weiss 1965b), which deviates from the German in crucial ways.

44. See Mennel on masochistic aesthetics as a central feature of West German culture (1998).
45. See Kaiser on tropes of deferral specific to Marxism.
46. Skelton renders this as "forgive us our good deeds" (Weiss 1965b: 38).
47. In the English this scene is numbered 21 instead (58–59).
48. Without having thoroughly examined the vast scholarship on *Marat/Sade*, I am not prepared to claim this as an original question. I raise it to establish one interpretive framework in which some German literature of migration must be understood.
49. Butler's study critically engages Austin's account of linguistic acts and Althusser's concept of interpellation.
50. Without citing Butler, Ha makes a similar argument under the rubric of postcolonialism.
51. As Cheesman notes, " '*Kanake*' is powerful hate speech . . . appropriated by some racialized Germans . . . as a group self-ascription" (2004: 83). Çağlar notes that the music group Islamic Force once considered naming itself "Kan.Ak," a pun invoking both the derogatory German word for Turk (*Kanake*) and a Turkish expression for spilling blood (*Kan ak*) (2001: 240, n. 4). The German "Kanake" derives from the Hawaiian word for human being, but the means by which it became associated with Turks (meant to be disparaged by the term) are unclear. See Pukui and Elbert on related Hawaiian words and nuances (127). For speculations on links between the word's Hawaiian provenance, its German usage, and colonial histories, see Cheesman 2004: 83, n. 10; Yıldız 2005; and Fachinger 2001: 121, n. 32. See Yıldız on the German interpellation of migrants and minorities more generally (1999).
52. See n. 36 of introduction for distinctions between the antiracist organization established in 1999 called "Kanak Attak" and Zaimoğlu's subsequent treatise titled "KanakAttack." Although Zaimoğlu is no spokesperson for the organization or Turkish–German youth, *Kanak Sprak* reflected and contributed to attitudinal changes following lethal attacks on Turkish homes a few years earlier. Cheesman does an especially good job analyzing Zaimoğlu's actual work, the antiracist coalition it inspired, and the Zaimoğlu effect in media and commerce (2002, 2004).
53. Lottmann also mentions Malcolm X in apposition to Zaimoğlu. Designating Zaimoğlu a "writer of color" foregrounds political affiliations rather than ethnicity or race. Such an understanding underwrites the antiracist platform of Kanak Attak, but the ascription is neither self-evident nor unproblematic. Most Turks would not categorize themselves as persons "of color," even though many Germans see them that way. Cheesman explicitly includes Turks when speaking of "people 'of colour' " as " 'visible others' whose belonging . . . is constantly called into question in one way or another" (2003: 146). Frequent references in Zaimoğlu's writing and its reception to African American figures, rap culture, and hip-hop suggest in any event that many more touching tales are at stake than those for which this chapter accounts. Cheesman discusses Zaimoğlu in relation to transnational liberal multiculturalism and minority critiques thereof (2002). Fachinger loosely categorizes Zaimoğlu as "postcolonial" in this connection (2001).
54. Sieg remarks on a postwar "taboo on investigating 'race' and its legacies in official contexts," which coexisted with artistic and other attempts by Germans to

address the racist legacy of the Third Reich "even in the absence of an official language about it" (22). Cheesman discusses the vapid "Kanakisch" developed by two German comedy teams and marketed by a mainstream publisher (2004: 98–99). See Loh and Güngör on the nexus of commerce, culture, and politics from the vantage point of hip-hop artists and antiracist activists associated with *Kanak Attak*.

55. This information is based on Zaimoğlu's autobiographical essay (2001: 8–21). The dates conflict with information provided on the dust jacket of *Kanak Sprak* in 1995. The autobiographical essay diverges in tone from the "stylized slang" as which Cheesman correctly characterizes the work that made the author famous. The essay invokes multiple touching tales of Turkish migration when Zaimoğlu discusses the effects of Stalinist deportations and Balkan politics on family history.

56. Cheesman makes a persuasive case for understanding Zaimoğlu's work in the context of pop literature (2004: 99), but here too I would plead for a scalar model of contextualization. In my view pop literature and the literature of migration represent interactive rather than mutually exclusive frames of reference.

57. Zaimoğlu includes a transsexual without commentary in his otherwise pointedly masculinist selection, even though this interviewee concludes, "I am now a blessed bitch, sweetheart, and whatever happens to me now, it happens to me as a woman" (38).

58. Commenting on this social landscape, Fachinger (2001) and Cheesman (2002) rightly recall Wallraff's exposé of working conditions for migrant laborers in Germany of the 1980s (1988). Cheesman contrasts Zaimoğlu's " 'protocols' " with Dursun Akçam's bilingual documentation of interviews with a broad spectrum of Turkish citizens living in Germany, noting that *Kanak Sprak* focuses on "social outsiders" instead (Cheesman 2002: 183–184).See Moray McGowan on *Kanak Sprak* in relation to the "multiple masculinities" of the literature of Turkish migration (2001). Yıldız analyzes gender, affect, and multilingualism in the text (2005).

59. Despite the near absence of Turkish language traces, this literary German is complexly multilingual (Yıldız 2004, 2005). See also Cheesman (2002: 195). If Zaimoğlu's claim to have destroyed all interview tapes is true, there is no way to compare the multilingualism in the original interviews with the multilingualism in *Kanak Sprak*.

60. See Günter on *Kanak Sprak*'s authorship in terms of a collective process of articulation. For Günter, however, it is "impossible" to speak of *Kanak Sprak* as one text rather than several (18).

61. "Brotherhood" does not refer to an actual organization but reflects the mode of address foregrounded in *Kanak Sprak*. Sieg regards the parodic stance of Özdamar's *Keloglan* as a forerunner to the *Kanak Attak* movement (253). In using *Kanak, Kanake*, and *Kanaken*—which remain problematic as racist signifiers—I cite Zaimoğlu's critical appropriation of the category. Readers are asked to imagine the terms in quotation marks here.

62. Zaimoğlu attacks "the fairy tale of multiculturalism" for relegating *Kanaken* to "the great zoo of ethnic identities," where caged creatures can be "observed and admired" (11). Citing Berger on looking at animals in zoos, Chow notes,

"marginalized existence is a relation of visuality" (96). For Zaimoğlu, multicultural discourse of ethnic identity belongs "to the vocabulary of oppression" (Cheesman 2004: 87).

63. Tuschick clarifies that Zaimoğlu is concerned with " 'social problems' " that cannot be reduced to " 'ethnic difference' " (2000a: 108), adding that fans "cleave to him because they seek a community that they themselves define as ethnic" (115).

63. Günter discusses *Kanak Sprak* as a work in which " 'the others' " precisely do not disappear from view; she stresses visible "seams" or "sutures" between external ascriptions of ethnic identity and those mobilized by migrants to counter hate speech (16–17).

64. Zaimoğlu's *Kanaken* refer to Germans as *alemannen*, one of the few instances of trace elements from Turkish in the text.

65. This is similar to *halal* distinctions in Islamic dietary laws, but "halal" does not figure in Zaimoğlu's "Kanak" vocabulary.

66. Fachinger discusses Zaimoğlu's rhetoric of scatology in terms of a Bakhtinian, Rabelaisian "grotesque body" that effectively "writes back" in a gesture of postcolonial self-assertion (2001). Yeşilada plays with a similar notion of "writing back" for minority writing in Germany (2001). Invoking Gökberk (1991), Bachmann-Medick alludes to the gesture as well (1996a: 43). For Teraoka, the *Gastarbeiterliteratur* of the 1980s "speaks" rather than "writes" back to Germany (1987).

67. Cheesman makes a similar point about "angry young Turks" in *Kanak Sprak* (2002: 187), as does Ha in reference to *Abschaum* (50). Chow speaks generally of "coercive mimeticism" that produces marginalized subjects "as ethnics" (107).

68. Sellars examines "dreckology" and waste management in Freud, Adorno, and Wallace Stevens.

69. See Gilman on the circumcised Jewish body in German-speaking cultures (1991b) and recent representations of Jewish sexuality in German culture (1995).

70. Remarking on Gómez-Peña's "racialized scenarios" in cyber-art, Foster notes, "minoritized subjects often experience real life as a kind of virtual fantasy" projected onto them by the majority (62). The German fantasy projected onto the Turkish gigolo in *Kanak Sprak* departs significantly from the high moral chord struck in a Böll novel when the protagonist chooses a guest worker as her life's companion, thereby cementing her own status as an icon of antifascist integrity (Durzak 1993: 291; Chin 59; Akbulut 82–97). The scenario of German fantasy and *Kanak* critique in *Kanak Sprak* also entails a type of triangulated "ethnic drag" in the sense that "surrogation in postwar German theater primarily captures the ambivalence of memory and mourning, and denial and historical revisionism" (Sieg 13). Yet Zaimoğlu's "christ lady" renders "her" Jew figurally present by denying the literal presence of a Turk, and the effaced party in this triangle of ethnic surrogation speaks more assertively than the German fantasy.

71. Regarding "excitable speech" and cultural taboos, one might also consider the performative satire of Somuncu, a Turkish-born artist educated in Europe who has been performing critical readings in Germany of Hitler's *Mein Kampf* since 1996 and a notorious Goebbels's tirade since 2000.

72. The invisibility of living Jews in *Kanak Sprak* also reflects a broader phenomenon in postwar German literature. See Gilman (1991a).

73. Şenocak considers "the destruction of images" an important feature of his writing generally (Konzett 2003b: 133). The author uses this term in the sense of unsettling stereotypical images of "the other." My analysis of iconoclastic narration targets something beyond this.
74. Gellately and Kiernan's volume does not confine "the murderous side of the modern world" to the twentieth century, but probes the historical significance of genocide in that century. For thoughtful analyses of *Perilous Kinship* stressing its structure as a family history intervening in the German culture of postwar memory, see Gerstenberger and Eigler (2005).
75. Lamenting the absence of an Armenian "novel of novels" on the topic of genocide, Peroomian gives pride of place to Werfel and Hilsenrath, especially the latter (158–159). Kirby and Lorenz (1992: 270–275; 1998) elaborate on these texts by Jewish authors.
76. See Yeşilada's "outline biography" and her extensive international bibliography of relevant publications (Cheesman and Yeşilada 160–183). For additional background, overviews, and interviews, see Yeşilada 1998; Adelson 2000a; Konzett 2000b; Konzett 2003b; Waldhoff; Bullivant 2004; and Cheesman and Yeşilada.
77. Şenocak collaborated on the translation of the Ören novel, which appeared in German as *Eine verspätete Abrechnung* [A Belated Settling of Accounts]. The Turkish original and the German translation were both published in Germany. Şenocak has published or copublished important volumes that mediate Turkish culture for a largely ignorant German readership (Göktürk and Şenocak; Şenocak 1994a).
78. Şenocak 1992 and 2000 are not identical in content despite similar titles. According to various publications, the author moved to Berlin in 1988 (Şenocak 2003: 145), 1989 (Konzett 2003b: 131), or 1990 (Yeşilada 2003b: 16). Personal correspondence with the author clarifies that he moved to Berlin late in 1989 after having spent time there in 1988.
79. Cheesman has translated several excerpts from the first item under the rubric "The Man in a Vest" <http://www.swan.ac.uk/german/cheesman/senocak/man.htm>. Because the discussion here involves passages that Cheesman has not translated, I rely on my own translations for all citations from Şenocak 1995 to facilitate documentation. Page references are to the original text. Pagination for *Perilous Kinship* likewise refers to the German original, since Cheesman's translation has no pagination. In the case of *Perilous Kinship*, I rely on Cheesman's translation unless otherwise indicated.
80. For extended insights into Şenocak's poetry, including the Karpat collaborations, see Yeşilada 2002, 2003, and 2005. "Futurist epilogue" stems from Karpat and Şenocak (Yeşilada 2003: 127).
81. Yeşilada's bibliography includes journalistic publications on these topics. While *Mann* appeared in Turkish in 1997 as *Atletli Adam, Gefährliche Verwandtschaft* has to date been translated into only English and French. Newer literary works in German are expected soon; the author's first book of poetry written in Turkish has recently appeared (2004). A manuscript for the author's first novel in Turkish has also been completed.
82. Konzett makes a related observation (2003a: 51). Cheesman provides an amusing account of related difficulties beginning with the spelling of Şenocak's name (2003: 157).

83. See especially Şenocak 2000 (43–48, 62–65) and Şenocak 2001c (62–63). Elsewhere Şenocak calls for critical studies of discourse that could alter our understanding of migration in the same way that Foucault radically altered our understanding of sexuality (2000: 25).
84. Interviewing Şenocak for a Turkish audience in 1994, Halil Gökhan noted the frequency of spatial metaphors (houses, doors, windows, and the like) in the author's poetry (Şenocak 2000: 49–52). For additional remarks on spatial coordinates in *Mann*, see my manifesto "Against Between" (2001). Dollinger highlights house metaphors in his discussion of hybrid and "staged identities" (2003: 5–8, 24).
85. These details are not recounted. Indirectly the text associates the year of Sascha's birth with a renewal of German identity. References to 1954, 1972, and 1989 are thus hardly coincidental.
86. Here I deviate from Cheesman's translation, which yields "the fresh side" of history as opposed to its "worn-out side." The German terms *verbraucht* and *unverbraucht* connote a relationship to usage and residue that I stress.
87. Whether this information functions in the textual world as a historical fact or something that Sascha imagines for the purposes of writing his novel is unclear.
88. The theme of detective work as anything but evidentiary is not new in Şenocak's work (see especially Şenocak 1995: 7–21; 1999). See Teraoka on hard-boiled detective fiction in relation to post-fascist Germany and Turkish migration (1999).
89. Observing the privileged status of this motif in *Perilous Kinship*, Gerstenberger argues that Şenocak helps "rewrite the project of *Vergangenheitsbewältigung*" at a time when many other German writers are more interested in German "normalcy" instead (235–241).
90. My rendering of this last clause deviates from Cheesman's translation, which resolves the referential ambiguity of the German. I also retain the archival allusion of *Speicher*, which Cheesman renders as a "loft" rather than a "storage room."
91. In Cheesman's translation Sascha asks: "Why did I need the archives?" The rhetorical nature of the question in German suggests that Sascha feels no need for the historian's archive. See Grimm on the shifting trope of the archive (documentary, psychological, digital) in German poetry of the 1990s.
92. This indexes another rupture in historical consciousness in Turkey. The Kemalist language reforms of 1928 were introduced so quickly that "future generations were barred access to the written testimony of the past" (Taner Akçam 2001: 88). Özdamar's "tongue stories" revolve around this rupture, which Akçam identifies as a major obstacle in dealing with the Armenian genocide.
93. The opening of Tolstoy's *Anna Karenina* is tagged as such.
94. Cheesman translates *unaufgeklärt* as "ultimately unsolved." Adelson 1997a discusses unruly corpses that must literally be kept secret in novels by Hans Keilson and Güney Dal.
95. Cheesman notes that the novel "includes parodic life-story interviews with Turks" (2002: 183); see also Jordan 105. Nadolny's Selim similarly explains that he is only "playing" a Turk when recounting an anecdote involving a German bureaucrat (237).
96. See n. 24 for Santner's definition of "narrative fetishism" and Cheesman's somewhat different translation of this passage. Sascha expresses "a deeply felt distaste

for any kind of fetishistic treatment of suffering" (36). Commenting on the rhetorical "community of fate" that ostensibly links perpetrators, victims, and survivors after the Holocaust in Germany, Sascha refers to candlelight demonstrations with which many Germans protested the arson attacks on Turkish homes in the early 1990s. The demonstrators strike him as "caricatures of the killers," the "trembling candle-flames" of solidarity only feebly protected "against the rampant flames of the arsonists" (121). Neumann cites Henscheid's extensive entry on *Betroffenheit* in the latter's pop dictionary of 1993. According to Neumann, this reflects "the prominence of the term in West German political culture since the early 1980s" (10; 269).

97. Begemann's primary example is Tekinay. Biondi and Schami's programmatic essay of 1981 makes it clear, however, that the guest worker literature of *Betroffenheit* was intended to interpellate German laborers and foreign laborers of all nationalities as proletarians. Tekinay's appeal to German empathy is predicated on liberal humanism rather than class politics. Begemann notes that Şenocak's poetry and early prose break with the widespread expectation that migrant authors will write in styles easy to understand (220). For additional reflections on the "literature of being moved," see Burns and Horn. Referring to a certain kind of first-person narration more generally, Seyhan notes, "Modern immigrant writing is almost exclusively autobiographical in nature" (1996a: 180).

98. Individual scholars do so to different ends. For Dollinger, the novel advances "hybrid identities" as an antidote to strong multiculturalism (2002: 71; see also Dollinger 2003). Hall makes similar points but stresses the importance of individual biographies to counter an understanding of identities as representative of ethnic groups or national communities, especially after 9/11. Eigler's focus on identity serves a more complex analysis of national discourses of guilt and cultures of memory that acquire new contours in the 1990s. Challenging Dollinger's celebratory account of "hybrid identities," she highlights the novel's "oscillation between lifting taboos and upholding them" in reference to the Armenian genocide. According to Eigler, this fundamental ambivalence signals cultural memory no longer fueled by the production of identity, but by a continual questioning of identity (2005). Eigler understands this questioning and the strength of the novel in terms of dynamic intercultural dialogue and postpositivist epistemology.

99. This figural allusion recalls an earlier passage when the autobiographical voice speaks of tying the "threads" in his head together to yield a novel (51). My translation of the "void" passage differs from Cheesman's, which reads: "I live in a void which offers me nothing to which to attach the fraying threads which are meant to connect me to the three parts of my self."

100. Besides collecting German handwriting from the 1930s, Sascha also collects old maps. These maps record "all the mute borders . . . that have been drawn with much blood" (75). Because of the connotations of *nichtssagend* (literally, saying nothing), my translation characterizes these borders as "mute." Cheesman renders them "meaningless."

101. Bettina Brandt is preparing an article on the language of dreams in *Perilous Kinship*. Yeşilada notes the conjoined themes of sleepwalking and disorientation in Şenocak's poetry (2003: 119–121).

102. In Cheesman's translation, Sascha hears "people breathing."
103. The German adjective *langatmig* has a negative connotation and is usually translated as *long-winded*. Literally it means characterized by a long breath.
104. Addressing the relationship between culture and barbarism, realism and antirealism, the everyday and the extreme in Holocaust studies and cultural studies, Rothberg focuses precisely on this interlocking network of what must be documented, what cannot be represented, and what circulates in the public domain.
105. Surnames were not commonly used in Turkish culture until a Republican reform of 1934 required them. *Pasha* is the military honorific by which this historical figure was known.
106. The question does not appear in Cheesman's translation.
107. Regarding the German rhetoric of a "community of fate," see n. 96. Sascha's remark about coming along "later" indirectly indexes controversy over a commemorative speech given by the German Chancellor to the Israeli parliament in 1984. On that occasion Helmut Kohl (b. 1930) coined "the grace of late birth."
108. Skare discusses other protagonists in post-Wall fiction who "had pretty much slept through the events of the autumn of 1989" (194). See Grünbein for a figure of an author desiring "to sleep through history this one time" (22–23).
109. Cheesman and I translate this key passage differently. For Cheesman the first sentence reads: "I'm not traveling in pursuit of my characters."
110. Şenocak has described Berlin as a uniquely "phlegmatic" German city (2003: 141–142). The author claims elsewhere that "lability" is the precondition for "every poetic reflection" (Konzett 2003b: 134).
111. Eshel suggests instead that Sebald's prose "exceeds" the aesthetic tradition of elegiac modernism by articulating an existential "poetics of suspension" (2003: 73–74). Even if one agrees with Eshel, the atmospheric contrast between *Austerlitz* and *Perilous Kinship* remains striking. Eshel astutely analyzes a constitutive "tension between fact and fiction, authorial or autobiographical narration and fictional narrative, between the mediation of data and its metaphorical figuration" in Sebald's work (76). For additional reflections on visible and invisible histories in Sebald's writing, see Huyssen (2003b, 2005); Hell (2003); Schlant. Other publications are too numerous to mention here.
112. Regarding the limit-figure of the *Muselmann* in Auschwitz, Agamben addresses an "impossibility of vision" in reference to "what cannot *not* be seen" (53).
113. The reference is to Martin Walser (1998b); see especially Eshel (2000). Eigler breaks new critical ground by examining Walser and Şenocak together (2002, 2005).
114. Hell discusses Sebald in terms of "a visual literature informed by the gaze of one born after" (34). According to Hell, three primary forms of unsettlement characterize this gaze: the need to see photographs of the death camps, fear of becoming a ghoulish voyeur, and exposure to the survivors' gaze. Sascha represents a different after-effect, partly because of his German–Jewish family, and partly because of his Turkish–Armenian legacy. *Perilous Kinship* also reflects the broader obsession in Germany with disturbed vision, patriarchal legacies, and belated birth. See Jerome for a range of perspectives on German masculinity after 1945. On patrilineal motifs in Şenocak's work, see Adelson

(2002); Gerstenberger; Huyssen (2003a); Moray McGowan (2003); Eigler (2005); and chapter three. Hall characterizes *Perilous Kinship* as "grandfathers' literature" in contrast to the "fathers' literature" of the 1970s and 1980s (79–80). See Santner (1990: 35–46) on related transgenerational legacies and Moray McGowan (2001) on tropes of masculinity in the literature of Turkish migration written by other male authors.

115. I disagree with Dollinger, who claims Sascha "transcends... the moral opposition between 'victims' and 'perpetrators' " (2002: 70–71). One might contrast *Perilous Kinship* on this score with Keilson's psychological thriller about a Jew in hiding identifying with Hitler, Hilsenrath's satire about a German Nazi passing as a Jewish survivor in Israel, or Dische's quirky stories about more recent "pious secrets."

116. On historical relationships between Wilhelminian Germany and the Ottoman Empire, especially in reference to the Armenian genocide, see Trumpener; Dadrian (1996); and Hull (2005). Weitz begins his study of "a century of genocide" by referring to a German missionary whose report of 1916 is widely referenced in studies of the Armenian case.

117. Taner Akçam identifies several international and domestic phenomena around 2000 as indicating that the entrenched national taboo against acknowledging the Armenian genocide may be slowly lifting (2001: 1–4). Hovannisian expresses a similar view (2003: 3). See Torbakov for an update on pertinent developments related to Turkey's bid for membership in the European Union and the ninetieth anniversary of the genocide in April 2005. Scholars generally agree that 1915 was the decisive year for "a centrally controlled policy of extermination" orchestrated by key members of the Committee of Union and Progress, known colloquially as Young Turks, with Talât Pasha foremost among them (Zürcher 121). Because the killing and deportation of Armenians did not end in 1915, scholars sometimes include the years between 1915 and 1923 in their discussion of the genocide. 1923 marked the founding of the Republic of Turkey and the Treaty of Lausanne, which recognized the new nation's territorial parameters "without reference to the Armenians" (Helmut Smith 176). As Joel Dark notes in his brief overview of the Armenian genocide, deportation in this context was and is often understood as "another word for annihilation" (Helmut Smith 153). For more commentaries on this controversial subject, see Dadrian (1995, 1996, 1999); Hovannisian (1986, 2003); Melson; Chaliand and Ternon; Gellately and Kiernan (esp. Jay Winter's "Under Cover of War," 189–213); Weitz (2003a); and Hull (2005). This is only a smattering of the relevant scholarship. See Dadrian (1995) for an extensive bibliography of Turkish, English, German, French, and Armenian materials. For a rebuttal by the Turkish ambassador on the occasion of renewed efforts to pass a resolution on the Armenian genocide in the U.S. Congress, see Dadrian (1999: 59–74). The ambassador recommends readings deemed to counter the charge of genocide. Among these are historical studies by McCarthy, who "tells the story of Turks as victims" in his book on "ethnic cleansing" and Ottoman Muslims (1995: 3) and elsewhere speaks of an "Armenian–Muslim civil war" rather than genocide (1997: 365).

118. A political refugee in Germany in the late 1970s, Akçam later received his doctorate from the University of Hannover and is now affiliated with the

Institute for Social Research in Hamburg. This suggests more entangled histories. The frequency with which Akçam cites Norbert Elias and T. W. Adorno in his discussion of Turkish history, e.g., is striking (2001: 75–101).
119. Keyder speaks of "embarrassment and shame, covered up in official discourse as much as in the national psyche" (44).
120. Diasporic positions are heterogeneous and sometimes at odds with the Armenian state (Taner Akçam 2001: 12–13).
121. A National Day of Remembrance of the Armenian Genocide of 1915–1923 was declared in 1987, e.g., while a Congressional resolution of 2000 reflected dissenting views as well, partly because of objections raised by the Turkish government and the U.S. President. See Balakian (1997) for an autobiographical account of life in the U.S.-Armenian diaspora following World War II and Balakian (2003) for longer historical views on the U.S. response to the Armenian genocide.
122. To recall Appadurai, an ethnoscape is "the landscape of persons who constitute the shifting world in which we live" (1996: 33). See chapter one for additional commentary. Cultural taboos at stake in this chapter regulate relations between the living and the dead in reference to the Holocaust in mid century and the Armenian genocide roughly two decades earlier. One might contrast such taboos with the historical amnesia that prevails in Germany regarding German colonial history, which includes the first genocide of the twentieth century. Zantop coined the term "postcolonial amnesia" in a posthumously published article on German culture and Nazi cinema (2001). On the relationship between "military culture" and the Herero-Nama genocide of 1904–1907 in the area known today as Namibia, see Hull (2003, 2005). Hull's book on "military culture" additionally discusses the Armenian genocide. Şenocak refers to Turkey as "a revolutionary state founded on amnesia" (Konzett 2003b: 135). *Perilous Kinship* nonetheless foregrounds taboo rather than amnesia.
123. Dollinger stresses instead "a familial taboo" in the sense that Sascha's family had not explained the nature of his grandfather's involvement in the Armenian genocide to him (2002: 70).
124. Frequent allusions to finances in the text are nonetheless striking and warrant analysis. See Weigel on *Schuld* as guilt and *Schulden* (pl.) as debts in the culture of the Federal Republic (1996). See also Tanner and Weigel on memory, money, and law. On Eastern European approaches to "settling accounts" following the collapse of communist regimes, see Borneman (1997).
125. See n. 98 regarding Eigler's analysis of the Armenian motif. The letter that prompts Sascha's protagonist to commit suicide includes catchwords for separation, flight, rape, and other violence perpetrated by "bastards, traffickers and soldiers" (136), but no extended narration or descriptive detail. On the novel's Armenian motif, Huyssen observes that the Armenian genocide appears as "a gap" in narration, which he considers as "a metaphor perhaps" for Turkey's political refusal to acknowledge the genocide (163). This reading would be supported by Şenocak's own remarks about the novel in an interview with Cheesman, where the author describes his intention to juxtapose an "absolute silence" in Turkey about the Armenian genocide with continual talk about the Holocaust in Germany (Cheesman and Yeşilada 28), even though Sascha's

mother steadfastly refuses to discuss the latter. (Waldhoff suggests that the mother's silence in general represents a "killing off of collective memory" specific to the Kemalist revolution [333].) My reading of the Armenian leitmotif suggests that more intricate structures of figural reference and historical narrative are at play than Huyssen, Şenocak, or Waldhoff indicate. Eigler makes the intriguing suggestion that the novel's limited engagement with the Armenian genocide reflects "a secondary taboo" (2005).

126. In this sense I agree with Şenocak's assertion elsewhere that "the book's real protagonist" is the confluence of history and story (2003: 146). But as my analysis demonstrates, this agreement does not rest on any generic sense that "the truth cannot easily be documented" or that fragmented stories comprise a "modern form of narrative," as the author contends.
127. In the German original Sascha refers to "German Jews" in the final sentence of this passage.
128. "German" and "Jew" do not function as mutually exclusive categories in *Perilous Kinship*. Public rhetoric of a sad "community of fate" tends to inscribe them as such despite the reference to "community."
129. Dollinger and I thus differ in our interpretations of this "trialogue."
130. While the history of Kurdish conflicts with the Turkish state erupted on German streets in the 1990s, this history has no face in *Perilous Kinship*. Taner Akçam lists the existence of Kurds as one of five foundational taboos in Turkey, the others involving class, religion, genocide, and the military (2001: 4–5). *Perilous Kinship* breaks with the latter two. Özdamar defies "the laicist ideology that underwrites modern Turkish education" when the Turkish narrator of *Mother Tongue* begins to learn Arabic, the language of the Qur'an, in a divided Berlin (Seyhan 2001: 122). Moray McGowan inverts the title of one of Şenocak's anthologies to speak of a " 'fractured gaze from' rather than at 'the west' " (2000b: 57).
131. Cheesman translates "triangular relationships" (*Dreiecksbeziehungen*) as "ménages à trois," which obscures the allusion to geometrical lines.

Chapter Three: Capital and Labor

1. Sassen similarly approaches gender in a global economy as "a strategic nexus" of structural developments rather than a predominantly experiential category (85).
2. Appadurai takes the extreme position that "*the imagination as a social practice*" becomes "the key component of the new global order" (1996: 31). Highlighting a "new stage in the history of capitalism" dating from 1973, Lee and LiPuma argue that financial risk and speculation displace production-based labor as the driving force of global capital (204–211; see also n. 20 of introduction). All three ascribe an "unprecedented" rate of acceleration to structural changes in labor widely underway late in the twentieth century (Appadurai 3; Lee and LiPuma 209). The labor of literature is also subject to change at this time.
3. See Theisen on "indexical" realism in postwar Austrian literature.
4. The essay cited is "Überfremdung I." A longer essay by the prominent Swiss author, written in 1966 and titled "Überfremdung 2," satirically targets a similar distinction between labor and humans (387).

5. Ha underscores dehumanization by likening the experience of migrant laborers in Germany to both Nazi mechanisms of genocidal "selection" and "a modern 'slave market' " (20). Only the initial emphasis on dehumanization is characteristic of citations of Frisch generally.
6. Wallraff squarely blames capitalism for such degradation (1972).
7. National narratives of the two postwar German states are shaped by similar regimes of rhetorical incorporation. The Basic Law of the Federal Republic asserts the inviolability of human dignity for individuals, and the German Democratic Republic was formally conceived as a state of workers and farmers. Touching tales of Turkish migration and German citizenship are multiply entangled along incorporative axes of labor and humanity.
8. As Levent Soysal observes, "the migration story differentiates its subject, the migrant, along gender and ethnic lines" (2003a: 496).
9. These questions indirectly entail a critical engagement with "intersectional analysis" (Crenshaw; Wiegman 1999: 366), which studies gender, race, class, sexuality, and nationality as conceptually, phenomenologically, and culturally entwined. When the matter of culture is reduced to the embodiment of identity, intersectional analysis becomes problematic. See Wiegman and Valerie Smith for related debates among U.S.-based feminists; on intersectional analysis in Germany, see Hark; del Mar Castro Varela and Gutiérrez Rodríguez; Gelbin et al.
10. This competes with other national narratives and policies. Turkish residents without German citizenship are technically foreigners, a national minority but not necessarily an ethnic grouping. The Kemalist paradigm of citizenship is predicated on Turkishness as a national identity in contradistinction to ethnic affinity. By contrast, some Young Turks passionately favored Pan-Turkism (Melson 163–169).
11. For different reasons from those adduced here (see n. 61), Mani also uses a spectral metaphor to account for the ongoing significance of guest worker literature, which he considers a genre (2002).
12. Changing labor needs in computer and information industries have not yet affected popular images of Turkish labor. For German representations of foreign laborers prior to 1995, see Wise; Chin (2002).
13. A poor man is not necessarily a trash man, but the images are often linked in German representations of Turks.
14. I thank Karin Yeşilada for alerting me to this postcard.
15. Çağlar (1994) draws on Bourdieu's categories of capital to make this general point. Journalistic reminders that Turks contribute to the German economy in vital ways make few dents in the popular perception that the relationship of Turks to German capital is parasitical. Goldberg remarks an ongoing "process of diversification" among Turkish-owned businesses in Germany adapting to new economic structures overall (2002: 37). See Clark on sexualized sites of abjection regarding Turkish migration.
16. Bourdieu famously discerns four forms of capital (economic, social, cultural, symbolic) and the means by which one is converted into another (1984, 1986). Economic capital is "immediately and directly controvertible into money" (1986: 243). This is not true of cultural capital, which Bourdieu identifies in embodied dispositions, cultural artifacts, and institutionalized credentials, or of

social capital, which consists of aggregated resources associated with membership in particular groups. According to Bourdieu, symbolic capital is both "unrecognized as capital and recognized as legitimate competence" in a given field (245). For the moment, I use the term cultural capital to index some type of value encoded in cultural terms of difference and exchange.
17. See Kandiyoti for related remarks in a broader context. Mushaben illuminates the centrality of security questions for national identity in the Federal Republic since 1949 (1998). For transnational perspectives on migration, security, and globalization, see Weiner (1993, 1995). These studies predate heightened attention to migration and security since 9/11/2001.
18. "Stories about Turks in Germany often operate in terms of gender relations. The liberation of the poor Turkish woman from imprisonment, oppression, dependency, or even prostitution is a popular fantasy, which derives from the German public's feeling of superiority" (Göktürk 336). Jenny White refers to the "almost iconic quality" of many stories about young Turkish women, interventionist social programs, and Turkish family life in Germany (1997: 759). See also Yeşilada (1997a: 97); Sieg (241); Ha (42); and Karpf et al. Public commentary on Sibel Kekilli, who secretly acted in pornographic films before achieving fame at the Berlin Film Festival of 2004 for her performance in a prize-winning film by Fatih Akın, echoes elements of this earlier discourse of emancipation in Germany.
19. Adelson 1997b compares the rhetoric of gender and migration in Schwarzer's essay and Schönhuber's book on Turks. A former member of the *Waffen-SS*, Schönhuber founded a right-wing party known for its anti-immigration platform. On *Emma*'s overall stance on feminism and Islam, see Kreile.
20. This will surprise no one. For related commentaries, see Kaplan et al. Mandel (1989) offers the most comprehensive insights into German headscarf debates prior to 1989; Tibi (1998a: 320–339); Henkel (2004b); and Spuler-Stegemann assess more recent developments. Kandiyoti targets core contradictions concerning gender in modernist, antimodernist, nationalist, and anticolonial discourses. From Schönhuber's vantage point, the problem with Turkish migration is not that migrant men are too patriarchal but that male guest workers are insufficiently masculinized traitors to Kemalist ideals (Adelson 1997b: 310–311).
21. These stereotypes are oblivious to the secular culture and history of modern Turkey, where religious headscarves have traditionally been banned in official domains such as schools and government offices. See Göle (1996) on veiling in Turkey. Göle (2002) analyzes the controversy that exploded in 1999 when an Islamic woman elected to the Turkish parliament entered the National Assembly wearing a headscarf.
22. Comparing French headscarf debates and the German crucifix controversy of the 1990s, Ausländer speaks of "the wearing and the tearing of the social fabric" (283). Recent crises over religious symbols in France and Germany, she argues, derive from new challenges to national sovereignty posed by immigration, Europeanization, and globalization.
23. The court's ruling in September 2003 relegates a principled decision regarding headscarves in civil service to the legislative bodies of individual states, which regulate public education within the federation. German media were filled with reports about these developments in fall 2003. For an overview of state inclinations

in this regard, see Cziesche et al. One color photograph included in this article was clearly taken at the same scene of ritual slaughter depicted in *Emma* in 1993.
24. In her contribution to a book on "false tolerance" Schwarzer reiterates her equation between German fascism and Islamic fundamentalism (Badinter et al). This echoes the "beleaguered tolerance" featured in Heitmeyer and Dollase.
25. Şenocak criticized liberal tolerance blind to real conflict shortly after 9/11/2001 without taking a position on the headscarf (2001a). Tibi contends that Islamic scripture does not require veiling, as some claim. Balić also argues for the compatability of Islam and European democracy.
26. Germans generally do not distinguish between secular and Muslim Turks. Debates about the Turkish population often refer to Islam as either the second or third largest religion in Germany. Goldberg calls Islam "the second largest religion in Germany after Christianity" and "the third largest religion in Germany after Catholicism and Protestantism" in the same article (2002: 29, 44).
27. Stressing ocular functions in social imaginaries, Göle focuses on new forms of visibility in Turkey but casts a conceptual eye on European developments too. Sassen discusses the "expansion of an international civil society" in terms of changing conditions of visibility and invisibility (1998: 98–99).
28. See Brady on contemporary German discourses of "threat" as a medium of incorporation rather than exclusion. Chow explicitly evaluates victimization as cultural capital (179).
29. See n. 37, n. 45 of introduction. Ha similarly criticizes sociological theories of cultural conflict (49–54). Challenging the presumption of "unbridgeable cultural" differences between Turkish Muslims and German society, Henkel argues that "conflict is only one facet" of this relationship (2004b: 975). Çağlar analyzes related issues in Turkish–German rap and hip-hop (2001).
30. Kolinsky notes that *Verlockender Fundamentalismus* "equates Islam with anti-modernism" (2002: 216, n. 3). For present purposes, these references are invoked only to sketch a grid of imaginative labor and cultural capital that exerts considerable pressure on public perceptions of Turkish migration. These pressures have intensified since September 2001, partly because some Saudi terrorists had lived in Germany.
31. Breger observes that masculinity becomes "the quintessential subject" of gender studies and queer studies in Germany and elsewhere around 2000 (2003b). Moray McGowan draws important connections between Şenocak's writing and "the question of masculinity in a time of its crisis" (2003: 76).
32. Together with Harald Weinrich at the University of Munich, Ackermann played a prominent role in publishing migration stories in the early 1980s. See Teraoka (1987: 92–97).
33. See Nazan Aksoy; Göktürk (1999a); Henderson (1997); Seyhan (1997); and Yeşilada (1997a) for related commentary. Regarding the reception of these writers, Yeşilada coins the term "Suleikalism," a peculiarly German and gendered version of Orientalism. For additional analyses of their work, see Frederking; Wierschke (1996); Veteto-Conrad; Zielke-Nadkarni; and Gökberk (1997b).
34. One little known exception is Nazan Aksoy's chapter on Turkish women writers in Germany, which plays a minor role in her study of Russian formalism and postmodernism, but which situates these writers in German rather than Turkish contexts (111).

35. Veteto-Conrad contrasts Scheinhardt, Özakın, and Çırak on this point (59–77); Göktürk adds Tekinay, Demirkan, and Özdamar to the mix. Yeşilada skewers Scheinhardt for fueling German perceptions of Turkish women as victims well into the 1990s (1999: 151–152). Unlike Scheinhardt, Özakın focuses on Turkish women's relationship to bourgeois secularism, European modernism, and cosmopolitan affinities. Özakın eventually moved to England when she could no longer stand the stereotypical expectations that Germans brought to her writing (Wierschke 1996). Özakın especially chastised the German left for casting Turks as a "symbol of suffering" (7).
36. Ghaussy combines an interest in *écriture féminine* with a focus on female embodiment to highlight what she considers the "hybrid" or "nomadic" subjectivity of the novel. (Contrast Breger 2003a on nomadism.) Ackermann also speaks of "feminine writing" in relation to Özdamar and others.
37. Ghaussy, e.g., compares Özdamar and Irigaray regarding "embodied" language as a feminist counterpoint to masculinist abstraction (11).
38. See Adelson (1997a, 2005) on "epochal disorientation" in reference to Dal. Clarke compares the German and Turkish versions of the strike story. Moray McGowan reviews "multiple masculinities in Turkish-German men's writings" (2001). See also Fischer and McGowan (1996).
39. Occasionally Chow uses gender and sexuality interchangeably in reference to minority subjects, but her overarching arguments focus on gender and ethnicity. Contrast this with Butler's account of sociolinguistic interpellation, which stresses the production of abjection that minority subjects struggle to counter (1997), while Chow foregrounds the production of ethnicity as a commodity. For Chow, "feminism in the West" is complicit with liberalism, her primary target (154). Both Butler and Chow draw on Althusser's concept of interpellation.
40. "In this context, *to be ethnic is to protest*—but perhaps less for actual emancipation of any kind than for the benefits of worldwide visibility, currency, and circulation" (48). In Germany this bald equation does not apply. Chow's emphasis on tensions between personhood and currency, however, reveals how unexamined premises can hobble cultural studies of migration.
41. Other aspects of Chow's project and mine are incompatible or simply different. For example, Chow faults liberal tolerance for "recurrent antagonisms, atrocities, and genocides that take place every day around the world" (26). I am not persuaded that liberal forms of violence are the root cause of "racial and ethnic unrest in the contemporary world today" (15). This is in any event not the subject of this book.
42. Citing Seyhan on the "almost exclusively autobiographical" form of migrant writing today (1996a: 180), Chow illuminates the problematic relationship between celebrations of hybridity and the genre of autobiography (138–146).
43. Despite her title, even Wierschke does not have the self-assertion in mind that Chow ascribes to protestant ethnics (1996).
44. Nadolny's Selim is formally arrested, convicted, imprisoned, and deported. More commonly, this motif conjures an amorphous fear of being accused of something illegal or improper, especially murder. For additional commentary and references, see Teraoka (1987: 82; 1999); Riemann 13; Şölçün (1992: 25–29); Simpson; Adelson (1994: 326; 1997a: 126–127); Wise 5.

45. Like Chow, Seyhan speaks of a "confessional idiom," especially for women writers of Turkish migration. "Writing the self . . . is an act of symbolic unveiling" (2001: 136).
46. For Chow "the ethnic community" seems to refer to a second-order source of pressure on individuals to perform as protestant ethnics (190–191). It is not clear how Chow understands the relationship between community and capitalism.
47. This functional definition of cultural capital strays from Bourdieu's structural account without being radically incompatible (see n. 16). Beyond ideology, Taylor characterizes "the social imaginary" as "that common understanding that makes possible common practices and a widely shared sense of legitimacy" (2002: 91, 106). Guillory's approach to cultural capital is most relevant to this chapter's concerns. This is partly because Taylor stresses the "making sense of" societal practices, whereas Guillory highlights the non-sense of social relations.
48. One looks in vain, however, for a definition of cultural capital in Guillory's book, for Guillory claims to follow "Bourdieu's own practice in constructing the concept through the contexts of its deployment" (341, n. 1). Fennell makes only passing reference to Bourdieu, canon wars, and "literature as capital" in her study of the language and literature of foreign laborers in Germany (132). For Fennell, debates about this literature revolve around a "struggle for identity" (135).
49. Guillory also understands this remainder in historical terms. Others rethinking Marxist categories of labor and capital to address formations of difference in globalization include Chakrabarty; Lowe and Lloyd. The latter two reject "the 'center-periphery' model of both economic and cultural relations" because it cannot account for the intrinsic "heterogeneity of the contemporary capitalist mode of production" (2–3, 15). Chow similarly rejects the notion of a resistant "elsewhere" independent of capitalist production. By contrast, Ha stresses resistant "capitalist peripheries" (84).
50. Arguing against the presumption of monosemia in GDR cultural politics, Bathrick demonstrates that the presumption of binary antagonisms fails to grasp how East and West German cultures were reciprocally referential (16 and passim). Hell's ongoing critical project dismantles the mirror approach to East and West German forms of Holocaust memory.
51. A "story of similarities" is not a story of equivalence. Buck-Morss establishes a different frame of reference with which the story of the twentieth century may be told. Scribner stresses the difference that "the second world" makes in cultures of memory since its disintegration.
52. See Moray McGowan on masculinity in Şenocak's oeuvre (2003). Cheesman discusses related tropes in terms of a "Turco-German shared history" (2003: 148–149, 154–157). McGowan jointly discusses "[c]ultural ambiguity and gender ambiguity" (2001: 304; see also 2003: 62).
53. The Turkish version was subsequently published in 1985 by a German press. Adapted from the Turkish, the English translation differs greatly from the German, on which my analysis is based. I provide my own translations for passages cited where such details matter but page references to the German and English publications.
54. The novels in the series may also be understood in terms of a technology of localization. The series includes Ören (1988/I), (1998/II), (1999b/IV), (1995/V), (1997/VI). To date available only in Turkish, the intended third item

appeared in 1990. Proust's project "in search of the past" appeared in fifteen volumes between 1913 and 1927. Ackermann (1997) and Mani (2002) compare Ören's novella with some of his novels.
55. In the 1970s persecution of the left was especially harsh (Zürcher 272). According to Lipovsky, however, Turkish socialists could resume legal activities when martial law was lifted in 1973 and were "outlawed" only after the coup of 1980 (2).
56. The trilogy consists of Ören 1973, 1974, and 1980b. Only the Turkish version was tagged as a trilogy (1980a).
57. Edited by Deniz Göktürk and Barbara Wolbert, a special issue of *New German Critique* in 2004 addresses multicultural media in Germany.
58. Between 1990 and 1991 Ören also corresponded with a prominent public intellectual about unification, human rights, and the twenty-first century (Ören and Schneider). The published exchange casts Berlin and Istanbul "less as polar opposites than twin places of complex interchange in European metropolitan culture" (Moray McGowan 2000a).
59. McGowan rightly notes that "migrant labourers are doubly feminised, as migrants and as labourers," in Ören's work. That is to say, his Marxist perspective relies on gender as a metaphor for the experience of migration (2001: 297). Concluding that ethnicity bespeaks "resistance" to capitalist effacement of historical specificity (190), Gott favors the kind of "protestant" claim that Chow disparages. Chin credits the trilogy with giving guest workers in Germany a public face but finds that ethnicity marks political tensions within the working class. Chin contends that the author's work overall prompted major changes in German attitudes toward identity, migration, and citizenship. While her causal claims may be overstated, she is not alone in thinking that Ören "perhaps more than anyone else reshaped the boundaries of public debate about the guest worker after 1970" (45).
60. Mani makes a similar point when contrasting *Please, No Police* with Wallraff's *Lowest of the Low* (2002: 117).
61. Mani discusses *Please, No Police* and *Berlin Savignyplatz* against the foil of *Kanak Sprak*, Zaimoğlu's "death knell" for guest worker literature and the victim narratives of cultural difference it ostensibly represented (2002: 113; see also Wertheimer 131). According to Mani, Ören's novella revolves around "financial troubles" experienced by German and Turkish characters in an earlier phase of West German history, while the later novel is "symptomatic" of changed material circumstances in the 1990s (117, 125). To the degree that Ören's evolving depiction of Ali Itir challenges cultural and economic stereotypes, then and now, Mani argues, the specter of guest workers "will continue to haunt the house of German literature for years to come" (129). Mani and I agree that the figure of the guest worker is spectral but not peripheral to contemporary German culture. Yet Mani's largely thematic discussion of economy and ethnicity cannot explain how the narrative embrace of these motifs comes to "matter" in Ören's work. The discussion here thus articulates the materiality of the text in terms of literary labors of imagination and the cultural capital of migration.
62. Rosa Luxemburg's body was found in this canal in 1919 after she and Karl Liebknecht, another founding member of the German Communist Party, had

been murdered by right-wing militia. The dead of Berlin's canals also figure in Şenocak (1995) and Kutluğ Ataman's film on "trans" subcultures in Berlin (Clark 207–208).
63. In the German, police are convinced that a rape occurred despite "a few things that don't match up in the depiction of the event" (1983: 79). In the more tenuous English version, police "sensed that an assault might have taken place" but doubt "the credibility" of certain details in the woman's report (1992: 118). Ören may have taken some cues for this story from a rape trial resulting from events in 1978 involving a German woman and Turkish youths. The trial became ensconced in public lore when a social scientist used it to situate sexuality at the center of cultural conflict (Schiffauer). Rösch explicitly compares Schiffauer and Ören in intercultural terms (101–108).
64. Suggesting that only the manner of death is uncertain, Mani assumes that the corpse fished from the canal is Ali Itir (2002: 117). The English translation explicitly lists suicide, accident, and murder as possible causes of death; the German indicates only that the deceased may have been the " 'victim of a crime' " (87).
65. The narrator of Ören's first novel "in search of the present" refers to himself as "a nobody" and "a nothing" (1988: 267, 278). Loentz discusses these appellations in terms of intertextual references to Homer's *Odyssey*. See also Adelson (2005: 917). Fachinger discusses the same motif in a novella by Franco Biondi, prominent in German literature of Italian migration (2001: 24). Moray McGowan discusses Şenocak's "imagined masculinities" in terms of "a new Odysseus" (2003: 76–77). I argue that the economy of representation in Ören's novella rests on Ali's status as a "non-person."
66. The case is never investigated as murder. Only the rumor mill produces the image of the brutal foreigner, which is missing in the English translation.
67. Borrowing a term from Trinh T. Minh-ha, Anderson reads Ali Itir as an " 'Inappropriate Other,' an outsider who steps inside and calls into question the very difference between those living at the center of a system and those on the margins" (145). Breger cites Bhabha in her discussion of mimicry as "inappropriate behavior" in Özdamar's prose (1999: 37).
68. In German this is rendered "Unperson" (1983: 20). The English translation weakens this: "not even a 'person' " (1992: 25). A passing reference to ritual ablutions identifies Ali Itir as a Muslim, but this attribution never becomes a narrative motif.
69. Bruno Gramke articulates a parallel between this situation and his own in the early 1950s, when Germans who came west from the " 'Soviet Zone' " were treated " 'like illegals' " (1983: 59; 1992: 87).
70. According to Sassen, citizenship was also "of minor importance in the 1970s and 1980s" where social services for migrant laborers were concerned. "What mattered above all was residence and legal alien status" (1998: 23).
71. The German text uses two different words for contraband, one denoting goods that are smuggled and one for goods traded on the black market.
72. In linguistic terms Benveniste considers "the 'third person' . . . literally a 'non-person' " (221). See also Theisen (109).
73. This last example conjoins heterosexual normativity, economic solvency, and symbolic personhood.

74. Susan Anderson rightly registers the importance of snow and ice in Ören's narrative, but our assessments of these motifs diverge. For Anderson, the snow dangerously obscures "distinctions between Turks and Germans" (150). I emphasize an indexical economy of representation that cannot be grasped in terms of personal or collective identities.
75. The German words *Tathergang* and *Täter* derive from the verb *tun*, "to do." The standard translation of *Täter* is "perpetrator," but literally it means "one who commits an act." *Tathergang* literally means "the course of an action." Ali's surname derives from the transitive Turkish verb *itmek*, to "push" or "compel," which connotes an effect exerted by action.
76. Bayazitoğlu discusses Özdamar's use of Arabic in *Mother Tongue* as "an active reconstruction rather than a rediscovery" (115).
77. By "post-ethnic" I mean interactive ethnoscapes unbounded by ethnic identities as strong multiculturalism construes them.
78. Both the German (1990) and English (1994) versions of *Mother Tongue* will be cited.
79. See Brandt for a notable exception (2004).
80. Zürcher expresses the widely held view that "the adoption of the Latin alphabet in 1928" was possibly "the most drastic measure" of Atatürk's modernization program, which radically refashioned the Ottoman Empire into the secularist Republic of Turkey (196). Benhabib summarizes these consequential reforms (2002b: 9–10), as does Bayazitoğlu (104–109). See also n. 92 in chapter two.
81. Something closer to taboo than proscription is meant here, though Özdamar uses various forms of *verbieten* (to forbid) in explicit reference to Kemalist language reforms.
82. See also Wierschke (1996: 177) and Konuk (2001: 88). As Bayazitoğlu observes, because the national figure of fatherhood is still occupied by Atatürk and his generational cohorts, there is no "father tongue" among Özdamar's tongue stories (129–130).
83. Littler also differs from Seyhan by favoring "a postcolonial perspective" on the literature of migration (221). See n. 32 of introduction.
84. Seyhan and Konuk also characterize Özdamar's work in terms of palimpsests, but they speak of "a palimpsest of . . . signifying practices" (Seyhan 2001: 144) or "a palimpsest-like weave" of text and "sub-text" (Konuk 1997: 149). These are not palimpsests of identity. (Konuk's book of 2001, however, is organized around concepts of identity.)
85. The German word commonly means *poet* or *writer*. Literally, it means someone who makes something tight, dense, thickly packed, or solid.
86. I thank Geoffrey Waite for alerting me to related disagreements among Hölderlin scholars.
87. The coupling is itself split, since the two words appear in the same sentence but at some remove from each other. In Hölderlin they are separated only by a definite article.
88. See Yıldız on intralingual translations in *Kanak Sprak* (2005). Brandt assesses Özdamar's surrealist strategies of "collection" in terms of anticipation (2004).
89. My reading of affect thus deviates from Bird's emphasis on the "physicality of language" (160) in the tongue stories and Bayazitoğlu's discussion of "the unruly body" in terms of "oppositional vitality" (118–119), or Ghaussy's

approach to "embodied language" in *Life* (9). German audiences and critics tend to see Özdamar's protagonists as naïve and child-like; some scholars rely on this vocabulary (e.g., Seyhan 1996c, 2001; Müller). Others challenge the presumption of naïveté to varying degrees (e.g., Breger 1999; Konuk 1999; Şölçün 2002; Bayazitoğlu 112). Primarily concerned with mimicry, Breger finds no Turkish woman speaking in Özdamar's texts, "but a figure that poses as a foreign woman" (46). Göktürk speaks here of "role play" and a "mask" of naïveté (1999a: 532). See also Göktürk on "role play beyond identity politics" in film (2004).
90. One can also say that erotic desire is voiced in the language of spiritual longing. Littler rightly notes the confluence of sexual and sacred desire in Özdamar's story (228–229).
91. Konuk designates German as "the medium" of communication and subversion in this text (1999: 61; 2001: 85, 87). Brandt regards Arabic as the "mediator between Turkish and German" (2004).
92. Founded by Hassan al-Banna in Cairo in 1928, the Muslim Brotherhood has often been at serious odds with the Egyptian government. References to a war in which an Israeli soldier almost killed Ibni Abdullah could index the "Yom Kippur" war of 1973, which pitted Egypt and Syria against Israel. Although the Palestinian conflict is mentioned in terms of an aporia—"Palestine will not be founded and not be murdered" (1990: 28–29; 1994: 35)—this does not justify the conclusion that the teacher is Palestinian (Konuk 2001: 87; Neubert 159).
93. Because these words in print appear as homonyms or " 'false friends' " (Littler 229), the Thomas translation adds clarifying prose. Yıldız indicates that only readers familiar with Turkish pronunciation will recognize that the words are not homonyms at all (2001: 32); see also Brandt (2004: 307). The sound of breath is required to animate social relations suspended here in form. Against readings of this scene proposed by Wierschke (1996) and Neubert, Littler finds hybridity underscored rather than difference "overcome" (230). Bird notes only in passing the nonsense of another conversation (170).
94. Littler discusses a subsequent pun on "divan" (225).
95. Raffman even uses a color schematic to exemplify vagueness as a philosophical problem.
96. See Şenocak (2000) for the most extensive collection of the author's essays available in English.
97. This author typically conjures men who either do not work or work by writing (Moray McGowan 2003: 64).
98. For more comprehensive discussion of German literary authors on the subject of Europe (including a wider range of contemporary authors), see Lützeler (1992, 1994).
99. For the German text of the island essay, see Şenocak (1992: 50–55). For the German text of "Thoughts on May 8, 1995," see Şenocak (2001c: 25–28).
100. See Eigler (2005) and Gerstenberger on these motifs in *Perilous Kinship*.
101. Şenocak (1995, 1998, and 1999) writes such "generational" (but not simply patrilineal) narratives. For recent critiques of Group 47, see Braese (2001a) and Briegleb (2003).
102. Weigel's original German refers to the "secret" (*heimlich*) first generation. This generation is "secret" or "concealed" because it is discursively positioned as

a "point of origin" for West German culture rather than something following from what came before (2002: 265).
103. Although Weigel highlights generation as a "symbolic" form, her use of the term is closer to "emblematic" in the context of this chapter. That is to say, she discusses a strategic nexus that indexes social relations without representing them.
104. Von Molo's rhetoric is also infused with references to humanity and personhood. Thieß sharpens this rhetoric and criticizes Mann by proposing, "it was more difficult to maintain one's personhood here than to send messages to the German people from over there" (Grosser 25).
105. In other essays Şenocak crafts affective and critical ties to various literary figures who had a notoriously conflicted relationship with the Group 47, notably Paul Celan and Ingeborg Bachmann.
106. Konuk cites Spivak's characterization of Atatürk as "the 'visionary mimic man as father of the nation' " (Konuk 2001: 44, n. 61; Spivak 1993: 264).
107. See Yeşilada (2002) for extended insights into intermedial collaboration involving Şenocak and others in reference to Atatürk and Hikmet.
108. Moray McGowan discusses how this volume challenges normative paradigms of masculinity (2003).
109. The picture painted by Şenocak is subject to change over time. See Klopp (188–193) and Georgi on related issues of memory and migration.
110. Katzenstein cites "old fears about Europe's domination by an unpredictable German giant" (1). Schieb and Wedekind discuss a different island as a German *lieu de mémoire*.
111. The reference to Hauptmann's notes pairs aesthetics and history. Some Germans buried valuables at war's end to prevent Allied troops from finding them. Guy Stern tells an anecdote about GIs disappointed to find Hauptmann's box full of paper. References to the naturalist author also connote a multiply divided literary tradition in Germany, albeit less rigorously than in "Thoughts." "The Island" also alludes in passing to the aesthetics of socialist realism (22).
112. Citing Liss, Morris approaches postmemory by contrast "as part of an ongoing process of intertextuality, translation, metonymic substitution, and a constant interrogation of the nature of the original" (Morris 293; Liss 86). Şenocak's essays do not radically question "the nature of the original" in reference to the Nazi past.
113. The Winston translation is cited here.
114. A former student of logic, Hein conjures the "false premises" on which generations are based and "[t]he devil as past master of the syllogism" (8).

Postscript

1. Sykora addresses "uncanny couplings" in the history of art.
2. For more cerebral pairings of Gregor Samsa and great thinkers of the twentieth century, see Estrin. For divergent approaches to pastiche, globalization, and cyberspace, see Appadurai 1996 (30–31) and Hoesterey (103).
3. See introduction for Benhabib's critique of this philosophical conceit.

Works Cited

Abraham, Nicolas and Maria Torok (1980). "Introjection—Incorporation: Mourning *or* Melancholia." *Psychoanalysis in France*. Ed. Serge Lebovici and Daniel Widlöcher. New York: International Universities Press. 3–16.
—— (1994). *The Shell and the Kernel: Renewals of Psychoanalysis*. Trans. and ed. Nicolas T. Rand. Chicago: University of Chicago Press.
Ackermann, Irmgard (1997). "Ali Itırs Wandlungen: Aras Örens Romanheld zwischen Wirklichkeit und Phantasie." Howard 17–30.
—— (2002). "Mit einem Visum für das Leben: Formen weiblichen Schreibens am Beispiel dreier türkischer Autorinnen." Blioumi 147–157.
Adelson, Leslie A. (1990). "Migrants' Literature or German Literature? TORKAN's *Tufan: Brief an einen islamischen Bruder*." *German Quarterly* 63: 382–389.
—— (1993). *Making Bodies, Making History: Feminism and German Identity*. Lincoln, NE: University of Nebraska Press.
—— (1994). "Opposing Oppositions: Turkish-German Questions in Contemporary German Studies." *German Studies Review* 17.2: 305–330.
—— (1997a). "Minor Chords? Migration, Murder, and Multiculturalism." *Zeitenwenden/Wendezeiten*. Ed. Robert Weninger and Brigitte Rossbacher. Tübingen: Stauffenburg. 115–129.
—— (1997b). "The Price of Feminism: Of Women and Turks." *Gender and Germanness*. Ed. Patricia Herminghouse and Magda Mueller. Oxford: Berghahn Books. 303–317.
—— (1997c). "Response to Ülker Gökberk, '*Culture Studies* und die Türken.'" *German Quarterly* 70.3: 277–282.
—— (1998). "History By Proxy or Proximate Histories? Touching Tales of Turks, Germans, and Jews." Paper presented at the Modern Language Association Annual Convention (San Francisco). December 28.
—— (2000a). "Coordinates of Orientation: An Introduction." Şenocak 2000: xi–xxxvii.
—— (2000b). "Touching Tales of Turks, Germans, and Jews: Cultural Alterity, Historical Narrative, and Literary Riddles for the 1990s." *New German Critique* 80: 93–124.
—— (2001). "Against Between: A Manifesto." *Unpacking Europe: Towards a Critical Reading*. Ed. Salah Hassan and Iftikhar Dadi. Rotterdam: NAi Publishers. 244–255.
—— (2002). "The Turkish Turn in Contemporary German Literature and Memory Work." *Germanic Review* 77.4: 326–338.

Adelson, Leslie A. (2005). "Migrants and Muses." *The New History of German Literature*. Ed. David E. Wellbery, Judith Ryan, Hans Ulrich Gumbrecht, Anton Kaes, Joseph Leo Koerner, and Dorothea E. von Mücke. Cambridge, MA: Harvard University Press. 912–917.

Adorno, Theodor W. (1977). *Gesammelte Schriften*. Ed. Rolf Tiedemann. Vol. 10.1–2. Frankfurt a. M.: Suhrkamp.

Agamben, Giorgio (1999). *Remnants of Auschwitz: The Witness and the Archive*. Trans. Daniel Heller-Roazen. New York: Zone Books.

Akbulut, Nazire (1993). *Das Türkenbild in der neueren deutschen Literatur 1970–1990*. Berlin: Köster.

Akçam, Dursun (1993). *Deutsches Heim—Glück allein: Wie Türken Deutsche sehen/ Alaman Ocağı: Türkler Almanları anlatıyor*. 1982. Göttingen: Lamuv.

Akçam, Taner (1993). *Türk Ulusal Kimliği ve Ermeni Meselesi*. Istanbul: İletişim.

—— (2001). *Dialogue Across an International Divide: Essays Towards a Turkish-Armenian Dialogue*. Trans. Vahakn N. Dadrian, Dzovig Chakarian, and Harutun Vaporciyan. Cambridge, MA: The Zoryan Institute for Contemporary Armenian Research and Documentation.

—— (2002). *Ermeni tabusu arlanırken: diyalogdan başka bir çözüm var mı?* Istanbul: Su Yayınları.

Aksoy, Asu, and Kevin Robins (2000). "Thinking Across Spaces: Transnational Television from Turkey." *European Journal of Cultural Studies* 3.3: 343–365.

Aksoy, Nazan (1996). *Batı ve Başkaları*. Istanbul: Düzlem Yayınları.

Althusser, Louis (1971). "Ideology and Ideological State Apparatuses." *Lenin and Philosophy*. Trans. Ben Brewster. New York: Monthly Review. 170–186.

Amodeo, Immacolata (1996). *"Die Heimat heisst Babylon": Zur Literatur ausländischer Autoren in der Bundesrepublik Deutschland*. Opladen: Westdeutscher Verlag.

Anderson, Benedict (1991). *Imagined Communities: Reflections on the Origin and Spread of Nationalism*. 1983. Rev. ed. London: Verso.

—— (1998). *The Spectre of Comparisons: Nationalism, Southeast Asia and the World*. London: Verso.

Anderson, Susan C. (2002). "Outsiders, Foreigners, and Aliens in Cinematic or Literary Narratives by Bohm, Dische, Dörrie, and Ören." *German Quarterly* 75.2: 144–159.

Angress, Ruth (1985). "A 'Jewish Problem' in German Postwar Fiction." *Modern Judaism* 5: 215–233.

Appadurai, Arjun (1996). *Modernity at Large: Cultural Dimensions of Globalization*. Minneapolis: University of Minnesota Press.

—— (2000). "Grassroots Globalization and the Research Imagination." *Public Culture* 12.1: 1–19.

Apter, Emily (1999). *The Translation Zone: Language Wars and Literary Politics*. Princeton, NJ: Princeton University Press.

—— (2001a). "Balkan Babel: Translation Zones, Military Zones." *Public Culture* 13.1: 65–80.

—— (2001b). "On Translation in a Global Market." *Public Culture* 13.1: 1–12.

Ardagh, John (1987). *Germany and the Germans: An Anatomy of Society Today*. New York: Harper and Row.

Arens, Hiltrud (2000). *"Kulturelle Hybridität" in der deutschen Minoritätenliteratur der achtziger Jahre*. Tübingen: Stauffenburg.

Argun, Betigül Ercan (2003). *Turkey in Germany: The Transnational Sphere of Deutschkei.* New York: Routledge.
Assmann, Aleida and Ute Frevert (1999). *Geschichtsvergessenheit—Geschichtsversessenheit: Vom Umgang mit deutschen Vergangenheiten nach 1945.* Stuttgart: Deutsche Verlags-Anstalt.
Ausländer, Leora (2000). "Bavarian Crucifixes and French Headscarves: Religious Practices and the Postmodern European State." *Cultural Dynamics* 12.3: 183–209.
Austin, J. L. (1975). *How to Do Things with Words.* Second ed. Oxford: Clarendon.
Axel, Brian (2001). *The Nation's Tortured Body: Violence, Representation, and the Formation of a Sikh 'Diaspora'.* Durham, NC: Duke University Press.
—— (2002). "The Diasporic Imaginary." *Public Culture* 14.2: 411–428.
Ayim, May (1993). "Das Jahr 1990: Heimat und Einheit aus afro-deutscher Perspektive." *Entfernte Verbindungen: Rassismus, Antisemitismus, Klassenunterdrückung.* Ed. Ika Hügel, Chris Lange, May Ayim, Ilona Bubeck, Gülsen Aktaş, and Dagmar Schultz. Berlin: Orlanda. 206–222.
Aytaç, Gürsel (1997). "Sprache als Spiegel der Kultur: Zu Emine Sevgi Özdamars Roman *Das Leben ist eine Karawanserai.*" Howard 171–177.
Bachmann-Medick, Doris (1987). "Kulturelle Texte und interkulturelles (Miß–) Verstehen: Kulturanthropologische Herausforderungen für die interkulturelle Literaturwissenschaft." Wierlacher, *Perspektiven und Verfahren* 653–664.
—— (1996a). "Einleitung." Bachmann-Medick, *Kultur als Text* 7–64.
—— (ed.) (1996b). *Kultur als Text: Die anthropologische Wende in der Literaturwissenschaft.* Frankfurt a. M.: Fischer.
—— (1996c). "Multikultur oder kulturelle Differenzen? Neue Konzepte von Weltliteratur und Übersetzung in postkolonialer Perspektive." Bachmann-Medick, *Kultur als Text* 262–296.
Bade, Klaus J. (ed.) (1992). *Deutsche im Ausland—Fremde in Deutschland: Migration in Geschichte und Gegenwart.* Munich: Beck.
Bade, Klaus J. and Myron Weiner (eds.) (1997). *Migration Past, Migration Future: Germany and the United States.* Providence, RI: Berghahn.
Badinter, Elisabeth, Johannes von Dohnanyi, Cornelia Filter, Wilhelm Heitmeyer, Robin Morgan, and Alice Schwarzer (2002). *Die Gotteskrieger und die falsche Toleranz.* Cologne: Kiepenheuer & Witsch.
Balakian, Peter (1997). *Black Dog of Fate: An American Son Uncovers His Armenian Past.* New York: Broadway Books.
—— (2003). *The Burning Tigris: The Armenian Genocide and America's Response.* New York: Harper Collins.
Balibar, Étienne (2004). *We, the People of Europe? Reflections on Transnational Citizenship.* Trans. James Swenson. Princeton, NJ: Princeton University Press.
Balić, Smail (2001). *Islam für Europa: Neue Perspektiven einer alten Religion.* Cologne: Böhlau.
Barbieri, William A., Jr. (1998). *Ethics of Citizenship: Immigration and Group Rights in Germany.* Durham, NC: Duke University Press.
Barnouw, Dagmar (1996). *Germany 1945: Views of War and Violence.* Bloomington, IN: Indiana University Press.
Bartov, Omer (1997). "'Seit die Juden weg sind...': Germany, History, and Representations of Absence." Denham, Kacandes, and Petropoulos 209–226.

Bartov, Omer (1998). "Defining Enemies, Making Victims: Germans, Jews, and the Holocaust." *The American Historical Review* 103.3: 771–816.
Bathrick, David (1995). *The Powers of Speech: The Politics of Culture in the GDR.* Lincoln, NE: University of Nebraska Press.
Baudelaire, Charles (1966). *Oeuvres Complètes.* Vol. I. Ed. Yves Florenne. Paris: le club français du livre.
Bauman, Zygmunt (1989). *Modernity and the Holocaust.* Ithaca, NY: Cornell University Press.
Bayazitoğlu, Ahmet Sitki (2001). "Motion Sickness: Literatures of Migration and Minorities." Diss. Princeton University.
Bayer, Gerd (2004). "Theory as Hierarchy: Positioning German Migrantenliteratur." *Monatshefte* 96.1: 1–19.
Beck, Ulrich (2000). "The Cosmopolitan Perspective: The Sociology of the Second Age of Modernity." Trans. Martin Chalmers. *British Journal of Sociology* 51.1: 79–105.
Becker, Thorsten (2003). "Die Türken—Wie ich sie lieben lernte." *Frankfurter Allgemeine Sonntagszeitung* [Feuilleton]. June 22: 21.
——— (2004). *Sieger nach Punkten.* Reinbek bei Hamburg: Rowohlt.
Begemann, Christian (1999). " 'Kanakensprache': Schwellenphänomene in der deutschsprachigen Literatur ausländischer AutorInnen der Gegenwart." Saul, Steuer, Möbus, and Illner 209–220.
Beitter, Ursula E. (ed.) (2000). *Literatur und Identität: Deutsch-deutsche Befindlichkeiten und die multikulturelle Gesellschaft.* New York: Lang.
Benhabib, Seyla (2002a). "Citizens, Residents, and Aliens in a Changing World: Political Membership in the Global Era." Hedetoft and Hjort 85–119.
——— (2002b). *The Claims of Culture: Equality and Diversity in the Global Era.* Princeton, NJ: Princeton University Press.
Benveniste, Emile (1971). *Problems in General Linguistics.* Trans. Mary Elizabeth Meek. Coral Gables, FL: University of Miami Press.
Berezin, Mabel and Martin Schain (eds.) (2003). *Europe without Borders: Remapping Territory, Citizenship, and Identity in a Transnational Age.* Baltimore, MD: Johns Hopkins University Press.
Berg, Nicolas (2003). "Eine deutsche Sehnsucht." *Die Zeit* 46 (November 6): 38.
Berger, John (1975). *A Seventh Man: Migrant Workers in Europe.* New York: Viking.
——— (1985). *The Sense of Sight: Writings by John Berger.* Ed. Lloyd Spencer. New York: Pantheon.
Berger, John, Sven Blomberg, Chris Fox, Michael Dibb, and Richard Hollis (1972). *Ways of Seeing.* Harmondsworth (UK): British Broadcasting Corporation and Penguin.
Berkenbusch, Gisela (1985). *Zum Heulen: Kulturgeschichte unserer Tränen.* Berlin: TRANSIT.
Bhabha, Homi K. (1990a). "DissemiNation: time, narrative, and the margins of the modern nation." *Nation and Narration* 291–322.
——— (ed.) (1990b). *Nation and Narration.* London: Routledge.
——— (1994). *The Location of Culture.* London: Routledge.
Biondi, Franco (1984). *Abschied der zerschellten Jahre: Novelle.* Kiel: Neuer Malik.
Biondi, Franco and Rafik Schami (1981). "Literatur der Betroffenheit: Bemerkungen zur Gastarbeiterliteratur." Unter Mitarbeit von Jusuf Naoum und Suleman Taufiq. *Zu Hause in der Fremde: Ein bundesdeutsches Ausländer-Lesebuch.* Ed. Christian Schaffernicht. Fischerhude: Atelier im Bauernhaus. 124–136.

WORKS CITED / 217

Bird, Stephanie (2003). *Women Writers and National Identity: Bachmann, Duden, Özdamar*. Cambridge, UK: Cambridge University Press.
Blackshire-Belay, Carol Aisha (ed.) (1994). *The Germanic Mosaic: Cultural and Linguistic Diversity in Society*. Westport, CT: Greenwood.
Blioumi, Aglaia (ed.) (2002). *Migration und Interkulturalität in neueren literarischen Texten*. Munich: Iudicium.
Boa, Elizabeth (1997). "Sprachenverkehr: Hybrides Schreiben in Werken von Özdamar, Özakin und Demirkan." Howard 115–138.
Boa, Elizabeth and Janet Wharton (eds.) (1994). *Women and the Wende: Social Effects and Cultural Reflections of the German Unification Process*. Amsterdam: Rodopi.
Böll, Heinrich (1973). *Group Portrait with Lady*. Trans. Leila Vennewitz. New York: McGraw Hill. Trans. of *Gruppenbild mit Dame*. Cologne: Kiepenheuer & Witsch, 1971.
Bohnenkamp, Anne (1996). "Von der Freiheit des Erzählens: Zur Poetik Sten Nadolnys." Bunzel, *Sten Nadolny* 17–39.
Borges, Jorge Luis (2000). *The Library of Babel*. 1941. Trans. Andrew Hurley. Boston: David R. Godine. Trans. of "La biblioteca de Babel."
Borneman, John (1992). *Belonging in the Two Berlins: Kin, State, Nation*. Cambridge, UK: Cambridge University Press.
—— (1997). *Settling Accounts: Violence, Justice, and Accountability in Postsocialist Europe*. Princeton, NJ: Princeton University Press.
Bosse, Anke (1996). "Ost und West im Fadenkreuz des Erzählens: 'Selim oder Die Gabe der Rede.' " Bunzel, *Sten Nadolny* 192–219.
Bourdieu, Pierre (1984). *Distinction: A Social Critique of the Judgement of Taste*. Trans. Richard Nice. Cambridge, MA: Harvard University Press.
—— (1986). "The Forms of Capital." Trans. Richard Nice. *Handbook of Theory and Research for the Sociology of Education*. Ed. John G. Richardson. Westport, CT: Greenwood Press. 241–258.
Brady, John (2004). "Dangerous Foreigners: The Discourse of Threat and the Contours of Inclusion and Exclusion in Berlin's Public Sphere." Göktürk and Wolbert 194–224.
Braese, Stephan (ed.) (1998). *In der Sprache der Täter: Neue Lektüren deutschsprachiger Nachkriegs- und Gegenwartsliteratur*. Opladen: Westdeutscher Verlag.
—— (2001a). *Die andere Erinnerung: Jüdische Autoren in der westdeutschen Nachkriegsliteratur*. Berlin: Philo.
—— (2001b). " 'In einer deutschen Angelegenheit'—Der Frankfurter Auschwitz-Prozess in der westdeutschen Nachkriegsliteratur." Wojak 217–243.
Brandt, Bettina (2003). "Chance Encounters or Poetic Transformations in the Works of Herta Müller, Emine Sevgi Özdamar and Yoko Tawada." Paper presented at the German Studies Association Annual Convention (New Orleans). September 21.
—— (2004). "Collecting Childhood Memories of the Future: Arabic as Mediator Between Turkish and German in Emine Sevgi Özdamar's *Mutterzunge*." *Germanic Review* 79.4: 295–315.
Brecht, Bertolt (1990). *Poems & Songs from the Plays*. Ed. and mainly trans. John Willett. London: Methuen.
Breger, Claudia (1999). " 'Meine Herren, spielt in meinem Gesicht ein Affe?' Strategien der Mimikry in Texten von Emine S. Özdamar und Yoko Tawada." Gelbin, Konuk, and Piesche 30–59.

Breger, Claudia (2003a). "Narratives of Nomadism or Copying German Culture." Kosta and Kraft 47–60.
—— (2003b). "Theorizing Femininities@2003." Paper presented at annual conference of Women in German. Carrollton, KY. October 17.
Briegleb, Klaus (2003). *Mißachtung und Tabu, Eine Streitschrift zur Frage: 'Wie antisemitisch war die Gruppe 47?'*. Berlin: Philo.
Briegleb, Klaus and Sigrid Weigel (eds.) (1992). *Gegenwartsliteratur seit 1968*. Munich: Deutscher Taschenbuch Verlag.
Brockmann, Stephen (1999). *Literature and German Reunification*. Cambridge, UK: Cambridge University Press.
Brodsky Lacour, Claudia (1996). *Lines of Thought: Discourse, Architectonics, and the Origin of Modern Philosophy*. Durham, NC: Duke University Press.
Bronfen, Elisabeth, Benjamin Marius, and Therese Steffen (eds.) (1997). *Hybride Kulturen: Beiträge zur anglo-amerikanischen Multikulturalismusdebatte*. Trans. Anne Emmert and Josef Raab. Tübingen: Stauffenburg.
Brown, Gillian and George Yule (1983). *Discourse Analysis*. Cambridge, UK: Cambridge University Press.
Brown, Laura (2001a). "The City Sewer: Fables of Modernity." Annual Invitational Lecture (Society for the Humanities). Cornell University (Ithaca, NY). February 22.
—— (2001b). *Fables of Modernity: Literature and Culture in the English Eighteenth Century*. Ithaca, NY: Cornell University Press.
Brubaker, Rogers (ed.) (1989). *Immigration and Politics of Citizenship in Europe and North America*. Lanham, MD: University Press of America.
—— (1992). *Citizenship and Nationhood in France and Germany*. Cambridge, MA: Harvard University Press.
—— (1998). "Immigration, Citizenship, and the Nation-State in France and Germany." Shafir 131–164.
Brumlik, Micha (1991). "Antisemitismus, Rassismus und Ausländerfeindlichkeit." *Die multikulturelle Versuchung: Ethnische Minderheiten in der deutschen Gesellschaft*. Ed. Doron Kiesel and Rosi Wolf-Almanasreh. Frankfurt am Main: Haag & Herchen. 29–38.
Buck-Morss, Susan (2000). *Dreamworld and Catastrophe: The Passing of Mass Utopia in East and West*. Cambridge, MA: MIT Press.
Bude, Heinz (2001). "Achtundsechzig." *Deutsche Erinnerungsorte II*. Ed. Etienne François and Hagen Schulze. Munich: Beck. 122–134.
Bullivant, Keith (1994). *The Future of German Literature*. Oxford: Berg.
—— (ed.) (1997). *Beyond 1989: Re-reading German Literature Since 1945*. Providence, RI: Berghahn.
—— (2004). "Zafer Şenocaks *Atlas des tropischen Deutschland*: damals und heute." Durzak and Kuruyazıcı 91–96.
Bullivant, Keith and Klaus Briegleb (1992). "Die Krise des Erzählens—'1968' und danach." Briegleb and Weigel 302–339.
Bunzel, Wolfgang (1996a). "Sten Nadolnys 'Selim oder Die Gabe der Rede': Aufbau, Struktur, Erzählweise." Bunzel, *Sten Nadolny* 147–169.
—— (ed.) (1996b). *Sten Nadolny*. Eggingen: Isele.
Burns, Rob (1999). "Images of Alterity: Second Generation Turks in the Federal Republic." *Modern Language Review* 94: 744–757.

Butler, Judith (1990). *Gender Trouble: Feminism and the Subversion of Identity*. New York: Routledge.
—— (1997). *Excitable Speech: A Politics of the Performative*. New York: Routledge.
Campt, Tina (1993). "Afro-German Cultural Identity and the Politics of Positionality: Contexts and Contests in the Formation of a German Ethnic Identity." *New German Critique* 58: 109–126.
—— (2003). *Other Germans, Black Germans, and the Politics of Race, Gender, and Memory in the Third Reich*. Ann Arbor, MI: University of Michigan Press.
Çağlar, Ayşe (1994). "German Turks in Berlin: Migration and Their Quest for Social Mobility." Diss. University of Montréal.
—— (2001). "Management kultureller Vielfalt: Deutsch-türkischer Hip-Hop, Rap und Türkpop in Berlin." *Geschlecht und Globalisierung: Ein kulturwissenschaftlicher Streifzug durch transnationale Räume*. Ed. Sabine Hess and Ramona Lenz. Königstein/Taunus: Ulrike Helmer. 221–241.
Carbe, Monika (2003). "*Der Erottomane*: Ein Vexierspiel mit der Identität." Cheesman and Yeşilada 80–90.
Carbe, Monika and Wolfgang Riemann (eds.) (2002). *Hundert Jahre Nâzim Hikmet, 1902–1963*. Hildesheim [Germany]: Georg Olms.
Carroll, Lewis [Charles Lutwidge Dodgson] (1963). *Alice im Wunderland, Alice hinter den Spiegeln: Zwei Romane*. Trans. and ed. Christian Enzensberger. Frankfurt a. M.: Insel.
—— (1965). *Alice in Wonderland; Through the Looking-Glass, etc*. New York: Dutton.
Castles, Stephen, Heather Booth, and Tina Wallace (eds.) (1984). *Here for Good: Western Europe's New Ethnic Minorities*. London: Pluto.
Castles, Stephen and Mark J. Miller (2003). *The Age of Migration: International Population Movements in the Modern World*. Third ed. New York: Guilford.
Chakrabarty, Dipesh (2000a). *Provincializing Europe: Postcolonial Thought and Historical Difference*. Princeton, NJ: Princeton University Press.
—— (2000b). "Universalism and Belonging in the Logic of Capital." *Public Culture* 12.3: 653–678.
Chaliand, Gérard and Jean-Pierre Rageau (1995). *The Penguin Atlas of Diasporas*. Trans. A. M. Berrett. New York: Viking.
Chaliand, Gérard and Yves Ternon (2002). *1915, le génocide des arméniens*. Brussels: Complexe.
Chapin, Wesley D. (1996). "The Turkish Diaspora in Germany." *Diaspora* 5.2: 273–301.
Cheah, Pheng and Bruce Robbins (eds.) (1998). *Cosmopolitics: Thinking and Feeling Beyond the Nation*. Minneapolis, MN: University of Minnesota Press.
Cheesman, Tom (1998). "Polyglot Politics: Hip Hop in Germany." *Debatte* 6.2: 191–214.
—— (2002). "Akçam—Zaimoğlu—Kanak Attak: Turkish Lives and Letters in German."*German Life and Letters* 40: 180–195.
—— (2003). "Ş/ß: Zafer Şenocak and the Civilization of Clashes." Cheesman and Yeşilada 144–159.
—— (2004). "Talking '*Kanak*': Zaimoğlu contra *Leitkultur*." Göktürk and Wolbert 82–99.
Cheesman, Tom and Karin E. Yeşilada (eds.) (2003). *Zafer Şenocak*. Cardiff, UK: University of Wales Press.

Chiellino, Carmine (ed.) (1988). *Die Reise hält an: Ausländische Künstler in der Bundesrepublik*. Munich: Beck.
—— (1998). "La nascita della memoria biculturale." *Letteratura e immigrazione*. Ed. Giovanni Scimonello. Spec. issue of *Cultura tedesca* 10: 23–32.
—— (2000). *Interkulturelle Literatur in Deutschland: Ein Handbuch*. Stuttgart: Metzler.
Chin, Rita C.-K. (2002). "Imagining a German Multiculturalism: Aras Ören and the Contested Meanings of the 'Guest Worker,' 1955–1980." *Radical History Review* 83: 44–72.
—— (2003). "Toward a 'Minor Literature'? The Case of *Ausländerliteratur* in Postwar Germany." *New Perspectives on Turkey* 28–29: 61–84.
Chow, Rey (2002). *The Protestant Ethnic & the Spirit of Capitalism*. New York: Columbia University Press.
Cixous, Hélène (1997). "My Algeriance, in other words, to Depart not to Arrive from Algeria." Trans. Eric Prenowitz. *TriQuarterly* 100: 259–279.
Clark, Christopher (2003). "Sexuality and Alterity in German Literature, Film, and Performance, 1968–2000." Diss. Cornell University.
Clarke, Alexandra (2003). "Nicht nur Gastarbeiterliteratur: A Reading of Güney Dal's *İş Sürgünleri/Wenn Ali die Glocken läuten hört*." Paper presented at Conference of University Teachers of German in the United Kingdom and Ireland, National University of Ireland (Maynooth). September 8–10.
Cohen, Margaret and Carolyn Dever (eds.) (2002). *The Literary Channel: The Inter-National Invention of the Novel*. Princeton, NJ: Princeton University Press.
Cohen, Robert (1998). "The Political Aesthetics of Holocaust Literature: Peter Weiss's *The Investigation* and Its Critics." *History and Memory* 10.2: 43–67.
Cohn, Dorrit (1999). *The Distinction of Fiction*. Baltimore, MD: Johns Hopkins University Press.
Constantine, David (trans.) (1990). "Half of Life." By Friedrich Hölderlin. *Friedrich Hölderlin: Selected Poems*. Newcastle upon Tyne: Bloodaxe Books. 56.
Corngold, Stanley (1998). *Complex Pleasure: Forms of Feeling in German Literature*. Stanford: Stanford University Press.
Crenshaw, Kimberlé Williams (1995). "Mapping the Margins: Intersectionality, Identity Politics, and Violence Against Women of Color." *Critical Race Theory: The Key Writings That Formed the Movement*. Ed. Kimberlé Williams Crenshaw, Neil Gotanda, Gary Peller, and Kendal Thomas. New York: New Press. 357–383.
Cuddon, J. A. (ed.) (1991). *A Dictionary of Literary Terms and Literary Theory*. Third ed. Oxford, UK: Blackwell Reference.
Culler, Jonathan (1988). "The Call of the Phoneme: Introduction." *On Puns: The Foundation of Letters*. Ed. Jonathan Culler. Oxford, UK: Basil Blackwell. 1–16.
—— (1999). "Anderson and the Novel." *Diacritics* 29.4: 20–39.
Cziesche, Dominik, Dietmar Hipp, Felix Kurz, Barbara Schmid, Matthias Schreiber, Martin Sümening, Silvia Tyburski, and Andreas Ulrich (2003). "Das Kreuz mit dem Koran." *Der Spiegel* 40 (September 29): 82–97.
Dadrian, Vahakn N. (1995). *The History of the Armenian Genocide: Ethnic Conflict from the Balkans to Anatolia to the Caucasus*. Oxford: Berghahn.
—— (1996). *German Responsibility in the Armenian Genocide: A Review of the Historical Evidence of German Complicity*. Watertown, MA: Blue Crane.
—— (1999). *The Key Elements in the Turkish Denial of the Armenian Genocide: A Case Study of Distortion and Falsification*. Toronto: The Zoryan Institute.

Dal, Güney (1979). *Wenn Ali die Glocken läuten hört.* Trans. Brigitte Schreiber-Grabitz. Berlin: Edition der 2. Trans. of *İş Sürgünleri.* Istanbul: Milliyet Yayınları, 1976.
—— (1981). *Europastraße 5.* Hamburg: Buntbuch.
Delabar, Walter, Werner Jung, and Ingrid Pergande (eds.) (1993). *Neue Generation—neues Erzählen: Deutsche Prosa-Literatur der achtziger Jahre.* Opladen: Westdeutscher Verlag.
Deleuze, Gilles and Félix Guattari (1986). *Kafka: Toward a Minor Literature.* 1975. Trans. Dana Polan. Minneapolis, MN: University of Minnesota Press.
del Mar Castro Varela, María and Encarnación Gutiérrez Rodríguez (2000). "Queer Politics im Exil und in der Migration." *Queering Demokratie [sexuelle politiken].* Ed. quaestio: Nico J. Beger, Sabine Hark, Antke Engel, Corinna Genschel, and Eva Schäfer. Berlin: Querverlag. 100–112.
De Man, Paul (1979). *Allegories of Reading: Figural Language in Rousseau, Nietzsche, Rilke, and Proust.* New Haven: Yale University Press.
—— (1984). *The Rhetoric of Romanticism.* New York: Columbia University Press.
Denham, Scott, Irene Kacandes, and Jonathan Petropoulos (eds.) (1997). *A User's Guide to German Cultural Studies.* Ann Arbor, MI: University of Michigan Press.
Derrida, Jacques (1996). *Archive Fever: A Freudian Impression.* Trans. Eric Prenowitz. Chicago: University of Chicago Press.
Diez, Georg (2003). "Der Halbmond ist aufgegangen." *Frankfurter Allgemeine Sonntagszeitung* 25 (June 22): 19.
Dikmen, Şinasi (1995). *Hurra, ich lebe in Deutschland: Satiren.* Munich: Piper.
Diner, Dan (1999). *Das Jahrhundert verstehen: Eine universalhistorische Deutung.* Munich: Luchterhand.
—— (2003a). "The Destruction of Narrativity: The Holocaust in Historical Discourse." *Catastrophe and Meaning: The Holocaust and the Twentieth Century.* Ed. Moishe Postone and Eric Santner. Chicago: University of Chicago Press. 67–80.
—— (2003b). "Restitution and Memory—The Holocaust in European Political Cultures." *New German Critique* 90: 36–44.
Dische, Irene (1991). *Pious Secrets.* New York: Viking.
Dollinger, Roland (2002). "Hybride Identitäten: Zafer Şenocaks Roman *Gefährliche Verwandtschaft.*" *Seminar* 38.1: 59–73.
—— (2003). "'Stolpersteine': Zafer Şenocaks Romane der neunziger Jahre." *Gegenwartsliteratur* 2: 1–28.
Draper, Hal (1982). *The Complete Poems of Heinrich Heine: A Modern English Version.* Boston: Suhrkamp/Insel.
Drawert, Kurt (1992). *Spiegelland: Ein deutscher Monolog.* Frankfurt a. M.: Suhrkamp.
Droste, Wiglaf (1998). "Elefanten im Paul-Celan-Laden (1)." *die tageszeitung* [Berlin]. July 24: 16.
Dümcke, Wolfgang and Fritz Vilmar (eds.) (1995). *Kolonisierung der DDR: Kritische Analysen und Alternativen des Einigungsprozesses.* Münster: Agenda.
Durzak, Manfred (1980). *Die deutsche Kurzgeschichte der Gegenwart: Autorenporträts, Werkstattgespräche, Interpretationen.* Stuttgart: Reclam.
—— (1993). "Schnittpunkte interkultureller Erfahrung: Am Beispiel deutsch-türkischer Begegnung in Sten Nadolnys Roman 'Selim oder Die Gabe der Rede.'" *Praxis interkultureller Germanistik: Forschung—Bildung—Politik.*

Beiträge zum II. Internationalen Kongreß der Gesellschaft für Interkulturelle Germanistik, Straßburg 1991. Ed. Bernd Thum and Gonthier-Louis Fink. Munich: Iudicium. 291–304.

Durzak, Manfred (2004). "Deutschland-Bilder in den Kurzgeschichten von Şinasi Dikmen." Durzak and Kuruyazıcı 111–117.

Durzak, Manfred and Nilüfer Kuruyazıcı (eds.) (2004). *Die andere Deutsche Literatur: Istanbuler Vorträge*. Würzburg: Königshausen & Neumann.

Edgar Medien AG (2003). "Münih'in yakışıklı çöpçüsü/Münchens schöner Müllmann." Public Relations Image #6.119.

Eigler, Friederike (2002). "Memory, Moralism, and the Role of Intellectuals in the Unified Germany." Paper presented at the German Studies Association Annual Convention (San Diego). October 4.

—— (2005). *Generation und Gedächtnis in der deutschsprachigen Literatur um 2000*. Berlin: Erich Schmidt.

Elias, Norbert (1996). *The Germans: Power Struggles and the Development of Habitus in the Nineteenth and Twentieth Centuries*. Ed. Michael Schröter. Trans. Eric Dunning and Stephen Mennell. New York: Columbia University Press. Trans. of *Studien über die Decutschen: Machtkämpfe und Habitusentwicklung im 19. und 20. Jahrhundert*. Ed. Michael Schröter. Frankfurt a. M.: Suhrkamp, 1989.

—— (2000). *The Civilizing Process: Sociogenetic and Psychogenetic Investigations*. Trans. Edmund Jephcott with some notes and corrections by the author. Ed. Eric Dunning, Johan Goudsblom, and Stephen Mennell. Rev. ed. Oxford, UK: Blackwell. Trans. of *Über den Prozess der Zivilisation: Soziogenetische und psychogenetische Untersuchungen*. Basel: Haus zum Falken, 1939.

Elliott, Emory, Louis Freitas Caton, and Jeffrey Rhyne (eds.) (2002). *Aesthetics in a Multicultural Age*. New York: Oxford University Press.

El-Tayeb, Fatima (2001). *Schwarze Deutsche: Der Diskurs um 'Rasse' und nationale Identität 1890–1933*. Frankfurt a. M.: Campus.

Emmerich, Wolfgang (1997). *Kleine Literaturgeschichte der DDR*. Erweiterte Neuausgabe. Leipzig: Gustav Kiepenheuer.

Eryılmaz, Aytaç and Mathilde Jamin (eds.) (1998). *Fremde Heimat/Yaban, Sılan olur: Eine Geschichte der Einwanderung aus der Türkei/Türkiye'den Almanya'ya Göçün Tarihi*. Exhibit catalogue sponsored by DoMIT [Dokumentationszentrum und Museum über die Migration aus der Türkei]. Essen: Klartext.

Eshel, Amir (2000). "Vom einsamen Gewissen: Die Walser-Debatte und der Ort des Nationalsozialismus im Selbstbild der Berliner Republik." *Deutsche Vierteljahrsschrift* 74: 333–360.

—— (2003). "Against the Power of Time: The Poetics of Suspension in W.G. Sebald's *Austerlitz*." *New German Critique* 88: 71–96.

Esselborn, Karl (1995). "Deutschsprachige Literatur von Autoren nichtdeutscher Muttersprache und der Adelbert-von-Chamisso Preis." *Jahrbuch Deutsch als Fremdsprache* 21: 411–427.

—— (1997). "Von der Gastarbeiterliteratur zur Literatur der Interkulturalität: Zum Wandel des Blicks auf die Literatur kultureller Minderheiten in Deutschland." *Jahrbuch Deutsch als Fremdsprache* 23: 47–75.

Estrin, Marc (2002). *Insect Dreams: The Half Life of Gregor Samsa*. New York: Blue Hen.

Ewing, Katherine Pratt (2003). "Living Islam in the Diaspora: Between Turkey and Germany." Irzık and Güzeldere 405–431.

Fachinger, Petra (1999). "Orientalism Reconsidered: Turkey in Barbara Frischmuth's *Das Verschwinden des Schattens in der Sonne* and Hanne Mede-Flock's *Im Schatten der Mondsichel.*" *Studies in Twentieth-Century Literature* 23.2: 239–254.

——— (2001). *Rewriting Germany from the Margins: "Other" German Literature of the 1980s and 1990s.* Montreal: McGill-Queen's University Press.

Faist, Thomas (1995). *Social Citizenship for Whom? Young Turks in Germany and Mexican Americans in the United States.* Aldershot, UK: Avebury.

——— (ed.) (2000a). *Transstaatliche Räume: Politik, Wirtschaft und Kultur in und zwischen Deutschland und der Türkei.* Bielefeld: transcript.

——— (2000b). *The Volume and Dynamics of International Migration and Transnational Social Spaces.* Oxford, UK: Clarendon.

Fennell, Barbara A. (1997). *Language, Literature, and the Negotiation of Identity: Foreign Worker German in the Federal Republic of Germany.* Chapel Hill, NC: University of North Carolina Press.

Fenner, Angelica and Eric D. Weitz (eds.) (2004). *Fascism and Neofascism: Critical Writings on the Radical Right in Europe.* New York: Palgrave.

Fergar, Feyyaz Kayacan (ed.) (1993). *The Poetry of Can Yücel: A Selection/Can Yücel'in Şiirleri: Seçmeler.* Trans. Feyyaz Kayacan Fergar, with supplementary translations by Richard McKane, Ruth Christie, and Talat S. Halman. Istanbul: Papirus.

Fischer, Gerhard and David Roberts (eds.) (2001). *Schreiben nach der Wende: Ein Jahrzehnt deutscher Literatur 1989–1999.* Tübingen: Stauffenburg.

Fischer, Sabine and Moray McGowan (1996). "From *Pappkoffer* to Pluralism: on the Development of Migrant Writing in the German Federal Republic." Horrocks and Kolinsky 1–22.

——— (eds.) (1997). *Denn du tanzt auf einem Seil: Positionen deutschsprachiger MigrantInnenliteratur.* Tübingen: Stauffenburg.

Foster, Thomas (2002). "Cyber-Aztecs and Cholo-Punks: Guillermo Gómez-Peña's Five-Worlds Theory." *PMLA* 117.1: 43–67.

Foucault, Michel (1966). *Les mots et les choses.* Paris: Seuil.

Fox, Thomas C. (1999). *Stated Memory: East Germany and the Holocaust.* Rochester, NY: Boydell & Brewer.

Frantz, Douglas (2001). "Breaking Old Soviet Ties, Letter by Letter." *New York Times* (September 2): A 10.

Frederking, Monika (1985). *Schreiben gegen Vorurteile: Literatur türkischer Migration in der Bundesrepublik Deutschland.* Berlin: EXpress Edition.

Friedlander, Saul (ed.) (1992). *Probing the Limits of Representation: Nazism and the "Final Solution."* Cambridge, MA: Harvard University Press.

Friedrich, Jörg (2002). *Der Brand: Deutschland im Bombenkrieg 1940–1945.* Berlin: Propyläen.

Frisch, Max (1976). *Gesammelte Werke in zeitlicher Folge.* Werkausgabe Edition Suhrkamp in zwölf Bänden. Vol. V.2. Ed. Hans Mayer (and Walter Schmitz). Frankfurt a. M.: Suhrkamp.

Frischmuth, Barbara (1998a). *Die Schrift des Freundes.* Salzburg: Residenz.

——— (1998b). *The Shadow Disappears in the Sun.* Trans. Nicholas J. Meyerhofer. Riverside, CA: Ariadne.

Fröhling, Jörg, Reinhild Meinel, and Karl Riha (eds.) (1999). *Wende-Literatur: Bibliographie und Materialien zur Literatur der deutschen Einheit*. Third rev. ed. Frankfurt a. M.: Lang/Europäischer Verlag.

Frölich, Margrit (1997). "Reinventions of Turkey: Emine Sevgi Özdamar's *Life is a Caravanserai*." Jankowsky and Love 56–73.

Gadamer, Hans-Georg (1975). *Truth and Method*. Trans. Garret Barden and William G. Doerpel. New York: Seabury.

—— (1977). *Philosophical Hermeneutics*. Trans. and ed. David E. Linge. Berkeley, CA: University of California Press.

Gaonkar, Dilip Parameshwar (ed.) (2001). *Alternative Modernities*. Durham, NC: Duke University Press.

Gaonkar, Dilip Parameshwar and Benjamin Lee (eds.) (2002). *New Imaginaries*. Spec. issue of *Public Culture* 14.1.

Gelbin, Cathy S., Kader Konuk, and Peggy Piesche (eds.) (1999). *AufBrüche: Kulturelle Produktionen von Migrantinnen, Schwarzen und jüdischen Frauen in Deutschland*. Königstein/Ts.: Ulrike Helmer.

Gellately, Robert and Ben Kiernan (eds.) (2003). *The Specter of Genocide: Mass Murder in Historical Perspective*. Cambridge, UK: Cambridge University Press.

Georgi, Viola B. (ed.) (2003). *Entliehene Erinnerung: Geschichtsbilder junger Migranten in Deutschland*. Hamburg: Hamburger Edition.

Gerstenberger, Katharina (2002). "Difficult Stories: Generation, Genealogy, Gender in Zafer Şenocak's *Gefährliche Verwandtschaft* and Monika Maron's *Pawels Briefe*." Taberner and Finlay 235–249.

Geyer, Michael (1996). "The Politics of Memory in Contemporary Germany." *Radical Evil*. Ed. Joan Copjec. London: Verso. 169–200.

Ghaussy, Soheila (1999). "Das Vaterland verlassen: Nomadic Language and 'Feminine Writing' in Emine Sevgi Özdamar's *Das Leben ist eine Karawanserai*." *German Quarterly* 72.1: 1–16.

Gilman, Sander L. (1985). *Difference and Pathology: Stereotypes of Sexuality, Race, and Madness*. Ithaca, NY: Cornell University Press.

—— (1991a). *Inscribing the Other*. Lincoln, NE: University of Nebraska Press.

—— (1991b). *The Jew's Body*. New York: Routledge.

—— (1995). *Jews in Today's German Culture*. Bloomington, IN: Indiana University Press.

Gilman, Sander L. and Jack Zipes (eds.) (1997). *Yale Companion to Jewish Writing and Thought in German Culture, 1096–1996*. New Haven, CT: Yale University Press.

Godoy, Julio (1990). "Nowhere at Home." *Mother Jones* (February/March): 16.

Gökberk, Ülker (1991). "Understanding Alterity: *Ausländerliteratur* Between Relativism and Universalism." *Theoretical Issues in Literary History*. Ed. David Perkins. Harvard English Studies 16. Cambridge, MA: Harvard University Press. 143–172.

—— (1997a). "*Culture Studies* und die Türken: Sten Nadolnys *Selim oder die Gabe der Rede* im Lichte einer Methodendiskussion." *German Quarterly* 70.2: 97–122.

—— (1997b). "Encounters with the Other in German Cultural Discourse: *Interkulturelle Germanistik* and Aysel Özakin's *Journeys of Exile*." Jankowsky and Love 19–55.

Göktürk, Deniz (1993). "Schwarzes Buch in weißer Festung: Entschwindende Erzähler auf postmodernen Pfaden in der türkischen Literatur." *Der Deutschunterricht* 45.5: 32–45.

Göktürk, Deniz (1994). "Multikültürelle Zungenbrecher: Literatürken aus Deutschlands Nischen." *Sirene* 12/13: 77–92.

——— (1999a). "Kennzeichen: weiblich/türkisch/deutsch; Beruf: Sozialarbeiterin/ Schriftstellerin/Schauspielerin." *Frauen Literatur Geschichte: Schreibende Frauen vom Mittelalter bis zur Gegenwart*. Ed. Hiltrud Gnüg and Renate Möhrmann. Second ed. Stuttgart: Metzler. 516–532.

——— (1999b). "Turkish Delight—German Fright: Migrant Identities in Transnational Cinema." *Transnational Communities—Working Paper Series* (January) [An Economic & Social Research Council Research Programme at the University of Oxford]: 1–14.

——— (2000). "Migration und Kino—Subnationale Mitleidskultur oder transnationale Rollenspiele?" Chiellino, *Handbuch* 329–347.

——— (2004). "Strangers in Disguise: Role-Play beyond Identity Politics in Anarchic Film Comedy." Göktürk and Wolbert 100–122.

Göktürk, Deniz and Barbara Wolbert (eds.) (2004). *Multicultural Germany: Arts, Media, and Performance*. Spec. issue of *New German Critique* 92.

Göktürk, Deniz and Zafer Şenocak (eds.) (1991). *Jedem Wort gehört ein Himmel: Türkei literarisch*. Berlin: Babel.

Göle, Nilüfer (1996). *The Forbidden Modern: Civilization and Veiling*. Ann Arbor, MI: University of Michigan Press.

——— (2002). "Islam in Public: New Visibilities and New Imaginaries." Gaonkar and Lee 173–190.

Goldberg, Andreas (1996). "Status and Problems of the Turkish Community in Germany." Unpublished document. Essen: Zentrum für Türkeistudien.

——— (2002). "Islam in Germany." Hunter 29–50.

Goldberg, Andreas and Faruk Şen (eds.) (1999). *Deutsche Türken—Türkische Deutsche? Die Diskussion um die doppelte Staatsbürgerschaft*. Münster: LIT.

Gómez-Peña, Guillermo (1996). *The New World Border*. San Francisco: City Lights.

——— (2000). *Dangerous Border Crossers: The Artist Talks Back*. New York: Routledge.

Gott, Gil Michael (1994). "Migration, Ethnicization and Germany's New Ethnic Minority Literature." Diss. University of California [Berkeley].

Gram, Ole (2003). "The King of Marxloh: Ahmet Öner, Boxing, and Turkish-German Regionalism." Paper presented at the German Studies Association Annual Convention (New Orleans). September 20.

Grass, Günter (2002). *Crabwalk*. Trans. Krishna Winston. Orlando, FL: Harcourt. Trans. of *Im Krebsgang*. Göttingen: Steidl, 2002.

Green, André (1999). *The Fabric of Affect in the Psychoanalytic Discourse*. Trans. Alan Sheridan. London: Routledge.

Grenoble, Lenore A. (2003). *Language Policy in the Soviet Union*. Dordrecht [The Netherlands]: Kluwer Academic Publishers.

Grice, Paul (1989). *Studies in the Way of Words*. Cambridge, MA: Harvard University Press.

Grimm, Erk (2003). "Fathoming the Archive: German Poetry and the Culture of Memory." *New German Critique* 88: 107–140.

Grosse, Pascal (2000). *Kolonialismus, Eugenik und bürgerliche Gesellschaft in Deutschland 1850–1918*. Frankfurt a. M.: Campus.

Grosser, J. F. G. (ed.) (1963). *Die grosse Kontroverse: Ein Briefwechsel um Deutschland*. Hamburg: Nagel.

Grünbein, Durs (1995). *Den Körper zerbrechen*. Frankfurt a. M.: Suhrkamp.

Grünefeld, Hans-Dieter (1995). "Deutsche Literatur oder Literatur in Deutschland? Rezeption und Bedeutung literarischer Texte der Migration." *Sirene* 14: 88–104.

Günter, Manuela (1999). " 'Wir sind bastarde, freunde...': Feridun Zaimoglus *Kanak Sprak* und die performative Struktur von Identität." *Sprache und Literatur in Wissenschaft und Didaktik* 83: 15–28.

Günther, Petra (1993). " 'Langsam komme ich zu mir und überlege, ob ich das aufschreiben soll': Der Erzähler Sten Nadolny." Delabar, Jung, and Pergande 35–44.

Guillory, John (1993). *Cultural Capital: The Problem of Literary Canon Formation*. Chicago: University of Chicago Press.

Ha, Kien Nghi [Hà Kiên Nghi—Ho Gin Ngai] (1999). *Ethnizität und Migration*. Münster: Westfälisches Dampfboot.

Habermas, Jürgen (1989). *The Structural Transformation of the Public Sphere: An Inquiry into a Category of Bourgeois Society*. Trans. Thomas Burger with Frederick Lawrence. Cambridge, MA: MIT Press. Trans. of *Stukturwandel der Öffentlichkeit*. Neuwied, Germany: Luchterhand, 1962.

Hall, Katharina (2003). " 'Bekanntlich sind Dreiecksbeziehungen am kompliziertesten': Turkish, Jewish and German Identity in Zafer Şenocak's *Gefährliche Verwandtschaft*." *German Life and Letters* 56.1: 72–88.

Halman, Talat Sait (ed.) (1982). *Contemporary Turkish Literature: Fiction and Poetry*. Rutherford: Fairleigh Dickinson University Press.

Hamburger, Michael (trans.) (1967). "The Middle of Life." By Friedrich Hölderlin. *Friedrich Hölderlin: Poems and Fragments*. Ann Arbor, MI: University of Michigan Press. 371.

Hark, Sabine (2005). *Dissidente Partizipation: Eine Diskursgeschichte des Feminismus*. Frankfurt a. M.: Suhrkamp.

Hassan, Salah and Iftikhar Dadi (eds.) (2001). *Unpacking Europe: Towards a Critical Reading*. Rotterdam: NAi Publishers.

Hedetoft, Ulf and Mette Hjort (eds.) (2002) *The Postnational Self: Belonging and Identity*. Public Worlds 10. Minneapolis, MN: University of Minnesota Press.

Heidenreich, Nanna (2000). "Das sieht man doch! Die Erkennungsdienste des Ausländerdiskurses am Beispiel von 'Berlin in Berlin.' " *Ästhetik & Kommunikation* 31.111: 31–38.

Hein, Christoph (1989). *The Distant Lover*. Trans. Krishna Winston. New York: Pantheon. Trans. of *Der fremde Freund*. Berlin (East) and Weimar: Aufbau, 1982.

Heine, Heinrich (1975). *Historisch-kritische Gesamtausgabe der Werke*. Ed. Manfred Windfuhr and Pierre Grappin. Vol. I/1. Buch der Lieder. Hamburg: Hoffmann and Campe.

—— (1983). *Historisch-kritische Gesamtausgabe der Werke*. Ed. Manfred Windfuhr and Elisabeth Genton. Vol. II. Neue Gedichte. Hamburg: Hoffmann and Campe.

Heinze, Hartmut (1986). *Migrantenliteratur in der Bundesrepublik Deutschland: Bestandsaufnahme und Entwicklungstendenzen zu einer multikulturellen Literatursynthese*. Berlin: EXpress Edition.

Heitmeyer, Wilhelm and Rainer Dollase (eds.) (1996). *Die bedrängte Toleranz: Ethnisch-kulturelle Konflikte, religiöse Differenzen und die Gefahren politisierter Gewalt*. Frankfurt a. M.: Suhrkamp.

Heitmeyer, Wilhelm, Joachim Müller, and Helmut Schröder (1997). *Verlockender Fundamentalismus: Türkische Jugendliche in Deutschland.* Frankfurt a. M.: Suhrkamp.
Hell, Julia (1992). "Christoph Hein's *Der fremde Freund / Drachenblut* and the Antinomies of Writing Under 'Real Existing Socialism.'" *Colloquia Germanica* 25.3/4: 307–337.
—— (1997). *Post-Fascist Fantasies: Psychoanalysis, History and the Literature of East Germany.* Durham, NC: Duke University Press.
—— (1999). "Holocaust Memory, Femininity, and Cold War Rhetoric." Paper presented at conference on Fifty Years of the Federal Republic of Germany through a Gendered Lens. University of North Carolina (Chapel Hill). September 26.
—— (2003). "Eyes Wide Shut: German Post-Holocaust Authorship." *New German Critique* 88: 9–36.
Heller, Agnes (1982). *A Theory of History.* London: Routledge and Kegan-Paul.
Henderson, Heike (1997). "Re-Thinking and Re-Writing *Heimat*: Turkish Women Writers in Germany." *Women in German Yearbook* 13: 225–243.
—— (2000). "Geschichte(n) erzählen: Literarische Erinnerungen an eine Kindheit in der Türkei." Beitter 81–95.
Henkel, Heiko (2004a). "Pious Disciplines and Modern Lives: The Culture of Fiqh in the Turkish Islamic Tradition." Diss. Princeton University.
—— (2004b). "Rethinking the *dâr al-harb*: Social Change and Changing Perceptions of the West in Turkish Islam." *Journal of Ethnic and Migration Studies* 30.5: 961–977.
Henscheid, Eckhard (1993). *Dummdeutsch: Ein Wörterbuch.* Stuttgart: Reclam.
Herf, Jeffrey (1997). *Divided Memory: The Nazi Past in the Two Germanys.* Cambridge, MA: Harvard University Press.
—— (2002). "Traditions of Memory and Belonging: The Holocaust and the Germans since 1945." Hedetoft and Hjort 275–294.
Herman, David (2002). *Story Logic: Problems and Possibilities of Narrative.* Lincoln, NE: University of Nebraska Press.
Hess, Sabine and Ramona Lenz (eds.) (2001). *Geschlecht und Globalisierung: Ein kulturwissenschaftlicher Streifzug durch transnationale Räume.* Königstein/ Taunus: Ulrike Helmer.
Hielscher, Martin (2001). "Kritik der Krise: Erzählerische Strategien der jüngsten Gegenwartsliteratur und ihre Vorläufer." *Literarisches Krisenbewußtsein: Ein Perzeptions- und Produktionsmuster im 20. Jahrhundert.* Ed. Keith Bullivant and Bernhard Spies. Munich: Iudicium. 314–334.
Hilsenrath, Edgar (1971). *The Nazi and the Barber.* Trans. Andrew White. Garden City, NY: Doubleday. Trans. of *Der Nazi und der Friseur.*
—— (1990). *The Story of the Last Thought.* Trans. Hugh Young. London: Scribners. Trans. of *Das Märchen vom letzten Gedanken.* Munich: Piper, 1989.
Hirsch, Marianne (1997). *Family Frames: Photography, Narrative, and Postmemory.* Cambridge, MA: Harvard University Press.
Hochstadt, Steve (1999). *Mobility and Modernity: Migration in Germany, 1820–1989.* Ann Arbor, MI: University of Michigan Press.
Hölderlin, Friedrich (1944). *Werke.* Vol. I: *Gedichte.* Ed. Emil Staiger. Zürich: Atlantis.

Hoesterey, Ingeborg (2001). *Pastiche: Cultural Memory in Art, Film, Literature*. Bloomington, IN: Indiana University Press.

Hoffmann, Dieter (2001). *Postmoderne Erzählstrukturen und Interkulturalität in Sten Nadolnys Roman* Selim oder Die Gabe der Rede: *Interpretation, Kommentar, Materialien*. Europäische Hochschulschriften, Series 1: Deutsche Sprache und Literatur 1786. Frankfurt a. M.: Lang.

Hohoff, Ulrich and Irmgard Ackermann (1999). "Aras Ören." *Kritisches Lexikon zur deutschsprachigen Gegenwartsliteratur*. Ed. Heinz Ludwig Arnold. Munich: edition text + kritik. 61. Nachlieferung.

Hollinger, David A. (1995). *Postethnic America: Beyond Multiculturalism*. New York: Basic Books.

Horn, Dieter (1986). "Schreiben aus Betroffenheit: Die Migrantenliteratur in der Bundesrepublik." *Migration und Integration: Ein Reader*. Ed. Alfred J. Tumat. Baltmannsweiler: Pädagogischer Verlag Burgbücherei Schneider. 213–233.

Horrocks, David and Eva Kolinsky (eds.) (1996). *Turkish Culture in German Society Today*. Providence, RI: Berghahn.

Hovannisian, Richard G. (ed.) (1986). *The Armenian Genocide in Perspective*. New Brunswick, NJ: Transaction.

—— (ed.) (2003). *Looking Backward, Moving Forward: Confronting the Armenian Genocide*. New Brunswick, NJ: Transaction.

Howard, Mary (ed.) (1997). *Interkulturelle Konfigurationen: Zur deutschsprachigen Erzählliteratur von Autoren nichtdeutscher Herkunft*. Munich: Iudicium.

Hull, Isabel V. (2003). "Military Culture and the Production of 'Final Solutions' in the Colonies: The Example of Wilhelminian Germany." Gellately and Kiernan 141–62.

—— (2005). *Absolute Destruction: Military Culture and the Practices of War in Imperial Germany*. Ithaca, NY: Cornell University Press.

Hunter, Shireen T. (ed.) (2002). *Islam, Europe's Second Religion: The New Social, Cultural, and Political Landscape*. Westport, CT: Praeger.

Huntington, Samuel (1993). "The Clash of Civilizations?" *Foreign Affairs* 72.3: 22–49.

—— (1996). *The Clash of Civilizations and the Remaking of World Order*. New York: Simon and Schuster.

Huyssen, Andreas (1995). *Twilight Memories: Marking Time in a Culture of Amnesia*. New York: Routledge.

—— (2000). "Present Pasts: Media, Politics, Amnesia." *Public Culture* 12.1: 21–38.

—— (2003a). "Diaspora and Nation: Migration Into Other Pasts." *New German Critique* 88: 147–164.

—— (2003b). *Present Pasts: Urban Palimpsests and the Politics of Memory*. Stanford: Stanford University Press.

—— (2005). "Gray Zones of Remembrance." *New History of German Literature*. Ed. David Wellbery, Judith Ryan, Hans Ulrich Gumbrecht, Anton Kaes, Joseph Leo Koerner, and Dorothea E. von Mücke. Cambridge, MA: Harvard University Press. 970–975.

Irzık, Sibel and Güven Güzeldere (eds.) (2003). *Relocating the Fault Lines: Turkey beyond the East-West Divide*. Spec. issue of *South Atlantic Quarterly* 102. 2/3. Durham, NC: Duke University Press.

Jacobson, David (1996). *Rights from Across Borders: Immigration and the Decline of Citizenship*. Baltimore, MD: Johns Hopkins University Press.

Jankowsky, Karen (1997). "'German' Literature Contested: The 1991 Ingeborg-Bachmann-Prize Debate, 'Cultural Diversity,' and Emine Sevgi Özdamar." *German Quarterly* 70.3: 261–276.
Jankowsky, Karen and Carla Love (eds.) (1997). *Other Germanies: Questioning Identity in Women's Literature and Art.* Albany, NY: SUNY Press.
Jarausch, Konrad H. and Michael Geyer (2003). *Shattered Past: Reconstructing German Histories.* Princeton, NJ: Princeton University Press.
Jerome, Roy (ed.) (2001). *Conceptions of Postwar German Masculinity.* Albany, NY: SUNY Press.
Johnson, Sheila (1997a). "Literatur von deutschschreibenden Autorinnen islamischer Herkunft." *German Studies Review* 20.2 (May): 261–278.
—— (1997b). "Von 'Betroffenheit' zur Literatur: Frauen islamischer Herkunft, die auf deutsch schreiben." Howard 153–169.
—— (2001). "Transnational *Ästhetik des türkischen Alltags*: Emine Sevgi Özdamar's *Das Leben ist eine Karawanserai.*" *German Quarterly* 74.1: 37–57.
Jordan, James (2003). "Zafer Şenocak's Essays and Early Prose Fiction: From Collective Multiculturalism to Fragmented Cultural Identities." Cheesman and Yeşilada 91–105.
Judt, Tony (2002). "The Past Is Another Country: Myth and Memory in Post-War Europe." *Memory and Power in Post-War Europe: Studies in the Presence of the Past.* Ed. Jan-Werner Müller. Cambridge, UK: Cambridge University Press. 157–183.
Kacandes, Irene (2001). *Talk Fiction: Literature and the Talk Explosion.* Lincoln, NE: University of Nebraska Press.
Kaiser, Volker (2003). "Karl Marx: Darstellung und Kritik als Versprechen zur Moderne." *1848 und das Versprechen der Moderne.* Ed. Jürgen Fohrmann and Helmut J. Schneider. Würzburg: Königshausen & Neumann. 65–84.
Kakutani, Michiko (2003). "Setting Out With a Dream And a Lot Of Sausages." *New York Times.* February 4: E1.
Kanak Attak (1998). "Kanak Attak und basta!"/"Kanak Attak—ve işte o kadar!" October 2, 2003 <http://www.kanak-attak.de/ka/down/ pdf/textos. pdf >.
Kandiyoti, Deniz (1991). "Identity and Its Discontents: Women and the Nation." *Millennium: Journal of International Studies* 20.3: 429–443.
Kaplan, Caren, Norma Alarcón, and Minoo Moallem (eds.) (1999). *Between Woman and Nation: Nationalisms, Feminist Transnationalisms, and the State.* Durham, NC: Duke University Press.
Kara, Yadé (2003). *Selam Berlin.* Zurich: Diogenes.
Karakuş, Mahmut (1994). "Zafer Şenocak in türkischer Übersetzung." *Diyalog: Interkulturelle Zeitschrift für Germanistik* 2: 231–234.
—— (2001). "Sıra Dışı Bir Yazar: Feridun Zaimoğlu." Karakuş and Kuruyazıcı 273–284.
Karakuş, Mahmut and Nilüfer Kuruyazıcı (eds.) (2001). *Gurbeti Vatan Edenler: Almanca Yazan Almanyalı Türkler.* Ankara: Kültür Bakanlığı.
Karpat, Berkan and Zafer Şenocak (1998). *Nâzım Hikmet: Auf dem Schiff zum Mars.* Munich: Babel.
—— (1999). *Tanzende der Elektrik: Szenisches Poem.* Munich: Verlag im Gleisbau.
—— (2000). *wie den vater nicht töten: Ein Sprechlabyrinth.* Tuschick, *Morgen Land* 179–190.

Karpen, Ulrich (ed.) (1988). *The Constitution of the Federal Republic of Germany: Essays on the Basic Rights and Principles of the Basic Law with a Translation of the Basic Law*. Baden-Baden: Nomos Verlagsgesellschaft.

Karpf, Ernst, Doron Kiesel, and Karsten Visarius (eds.) (1995). *"Getürkte Bilder": Zur Inszenierung von Fremden im Film*. Arnoldshainer Filmgespräche 12. Marburg: Schüren.

Katzenstein, Peter (ed.) (1997). *Tamed Power: Germany in Europe*. Ithaca, NY: Cornell University Press.

Keilson, Hans (1947). *Komödie in Moll*. Amsterdam: Querido Verlag N.V.

—— (1962). *The Death of the Adversary*. Trans. Ivo Jarosy. New York: Arion Press.

Keim, Walter and Hans Dollinger (eds.) (1991). *Flitterwochen: Karikaturisten sehen das Jahr nach der deutsch-deutschen Hochzeit*. Munich: Süddeutscher.

Kellman, Steven G. (2000). *The Translingual Imagination*. Lincoln, NE: University of Nebraska Press.

Keyder, Çağlar (1997). "Whither the Project of Modernity? Turkey in the 1990s." *Rethinking Modernity and National Identity in Turkey*. Ed. Sibel Bozdoğan and Reşat Kasaba. Seattle, WA: University of Washington Press. 37–51.

Kirby, Rachel (1999). *The Culturally Complex Individual: Franz Werfel's Reflections on Minority Identity and Historical Depiction in* The Forty Days of Musa Dagh. London: Associated University Presses.

Klopp, Brett (2002). *German Multiculturalism: Immigrant Integration and the Transformation of Citizenship*. Westport, CT: Praeger.

Koch, Gertrud (1992). *Die Einstellung ist die Einstellung: visuelle Konstruktionen des Judentums*. Frankfurt a. M.: Suhrkamp.

—— (ed.) (1999a). *Bruchlinien: Tendenzen der Holocaustforschung*. Cologne: Böhlau.

—— (1999b). "Handlungsfolgen: Moralische Schlüsse aus narrativen Schließungen: Populäre Visualisierungen des Holocaust." Trans. Sissi Tax and Irmelin Hoffer. Koch, *Bruchlinien* 295–313.

—— (2003). "Between Fear of Contact and Self-Preservation: Taboo and Its Relation to the Dead." Trans. Rachel Leah Magshamhrain. *New German Critique* 90: 71–83.

Kocka, Jürgen (2003). "Comparison and Beyond." *History and Theory* 42.1 (February): 39–44.

Kolinsky, Eva (2000). *Deutsch und türkisch leben: Bild und Selbstbild der türkischen Minderheit in Deutschland*. German Linguistic and Cultural Studies 4. Oxford, UK: Lang.

—— (2002). "Migration Experience and the Construction of Identity among Turks Living in Germany." Taberner and Finlay 205–218.

Konuk, Kader (1997). "Das Leben ist eine Karawanserai: Heim-at bei Emine Sevgi Özdamar." *Kein Land in Sicht: Heimat—weiblich?* Ed. Gisela Ecker. Munich: Wilhelm Fink. 143–157.

—— (1999). " 'Identitätssuche ist ein [sic!] private archäologische Graberei': Emine Sevgi Özdamars inszeniertes Sprechen." Gelbin, Konuk, and Piesche 60–74.

—— (2001). *Identitäten im Prozeß: Literatur von Autorinnen aus und in der Türkei in deutscher, englischer und türkischer Sprache*. Essen: Die Blaue Eule.

Konzett, Matthias (ed.) (2000a). *Encyclopedia of German Literature*. Chicago: Fitzroy Dearborn.

Konzett, Matthias (2000b). "Zafer Şenocak (1961-)." Konzett, *Encyclopedia* 895–897.
—— (2003a). "Writing Against the Grain: Zafer Şenocak as Public Intellectual and Writer." Cheesman and Yeşilada 43–60.
—— (2003b). "Zafer Şenocak im Gespräch: Interview." *German Quarterly* 76.2: 131–139.
Kosta, Barbara and Helga Kraft (eds.) (2003). *Writing Against Boundaries: Nationality, Ethnicity and Gender in the German-speaking Context.* Amsterdam: Rodopi.
Kramsch, Claire (1999). "Thirdness: The Intercultural Stance." *Language, Culture and Identity.* Ed. Torben Vestergaard. Aalborg, Denmark: Aalborg University Press. 41–58.
Kreile, Renate (1993). "EMMA und die 'deutschen Frauen': 'an's Vaterland, an's teure, schließt euch an . . . .' " *Beiträge zur feministischen Theorie und Praxis* 35: 123–130.
Krusche, Dietrich (1985). *Literatur und Fremde: Zur Hermeneutik kulturräumlicher Distanz.* Munich: Iudicium.
Krusche, Dietrich and Alois Wierlacher (1990). *Hermeneutik der Fremde.* Munich: Iudicium.
Kurt, Kemal (1998). *Ja, sagt Molly.* Berlin: Hitit.
Kurthen, Hermann, Werner Bergmann, and Rainer Erb (eds.) (1997). *Antisemitism and Xenophobia in Germany After Unification.* New York: Oxford University Press.
Kuruyazıcı, Nilüfer (1995). " 'Selim oder die Gabe der Rede' (Verschiedene Lesemöglichkeiten des Romans von Sten Nadolny)." *Alman Dili ve Edebiyatı Dergisi* 9: 21–31.
—— (1997). "Emine Sevgi Özdamars *Das Leben ist eine Karawanserai* im Prozeß der interkulturellen Kommunikation." Howard 179–188.
—— (2001). "Almanya'da Oluşan Yeni Bir Yazının Tartışılması." Karakuş and Kuruyazıcı 3–24.
La Belle, Jenijoy (1988). *Herself Beheld: The Literature of the Looking Glass.* Ithaca, NY: Cornell University Press.
LaCapra, Dominick (1992). "Representing the Holocaust: Reflections on the Historians' Debate." Friedlander 108–127.
—— (1994). *Representing the Holocaust: History, Theory, Trauma.* Ithaca, NY: Cornell University Press.
—— (1997). "1986." Gilman and Zipes 812–819.
—— (1998). *History and Memory After Auschwitz.* Ithaca, NY: Cornell University Press.
—— (2003). "History, Psychoanalysis, Critical Theory." Lecture at School of Criticism and Theory, Cornell University, June 17.
—— (2004a). *History in Transit: Experience, Identity, Critical Theory.* Ithaca, NY: Cornell University Press.
—— (2004b). "Tropisms of Intellectual History." *Rethinking History* 8.4: 499–529.
Langenbacher, Eric (2002). "Memory Regimes in Contemporary Germany." Diss. Georgetown University.
Lankowski, Carl (2003). "Testimony Prepared for the Subcommittee on Europe of the US House of Representatives Committee on International Relations,

Hearing on the European Union, 22 July 2003." September 5, 2003 <www.aicgs.org/carl/shtml>.
Lee, Benjamin and Edward LiPuma (2002). "Cultures of Circulation: The Imaginations of Modernity." Gaonkar and Lee 191–213.
Leggewie, Claus (2000). "Hybridkulturen." *Merkur* 54.9/10: 878–889.
—— (2002). "German-Turks and the Holocaust: How Immigrants Deal with Their Host Country's 'Burden of the Past.' " Lecture presented at Cornell University, Einaudi Seminar on *Remembering Europe*, October 31.
—— (2005). "Bindestrich-Deutsche, Euro-Muslime und Unions-Bürger: Eine Forschungsskizze zu den Erinnerungsorten von 'Deutsch-Türken.' " *Nationale Mythen—kollektive Symbole: Funktionen, Konstruktionen und Medien der Erinnerung*. Ed. Klaudia Knabel, Dietmar Rieger, and Stephanie Wodianka. Göttingen: Vandenhoeck & Ruprecht. 67–99.
Leggewie, Claus and Zafer Şenocak (eds.) (1993). *Deutsche Türken/Türk Almanlar: Das Ende der Geduld/Sabrın Sonu*. Reinbek bei Hamburg: Rowohlt.
Lejeune, Philippe (1989). *On Autobiography*. Trans. Katherine Leary. Minneapolis, MN: University of Minnesota Press.
Lepsius, M. Rainer (1989). "Das Erbe des Nationalsozialismus und die politische Kultur der Nachfolgestaaten des 'Großdeutschen Reiches.' " *Kultur und Gesellschaft*. Ed. Michael Haller, Hans-Joachim Hoffmann-Nowotny, and Wolfgang Zapf. Frankfurt a. M.: Campus. 247–264.
Levy, Daniel and Natan Sznaider (2001). *Erinnerung im globalen Zeitalter: Der Holocaust*. Frankfurt a. M.: Suhrkamp.
—— (2002). "Memory Unbound: The Holocaust and the Formation of Cosmopolitan Memory." *European Journal of Social Theory* 5.1: 87–106.
Linke, Uli (1995). "Murderous Fantasies: Violence, Memory, and Selfhood in Germany." *New German Critique* 64: 37–60.
Lipovsky, Igor P. (1992). *The Socialist Movement in Turkey 1960–1980*. Leiden: E. J. Brill.
Liss, Andrea (1998). *Trespassing through Shadows: Memory, Photography, and the Holocaust*. Minneapolis, MN: University of Minnesota Press.
Littler, Margaret (2002). "Diasporic Identity in Emine Sevgi Özdamar's *Mutterzunge*." Taberner and Finlay 219–234.
Loentz, Elizabeth (2003). "A Turkish-German Odyssey: Aras Ören's *Eine verspätete Abrechnung oder Der Aufstieg des Gündoğdus*." Kosta and Kraft 99–112.
Loh, Hannes and Murat Güngör (2002). *Fear of a Kanak Planet: HipHop zwischen Weltkultur und Nazi-Rap*. Höfen [Austria]: Hannibal.
Lorenz, Dagmar C. G. (1992). *Verfolgung bis zum Massenmord: Holocaust-Diskurse in deutscher Sprache aus der Sicht der Verfolgten*. New York: Lang.
—— (1998). "History, Identity, and the Body in Edgar Hilsenrath's *The Story of the Last Thought*." *Transforming the Center, Eroding the Margins: Essays on Ethnic and Cultural Boundaries in German-Speaking Countries*. Ed. Dagmar C. G. Lorenz and Renate S. Posthofen. Columbia, SC: Camden House. 146–154.
Lottmann, Joachim (1997). "Kanak Attack! Ein Wochenende in Kiel mit Feridun Zaimoglu, dem Malcolm X der deutschen Türken." *Die Zeit* 47 (November 14): 88.
Lowe, Lisa and David Lloyd (eds.) (1997). *The Politics of Culture in the Shadow of Capital*. Durham, NC: Duke University Press.

Lützeler, Paul Michael (1992). *Die Schriftsteller und Europa: Von der Romantik bis zur Gegenwart*. Munich: Piper.
—— (1993). "Von der Präsenz der Geschichte: Postmoderne Konstellationen in der Erzählliteratur der Gegenwart." *Neue Rundschau* 104.1: 91–106.
—— (1994). "Writers on European Identity." *Europe After Maastricht: American and European Perspectives*. Ed. Paul Michael Lützeler. Providence, RI: Berghahn. 295–306.
—— (ed.) (1995). *Multiculturalism in Contemporary German Literature*. Spec. issue of *World Literature Today* 69.3.
—— (ed.) (1996). *Schreiben zwischen den Kulturen: Beiträge zur deutschsprachigen Gegenwartsliteratur*. Frankfurt a. M.: Fischer.
Lyons, James (1977). *Semantics*. Vol. 2. Cambridge: Cambridge University Press.
Maier, Charles S. (1988). *The Unmasterable Past: History, Holocaust, and German National Identity*. Cambridge, MA: Harvard University Press.
Mandel, Ruth (1989). "Turkish Headscarves and the 'Foreigner Problem': Constructing Difference through Emblems of Identity." *New German Critique* 46: 27–46.
—— (2003). "Making *Ausländer*: Processes of Ethnicization in Germany." Presented at Lives In-Between? The Turkish Diaspora in Germany, An Interdisciplinary Conference at the University of Chicago, May 1–2.
—— (2006). *Cosmopolitan Anxieties*. Durham, NC: Duke University Press. Forthcoming.
Mani, Bala Venkat (2001). "On the Question, 'What is Turkish-German?': Minority Literatures and the Dialectics of Exclusion." Diss. Stanford University.
—— (2002). "Phantom of the 'Gastarbeiterliteratur': Aras Ören's Berlin Savignyplatz." Blioumi 112–129.
—— (2003). "The Good Woman of Istanbul: Emine Sevgi Özdamar's *Die Brücke vom Goldenen Horn*. *Gegenwartsliteratur* 2: 29–58.
Mattson, Michelle (1997). "The Function of the Cultural Stereotype in a Minor Literature: Alev Tekinay's Short Stories." *Monatshefte* 89.1: 68–83.
McCarthy, Justin (1995). *Death and Exile: The Ethnic Cleansing of Ottoman Muslims 1821–1922*. Princeton, NJ: Darwin Press.
—— (1997). *The Ottoman Turks: An Introductory History to 1923*. London: Longman.
McGann, Jerome (2001). *Radiant Textuality: Literature After the World Wide Web*. New York: Palgrave.
McGowan, James (trans.) (1993). *The Flowers of Evil*. By Charles Baudelaire. With an Introduction by Jonathan Culler. Oxford: Oxford University Press.
McGowan, Moray (1997). " 'Bosporus fließt in mir': Europa-Bilder und Brückenmetaphern bei Aras Ören und Zehra Çırak." Waldhoff, Tan, and Kürşat-Ahlers 21–39.
—— (2000a). "Aras Ören." Konzett, *Encyclopedia* 780.
—— (2000b). " 'The Bridge of the Golden Horn': Istanbul, Europe and the 'Fractured Gaze from the West' in Turkish Writing in Germany." *Beyond Boundaries: Textual Representations of European Identity*. Ed. Andy Hollis. Amsterdam: Rodopi. 53–69.
—— (2001). "Multiple Masculinities in Turkish-German Men's Writing." Jerome 289–312.

McGowan, Moray (2003) "Odysseus on the Ottoman, or 'The Man in Skirts': Exploratory Masculinities in the Prose Texts of Zafer Şenocak." Cheesman and Yeşilada 61–79.

—— (2004). "Brücken und Brücken-Köpfe: Wandlungen einer Metapher in der türkisch-deutschen Literatur." Durzak and Kuruyazıcı 31–40.

McLuhan, Marshall (1996). *Essential McLuhan*. Ed. Eric McLuhan and Frank Zingrone. New York: Basic Books.

Mecklenburg, Norbert (1990). "Über kulturelle und poetische Alterität: Kultur- und literaturtheoretische Grundprobleme einer interkulturellen Germanistik." Krusche and Wierlacher 80–103.

—— (1999). "Was ist Interkulturelle Literaturwissenschaft?" *Diyalog: Interkulturelle Zeitschrift für Germanistik*: 123–137.

Melas, Natalie (1995). "Versions of Incommensurability." *World Literature Today* 69.2: 275–288.

—— (2006). *All the Difference in the World: Postcoloniality and the Ends of Comparison*. Stanford, CA: Stanford University Press. Forthcoming.

Melson, Robert (1992). *Revolution and Genocide: On the Origins of the Armenian Genocide and the Holocaust*. Chicago: University of Chicago Press.

Mennel, Barbara (1998). "Seduction, Sacrifice, and Submission: Masochism in Postwar German Film and Literature." Diss. Cornell University.

—— (2002). "Bruce Lee in Kreuzberg and Scarface in Altona: Transnational Auteurism and Ghettocentrism in Thomas Arslan's *Brothers and Sisters* and Fatih Akin's *Short Sharp Shock*." *New German Critique* 87: 133–56.

Mignolo, Walter D. (2000a). *Local Histories/Global Designs: Coloniality, Subaltern Knowledges, and Border Thinking*. Princeton, NJ: Princeton University Press.

—— (2000b). "The Many Faces of Cosmo-polis: Border Thinking and Critical Cosmopolitanism." *Public Culture* 12.3: 721–748.

Migrationsmuseum (2003). "Deutschland braucht ein Migrationsmuseum!" October 23, 2003 <http://www.migrationsmuseum.de>.

Milich, Klaus (1983). " 'Sauber sind die alle nicht!' Zur Sozialgeschichte der Türkenwitze." Radio broadcast for Südwestfunk Baden-Baden, *Welt von heute*, 2. Program. 23 November.

Miller, Mark J. (1981). *Foreign Workers in Western Europe: An Emerging Political Force*. New York: Praeger.

Milz, Sabine (2000). "Comparative Cultural Studies and Ethnic Minority Writing Today: The Hybridities of Marlene Nourbese Philip and Emine Sevgi Özdamar." *Comparative Literature and Culture: A WWWeb Journal* [Purdue University Press]. June. April 24, 2003 <http://clcwebjournal.lib.purdue.edu/clcweb00-2/milz00.html>.

Mitscherlich, Alexander (1969). *Society without the Father: A Contribution to Social Psychology*. Trans. Eric Mosbacher. London: Tavistock. Trans. of *Auf dem Weg zur vaterlosen Gesellschaft*. Munich: Piper, 1963.

Mitscherlich, Alexander and Margarete Mitscherlich (1975). *The Inability to Mourn: Principles of Collective Behavior*. Trans. Beverley R. Placzek. New York: Grove Press.

Modarressi, Taghi (1992). "Writing with an Accent." *Chanteh* 1.1: 7–9.

Mohanty, Satya P. (1993). "The Epistemic Status of Cultural Identity: On *Beloved* and the Postcolonial Condition." *Cultural Critique* 24: 41–80.

Mohanty, Satya P. (1997). *Literary Theory and the Claims of History: Postmodernism, Objectivity, Multicultural Politics*. Ithaca, NY: Cornell University Press.

——— (2003). "Why I Am Not a Strategic Essentialist II: The Epistemic Status of Social Identity." Lecture presented at the School of Criticism and Theory, Cornell University, July 8.

Mohanty, Satya, Linda Alcoff, Michael Hames-García, and Paula Moya (2005). *Redefining Identity Politics*. New York: Palgrave.

Morris, Leslie (2002). "Postmemory, Postmemoir." *Unlikely History: The Changing German-Jewish Symbiosis, 1945–2000*. Ed. Leslie Morris and Jack Zipes. New York: Palgrave. 291–306.

Moya, Paula M. L. and Michael R. Hames-García (eds.) (2000). *Reclaiming Identity: Realist Theory and the Predicament of Postmodernism*. Berkeley, CA: University of California Press.

Müller, Regula (1997). " 'Ich war Mädchen, war ich Sultanin': Weitgeöffnete Augen betrachten türkische Frauengeschichte(n)/Zum Karawanserai-Roman von Emine Sevgi Özdamar." Fischer and McGowan, *Denn* 133–149.

Mushaben, Joyce (1998). *From Post-War to Post-Wall Generations: Changing Attitudes Toward the National Question and NATO in the Federal Republic of Germany*. Boulder, CO: Westview Press.

——— (2003). "Split Personalities or Dual Identities: Generational Change among Turkish-German Migrants." Paper presented at German Studies Association Annual Convention (New Orleans). September 20.

——— (2005). *The Changing Faces of Citizenship: Social Integration and Political Mobilization Among Ethnic Minorities in Germany*. New York: Berghahn.

Nadolny, Sten (1990). *Selim oder Die Gabe der Rede*. 1992 ed. Munich: Piper.

——— (1997a). *The Discovery of Slowness*. Trans. Ralph Freedman. 1987. New York: Penguin. Trans. of *Die Entdeckung der Langsamkeit*. Munich: Piper, 1983.

——— (1997b). *The God of Impertinence*. Trans. Breon Mitchell. New York: Viking. Trans. of *Ein Gott der Frechheit*. Munich: Piper, 1994.

Negt, Oskar and Alexander Kluge (1981). *Geschichte und Eigensinn: Geschichtliche Organisation der Arbeitsvermögen, Deutschland als Produktionsöffentlichkeit, Gewalt des Zusammenhangs*. Frankfurt a. M.: Zweitausendeins.

Neubert, Isolde (1997). "Searching for Intercultural Communication: Emine Sevgi Özdamar—A Turkish Woman Writer in Germany." *Post-War Women's Writing in German: Feminist Critical Approaches*. Ed. Chris Weedon. Providence, RI: Berghahn. 153–168.

Neumann, Klaus (2000). *Shifting Memories: The Nazi Past in the New Germany*. Ann Arbor, MI: University of Michigan Press.

Ong, Aihwa (1999). *Flexible Citizenship: The Cultural Logics of Transnationality*. Durham, NC: Duke University Press.

Ören, Aras (1973). *Was will Niyazi in der Naunynstraße: Ein Poem*. Trans. H. Achmed Schmiede and Johannes Schenk. Berlin: Rotbuch.

——— (1974). *Der kurze Traum aus Kagithane: Ein Poem*. Trans. H. Achmed Schmiede. Ed. Jürgen Theobaldy. Berlin: Rotbuch.

——— (1977). *Privatexil: Gedichte*. Trans. Gisela Kraft. Berlin: Rotbuch.

——— (1980a). *Berlin Üçlemesi*. Istanbul: Remzi.

——— (1980b). *Die Fremde ist auch ein Haus: Berlin-Poem*. Trans. Gisela Kraft. Berlin: Rotbuch.

Ören, Aras (1983). *Bitte nix Polizei: Kriminalerzählung.* Trans. Cornelius Bischoff. Düsseldorf: Claassen, 1981. Frankfurt a. M.: Fischer.
—— (1985). *Bütün Eserleri I: Manej, Bitte nix Polizei.* Frankfurt a. M.: Dağyeli.
—— (1986). "Dankrede zur Preisverleihung." *Chamissos Enkel: Zur Literatur von Ausländern in Deutschland.* Ed. Heinz Friedrich. Munich: dtv. 25–29.
—— (1988). *Eine verspätete Abrechnung oder Der Aufstieg der Gündoğdus.* In Search of the Present I. Trans. Zafer Şenocak and Eva Hund. Frankfurt a. M.: Dağyeli. Trans. of *Nilgün ya da Gündoğduların Yükselişi.* Frankfurt a. M.: Dağyeli, 1985.
—— (1990). *A'nın Gizli Yaşamı* [The Secret Life of A.]. In Search of the Present III. Istanbul: AFA.
—— (1992). *Please, No Police.* Trans. Teoman Sipahigil. Introduction by Akile Gürsoy Tezcan. Austin, TX: Center for Middle Eastern Studies, University of Texas at Austin.
—— (1995). *Berlin Savignyplatz.* In Search of the Present V. Trans. Deniz Göktürk. Berlin: Elefanten Press. Trans. of *Berlin Savignyplatz.* Istanbul: AFA, 1993.
—— (1997). *Unerwarteter Besuch.* In Search of the Present VI. Trans. Deniz Göktürk. Berlin: Elefanten Press. Trans. of *Beklenmedik Bir Ziyaretçi.* Istanbul: AFA, 1995.
—— (1998). *Granatapfelblüte.* In Search of the Present II. Trans. Eva Hund and Zafer Şenocak. Berlin: Elefanten Press. Trans. of *Nar Çiçeği.* Istanbul: AFA, 1988.
—— (1999a). *Privatexil: Ein Programm?.* Tübinger Poetik-Vorlesungen. Trans. Cem Dalaman. Tübingen: Konkursbuchverlag.
—— (1999b). *Sehnsucht nach Hollywood.* In Search of the Present IV. Trans. Deniz Göktürk. Trans. of *Hollywood Özlemi.* Istanbul: AFA, 1991.
Ören, Aras and Peter Schneider (1991). *Wie die Spree in den Bosporus fliesst: Briefe zwischen Istanbul und Berlin 1990/1991.* Ören entries trans. Eva Hund and Zafer Şenocak. Berlin: Babel Verlag Hund & Toker.
Özakın, Aysel (1986). "Ali hinter den Spiegeln." *literatur konkret* (October): 6–9.
Özdamar, Emine Sevgi (1990). *Mutterzunge: Erzählungen.* Berlin: Rotbuch.
—— (1991). *Keloglan in Alamania.* Franfurt a. M.: Verlag der Autoren.
—— (1992). *Das Leben ist eine Karawanserei: hat zwei Türen aus einer kam ich rein aus der anderen ging ich raus.* Cologne: Kiepenheuer & Witsch.
—— (1994). *Mother Tongue.* Trans. Craig Thomas. Toronto: Coach House.
—— (1998). *Die Brücke vom Goldenen Horn.* Cologne: Kiepenheuer & Witsch.
—— (2000a). *Keloglan in Alamania oder Die Versöhnung von Schwein und Lamm. Die deutsche Bühne* 71 (October): 30–37. Extant version of *Keloglan in Alamania.*
—— (2000b). *Life is a Caravanserai: Has Two Doors I Came In One I Went Out the Other.* Trans. Luise von Flotow. London: Middlesex University Press.
—— (2001). *Der Hof im Spiegel: Erzählungen.* Cologne: Kiepenheuer & Witsch.
—— (2003). *Seltsame Sterne starren zur Erde: Wedding—Pankow 1976/77.* Cologne: Kiepenheuer & Witsch.
Özdemir, Cem (1997). *Ich bin Inländer: Ein anatolischer Schwabe im Bundestag.* Ed. Hans Engels. Munich: dtv.
—— (2003). "Von den Latinos lernen: Die deutschen Türken sollten sich Amerikas Einwanderer zum Vorbild nehmen." *Die Zeit* 58.37 (September 4): 6.
Özoğuz, Yüksel (2001). "Zafer Şenocak—İki Kültürün Kesiştiği Noktada Yeni Bir Şiir Dili." Karakuş and Kuruyazıcı 201–208.

Partridge, Damani (2003). "Becoming Non-Citizens: Technologies of Exclusion and Exclusionary Incorporation after the Berlin Wall." Diss. University of California [Berkeley].
Pazarkaya, Yüksel (1986). "Über Aras Ören." *Chamissos Enkel: Zur Literatur von Ausländern in Deutschland.* Ed. Heinz Friedrich. Munich: dtv. 15–21.
—— (1989). *Rosen im Frost: Einblicke in die türkische Kultur.* Zurich: Unionsverlag.
Peck, Jeffrey (1997). "Turks and Jews: Comparing Minorities in Germany after the Holocaust." *German Cultures/Foreign Cultures: The Politics of Belonging.* Ed. Jeffrey Peck. Harry & Helen Gray Humanities Program Series 3. Washington, D.C.: American Institute for Contemporary German Studies. 1–16.
Pendas, Devin O. (2000). " 'I Didn't Know What Auschwitz Was': The Frankfurt Trial and the German Press 1963–1965." *Yale Journal of Law & the Humanities* 12: 397–446.
Peroomian, Rubina (2003). "New Directions in Literary Responses to the Armenian Genocide." *Looking Backward, Moving Forward: Confronting the Armenian Genocide.* Ed. Richard G. Hovannisian. New Brunswick, NJ: Transaction. 157–180.
Petersen, Christiane (1995). "Schnittpunkte türkisch-deutscher interkultureller Erfahrung am Beispiel Sten Nadolnys Roman 'Selim oder Die Gabe der Rede.' " *Alman Dili ve Edebiyatı Dergisi* 9: 191–197.
Phipps, Alison M. (1999). "Intercultural Germanistics: A Forum for Reconstruction?" Saul, Steuer, Möbus, and Illner 289–303.
Picco, Giandomenico, A. Kamal Aboulmagd, Lourdes Arizpe, Hanan Ashrawi, Ruth Cardoso, Jacques Delors, Leslie H. Gelb, Nadine Gordimer, Prince El Hassan bin Talal, Sergey Kapitza, Hayao Kawai, Tommy Koh, Hans Küng, Graça Machel, Amartya Sen, Song Jian, Dick Spring, Tu Weiming, Richard von Weizsäcker, and Javad Zarif (2001a). *Brücken in die Zukunft: Ein Manifest für den Dialog der Kulturen, Eine Initiative von Kofi Annan.* Trans. Klaus Kochmann and Hartmut Schickert. Frankfurt a. M.: Fischer.
—— (2001b). *Crossing the Divide: Dialogue Among Civilizations.* South Orange, NJ: School of Diplomacy and International Relations, Seton Hall University.
Posthofen, Renate S. (ed.) (1999). *Barbara Frischmuth in Contemporary Context.* Riverside, CA: Ariadne.
Prowe, Diethelm (2004). "The Fascist Phantom and Anti-Immigrant Violence: The Power of (False) Equation." Fenner and Weitz 125–140.
Pukui, Mary Kawena and Samuel H. Elbert (eds.) (1986). *Hawaiian Dictionary.* Honolulu: University of Hawaii Press.
Rabinovici, Doron (1997). *Suche nach M.: Roman in zwölf Episoden.* Frankfurt am Main: Suhrkamp.
Raffman, Diana (1994). "Vagueness Without Paradox." *The Philosophical Review* 103.1: 41–74.
Ramadan, Tariq (1999a). *Muslims in France: The Way Towards Coexistence.* Markfield, Leicester, UK: Islamic Foundation.
—— (1999b). *To Be a European Muslim: A Study of Islamic Sources in the European Context.* Leicester, UK: Islamic Foundation.
—— (2004). *Western Muslims and the Future of Islam.* Oxford, UK: Oxford University Press.
Rau, Johannes (2000). "Ohne Angst und ohne Träumereien: Gemeinsam in Deutschland leben." Speech held at the *Haus der Kulturen der Welt* [Berlin],

May 12. October 12, 2003 <http://www.bundespraesident.de/dokumente/ Rede/ ix_11961.htm>.
Rieger, Stefan, Schamma Schahadat, and Manfred Weinberg (eds.) (1999). *Interkulturalität—zwischen Inszenierung und Archiv*. Tübingen: Narr.
Riemann, Wolfgang (1990). *Über das Leben in Bitterland: Bibliographie zur türkischen Deutschland-Literatur und zur türkischen Literatur in Deutschland*. Wiesbaden: Harrassowitz.
Rimmon-Kenan, Shlomith (2002). *Narrative Fiction: Contemporary Poetics*. 1983. Second ed. London: Routledge.
Roach, Joseph (1996). *Cities of the Dead: Circum-Atlantic Performance*. New York: Columbia University Press.
Roberts, David (1990). "Surface and Depth: Christoph Hein's *Drachenblut*." *German Quarterly* 63: 478–489.
Robins, Kevin (2000). "Introduction: Turkish (Television) Culture Is Ordinary." *European Journal of Cultural Studies* 3.3: 291–295.
Robinson, Amy (1994). "It Takes One to Know One: Passing and Communities of Common Interest." *Critical Inquiry* 20: 715–736.
Römhild, Regina (2003). "welt raum frankfurt." *global heimat: ethnographische recherchen im transnationalen frankfurt*. Ed. Sven Bergmann and Regina Römhild. Frankfurt a. M.: Institut für Kulturanthropologie und Europäische Ethnologie der Universität Frankfurt am Main. 7–19.
Ronell, Avital (1989). *The Telephone Book: Technology—Schizophrenia—Electric Speech*. Lincoln, NE: University of Nebraska Press.
Rösch, Heidi (1992). *Migrationsliteratur im interkulturellen Kontext: Eine didaktische Studie zur Literatur von Aras Ören, Aysel Özakin, Franco Biondi und Rafik Schami*. Frankfurt a. M.: Verlag für Interkulturelle Kommunikation.
Rothberg, Michael (2000). *Traumatic Realism: The Demands of Holocaust Representation*. Minneapolis, MN: University of Minnesota Press.
Rudiger, Anja (ed.) (2001). *Voices of Change: European Minority Organisations in Civil Dialogue*. Berlin: Regionale Arbeitsstelle für Ausländerfragen, Jugendarbeit und Schule.
Rüsen, Jörn (2002). *Geschichte im Kulturprozeß*. Cologne: Böhlau.
Rushdie, Salman (1988). *The Satanic Verses*. New York: Viking.
Ryan, Judith (1983). *The Uncompleted Past: Postwar German Novels and the Third Reich*. Detroit, MI: Wayne State University Press.
Ryan, Marie-Laure (2001). *Narrative as Virtual Reality: Immersion and Interactivity in Literature and Electronic Media*. Baltimore, MD: Johns Hopkins University Press.
—— (2002). "Fiction and Its Other: How Trespassers Help Defend the Border." *Semiotica* 138–1/4: 351–369.
Sackmann, Rosemarie, Bernhard Peters, and Thomas Faist (eds.) (2003). *Identity and Integration: Migrants in Western Europe*. Hants [England]: Ashgate.
Santner, Eric L. (1990). *Stranded Objects: Mourning, Memory, and Film in Postwar Germany*. Ithaca, NY: Cornell University Press.
—— (1992). "History Beyond the Pleasure Principle: Some Thoughts on the Representation of Trauma." Friedlander 143–154.
Sappelt, Sven (2000). "Theater der Migrant/innen." Chiellino, *Handbuch* 275–293.
Sassen, Saskia (1988). *The Mobility of Labor and Capital: A Study in International Investment and Labor Flow*. Cambridge, UK: Cambridge University Press.

Sassen, Saskia (1996). *Migranten, Siedler, Flüchtlinge: Von der Massenauswanderung zur Festung Europa*. Trans. Irmgard Hölscher. Frankfurt a. M.: Fischer.
——— (1998). *Globalization and Its Discontents: Essays on the New Mobility of People and Money*. New York: New Press.
——— (1999). *Guests and Aliens*. New York: New Press.
——— (2000). "Spatialities and Temporalities of the Global: Elements for a Theorization." *Public Culture* 12.1: 215–232.
Saul, Nicholas, Daniel Steuer, Frank Möbus, and Birgit Illner (eds.) (1999). *Schwellen: Germanistische Erkundungen einer Metapher*. Würzburg: Königshausen & Neumann.
Sauzay, Brigitte, Heinz Ludwig Arnold, and Rudolf von Thadden (eds.) (1995). *Vom Vergessen, vom Gedenken*. Göttingen: Wallstein.
Schieb, Roswitha and Gregor Wedekind (eds.) (1999). *Rügen: Deutschlands mythische Insel*. Berlin: Berlin Verlag.
Schiffauer, Werner (1983). *Die Gewalt der Ehre: Erklärungen zu einem deutschtürkischen Sexualkonflikt*. Frankfurt a. M.: Suhrkamp.
Schlant, Ernestine (1999). *The Language of Silence: West German Literature and the Holocaust*. New York: Routledge.
Schmalz-Jacobsen, Cornelia (2001). "Wo sind die türkischen Lehrer und Ärzte?" *Die Zeit* 29 (July 12): 8.
Schmalz-Jacobsen, Cornelia and Georg Hansen (eds.) (1995). *Ethnische Minderheiten in der Bundesrepublik Deutschland: Ein Lexikon*. Munich: Beck.
Schmid, Thomas (1985). "Nicht sozial, aber bürokratisch: Über die Vergesellschaftung der Ohnmacht." *Das pfeifende Schwein: über weitergehende Interessen der Linken*. Ed. Thomas Schmid. Berlin: Wagenbach. 127–142.
Schmidt, Helmut (1989). "Der Teppich braucht keine neuen Flicken." *Die Zeit* 44.5 (January 27): 7.
——— (2002a). *Die Selbstbehauptung Europas: Perspektiven für das 21. Jahrhundert*. Stuttgart: Deutsche Verlags-Anstalt.
——— (2002b). "Sind die Türken Europäer? Nein, sie passen nicht dazu." *Die Zeit* 57.51 (December 12): 1–2.
Schneider, Peter (1983). *The Wall Jumper*. Trans. Leigh Hafrey. New York: Pantheon. Trans. of *Der Mauerspringer: Eine Erzählung*. Darmstadt: Luchterhand, 1982.
——— (1990). *Extreme Mittellage: Eine Reise durch das deutsche Nationalgefühl*. Reinbek bei Hamburg: Rowohlt.
——— (1991). *The German Comedy: Scenes of Life After the Wall*. Trans. Philip Boehm and Leigh Hafrey. New York: Farrar, Straus, Giroux.
——— (1995). "All My Foreigners." Trans. David Pan. Lützeler, *Multiculturalism* 487–493.
Schönhuber, Franz (1989). *Die Türken: Geschichte und Gegenwart*. Munich: Langen Müller.
Schwarzer, Alice (1993). "Hass: Wir gedenken der Opfer von Solingen." *Emma* 4 (July/August): 34–35.
——— (2003). "Islam: Die Machtprobe." *Der Spiegel* 26 (June 23): 88–90.
Scribner, Charity (2003). *Requiem for Communism*. Cambridge, MA: MIT Press.
Sebald, W. G. (2001). *Austerlitz*. Trans. Anthea Bell. NY: Random. Trans. of *Austerlitz*. Munich: Hanser, 2001.

Sebald, W. G. (2003). *On the Natural History of Destruction.* Trans. Anthea Bell. New York: Random. Trans. of *Luftkrieg und Literatur: Mit einem Essay zu Alfred Andersch.* Munich: Hanser, 1999.
Sedgwick, Eve Kosofsky and Adam Frank (eds.) (1995). *Shame and Its Sisters: A Silvan Tomkins Reader.* Durham, NC: Duke University Press.
Sellars, Roy (1995). "Theory on the Toilet: A Manifesto for Dreckology." *Angelaki* [Oxford] 2.1: 179–196.
Şen, Faruk (2002). "Längst in Europa." *Die Zeit* 57.49 (November 28): 6.
Şen, Faruk and Andreas Goldberg (1994). *Türken in Deutschland: Leben zwischen zwei Kulturen.* Munich: Beck.
Senders, Stefan (1996). "Laws of Belonging: Legal Dimensions of National Inclusion in Germany." *New German Critique* 67: 147–176.
Şenocak, Zafer (1992). *Atlas des tropischen Deutschland: Essays.* Berlin: Babel-Verlag Hund und Toker.
—— (ed.) (1994a). *Der gebrochene Blick nach Westen: Positionen und Perspektiven türkischer Kultur.* Berlin: Babel.
—— (1994b). *War Hitler Araber? IrreFührungen an den Rand Europas, Essays.* Berlin: Babel-Verlag Hund & van Uffelen.
—— (1995). *Der Mann im Unterhemd.* Berlin: Babel.
—— (1997a). *Atletli Adam.* Trans. Mustafa Tüzel. Istanbul: Kabalcı Yayınevi.
—— (1997b). *Die Prärie.* Berlin: Rotbuch.
—— (1998). *Gefährliche Verwandtschaft.* Munich: Babel.
—— (1999). *Der Erottomane: Ein Findelbuch.* Munich: Babel.
—— (2000). *Atlas of a Tropical Germany: Essays on Politics and Culture, 1990–1998.* Ed. and trans. Leslie A. Adelson. Lincoln, NE: University Nebraska Press.
—— (2001a). "Der Feind in unserer Mitte: Allzu lange haben die westlichen Gesellschaften den radikalen Islam toleriert." *Die Welt* [Berlin] (September 15): 9.
—— (2001b). *Perilous Kinship.* Trans. Tom Cheesman. September 29, 2003 <http://www.swan.ac.uk/german/cheesman/senocak/danger.htm> and <http://www.swan.ac.uk/german/cheesman/senocak/danger2.htm>.
—— (2001c). *Zungenentfernung: Bericht aus der Quarantänestation, Essays.* Munich: Babel.
—— (2002). "Meine drei Begegnungen mit Nâzım Hikmet." Carbe and Riemann 84–89.
—— (2003a). "The Capital of the Fragment." Trans. Tom Cheesman. *New German Critique* 88: 141–146.
—— (2004). *Kara Kutu.* Istanbul: Yapı Kredi Yayınları.
Seufert, Günter (2002). "Keine Angst vor den Türken!" *Die Zeit* 57.39 (September 19): 11.
Seyhan, Azade (1996a). "Ethnic Selves/Ethnic Signs: Invention of Self, Space, and Genealogy in Immigrant Writing." *Culture/Contexture: Explorations in Anthropology and Literary Studies.* Ed. E. Valentine Daniel and Jeffrey M. Peck. Berkeley, CA: University of California Press. 175–194.
—— (1996b). "From Minor Literature, Across Border Culture, to Hyphenated Criticisms." *Reading the Shape of the World: Toward an International Cultural Studies.* Ed. Henry Schwarz and Richard Dienst. Boulder, CO: Westview. 15–29.
—— (1996c). "Lost in Translation: Re-Membering the Mother Tongue in Emine Sevgi Özdamar's *Das Leben ist eine Karawanserai.*" *German Quarterly* 69.4: 414–426

Seyhan, Azade (1997). "Scheherazade's Daughters: The Thousand and One Tales of Turkish-German Women Writers." *Writing New Identities: Gender, Nation, and Immigration in Contemporary Europe.* Ed. Gisela Brinker-Gabler and Sidonie Smith. Minneapolis, MN: University of Minnesota Press. 230–248.
—— (1998). "Geographies of Memory: Protocols of Writing in the Borderlands." *Multiculturalism in Transit: A German-American Exchange.* Ed. Klaus J. Milich and Jeffrey M. Peck. New York: Berghahn. 193–212.
—— (2001). *Writing Outside the Nation.* Princeton, NJ: Princeton University Press.
Shafi, Monika (2001). *Balancing Acts: Intercultural Encounters in Contemporary German and Austrian Literature.* Tübingen: Stauffenburg.
Shafir, Gershon (ed.) (1998). *The Citizenship Debates: A Reader.* Minneapolis, MN: University of Minnesota Press.
Shore, Zachary (2003). *Uncommon Threats: Germany's Muslims, Transatlantic Relations, and the War on Terror.* AICGS Policy Report #5. Washington, D.C.: American Institute for Contemporary German Studies.
Sieg, Katrin (2002). *Ethnic Drag: Performing Race, Nation, Sexuality in West Germany.* Ann Arbor, MI: University of Michigan Press.
Simpson, Patricia Anne (1993). "Orchids and Mother Tongues: Telling Turkish-German Stories." Blackshire-Belay 45–55.
Smith, Helmut Walser (2002). *The Holocaust and Other Genocides: History, Representation, Ethics.* Nashville, TN: Vanderbilt University Press.
Smith, Michael G. (1998). *Language and Power in the Creation of the USSR 1917–1953.* Berlin: Mouton de Gruyter.
Smith, Valerie (1998). *Not Just Race, Not Just Gender: Black Feminist Readings.* New York: Routledge.
Şölçün, Sargut (1992). *Sein und Nichtsein: Zur Literatur in der multikulturellen Gesellschaft.* Bielefeld: Aisthesis.
—— (1998). *Unerhörter Gang des Wartenden: Dekonstruktive Wendungen in der deutschen Essayistik.* Würzburg: Königshausen & Neumann.
—— (2002). "Gespielte Naivität und ernsthafte Sinnlichkeit der Selbstbegegnung—Inszenierungen des Unterwegseins in Emine Sevgi Özdamars Roman 'Die Brücke vom Goldenen Horn'." Blioumi 92–111.
Sommer, Doris (1991). *Foundational Fictions: The National Romances of Latin America.* Berkeley, CA: University of California Press.
—— (1994). "Resistant Texts and Incompetent Readers." *Poetics Today* 15.4: 523–551.
—— (1999). *Proceed with Caution, When Engaged by Minority Writing in the Americas.* Cambridge, MA: Harvard University Press.
—— (ed.) (2003). *Bilingual Games: Some Literary Investigations.* New York: Palgrave Macmillan.
—— (2004). *Bilingual Aesthetics: A New Sentimental Education.* Durham, NC: Duke University Press.
Somuncu, Serdar (2001). *Serdar Somuncu liest aus dem Tagebuch eines Massenmörders—Mein Kampf.* Dramatisierte, kommentierte, satirische Lesung. CD. WortArt.
—— (2003). *Serdar Somuncu liest Joseph Goebbels: Diese Sünde der Idiotie, Wollt Ihr den Totalen Krieg?* Live-Lesung. CD. Lübbe.
Soysal, Levent (1999). "Projects of Culture: An Ethnographic Episode in the Life of Migrant Youth in Berlin." Diss. Harvard University.

Soysal, Levent (2003a). "Labor to Culture: Writing Turkish Migration to Europe." Irzık and Güzeldere 491–508.
—— (2003b). "Rap, Hip-Hop and the Topography of Migrant Youth Culture in the World City Berlin." Presented at Lives In-Between? The Turkish Diaspora in Germany, an Interdisciplinary Conference at the University of Chicago, May 1–2.
Soysal, Yasemin Nuhoğlu (1994). *Limits of Citizenship: Migrants and Postnational Membership in Europe*. Chicago: University of Chicago Press.
—— (1998). "Toward a Postnational Model of Membership." Shafir 189–217.
—— (2002). "Citizenship and Identity: Living in Diasporas in Postwar Europe?" Hedetoft and Hjort 137–151.
Spiegel (1993). "Weder Heimat noch Freunde." *Der Spiegel* 47.23 (June 7): 16–27.
Spivak, Gayatri Chakravorty (1993). *Outside in the Teaching Machine*. New York: Routledge.
—— (1999). *A Critique of Postcolonial Reason: Toward a History of the Vanishing Present*. Cambridge, MA: Harvard University Press.
Spuler-Stegemann, Ursula (2002). *Muslime in Deutschland: Informationen und Klärungen*. Freiburg: Herder.
Staeck, Klaus and Dieter Adelmann (1976). *Die Kunst findet nicht im Saale statt: Politische Plakate*. Reinbek bei Hamburg: Rowohlt.
Steiner, George (1974). *Language and Silence*. New York: Atheneum.
Stern, Frank (1991). *Im Anfang war Auschwitz: Antisemitismus und Philosemitismus im deutschen Nachkrieg*. Gerlingen: Bleicher.
—— (1992). *The Whitewashing of the Yellow Badge: Antisemitism and Philosemitism in Postwar Germany*. Trans. William Templer. Oxford: Pergamon.
Steyerl, Hito (2001). "Ornamente der neuen Mitte: Wo Widerstand zu Kanak-Chic wird." *iz3w: Blätter des Informationszentrums dritte Welt* [Freiburg] 253: 24–25.
Steyerl, Hito and Encarnación Gutiérrez Rodríguez (eds.) (2003). *Spricht die Subalterne Deutsch? Migration und postkoloniale Kritik*. Münster: Unrast.
Stoll, Georg (1998). "Immigrant Muslim Writers in Germany." *The Postcolonial Crescent: Islam's Impact on Contemporary Literature*. Ed. John C. Hawley. New York: Lang. 266–283.
Suhr, Heidrun (1989). "*Ausländerliteratur*: Minority Literature in the Federal Republic of Germany." *Minorities in German Culture*. Ed. Russell A. Berman, Azade Seyhan, and Arlene Akiko Teraoka. Spec. issue of *New German Critique* 46: 71–103.
—— (1990). "*Fremde* in Berlin: The Outsiders' View from the Inside." *Berlin: Culture and Metropolis*. Ed. Charles W. Haxthausen and Heidrun Suhr. Minneapolis, MN: University of Minnesota Press. 219–242.
Sykora, Katharina (1999). *Unheimliche Paarungen: Androidenfaszination und Geschlecht in der Fotografie*. Cologne: König.
Tabbi, Joseph, and Michael Wutz (eds.) (1997) *Reading Matters*. Ithaca, NY: Cornell University Press.
Taberner, Stuart and Frank Finlay (eds.) (2002). *Recasting German Identity: Culture, Politics, and Literature in the Berlin Republic*. Rochester, NY: Camden House-Boydell & Brewer.
Tanner, Jakob and Sigrid Weigel (eds.) (2002). *Gedächtnis, Geld und Gesetz: Vom Umgang mit der Vergangenheit des Zweiten Weltkriegs*. Zurich: vdf Hochschulverlag AG an der ETH Zürich.

Tarrow, Sidney (2002). "Rooted Cosmopolitans: Towards a Sociology of Transnational Contention." Lecture at University of California, Irvine, January 10.
—— (2005). *The New Transnational Activism*. Cambridge, UK: Cambridge University Press.
Taufiq, Suleman (1993). "Sehnsucht als Identität: Zur Emigranten-Literatur in der Bundesrepublik Deutschland." Delabar, Jung, and Pergande 237–244.
Taylor, Charles (1992). *Multiculturalism and the Politics of Recognition*. Ed. Amy Gutmann. Princeton, NJ: Princeton University Press.
—— (2002). "Modern Social Imaginaries." Gaonkar and Lee 91–124.
Taylor, Charles, K. Anthony Appiah, Jürgen Habermas, Steven C. Rockefeller, Michael Walzer, and Susan Wolf. *Multiculturalism: Examining the Politics of Recognition*. Ed. Amy Gutmann. Princeton, NJ: Princeton University Press.
Teraoka, Arlene Akiko (1987). "*Gastarbeiterliteratur*: The Other Speaks Back." *Cultural Critique* 7: 77–101.
—— (1989). "Talking 'Turk': On Narrative Strategies and Cultural Stereotypes." *New German Critique* 46: 104–128.
—— (1996a). *East, West, and Others: The Third World in Postwar German Literature*. Lincoln, NE: University of Nebraska Press.
—— (1996b). "Turks as Subjects: The Ethnographic Novels of Paul Geiersbach." *Culture and Contexture: Essays in Anthropology and Literary Studies*. Ed. E. Valentine Daniel and Jeffrey M. Peck. Berkeley, CA: University of California Press. 195–213.
—— (1999). "Detecting Ethnicity: Jakob Arjouni and the Case of the Missing German Detective Novel." *German Quarterly* 72.3: 265–289.
Terkessidis, Mark (1995). *Kulturkampf: Volk, Nation, der Westen und die Neue Rechte*. Cologne: Kiepenheuer & Witsch.
—— (1999). "Globale Kultur in Deutschland oder: Wie unterdrückte Frauen und Kriminelle die Hybridität retten." *parapluie* 6 (Summer). September 28, 2003 <http://parapluie.de/archiv/generation/hybrid>.
—— (2000). "Kabarett und Satire deutsch-türkischer Autoren." Chiellino, *Handbuch* 294–301.
Tertilt, Hermann (1996). *Turkish Power Boys: Ethnographie einer Jugendbande*. Frankfurt a. M.: Suhrkamp.
Theisen, Bianca (2003). *Silenced Facts: Media Montages in Contemporary Austrian Literature*. Amsterdam: Rodopi.
Thumann, Michael (2002). "Ja, sie gehören in die EU." *Die Zeit* 57.51 (December 12): 1.
Tibi, Bassam (1996). "Foreigners—Today's Jews? Xenophobic Right-Wing Radicalism and the Fundamentalism of the Other." *The Resurgence of Right-Wing Radicalism in Germany*. Ed. Ulrich Wank. Atlantic Highlands, NJ: Humanities Press International. 85–102.
—— (1998a). *Aufbruch am Bosporus: Die Türkei zwischen Europa und dem Islamismus*. Munich: Diana.
—— (1998b). *Europa ohne Identität? Die Krise der multikulturellen Gesellschaft*. Munich: Bertelsmann.
—— (2000). *Der Islam und Deutschland/Muslime in Deutschland*. Stuttgart: Deutsche Verlags-Anstalt.

Tibi, Bassam (2001). *Islam Between Culture and Politics*. New York: Palgrave.
—— (2002). "Muslim Migrants in Europe: Between Euro-Islam and Ghettoization." *Muslim Europe or Euro-Islam?* Ed. Nezar AlSayyad and Manuel Castells. Lanham, MD: Lexington Books. 31–52.
Todorov, Tzvetan (1987). *The Conquest of America*. New York: Harper.
Tomkins, Silvan (1962). *Affect, Imagery, Consciousness*. Vol. I. The Positive Affects. New York: Springer.
Torbakov, Igor (2005). "Turkish Scholars Seek to Engage Armenian Counterparts in Historical Debate." *Eurasianet.org* February 1. March 19, 2005 <http://www.eurasianet.org/departments/civilsociety/articles/eav020105.shtml>.
Trumpener, Ulrich (1968). *Germany and the Ottoman Empire 1914–1918*. Princeton, NJ: Princeton University Press.
Tuschick, Jamal (2000a). " 'Bruder, du bist meine Stimme': Feridun Zaimoglu, Kombattant im Kulturkampf." *aufgerissen: Zur Literatur der 90er*. Ed. Thomas Kraft. Munich: Piper. 105–116.
—— (ed.) (2000b). *Morgen Land: Neueste deutsche Literatur*. Frankfurt a. M.: Fischer.
Überhoff, Thomas (2002). "Sten Nadolny." *Kritsiches Lexikon zur deutschsprachigen Gegenwartsliteratur*. Ed. Heinz Ludwig Arnold. Munich: edition text + kritik.
Ueding, Gerd and Bernd Steinbrink (1994). *Grundriß der Rhetorik: Geschichte, Technik, Methode*. Third rev. ed. Stuttgart: Metzler.
Vertovec, Steven and Ceri Peach (1997). *Islam in Europe: The Politics of Religion and Community*. London: Macmillan.
Veteto-Conrad, Marilya J. (1996). *Finding a Voice: Identity and the Works of German-Language Turkish Writers in the Federal Republic of Germany to 1990*. New York: Lang.
Von Dirke, Sabine (1994). "West Meets East: Narrative Construction of the Foreigner and Postmodern Orientalism in Sten Nadolny's *Selim oder Die Gabe der Rede*." *Germanic Review* 49.2: 61–69.
Wägenbaur, Thomas (1996). "Hybride Hybridität: Der Kulturkonflikt im Text der Kulturtheorie." *arcadia: Zeitschrift für vergleichende Literaturwissenschaft* 31: 27–38.
Waldhoff, Hans-Peter (1997). "Ein Übersetzer: Über die sozio-biographische Genese eines transnationalen Denkstils." Waldhoff, Tan, and Kürşat-Ahlers 323–364.
Waldhoff, Hans-Peter, Dursun Tan, and Elçin Kürşat-Ahlers (eds.) (1997). *Brücken zwischen Zivilisationen: Zur Zivilisierung ethnisch-kultureller Differenzen und Machtungleichheiten, Das türkisch-deutsche Beispiel*. Frankfurt a. M.: IKO-Verlag für interkulturelle Kommunikation.
Wallraff, Günter (1972). " 'Gastarbeiter' oder der gewöhnliche Kapitalismus." *Neue Reportagen, Untersuchungen und Lehrbeispiele*. Cologne: Kiepenheuer & Witsch. 56–82.
—— (1988). *Lowest of the Low*. Trans. Martin Chalmers. London: Methuen. Trans. of *Ganz unten: Mit einer Dokumentation der Folgen*. Cologne: Kiepenheuer & Witsch, 1985.
Walser, Martin (1998a). *Erfahrungen beim Verfassen einer Sonntagsrede: Friedenspreis des deutschen Buchhandels*. Frankfurt a. M.: Suhrkamp.
—— (1998b). *Ein springender Brunnen*. Frankfurt a. M.: Suhrkamp.
Wehler, Hans-Ulrich (2002). "Das Türkenproblem." *Die Zeit* 57.38 (September 12): 9.

Weidauer, Friedemann (2003). "When Bobos Meet Bhabha: Do Minority Literatures Challenge the Concept of National Literatures?" *Monatshefte* 95.1: 19–32.

Weigel, Sigrid (1992). "Literatur der Fremde—Literatur in der Fremde." Briegleb and Weigel. 182–229.

——— (1996). "Shylocks Wiederkehr: Die Verwandlung von Schuld in Schulden oder: Zum symbolischen Tausch der Wiedergutmachung." *Fünfzig Jahre danach: Zur Nachgeschichte des Nationalsozialismus.* Ed. Sigrid Weigel and Birgit R. Erdle. Zurich: vdf Hochschulverlag AG an der ETH Zürich. 165–192.

——— (1999). "Die 'Generation' als symbolische Form: Zum genealogischen Diskurs im Gedächtnis nach 1945." *figurationen: gender literatur kultur* 0: 158–173.

——— (2002). " 'Generation' as a Symbolic Form: On the Genealogical Discourse of Memory since 1945." *Germanic Review* 77.4: 264–277.

Weiner, Myron (ed.) (1993). *International Migration and Security.* Boulder, CO: Westview Press.

——— (1995). *The Global Migration Crisis: Challenge to States and to Human Rights.* New York: HarperCollins College Publishers.

Weiss, Peter (1964). *Die Verfolgung und Ermordung Jean Paul Marats dargestellt durch die Schauspielgruppe des Hospizes zu Charenton unter Anleitung des Herrn de Sade: Drama in zwei Akten.* Frankfurt a. M.: Suhrkamp.

——— (1965a). *Die Ermittlung: Oratorium in 11 Gesängen.* Frankfurt a. M.: Suhrkamp.

——— (1965b). *The Persecution and Assassination of Marat as Performed by the Inmates of the Asylum of Charenton Under the Direction of the Marquis de Sade.* Trans. Geoffrey Skelton. Adapted by Adrian Mitchell. London: John Calder.

——— (1966). *The Investigation.* Trans. Jon Swan and Ulu Grosbard. New York: Atheneum.

——— (1967). "My Place." Trans. Christopher Middleton. *German Writing Today.* Ed. Christopher Middleton. Harmondsworth: Penguin. 20–28.

——— (1975–1981). *Die Ästhetik des Widerstands.* Frankfurt a. M.: Suhrkamp.

Weitz, Eric D. (2003a). *A Century of Genocide: Utopias of Race and Nation.* Princeton, NJ: Princeton University Press.

——— (2003b). "The Modernity of Genocides: War, Race, and Revolution in the Twentieth Century." Gellately and Kiernan 53–73.

Werfel, Franz (1934). *The Forty Days of Musa Dagh.* Trans. Geoffrey Dunlop. New York: Viking. Trans. of *Die letzten Tage des Musa Dagh.* Berlin: P. Zsolnay, 1933.

Wertheimer, Jürgen (2002). "Kanak/Wo/Man contra Skinhead—Zum neuen Ton jüngerer AutorInnen der Migration." Blioumi 130–135.

White, Hayden (1999). *Figural Realism: Studies in the Mimesis Effect.* Baltimore, MD: Johns Hopkins University Press.

White, Jenny B. (1995). "Turks in Germany: Overview of the Literature." *Middle East Studies Association Bulletin* 29.1: 12–15.

——— (1997). "Turks in the New Germany." *American Anthropologist* 99.4: 754–769.

Wiedmer, Caroline (1999). *The Claims of Memory: Representations of the Holocaust in Contemporary Germany and France.* Ithaca, NY: Cornell University Press.

Wiegman, Robyn (1999). "What Ails Feminist Criticism? A Second Opinion." *Critical Inquiry* 25: 362–379.

Wierlacher, Alois (ed.) (1985). *Das Fremde und das Eigene: Prolegomena zu einer interkulturellen Germanistik.* Munich: Iudicium.
—— (ed.) (1987). *Perspektiven und Verfahren interkultureller Germanistik.* Akten des I. Kongresses der Gesellschaft für Interkulturelle Germanistik. Munich: Iudicium.
—— (1994). "Zur Entwicklungsgeschichte und Systematik interkultureller Germanistik (1984–1994): Einige Antworten auf die Frage: Was heißt 'interkulturelle Germanistik?' " *Jahrbuch Deutsch als Fremdsprache* 20: 37–56.
Wierschke, Annette (1996). *Schreiben als Selbstbehauptung: Kulturkonflikt und Identität in den Werken von Aysel Özakin, Alev Tekinay und Emine Sevgi Özdamar: Mit Interviews.* Diss. University of Minnesota, 1994. Frankfurt a. M.: IKO—Verlag für Interkulturelle Kommunikation.
—— (1997). "Auf den Schnittstellen kultureller Grenzen tanzend: Aysel Özakin und Emine Sevgi Özdamar." Fischer and McGowan, *Denn* 179–194.
Winterson, Jeanette (2000). *night screen.* New York: Vintage Books.
Wise, Gail (1995). "Ali in Wunderland: German Representations of Foreign Workers." Diss. University of California [Berkeley].
Wittstock, Uwe (1994). "Der Autor und der Leser: Sten Nadolny, *Das Erzählen und die guten Absichten* (1990)." *Poetik der Autoren.* Ed. Paul Michael Lützeler. Frankfurt a. M.: Fischer. 262–278.
Wojak, Irmtrud (ed.) (2001). *"Gerichtstag halten wir über uns selbst . . .": Geschichte und Wirkung des ersten Frankfurter Auschwitz-Prozesses.* Frankfurt a. M.: Campus.
Yalçın-Heckmann, Lale (1997). "Zum kollektiven Gedächtnis türkischer Migranten." Waldhoff, Tan, and Kürşat-Ahlers. 183–195.
Yeşilada, Karin E. (1997a). "Die geschundene Suleika: Das Eigenbild der Türkin in der deutschsprachigen Literatur türkischer Autorinnen." Howard 95–114.
—— (1997b). "Schreiben mit spitzer Feder—Die Satiren der deutsch-türkischen Migrationsliteratur." *Spagat mit Kopftuch—Essays zur deutsch-türkischen Sommerakademie.* Ed. Jürgen Reulecke. Hamburg: Edition Körber-Stiftung. 529–564.
—— (1998). "Zafer Şenocak." *Kritisches Lexikon zur deutschsprachigen Gegenwartsliteratur.* Ed. Heinz Ludwig Arnold. Munich: edition text + kritik. 58. Nachlieferung.
—— (1999). "Literatur statt Tränen! Warum das Goethe-Institut Saliha Scheinhardt nicht mehr einladen sollte." *Diyalog: Interkulturelle Zeitschrift für Germanistik* [Ankara, n. vol.]: 151–154.
—— (2000). "Topographien im 'tropischen Deutschland': Türkisch-deutsche Literatur nach der Wiedervereinigung." Beitter 303–339.
—— (2001). "Das Empire schreibt zurück—Die deutschsprachige Migrationsliteratur." *Weltliteratur 2001: Vom Nobelpreis bis zum Comic.* Ed. Thomas Böhm and Martin Hielscher. Cologne: Könemann. 118–137.
—— (2002). "Nâzims Enkel schreiben weiter." Carbe and Riemann 180–211.
—— (2003a). "Poetry on its Way: aktuelle Zwischenstationen im lyrischen Werk Zafer Şenocaks." Cheesman and Yeşilada 112–129.
—— (2003b). "Zafer Şenocak: Outline Biography." Cheesman and Yeşilada 16–18.
—— (2005). "Deutsch-türkische Migrationslyrik der zweiten Generation" [Working Title]. Diss. University of Marburg [Germany]. In progress.

Yıldız, Yasemin (1999). "Keine Adresse in Deutschland? Adressierung als politische Strategie." *Gelbin, Konuk, and Piesche* 224–236.
—— (2001). Unpublished examination for doctoral candidacy at Cornell University.
—— (2004). "Critically 'Kanak': A Reimagination of German Culture." *Globalization and the Future of German*. Ed. Andreas Gardt and Bernd Hüppauf. Berlin: Mouton de Gruyter. 295–316.
—— (2005). "Beyond the Mother Tongue: Configurations of Multilingualism in 20th-Century German Literature." Diss. Cornell University. In progress.
Yücel, Can (1976). *Ölüm ve Oğlum: Şiirler*. Istanbul: Cem Yayınevi.
Zaimoğlu, Feridun (1995). *Kanak Sprak: 24 Mißtöne vom Rande der Gesellschaft*. Hamburg: Rotbuch.
—— (1996). "sicarim süppkültürünüze, züppeler! Ich scheiße auf eure Subkultur, ihr Schmöcke!" *Mainstream der Minderheiten: Pop in der Kontrollgesellschaft*. Ed. Tom Holert and Mark Terkessidis. Berlin: Edition ID-Archiv. 86–95.
—— (1997a). *Abschaum: Die wahre Geschichte von Ertan Ongun*. Hamburg: Rotbuch.
—— (1997b). "KümmelContra." *Kursbuch JugendKultur: Stile, Szenen und Identitäten vor der Jahrtausendwende*. Ed. SpoKK (Symbolische Politik, Kultur und Kommunikation). Mannheim: Bollmann. 174–181.
—— (1998a). "Gastarbeiterliteratur: Ali macht Männchen." *Globalkolorit: Multikulturalismus und Populärkultur*. Ed. Ruth Mayer and Mark Terkessidis. St. Andrä/Wördern [Austria]: Hannibal. 85–97.
—— (1998b). *Koppstoff: Kanaka Sprak vom Rande der Gesellschaft*. Hamburg: Rotbuch.
—— (2000). *Liebesmale, scharlachrot*. Hamburg: Rotbuch.
—— (2001). *Kopf und Kragen: Kanak—Kultur—Kompendium*. Frankfurt a. M.: Fischer.
—— (2002). *German Amok*. Cologne: Kiepenheuer & Witsch.
—— (2003a). "Häute." October 25, 2003 <http://studios.orf.at/ktn/bp2003/downloads>.
—— (2003b). *Leinwand*. Hamburg: Rotbuch.
—— (2004). *Zwölf Gramm Glück*. Cologne: Kiepenheuer & Witsch.
Zantop, Susanne (1997). *Colonial Fantasies: Conquest, Family, and Nation in Precolonial Germany, 1770–1870*. Durham, NC: Duke University Press.
—— (2001). "*Kolonie* and *Heimat*: Race, Gender, and Postcolonial Amnesia in Veit Harlan's *Opfergang* (1944)." *Women in German Yearbook* 17: 1–13.
Zielke-Nadkarni, Andrea (1996). *Frauenfiguren in den Erzählungen türkischer Autorinnen: Identität und Handlungs(spiel)räume*. Pfaffenweiler: Centaurus.
Zierau, Cornelia (2000). "Literarische Inter-Aktionen: Zur Literatur von MigrantInnen in Deutschland." *INTERaktionen: Formen und Mittel der Verständigung*. Ed. Heide Andres-Müller, Corinna Heipcke, and Leonie Wagner. Königstein/Taunus: Ulrike Helmer. 145–167.
Zimmermann, Peter (ed.) (1989). " 'Interkulturelle Germanistik'—Ein Phantom wird besichtigt." *"Interkulturelle Germanistik": Dialog der Kulturen auf Deutsch?* Ed. Peter Zimmermann. Second ed. Frankfurt a. M.: Lang. 13–26.
Zürcher, Erik J. (1993). *Turkey: A Modern History*. London: Taurus.

Index

Ackermann, Irmgard, 131, 141–142, 205n32, 205n36, 208n54
Adelbert von Chamisso Prize, for German Literature, 40, 105, 140
Adelson, Leslie A., 15, 19, 24, 32, 34, 83, 131, 175n18, 179n41, 181n59, 182n69, 182n74, 183n10, 189n2, 191n29, 196n76, 197n94, 199n114, 204n19–20, 206n38, 206n44, 209n65
Adorno, Theodor W., 195n68, 201n118
affect, 60, 181n57, 188n69, 188n73, 188n78; and Brian Axel's critique of diaspora studies, 10–11; and Laura Brown's definition of "cultural fable," 4; and literature of migration, 20, 26; and migration, 14, 135; and postcolonial contexts, 176n32; in "The Courtyard in the Mirror," 45, 46, 47, 53, 54, 57, 60, 63, 64, 66, 67, 68, 70, 72, 74, 75, 76; in *The Distant Lover*, 168; in "Grandfather Tongue," 149, 153–155, 157, 159, 170; in "The Island," 94, 165–170; in *Kanak Sprak*, 98–99, 101–103, 107, 120; in *Marat/Sade*, 94; in *Perilous Kinship*, 108, 115–116; in *Selim*, 36–39
Agamben, Giorgio, 179–180n44, 199n112
Akbulut, Nazire, 35, 195n70
Akçam, Dursun, 194n58
Akçam, Taner, 28, 117, 197n92, 200n117–118, 201n118, 201n120, 202n130
Aksoy, Nazan, 205n33–34
Alice in Wonderland, 15, 30, 47, 48, 50, 53, 62, 66, 68, 69, 71, 76; and fall of Berlin Wall, 16; and Turkish figures, 16; and Cheshire Cat, 66–67, 71, 76; and puns, 48, 53
Allen, Woody, 116
alphabet reforms, in Soviet Union, 151; in Turkey, 151
amnesia, 26, 173n6, 184n17, 201n122
Anderson, Benedict, 2, 42, 43, 49, 80, 185n35; *Imagined Communities*, 150; on "long-distance" national identifications, 42, 49, 80, 185n35; on mother tongues, 150
Anderson, Susan C., 141, 142, 144, 209n67, 210n74
Annan, Kofi, Secretary-General of the United Nations, and references to migration, 6
anti-Semitism, German, 92, 121, 192n42
Anzaldúa, Gloria, 151
Appadurai, Arjun, *Modernity at Large*, 1–3, 13–14, 29, 41–43, 49, 60, 124, 135, 138, 173n3, 173n9, 175n27, 185n31–34, 186n50, 187n66, 189n4, 201n122, 202n2, 212n2; and "community of sentiment," 60; and "ethnoscape," 3, 42, 135, 170, 185n33, 201n122; and " 'process'

Appadurai—*continued*
geographies," 13; and "production of locality," 3, 42–43, 49, 175n27, 186n50, 187n66; and work of imagination (imagination as labor), 1, 14, 41–42, 124, 173n3, 173n9, 185n31, 202n2
Appiah, K. Anthony, 123
Apter, Emily, 12, 176n30
Arabic, 108, 110, 150, 151, 152, 153, 155, 156, 159, 179n38, 202n130, 210n76, 211n91; alphabet, 155; as language of Islamic mysticism, 156
Arab-Israeli wars, 156
Armenian genocide, 20, 28, 82, 105, 108, 110, 113–115, 117–121, 159, 197n92, 198n98, 200n116–117, 201n121–123, 201–202n125; and diaspora, 11, 117–119, 201n120–121; and German novels, 105, 196n75; and Turkish denial, 117; and visibility, 119
Assmann, Aleida, 82, 189n7
Atatürk, 106, 108, 163, 164, 177n33, 178n38, 184n16, 210n80, 212n106–107; and language reforms, 150, 210n80
Auschwitz, 83, 86, 87, 91, 92, 94, 95, 176n32, 189n7, 192n41, 199n112; Auschwitz trials (1963–1965), 35, 92, 183n14
automaton, 89; Turkish laborer in Germany as, 90
Axel, Brian, 10, 11

Bachmann-Medick, Doris, 181n66, 181n68, 195n66
Bachmann Prize, for literature in German, 27, 40, 95, 185n24
barbarism, and civilization, 85, 87, 129, 199n104
Bardakjian, Kevork, 117
Bathrick, David, 137, 207n50

Baudelaire, Charles, 51, 72, 75; *Les Fleurs du mal*, 64, 186n47; "The Balcony," 64, 66
Bayazitoğlu, Ahmet, 150, 152, 155, 178n38, 210n76, 210n80, 210n82, 210–211n89
Becker, Thorsten, 32
Begemann, Christian, 111, 150, 184n22, 198n97
Behrens, Katja, 32
Benhabib, Seyla, and Atatürk, 177n34, 179n38, 210n80; and Bhabha, 177n34; and critique of "strong contextualism" and "mosaic multiculturalism," 10, 179n38, 187n67; and deliberative democracy, 10; and democratic vs. multicultural dialogue, 174–175n17; and "disaggregated" approach to migration and membership, in Europe, 7–8, 10, 124, 129, 175n22–23, 175n26, 176n29, 178n36, 180n47; and "fiction of a 'closed society'," 8; and figure of "seamless wholes," 23, 107, 173n10, 212n3; and Gadamer, 181n68; and "historical culture," in Germany, as contrasted with the Netherlands, 9; and Orientalization of Eastern Europe, in Cold War, 149; and Taylor, 175n28
Berger, John, 89, 90, 185n36, 191n33, 194n62
Berlin, 38, 51, 83, 105, 107, 149, 150, 153, 154, 157; Olympics, 108, 119
Berlin Wall, 79, 84, 123; effects of, upon Germany's labor force, 7; and Humpty Dumpty, 16; fall of, 109, 114, 132
Betroffenheit, culture of, 111, 116, 119, 191n24, 198n96–97
"between two worlds," as cultural fable of migration, 3–5, 7, 20, 27, 125,

INDEX / 251

127, 135, 172, 174n7, 176n32, 178n36
Beuys, Joseph, 51
Bhabha, Homi K., 2, 12, 86, 88, 89, 98, 114, 134, 155; and "the Turkish *Gastarbeiter*," 86, 88–90, 98, 177n32–33, 191n31
Biller, Maxim, 32
Bird, Stephanie, 151, 152, 155
birds, and "The Courtyard in the Mirror," 47, 53–55, 61, 65, 68–71; and death, 68; and feathers, in relation to reading, 30, 54, 68–70, 72, 74, 77; and love, 68; chickens, 44, 46, 73, 186n51; ducks, 1, 2, 30; parrots, 53–54, 76, 187n59–60
Bloom, Molly, 171–172
Bohm, Hark, *Yasemin*, 128
Böll, Heinrich, 160; *Billiards at Half-Past Nine*, 91, 163
"border gnosis," as defined by Walter Mignolo, 49, 176n32
Borges, Jorge Luis, 171–72
Bosse, Anke, 32, 33
"boundary work," as defined by David Herman, 49–50, 58, 72
Bourdieu, Pierre, 135, 136, 203n15–16, 204n16, 207n47–48
Braese, Stephan, 162, 183n14, 184n17, 192n37, 211n101
Brandt, Bettina, 150, 198n101, 210n79, 210n88, 211n91, 211n93
Brecht, Bertolt, 153; and "Sailor's Song," in "The Courtyard in the Mirror," 51; and theory of estrangement, 19
Breger, Claudia, 150, 153, 154, 186n41, 186n52, 187n56, 188n70, 188n81, 205n31, 206n36, 209n67, 211n89
bridge, rhetoric of, 5–6, 8, 24, 25, 34, 48, 127, 174n12, 175n18, 176n32, 205n29

Briegleb, Klaus, 183n7, 192n37, 211n101
Brodsky Lacour, Claudia, 104, 122; and figural representation, as distinguished from "an iconoclastic line," 22–23
Brown, Gillian, 63, 188n75
Brown, Laura, and concept of "cultural fable," 4–5, 54
Buck-Morss, Susan, *Dreamworld and Catastrophe*, 137, 207n51
Bullivant, Keith, 182n69, 183n7, 196n76
Burns, Rob, 198n97
Butler, Judith, 19, 193n49–50, 206n39; and "excitable speech," 94

Çağlar, Ayşe, 193n51, 203n15, 205n29
capital, cultural, 28, 123–138, 143–144; as understood by Bourdieu, 135, 136; as understood by Guillory, 133, 135–136, 145, 207n47–49; changing iconography of, in relation to Turks in Germany, 127–131
capitalism, 92, 123–124, 125, 139, 144, 148, 157, 158, 165, 175n20, 202n2, 203n6, 207n46
capitalist reconstruction, in Germany, 28, 124
Carroll, Lewis, 15, 67–69, 189n84
Central Office for Investigation of National Socialist Crimes, 35
Chakrabarty, Dipesh, 145, 207n49
Cheesman, Tom, and translations, 19, 189n2, 196n79, 197n86, 197n90–91, 197n94, 197n96, 198n99–100, 199n102, 199n106, 199n109, 202n131; on Turkish-German writers, 95, 97, 99, 130, 138, 158, 178n36, 180n43, 193n51–53, 194n54–56, 194n58–59, 195n62, 195n67,

Cheesman—*continued*
196n76, 196n82, 197n95, 201n125, 207n52
Chiellino, Carmine, 5, 23, 25, 131, 139, 179n41, 182n73
Chin, Rita, 140, 141, 208n59
Chow, Rey, *The Protestant Ethnic & the Spirit of Capitalism*, 126, 133–135, 136, 144, 145, 152, 158, 174n14, 206n41, 207n45, 207n49; and autobiography, 158, 206n42; and "coercive mimeticism," 134, 196n67; and ethnicity as alienated labor, 26, 133–135, 136, 144, 145, 152; and gender and sexuality, 133, 206n39; and hybridity, 158, 174n14; and stereotyping, 187n59; and victimization as cultural capital, 205n28; and visuality, 194n62, 206n40; on Bhabha as "iconophobic," 191n26; on ethnic community, 207n46
Churchill, Winston, 79
Cixous, Hélène, on Algeria, 3
Clark, Christopher, 130, 180n50, 203n15, 209n62
Clarke, Alexandra, 32, 206n38
Cohn, Dorrit, and "inner life" of characters, 186n43; and "separatist thesis" of narratology, 50, 186n42
Cold War, 2, 7, 15, 16, 20, 22, 28, 29, 79, 123–124, 137–138, 140, 149–150, 154–159, 165, 169–170; false mirror logic of, 137
comedy, 194n54
communism, 48, 149, 156–157, 167
Conrad, Joseph, 51, 189n84
contextualization, 1, 8–13, 20, 21, 23, 26, 28, 39–43, 48, 49–54, 58–60, 67, 68, 72–76, 80–81, 87–88, 90, 91, 107, 111–112, 115, 124, 126, 130, 134, 138, 140, 150–152, 155, 157–158, 161, 172, 184n21, 194n56, 207n51

Corday, Charlotte, 92–93
Corngold, Stanley, on literature and feeling, 186n45
"The Courtyard in the Mirror," 27, 30, 40, 42–49, 50–77, 99, 107, 112, 185n36, 185–186n40, 188n68–69; and affect, 45, 46, 47, 53, 54, 57, 60, 63, 64, 66, 67, 68, 70, 72, 74, 75, 76; and *Alice in Wonderland*, 30, 47–48, 50, 53, 62, 66–68, 69, 71, 76; and approximation of postnational intimacy, 20, 27, 40, 49, 50, 56, 58, 59, 60, 66, 76; and behavioral tracking, 45–46, 57, 60, 61, 72, 76, 99, 188n69; and "boundary work," 49–50, 52–54, 56, 58, 59, 72–76; and "personal city map," 40; and poetry, 51, 55–56, 62, 64, 65–66, 69, 70, 72, 74, 75, 186n46–47, 187n62, 188n76, 188n72; and production of locality, 42–44, 49–53, 59, 60, 69, 71, 74, ; and reading, 43, 47–48, 49, 50, 53, 56, 59–60, 62, 66, 67–72, 73–74, 76–77; and transubstantiation, 69–70, 71, 72, 189n83; importance of mirrors in, 43, 45, 47, 51–55, 57–58, 61–67, 70, 74; importance of telephone in, 43–46, 51, 54–55, 57–58, 61, 62, 68; importance of television in, 43–44, 56, 66, 69; old nun in, 47, 51–52, 55, 58, 61–62, 63, 65–71; stereotypes in, 53, 56; Turkey as frame of reference in, 43; unnamed setting of, 40, 51
Culler, Jonathan, on puns, 2, 48, 103, 157; on novels and nations, 49
"cultural fable," as defined by Laura Brown, 4–5; of "the nonhuman being," 54

Dal, Güney, 32, 131, 150, 197n94
Dante, *The Inferno*, 92

Defoe, Daniel, *Robinson Crusoe*, 132
de Man, Paul, 17, 112
Derrida, Jacques, 180n44
de Sade, Marquis, 92
Descartes, René, 22, 104
dialogic communication or exchange, 24–26, 33, 36, 61–66, 69, 72, 75, 156
dialogue, of cultures, 6, 24–26; and Benhabib on deliberative democracy, 10, 174–175n17; and chiastic exchange, in "Grandfather Tongue," 156; and presumption of coherence, 63; and the United Nations, on conflict resolution, 6; in "The Courtyard," 61–66; in *Selim*, 31–39
diaspora studies, critiques of, 10–11, 13
Diner, Dan, 189n7, 192n37
The Distant Lover, 167–168
Dollinger, Roland, 112, 159, 169, 197n84, 198n98, 200n115, 201n123, 202n129
dreck, 100–101, 195n68
Durzak, Manfred, 21, 32, 33, 34, 35, 39, 101, 183n9, 183n12, 184n16, 187n59, 195n70

Egoyan, Atom, *Ararat*, 119
Eichmann trial (1961), 35
Eigler, Friederike, 112, 196n74, 198n98, 199n113, 200n114, 201–202n125
Einwanderungsland, and Germany as land of immigration, 7
Elias, Norbert, 201n118
emblematic subjects, of migration and globalization, 13, 123, 131, 134, 141, 142, 148, 169, 170; as distinguished from symbolic subjects of migration, 126, 139, 212n103
Emma: The Magazine By Women for Human Beings, and popular German feminism, 129
"entangled histories," 21, 182n71

Enzensberger, Christian, and German translation of *Alice in Wonderland*, 67
Eshel, Amir, 190n10, 199n111, 199n113
ethnic cleansing (so-called), in the Balkans, 118; in Rwanda, 118
"ethnic drag," as defined by Katrin Sieg, 18–19; and referentiality, 18–20
ethnicity, as alienated labor, *see* Chow
ethnos, 126, 149, 176n32, 177n34; and changing concepts of ethnicity, 11, 150, 210n77
ethnoscape, as distinguished from ethnicity, 11, 135, 210n77; *see also* Appadurai
Euro-Islam, 129, 179n38, 205n25
Europe, after defeat of the Third Reich, 158
European Union, 84, 106, 131; and citizenship, 8

Fachinger, Petra, 97, 101, 137, 176–177n32, 193n51, 193n53, 194n58, 195n66, 209n65
Faist, Thomas, 173n2, 174n14, 177n34, 178n36, 181n66
fascism, 92, 129, 159, 165, 192n39, 205n24
feminism, 18, 29, 45, 129, 133, 155, 170, 188n81, 203n9, 204n19, 206n37, 206n39
Flaubert, Gustave, *Madame Bovary*, 132
Forty Days of Musa Dagh, The, 105
French Revolution, 92
Friedrich, Jörg, 83
Frisch, Max, 124–126, 142, 203n5
fundamentalism, 130, 205n24, 205n30
"fusion of horizons" (*Horizontverschmelzung*), 24–26

Gadamer, Hans-Georg, philosophy of hermeneutics, 24–25, 181n68, 182n70, 182n75

Gastarbeiter, 32, 130, 174n13; as anachronism, 126–127, 139; Turkish, spectral function of, 127, 128, 130, 139, 148, 203n11, 208n61; *see also* Bhabha
Gastarbeiterliteratur, 195n66
gender, 18, 28–29, 70–72, 135, 148–149, 155, 159–160, 168, 170, 194n58, 202n1, 203n9, 204n19–20, 205n31, 205n33, 207n52, 208n59; centrality of, to stories of Turkish migration, 125–132, 138, 203n8, 204n18; *see also* Chow and Sassen
generation, 96, 97, 98, 105, 110, 111, 140, 150, 159, 160–162, 166, 167, 184n20, 196n74, 197n92, 200n114, 210n82, 211n101–102, 212n103, 212n114
genocide, 28, 79–80, 82, 86, 90, 94, 102, 105, 110–112, 118, 120, 122, 144, 158; and speech-effects, 120; effect of, on non-Jewish German writers, 116; history of, in twentieth century, 105, 111; legacy of, 116; of Herero and Nama peoples, 201n122; *see also* Armenian genocide and Holocaust
genocide studies, 112, 115
German Democratic Republic (GDR), 96, 137, 138, 164–165, 167–168, 203n7, 207n50
German-Jewish exile, 108
German superiority, cultural capital of, 128–129; Turkish women's liberation in relation to, 129
Germany, Federal Republic of, 1; asylum laws in, 123; citizenship laws, 7, 8, 84; classification of minorities in, 6; crisis of authorship in, 116; growing Turkish presence in, literature and culture, 26, 84; Historians' Debate in, 84, 87, 117; importance of Turkish labor in, 123; in relation to Nazi past, 18, 20, 27, 35–37, 82, 85–86, 90, 153–154, 160, 164, 184n17, 192n35; national unification of 1990, 7, 79, 84, 108, 116; on admitting Turkey to EU, 85
Gerstenberger, Katharina, 21, 181n60, 196n74, 197n89, 200n114, 211n100
Geyer, Michael, 175n23, 184n17
Ghaussy, Soheila, 184n22, 206n36–37, 211n89
gigolo, Turkish, 100–103, 135, 195n70; as scene of German taboo, regarding murdered Jews, 101–102
globalization, 2, 6, 8, 10, 12, 15, 22, 41, 43, 49, 80–81, 83, 103, 106, 115, 123, 125–127, 139, 171
Göçek, Fatma Müge, 117
Goethe, J.W.v., 146
Gökberk, Ülker, 32–34, 38, 39, 90, 179n41, 181n63, 182n70, 182n74, 183n10, 184n21–22, 195n66, 205n33; on intercultural hermeneutics, 25, 182n73
Göktürk, Deniz, 128, 131, 175n21, 181n66, 187n52, 188n81, 196n77, 204n18, 205n33, 206n35, 208n57, 211n89; and critique of Bhabha's story of migration, 90, 177n33, 191n29, 191n33
Göle, Nilüfer, on Islamic visibility and changing public spheres, 129–30, 205n27; on veiling in Turkey, 204n21
Gómez-Peña, Guillermo, 2, 195n70
Göring, Hermann, 35, 36
"Grandfather Tongue," 138, 149–158, 170; and allusion to Hölderlin, 152–155; and Arabic, in relation to Cold War setting, 155–158; and chiasmus, 156–157; approaches to, with focus on identity, 149–152; approaches to, with focus on touching tales, 152–158; importance

of word play in, 156–157; *see also* affect

Grass, Günter, 83, 160; *Crabwalk*, 101; *The Tin Drum*, 91, 163

Green, André, on affect, 60, 188n69

Grice, Paul, and "cooperative principle" of conversation, 63, 188n75

Gruppe, 47, 160, 192n37, 211n101, 212n105

Guillory, John, on aesthetic experience, 136; on cultural capital, 126, 133, 135–136, 144, 145, 152, 157, 207n47–49

Günter, Manuela, 94, 97, 194n60, 195n63

Ha, Kien Nghi, 125, 176n32

Habermas, Jürgen, 14

Hall, Katharina, 112, 198n98, 200n114

Hallaç, Recai, 74, 186n46, 187n62, 188n82

hate speech, 94, 193n51, 195n63; as distinguished from love speech, 94

Hauptmann, Gerhart, 165–167, 212n111

headscarves, 128–130, 204n20–23, 205n25

Hein, Christoph, *The Distant Lover*, 167–168, 212n114

Heine, Heinrich, 51, 65–66, 69, 70, 72, 75, 188n76, 189n84; "Abroad" (In der Fremde), 55–56; "The Homecoming" (Die Heimkehr), 56

Heitmeyer, Wilhelm, 130, 205n24

Hell, Julia, 116, 132, 137, 148, 164, 168, 190n10, 191n24, 199n111, 199n114, 207n50

Henderson, Heike, 131, 205n33

Henkel, Heiko, 178n35–36, 204n20, 205n29

heritage, 6, 133, 135, 158–159, 161, 164–165, 179n38

Herman, David, 69, 180n54, 181n56, 188n72; and "contextual anchoring," 49–51, 58, 72; and deixis, 185n38; and "logic of conversation," 63, 188n75; *see also* "boundary work"

hermeneutic philosophy, critiques of, in relation to minorities, 24–26, 34, 40–41, 182n73, 182n75

Hermes, 33

Hielscher, Martin, 183n7

Hikmet, Nâzım, 106, 164, 212n107

Hilsenrath, Edgar, 105, 196n75, 200n115

hip-hop, popular culture of, 193n53, 194n54, 205n29

Historians' Debate, German, 84, 87, 117

historical narrative by proxy, as distinguished from proximate historical narratives, 18–19, 181n59

Hitchcock, Alfred, 186n40

Hitler, Adolf, 35, 37, 106, 108, 109, 160, 195n71, 200n115; and invasion of Soviet Union, 159; as orator, 36, 37

Hölderlin, Friedrich, 152–154, 210n86–87

Holocaust, 7, 20, 27, 29, 83, 84, 91, 93–94, 96, 105, 108, 113, 119, 148, 198n96; and changing significance of memory, 28, 80–82, 84, 102–103, 115, 189n7–8, 191n25, 192n38, 201n125, 207n50; and historiography, 86–87; and post-Holocaust authorship, 116, 190n10; and postmemory, 166, 212n112; and taboo, 80, 83, 102, 190n12, 201n122; and trauma, 87–88; and trials investigating, 35, 36, 92, 183n14, 192n40; and referentiality, 86, 93–94, 101, 112–113, 192n37, 199n104

Holthusen, Hans Egon, and essay on the Occident after 1945, 158
Horizontverschmelzung [fusion of horizons], 24–26
human rights, 6, 28, 80, 85, 118, 125, 131, 175n23, 208n58
Humpty Dumpty, 16
Huyssen, Andreas, on changing concept of diaspora, in relation to national formations, 11, 27, 81–82, 149; on Holocaust memory, 28, 79, 81, 189n7–8, 190n12; on *lieux de mémoire*, 184n20; on new beginnings in German literature, 190n14; on *Perilous Kinship*, 27, 181n60, 190n9, 200n114, 201–202n125; on Sebald, 199n111; on unprecedented memory culture of 1990s, 80, 81, 169, 179n44, 189n6
hybridity, and critiques of, 5, 10, 88, 90, 170, 174n14, 176n32, 181n66, 192n34, 206n42, 211n93

identity, 10, 24, 33, 39, 42, 49, 81, 85, 97, 98, 99, 112, 114, 124, 126, 127, 130, 133, 139–141, 143, 150, 151, 152, 154, 155, 158, 166, 170, 175n23, 176n32, 178n36, 181n61, 182n1, 191n23, 191n33, 195n62–63, 197n85, 198n98, 203n9–10, 204n17, 207n48, 208n59, 210n84
identity politics, 13, 20, 41, 56, 117, 121, 134, 178n36–37, 191n25; Deniz Göktürk and "role play beyond," in film, 211n89
imagination, 2, 5, 12, 42, 43, 46, 61, 62, 64, 66, 71, 72, 94, 107, 127, 139, 174n13, 185n31; labor of, 14, 29, 41, 77, 124, 132, 152, 166, 170, 173n3, 208n61; new role of, 1, 14, 41, 202n2
indexical reference, 145, 147–148, 155, 157, 202n3, 210n74

Ingeborg Bachmann Prize, *see* Bachmann Prize
intercultural hermeneutics, and historical orientation, 181n67; and justice, 174n17; and linguistic competence, 181n66; and literature, 5, 16, 21, 23–26, 33–34, 36, 39, 97, 179n41, 182n73, 184n16, 198n98, 209n63
Internet, 108
intersectional analysis, feminist, 203n9
intralingual translation, 156–157, 201n88
Iron Curtain, 79, 157
Islam, and cultural constellations, 2, 61, 72, 85, 96, 128, 129, 130, 131, 152, 193n51, 195n65, 204n19, 204n21, 205n24–26, 205n30; and Europe, 129, 179n38, 205n25; and mysticism, 155, 178n38; and phenomenology of Cold War, 155–156
Islamic mysticism, 155, 156
"The Island," 159, 165–168, 170, 211n99, 212n111; *see also* affect
Istanbul, 40, 44–45, 51, 55, 107, 108, 140, 142, 208n58
Italy, and effects of migration, 7, 92, 106, 124, 131, 209n65
ius sanguinis, 7

Jews, in Germany, since the Holocaust, 11, 19, 28, 79–95; in *Kanak Sprak*, 100–104, 195n72; in *Perilous Kinship*, 104–105, 109, 111, 114, 115–117, 121
jokes, 38, 190n20
Jordan, James, 112, 197n95
Joyce, James, 63, 187n53
Judt, Tony, "The Past Is Another Country," 115

Kacandes, Irene, 63, 185n38, 188n71, 188n77

Kanak Attak!, 94, 178n36, 193n52–53, 194n54, 194n61
Kanak Sprak, 79, 95–104, 148; absence of living Jews in, 103; allusions to Holocaust in, 96, 100; and German taboos, 101–103; and hate speech, 94; and inversion of social hierarchies, 99–100, 103; and powers of speech, 98; and production of presence, 98; and rap culture, 99; and rhetoric of *dreck*, 101; and storytelling, 98–99; sexual commerce in, 101–102, 104; *see also* affect
Kara, Yadé, 15
Karpat Berkan, 106, 163, 164, 196n80
Kellman, Steven G., and "the translingual imagination," 12, 13
Kiefer, Anselm, 30, 76
Kluge, Alexander, 83
Kocka, Jürgen, on "entangled histories," 21, 182n71
Konuk, Kader, 70, 150, 151, 152, 174n14, 176n32, 178n38, 181n62, 182n74, 184n22–23, 187n56, 188n70, 188n81, 192n34, 210n82, 210n84, 211n89, 211n91–92, 212n106
Konzett, Matthias, 182n69, 196n73, 196n76, 196n78, 196n82, 199n110, 201n122
Kurt, Kemal, 171
Kuruyazıcı, Nilüfer, 32, 33, 39, 179n43, 181n66, 182n74, 183n8

LaBelle, Jenijoy, 45
labor, and abjection, 130; and disorientation, associated with guest workers, 15, 132; and ethnicity, as alienation, *see* Chow; and gender, 29, 130–131, 170, 202n1; and globalization of capital, 123–125, 175n20, 175n26, 202n2, 207n49; and imagination, 14, 15, 17, 28–30, 41, 50, 60, 76–77, 83, 91, 107, 124, 126–128, 138, 149–150, 169–170, 172; and migration, 1, 6–7, 15, 21, 23, 27, 29, 40, 48, 81, 84, 88–90, 92, 96, 111, 123, 125, 139, 170, 172, 175n20, 194n58; and reading, 50, 60, 66, 70, 76–77; as distinguished from identity in story of migration, 126, 174n13, 198n97; in "Grandfather Tongue," 152, 154, 157; in "The Island" and "Thoughts on May 8, 1995," 159, 167; in *Please, No Police*, 140–145, 147–148; in *Selim*, 31, 35, 37, 39
LaCapra, Dominick, and contextualization, 12; and critique of absolute precepts of incommensurabilty, 58; and Hayden White, 181n57; and historiography of National Socialism and the Holocaust, 86–88, 190n15, 191n28; and language of silence, 91
Leggewie, Claus, 27, 106, 174n14, 175n24, 177n34, 178n36, 182n75, 182n77, 184n20
Levy, Daniel, and Natan Sznaider, and Holocaust memory, 79–81, 102, 189n3–4, 189n8
Liebknecht, Karl, 208n62
lieux de mémoire, 165, 184n20, 212n110
lines of thought, "Turkish," concept of, 20–23; 26, 81, 104, 105, 121, 124, 166, 167, 169
literature of migration, 1, 5, 9, 12, 14–16, 18–19, 20, 29, 87, 94, 95, 133–136, 150, 170, 179n41, 180n51; and concept of "touching tales," 20–21; and epochal disorientation, 15, 29, 82, 83, 132, 180n44, 186n50, 206n38; and figures of gender and ethnicity, 28, 138, *see also* chapter three; and German riddle of referentiality,

literature of migration—*continued*
90–95; and masculinist paradigms, 130–131; and pop literature, 194n56; and postcolonial categories, 49, 176n32, 210n83; and post-ethnic future, 150, 210n77; and transnational cultures of memory, 82; and Turkish figures, 16–17, 23; and Turkish riddle of referentiality, 88–90; and women writers, 131; as cultural archive, 15, 16, 179n44; as distinguished from "intercultural" literature, 23, 26; as revolving around something other than diaspora or politics of identity, 13, 20, 178n36; as transfigurative historical phenomenon, 26, 30, 86, 124–126, 138–139, 149; competing designations for, 23; Jewish figures in, 189n9, 191n25; need for disaggregated approach to, 124, 132; taboos addressed in, 28, 81, 83, 96, 100–102, 105, 109, 114, 117–118, 152, 155
Littler, Margaret, 150, 151, 152, 155, 156, 176n32, 177n35, 178n38, 210n83, 211n90, 211n93–94
localization, technology of, 9, 49, 51, 138, 175n27, 187n66, 207n54
long-distance modes of affiliation, 14, 43–44, 80, 83, 179n42, 187n65; *see also* Benedict Anderson
love, as motif, in "The Courtyard," 54–59
Lowe, Lisa, and David Lloyd, 207n49
Ludin, Fereshta, 129
Lukács, Georg, and Chow's critique of ethnic studies, 133
Luxemburg, Rosa, 208n62

Malcolm X, 95, 193n53
Mandel, Ruth, 127, 176n31, 178n36, 204n20

Mani, B. Venkat, 32, 33, 131, 141–142, 144, 179n44, 183n9, 188n70, 188n81, 203n11, 208n54, 208n60–61, 209n64
Mann, Thomas, and "the great controversy," for postwar Germany, 162–163
Marat, Jean Paul, 92–93
Marx Brothers, 51
Marxism, 124, 135–136, 141, 153, 157, 193n45, 207n49, 208n59
masculinity, 116, 148, 199–200n114, 205n31, 207n52, 212n108
McGann, Jerome, 171
McGowan, Moray, 97, 98, 132, 140, 141, 164, 175n18, 179n41, 194n58, 200n114, 202n130, 205n31, 206n38, 207n52, 208n58–59, 209n65, 211n97, 212n108
McLuhan, Marshall, 59
Mecklenburg, Norbert, 25, 32, 182n73
media, and culture of Turkish migration, in Germany, 95, 98, 106, 111, 128, 130, 131, 140, 182n72, 190n20, 193n52, 204n23, 208n57, 212n107; and globalization, 1–2, 14, 30, 41–42, 43, 76, 79–80, 171–172, 173n3, 173n5; distinction between hot and cool, 59–60
memory, cultures of, 15, 27, 80–82, 103, 105, 115–116, 120, 183n16, 189n3, 198n98, 207n51
Mennell, Barbara, 175n21, 193n44
migrant labor, *see* labor and migration
migration, *see* "between two worlds"; *see also* labor and migration; *see also* literature of migration
migration studies, 13, 22, 126, 134, 139, 174n13, 174n16, 177n34, 183n4, 206n40
Milich, Klaus, 190n20
minor literature, 184n22
Mitscherlich, Alexander, on "fatherless society" in Germany, 160; and

Margarete, on German "inability to mourn," 82
modernization theory, 2
Mohanty, Satya, and "postpositivist realism," 176n29
Mölln, 85–86, 106, 190n23
Moníková, Libuše, 131
Morocco, 7, 42
Morrison, Toni, 24
Mount Ararat, 119
mourning, in "The Courtyard in the Mirror," 45, 53, 70; in Germany, 82, 111, 180n55, 195n70; in *Perilous Kinship*, 111, 191n24
murder, 55, 80, 92, 105, 107, 108, 113, 114, 116, 117, 118, 129, 144, 206n44, 209n62, 209n64, 209n66, 211n92
Mushaben, Joyce, 7, 14, 204n17

Nadolny, Sten, 31–34, 39, 40, 111, 139, 148, 184n20, 184n24, 197n95, 206n44; as first German author to give sustained attention to Turkish migration, 27, 183n9; *Selim*, and sea change in German literature, 32–33, 39
"narraphasia," 33; as defined by B. Venkat Mani, 183n9
"narrative fetishism," as defined by Eric Santner, 191n24
narratology, postclassical, 180n54
National Monument for the Murdered Jews of Europe, in Berlin, 82, 84
National Socialism, 86, 111, 114, 160; *see also* fascism, genocide, Holocaust, Third Reich, and World War II
Negt, Oskar, 83
Netherlands, The, and Benhabib on treatment of minorities in, 9
Nuremberg trials (1946), 35

Ören, Aras, 28, 32, 105, 127, 131, 134, 135, 137, 138, 150, 170, 208n58; and *Bitte nix Polizei [Please, No Police]*, 138, 139–149, 171, 208n60–61; as alleged protagonist of guest worker literature in Germany, 141; as author of novel series "in search of the present," 105, 139, 141, 207–208n54, 209n65
Orientalism, 33, 35, 53, 56, 58, 97, 107, 130, 149, 187n56, 205n33
Ottoman Empire, 108, 113, 117, 149, 200n116, 210n80
Özakın, Aysel, 131, 206n35
Özdamar, Emine Sevgi, 11, 18, 27–30, 39–45, 48–50, 53, 55–56, 58–60, 62, 67, 69, 70–71, 75–76, 99, 106–108, 111, 127, 132, 137–139, 155, 178n38, 179n44, 182n74, 184n23, 185n29, 185n32, 185n37, 186n40, 186–187n52, 187n53; and Brecht, 153; and chiasmus, 156–157, 159; and conceit of naïveté, 131, 170, 188n81, 211n89; and focus on women characters and matrilinear motifs, 70, 138, 170; and tongue stories, 149–152, 157; *see also* "Grandfather Tongue"

Paris, 51, 70, 110
Pazarkaya, Yüksel, 25, 141, 182n72
Peck, Jeffrey, 190n20
Perilous Kinship, 19, 28, 41, 79, 104–122, 132, 159, 196n79, 199n111, 200n114–115, 201n122, 202n130, 211n100; and family history, in relation to genocide, 104–105, 108, 109, 113, 117, 119, 196n74, 199n114, 201n123; and German culture of *Betroffenheit*, 111, 116, 119, 191n24; and German-Jewish "community of fate," 114, 198n96, 199n107, 202n128; and film, 112, 116, 119; and national unification in

Perilous Kinship—continued
Germany, 108, 109, 114, 116, 132; and Turkish taboos, 117–118, 202n130; historical references in, 108, 113; motif of belatedness in, 114, 115, 120, 199n114; motif of secrets in, 110–112, 120, 159; motif of vision and visibility in, 113, 116, 120, 121; motif of writing in, 108–111, 113, 120, 122; narrator of, as abstract figure of history, 112–115; parodies of identity in, 111, 112; suspect trialogue in, 121–122; *see also* affect; *see also* Armenian genocide; *see also* Holocaust

personhood, 28, 81, 118, 126, 129–130, 133, 142–145, 147, 158, 167, 175n22, 206n40, 209n73, 212n104

philosemitism, 94

Please, No Police, 28, 135, 138, 139–149, 150, 171, 208n60–61; and Ali Itir as commodity, as distinguished from would-be person, 145; and class history, 141, 144; and novella form, 146–147; approaches to, with focus on identity, 141–142; approaches to, with focus on touching tales, 142–149; economic motifs in, 142–144; motif of ice in, 146, 149; motif of rape in, 142, 143, 146–148, 209n63

postcolonial phenomena and terminology, 3, 4, 7, 49, 125, 176n32, 193n53, 201n122, 210n83; *see also* Bhabha and "the Turkish *Gastarbeiter*"

post-Marxism, 135, 136

postmemory, 166, 212n112

prostitution, 96, 99, 104, 131–132, 143, 204n18

"the protestant ethnic," as defined by Rey Chow, 133–134, 206n40

proximate historical narratives, as distinguished from historical narrative by proxy, 18–19, 181n59

puns, 2, 43, 47, 48, 53, 71, 74, 99, 102, 103, 152, 157, 164, 186n47, 186n49, 193n51, 211n94

Qur'an, 155, 202n130

Raffman, Diana, 12, 211n95

rape, 117, 119, 142, 143, 146–148, 201n125, 209n63

reading, 1, 14, 18, 27, 29, 30, 32, 33, 35, 37, 41, 42, 43, 76–77, 92, 102, 113, 133, 139, 144, 177n35, 184n23, 186n42, 187n52, 187n60, 188n81, 195n71, 200n117, 201–202n125, 210n89, 211n93; *see also* "The Courtyard in the Mirror"; *see also* labor

referentiality, 17–20, 23, 47, 48, 50, 74, 91, 107, 187n55; operative definition of, 17; riddle of, 17, 19, 28, 85, 86–87, 88, 90, 93, 95, 172

Rothberg, Michael, 181n57, 190n15, 199n104

Rushdie, Salman, 2, 41, 89, 90, 177n33

Russian revolution, 108

Ryan, Marie-Laure, 50, 180n54, 187n55; on "phenomenology of reading" in digital age, 59

Samsa, Gregor, 171–172, 212n2

Santner, Eric, 180n46, 180n55, 185n40, 190n15, 200n114; and "narrative fetishism," 191n24

Sassen, Saskia, 8, 123–126, 134, 174n14, 175n20, 175n22, 175n26, 205n27, 209n70; on gender, 202n1

Scheinhardt, Saliha, 131, 206n35

Schiffauer, Werner, 209n63

Schlant, Ernestine, 184n17, 192n37, 199n111

Schönhuber, Franz, 204n19–20
Schwarzer, Alice, 128–129, 204n19, 205n24
Sebald, W.G., 83, 116, 199n111, 199n114
secularism, 129, 206n35
self-mimicry, *see* Chow on "coercive mimeticism"
Selim oder Die Gabe der Rede [Selim or the Gift of Speech], 31–40; and Alexander's obsession with speech, in relation to Nazi past, 36–39; and the "Auschwitz trial," 35; and "genius of storytelling," 31, 39; and German literary history, 27, 31, 32–34; dialogic scenarios in, 31–39; intercultural analyses of, 33–34, 35–36, 39; significance of train scene in, 31–32, 34–37, 38; "Turkish conversations" in, 37–38; *see also* affect
Şenocak, Zafer, 11, 20, 28, 39, 79, 82, 95, 96, 104–107, 127, 137, 139, 140, 158; and essays on turning points in German culture and history, 138, 149, 158–167; and focus on male figures and patrilinear motifs, 138, 159–161, 163–164, 170; and iconoclastic narration, 104, 122, 169–170, 196n73; and migration and memory, 27–29, 168–169; and new subject of German remembrance, 168–169; and philosophy of hermeneutics, 24–25, 41; and reputation, internationally and in Germany, 106; and "the wounds of communication," 24, 41; *Gefährliche Verwandtschaft [Perilous Kinship]*, different approaches to referentiality in, 19–20, 112; *see also Perilous Kinship*
Seyhan, Azade, and autobiography in literature of migration, 198n97,

206n42; and Benedict Anderson, 150; and comparison, 173n2; and critique of hermeneutic philosophy, 25–26, 182n70; and minor literature, 184n22; and Özdamar, 202n130, 210n84, 211n89; and Özdamar's tongue stories, 11, 150–151, 184n23; and skepticism concerning postcolonial labels, 176n32, 210n83; and Turkish national narrative, 178n38; and women writers, 205n33, 207n45; and "writing outside the nation," 25–26, 177n35
short-distance modes of affiliation, 14, 43, 56, 83, 179n42
Sieg, Katrin, 173n2, 177n32, 180n50, 180n53, 181n58, 181n61, 182n1, 184n23, 188n70, 191n33, 193n54, 195n70, 204n18; and referentiality, 18–20; on Özdamar's *Keloglan in Alamania*, 188n81, 194n61
Şölçün, Sargut, 141, 142, 147, 158, 179n41, 183n3, 188n81, 206n44, 211n89
Solingen, 85–86, 106, 129, 190n23
Sommer, Doris, and "bilingual games," 40, 182n71, 188n68; and critique of hermeneutics, 24–25, 40–41, 182n70; and national forms of intimacy, 59, 187n68; and "rhetoric of particularism," as corrective to "rhetoric of universalism," 24, 176n29, 181n68, 185n30
sorites paradox, 12, 157
South Africa, 42, 44, 56
Soviet Union, 151, 159
Soysal, Levent, and critique of Bhabha's story of migration, 177n33, 191n29, 191n33; and labor vs. identity as central category in story of migration, 126, 174n13, 177n33, 178n36, 180n51, 183n4, 203n8; and "symbolic" subjects of

Soysal, Levent—*continued*
 migration, 126, 134; and the
 Turkish *Gastarbeiter* as anachronism,
 127, 139
Soysal, Yasemin, 7; and critique of
 diaspora as analytical concept, 8,
 10–11; and "the limits of
 citizenship," regarding migration
 and membership, 8, 10, 14, 81, 125,
 126, 129, 175n20, 175n22–23,
 175n26, 176n29; and "symbolic"
 subjects of migration, 126, 134,
 174n13, 174n16
Spivak, Gayatri Chakravorty, and
 Atatürk, 212n106; and privileging of
 migrant in postcolonial theory, 4,
 177n32
Staeck, Klaus, 92, 128
Stalin, 151
Stalinism, 108, 194n55
Stern, Frank, 94, 184n17, 192n37
Stern, Guy, 212n111
Stoll, Georg, 13, 178n35, 178n38
Story of the Last Thought, The, 105
storytelling, 27, 32, 33, 35, 38, 39,
 108, 131, 132, 183n7
suffering, 26, 80, 183, 198n96;
 German, 83, 101, 190n11; Jewish,
 83, 116; Turks, as symbol of,
 206n35
Suhr, Heidrun, 140, 141, 142,
 179n41, 184n22
suicide, 36, 108, 110, 117, 119, 142,
 156, 201n125, 209n64
symbolic subjects, of migration, 6, 8,
 18, 23, 32, 128, 129, 134, 174n16;
 as distinguished from emblematic
 subjects of migration, 126, 139,
 212n103

Tabbi and Wutz, *Reading Matters*, 30,
 43, 76, 171
taboo, 20, 27, 28, 56, 79–83, 86, 90,
 96, 100–102, 105, 109, 114, 117,
 118, 122, 152, 154, 155,
 190n12–13, 193n54, 195n71,
 198n98, 200n117, 201n122–123,
 202n125, 202n130, 210n81
Talât Pasha, 113, 115, 117, 200n117
Tarrow, Sidney, and "rooted
 cosmopolitans," 175n25
Tawada, Yoko, 131
Taylor, Charles, 175n28, 182n75,
 207n47
television, 95, 106, 129, 130, 140,
 175n21, 185n37; *see also* "The
 Courtyard in the Mirror"
Teraoka, Arlene Akiko, 32, 53,
 179n41, 182n1, 183n5, 184n22,
 192n39, 195n66, 197n88, 205n32,
 206n44
Tertilt, Hermann, and presumption of
 delinquency in context of migration,
 180n45; and Turkish Power Boys,
 101, 130, 176n32, 178n37
Thieß, Frank, 162, 212n104
thingliness, of Turkish figures, in
 Germany, 16–17, 95, 98, 103, 120,
 124, 127, 134, 136, 141
Third Reich, 7, 9, 36, 81, 82, 84, 85,
 87, 91, 92, 100, 108, 114, 119, 154,
 158, 160, 161, 162, 184n20, 194n54
third space, trope of, 172, 181n66
"Thoughts on May 8, 1995," 159,
 161, 163–166, 211n99
Tibi, Bassam, 6, 129, 178n35, 179n38,
 192n42, 204n20, 205n25
Todorov, Tzvetan, 25
Tomkins, Silvan, and affect of shame,
 63, 188n73; and affect of interest,
 188n69; and face, as organ of
 affect, 188n78; and "interocular
 intimacy," 63
touching tales, as distinguished from
 story lines and "entangled histories,"
 21; concept of, 20, 22, 26, 138, 170,
 171, 181n59, 181n63; examples of,
 27, 28, 81, 86, 87, 90, 91, 124, 137,

141, 145, 150, 152, 193n53, 194n55, 203n7
transubstantiation, 47, 69, 71, 72, 189n83
Tulay, Bülent, 27, 159
Turkey, and colonization, 176n32; and controversy over Armenian genocide, 28, 117–118, 200n117; and European Union, 6, 84–85, 106; and labor migration, 7, 31, 40, 84; and language reforms, 150–151, 152; and war of liberation, 108; as alleged bridge "between two worlds," 174n12; as frame of reference, 11, 13, 21, 25, 43, 54, 72, 108, 115, 150, 159–160, 177n34; in "The Courtyard in the Mirror," 42–43; in *Selim*, 31, 34; military coup (1971) in, 40, 140; military coup (1980) in, 34, 140
Turkish figures, as and on face of things, 16, 104
Turkish language, 31, 32, 37, 38, 48, 71, 74, 75, 110, 156
"Turkish" lines of thought, definition of, 20–23, 26; *see also* Brodsky Lacour; *see also* lines of thought
Turkish turn, in German literature and culture, 1, 15, 17
Turks, and growing identification with German culture, 14; and migration to Germany, overview of, 5–15; as "Jews of today," 85, 92; as stock figures in cultural fables of migration, 88–90, 127–132; incoherent, trope of, in Germany, 88, 90; long-range effects of, on German culture, 7, 23; visibility of, in Germany, 32, 98, 103, 191n23

United Nations, 6, 118
Unpacking Europe, 13

Vergangenheitsbewältigung, 91, 160, 161, 192n35, 197n89

Versprechen, 110, 120
visibility, Armenian need for, 119; Göle on new forms of, 129–130, 205n27
vision, disturbance of, 116, 132, 199n112, 199n114
von Dirke, Sabine, 32, 33, 35
von Molo, Walter, 162, 212n104

Wallraff, Günter, 125, 126, 128, 194n58, 203n6, 208n60
Walser, Martin, 83, 116, 160, 199n113
Warsaw Ghetto, 36
Wehrmacht, 37, 101, 192n37
Weigel, Sigrid, 131, 160, 161, 162, 179n41, 184n22, 192n37, 201n124, 211n102, 212n103
Weiss, Peter, *The Investigation* and *Marat/Sade*, 28, 91–94, 192n39–41, 192n43, 193n46
welded for ware, 107
die Wende [the turn], in Germany, to national unification, 15
Wende-Literatur, commonly presumed to exclude Turkish-born authors, 15
Werfel, Franz, 105, 196n75
West Germany, and Holocaust trials, 35
White, Hayden, 17, 18, 181n57, 190n18
White, Jenny B., 137, 178n36, 185n33, 191n23, 204n18
Winterson, Jeanette, *night screen*, 3
World War I, 108, 159
World War II, 79, 83, 91, 101, 111, 138, 149, 159, 161, 190n11, 201n121; and Allied occupation, 143
writing, as motif, 164; *see also Perilous Kinship*

xenophobia, 32, 54, 97, 125, 131, 141, 144, 192n42

Yeşilada, Karin, 15, 106, 138, 163, 164, 180n50, 187n59, 195n66, 196n76, 196n78, 196n80–81,

Yeşilada—*continued*
    198n101, 201n125, 203n14,
    204n18, 205n33, 206n35,
    212n107
Yıldız, Yasemin, 194n59, 210n88,
    211n93
Yücel, Can, 48, 51, 55, 56, 62, 72, 75,
    185n36, 187n53, 187n62,
    189n84; "Casting Net," 72, 74, 75,
    186n46
Yugoslavia, 7, 42
Yule, George, 63, 188n75

Zaimoğlu, Feridun, 20, 28, 29, 79, 86,
    94–105, 107, 130, 139, 140, 178n36,
    179n43, 182n74, 189n2, 190n20,
    193n52–53, 194n55–62, 195n62–67,
    195n70, 208n61; and alleged
    untranslatability of *Kanak Sprak*, 99;
    and iconography of presence, 98, 148;
    and protestant ethnics, 134; and story
    of migration, 98–99; commercial
    success of, in Germany, 95, 106, 132;
    iconoclastic intentions of, 104; *see also*
    Kanak Attak!; *see also Kanak Sprak*